Enhancing Instruction with Visual Media:

Utilizing Video and Lecture Capture

Ellen G Smyth
Austin Peay State University, USA

John X. Volker
Austin Peay State University, USA

Managing Director:	Lindsay Johnston
Editorial Director:	Joel Gamon
Book Production Manager:	Jennifer Yoder
Publishing Systems Analyst:	Adrienne Freeland
Development Editor:	Austin DeMarco
Assistant Acquisitions Editor:	Kayla Wolfe
Typesetter:	Erin O'Dea
Cover Design:	Jason Mull

Published in the United States of America by
Information Science Reference (an imprint of IGI Global)
701 E. Chocolate Avenue
Hershey PA 17033
Tel: 717-533-8845
Fax: 717-533-8661
E-mail: cust@igi-global.com
Web site: http://www.igi-global.com

Library of Congress Cataloging-in-Publication Data

Enhancing instruction with visual media : utilizing video and lecture capture / Ellen G. Smyth and John X. Volker, editors.
   pages cm
 Includes bibliographical references and index.
 Summary: "This book offers unique approaches for integrating visual media into an instructional environment by covering the impact media has on student learning and various visual options to use in the classroom"--Provided by publisher.
 ISBN 978-1-4666-3962-1 (hardcover) -- ISBN 978-1-4666-3963-8 (ebook) -- ISBN 978-1-4666-3964-5 (print & perpetual access) 1. College teaching--Audio-visual aids. I. Smyth, Ellen G., 1973- II. Volker, John X., 1951-
 LB1043.E54 2013
 378.1'735--dc23
                              2012048657

British Cataloguing in Publication Data
A Cataloguing in Publication record for this book is available from the British Library.

Table of Contents

Section 3
Short Instructional Video

Section 4
Research-Based Best Practices

Section 5
Student-Centered Learning and Student-Created Videos

Detailed Table of Contents

Section 1
Setting the Stage

Chapter 1
Tom McBride, Beloit College, USA
Ron Nief, Beloit College, USA

This chapter projects how higher education will be systematically transformed once the practice of capturing lectures is widespread and common: in particular how the practice will affect the lecture format itself, bring about a reversal of homework and class work, influence the dialectic of interdisciplinary education, transform the communications ontology of the lecture, and affect small liberal arts colleges, for whom in-person pedagogy has been a hallmark—and to which captured lectures would appear to be alien.

Chapter 2
Julie A. DeCesare, Providence College, USA

The Web has quickly become a resource for multimedia and video content. Search engines have tools to mine for visual content, but finding video content creates different challenges than searching for text. This chapter presents a detailed guide on searching for visual multimedia content and provides a showcase of innovative collections and resources. The reader will learn research strategies, gain specific skills in navigating multimedia, and receive a list of resources for finding subject-specific and interdisciplinary video content. Resources are reviewed based on content quality, partnerships, technical specifications, and overall usability.

Chapter 3

Use of technological resources can greatly enhance the effectiveness of online instruction. Developing familiarity with these new resources can be time consuming and difficult for professors already overburdened with high class sizes and course load assignments. This chapter introduces the basic components of three general types of video lecture tools: lecture capturing tools, web conferencing tools, and video hosting and streaming tools by providing details of three specific software platforms: Tegrity™, Adobe® Connect™, and YouTube. Suggestions for their effective use in both online and hybrid classrooms are given.

Chapter 4

Visual media can be created using a plethora of software and hardware tools, including enterprise-wide deployed lecture capture system. Tools can be as simple as single click record software or require extensive knowledge of options, formats, or end-user devices. While this chapter does not cover all of the visual media creation tools available, it does give a brief overview of the tools for creating, editing, and delivering digital media content to enhance instruction.

Section 2
Lecture Capturing

Chapter 5

Emporia State University recently implemented a web-based presentation capture application for use in both a graduate and undergraduate counselor education program. Presentation capture, sometimes referred to as course capture or lecture capture, is most often used in traditional classrooms to record lectures by faculty for playback and review by students following class. However, in this educational scenario the students record sessions with assigned clients from the Emporia, Kansas community that are later played back by the faculty for review and evaluation – most often in a classroom environment where all the students gather to review and discuss the client recordings. The faculty critique the interview techniques, interview questions, and client engagement with the students as part of their training, research, and coursework. One of the unique needs of this approach is that the recordings conform to Health Insurance Privacy and Accountability Act (HIPAA) requirements and thus can only be replayed outside the counseling facility using an encrypted Virtual Private Network (VPN) access. Although this is a very small academic program at a modest-sized university, an empirical research study was conducted to gauge the effectiveness of capturing client sessions using a presentation capture application. Results from that study indicate that both students and faculty found the software and hardware to be very easy to use, and believed it significantly enhanced the quality of the counseling program.

Patrick Moskal, University of Central Florida, USA
Patricia Euzent, University of Central Florida, USA
Patsy Moskal, University of Central Florida, USA
Thomas Martin, University of Central Florida, USA

This research compared student performance and withdrawal rates in undergraduate business courses taught using lecture capture and face-to-face. Student perceptions of lecture capture are also described. Lecture capture refers to storing videos of live course lectures, which students may view at their convenience from anywhere with an Internet connection. Results indicate no significant difference in student performance between the lecture capture and face-to-face conditions. Withdrawal rates also were similar, although freshman and sophomores had higher withdrawal rates in lecture capture than in face-to-face. Student perceptions of lecture capture were quite positive. Students were satisfied with the video instruction they received, they liked having more control over their learning, they liked the convenience that lecture capture provided, and about 70% said they would take another course that used lecture capture. However, the majority of students did not feel that lecture capture enhanced their performance or their interest in the course.

Steve Garwood, Rutgers University, USA

LessonCapture is an approach to the creation and recording of presentation content (course lecture or demonstration), delivered either face-to-face or via screen-recording, and based on effective public speaking, presentation design, and multimedia learning principles. The combination of these principles with particular procedures and practices helps to ensure effective learning and reusability of content. The field of education faces many challenges: budgets, time limitations, new delivery approaches, and effectiveness. LessonCapture is one way to help maximize the return on the financial investment in recording technology and the instructor time needed to create high quality instructional materials.

Section 3
Short Instructional Video

Elizabeth J. Vincelette, Old Dominion University, USA

This chapter addresses students' preference for screencast assessment over traditional paper or digital text-based comments. Screencast assessment allows for asynchronous audio and visual commenting on student papers using screencast software. A pilot study using a qualitative approach has indicated that students prefer screencast assessment because of its multimodality and its ability to make the instructor's thought process while grading transparent. Multimodality involves multisensory and multimedia approaches, which can broaden student understanding of teacher feedback. The screencast, because of its multimodality, enhances students' understanding of the instructor's thought process and reasoning.

Because of the suggestion that students prefer this sort of feedback, the pilot study warrants a larger scale project in order to investigate the student preference for this feedback and whether the method leads to improvement in student performance.

Chapter 9

Curtis Kunkel, University of Tennessee Martin, USA

This chapter discusses the construction and implementation of a Virtual Math Lab for undergraduate students. The main technology used in the construction of the site was the Livescribe® SmartPen. Pros and cons of using this technology is discussed in detail. In addition, current usage numbers illustrate how the Virtual Math Lab has filled a need that this level of student desperately needed filled.

Chapter 10

Peter M. Jonas, Cardinal Stritch University, USA
Darnell J. Bradley, Cardinal Stritch University, USA

Capitalist economics posits that increased competition between entrepreneurs in an economy leads to better, more consumer friendly products. As colleges compete for students, the same could be said for how modern learners have driven traditional pedagogy to new heights. In the last 30 years, education has witnessed the transformation of distance learning via the internet and home computing, the growth and inclusion of non-traditional learning methods, and most recently, the growth of a ubiquitous video culture via the usage of digital video recording, phone cameras, and web vehicles such as YouTube. This chapter attempts to connect research with the practical components of using technology in the form of humorous, short videos as a new teaching technique called videagogy: from the words video and pedagogy, pronounced vid-e-ah-go-jee. Using humorous videos and allowing students to select video content brings self-directed learning to students in a non-threatening way that actually makes them laugh out loud.

Section 4
Research-Based Best Practices

Chapter 11

Paula Jones, Eastern Kentucky University, USA
Fred Kolloff, Eastern Kentucky University, USA
MaryAnn Kolloff, Eastern Kentucky University, USA

This chapter examines effective methods for using video and web conferencing tools to support online learning. The authors discuss the concept of presence, how web conferencing can be used to support presence in online courses, and why it is important to do so. Because of the impact web conferencing can have in learning, this chapter explores a variety of teaching roles that best leverage these conferencing tools. The chapter includes information on various web conferencing software programs (paid and open source). Best practices for using web conferencing tools in online learning are also explored.

Chapter 12

By definition, presence makes individuals feel connected and part of a community. Yet, creating presence among the students and their instructor does not happen automatically and can be especially challenging to develop in online courses. In these learning environments, interactions are frequently text-based and asynchronous. The visual and auditory cues generally associated with face-to-face interactions are absent. However, easy-to-use, inexpensive technologies to create audio and video content are emerging, and they can foster presence in educational settings. This chapter investigates the use of rich media to promote social, cognitive, and teaching presence. Specifically, instructor-created videos were used to enhance the sense of presence in a fully online course. Responses to surveys, reflections, and unstructured follow-up interviews suggest that students prefer the richer mode of communication, indicating that they felt a greater connection to the instructor as well as their classmates.

Chapter 13

We are immersed in a culture of spoken media, written media, and – like it or not – screen media. Just as writing and speaking skills are keys to functioning in society, we must consider that the future increasingly demands proficiency in "mediating" as well. Doing anything less leaves this powerful medium in the hands of a relative few. By offering instruction in what screen media is, how it is created, how it relates to other literacies, how the internet is changing it, and how this all informs everyday teaching and learning, the Rosebud Institute seeks to make screen media literacy more broadly understood and accessible. This chapter follows a program developed by the Rosebud Institute and looks at how – using simple, accessible technology – people can become more screen media literate by creating digital films and ePortfolios themselves. Developed along with Rosebud's program manager, Christine Wells, the creation process enables deeper, more authentic learning, allowing us all to communicate more effectively, to self assess more reflectively, and to thrive in a screen-based world.

Section 5
Student-Centered Learning and Student-Created Videos

Chapter 14

Learning design is critical to success when using visual media to enhance learning. This process involves beginning with the end goals in mind and working backwards to craft a thoughtful learning sequence. Through a pair of case studies, this chapter demonstrates the role student-generated digital stories can play in helping students make meaning of firsthand learning experiences. Digital story-making engages students in a multi-modal, multi-sensory experience that deepens engagement and improves the memorability of learning. Educators are under increasing pressure to provide evidence of the impact that coursework has on student learning, and student-generated digital stories provide valuable artifacts of learning.

    Marianne Castano Bishop, Indiana University South Bend, USA
    Jim Yocom, Indiana University South Bend, USA

Video projects offer valuable opportunities for students to engage in the academic enterprise and demonstrate what they are learning. This chapter explores what will be referred to as the Helix-Flow: an amalgam synthesizing and strengthening three theoretical frameworks of instruction, including Project-based Learning, Universal Design for Learning, and Bloom's Taxonomy of Cognitive Domain. The Helix-Flow captures the essence of these three theories and serves as a backdrop for understanding and appreciating video projects as a learning artifact. As a helix, the spirals wrap around the cylinder or cone. Each spiral represents one of the theories and the cylinder or cone represents student engagement with video projects. The spirals or theories support the cone or student engagement with video projects. Each theory or spiral has its own inherent and prescribed set of principles and guidelines. Each theory integrates with the others while keeping its own strengths, providing a comprehensive approach to instruction and student engagement. Each theory scaffolds differentiated instruction. This chapter will also examine the five Rs as guidelines for multimedia projects – Rationale, Roles, Resources, Rubric, and Readiness as well as the design of video assignments, assistance, production phases, and assessment.

    Christine Wells, Carthage College, Rosebud Institute, USA

Like learning to read or write, or acquiring the fundamentals of mathematics, screen media literacy is rapidly becoming an essential life skill. This dominant and expansive interface for contact, culture, and commerce has become the way we communicate now. Given the power and reach of the screen, it seems essential that as with any other fundamental skill, we must begin to understand and create within this medium in a more foundational, intentional way. But the language of the screen is complicated, rapidly becoming almost as multidimensional and multifaceted as the number of users it encompasses. Additionally, given its reliance on technology, it is an ever-changing landscape fraught with the challenges of chasing the elusive cutting edge. This chapter looks at a more back to basics approach to screen media literacy by offering instruction in what screen media really is and how to create it in a more foundational and transferable fashion. Using simple, accessible technology, people become more screen literate and the creation process enables deeper, more authentic learning, with the credence and accountability of a potentially world wide audience. Focusing on an integral part of a process developed by the Rosebud Institute – an organization committed to making screen media literacy more broadly understood and accessible – this step-by-step, integrated method delivers a new understanding of media literacy. Using simple, accessible technology, participants create dynamic, original ePortfolio websites themselves and distribute their work to an ever-expanding audience. Developed along with Rosebud's founder and director, Paul Chilsen, the process encourages individuals to find their own voice and embrace the me in media, moving us towards a future where people will instantly capture, identifiably own, intelligently store, and instinctively know what to do with their digital assets, allowing us all to communicate more effectively and thrive in a media-saturated world., more authentic learning, with the credence and accountability of a potentially world wide audience.

A number of researchers have explored the use of multimedia to support instruction in inverted classrooms providing a functional approach for university face-to-face and hybrid courses. Students in inverted learning work online before class listening to prerecorded lectures and completing related activities reserving class time for problem solving, projects, authentic applications, and reflection. The purpose of this chapter is to explore the value of cognitive and metacognitive elements in flipped – also known as inverted – learning that promote active learning. Practical strategies for course design and technical considerations related to how multimedia tools can be used to deliver and support instruction are also addressed.

Chapter 18

As more students bring powerful pocket-sized computers to class in the form of their smartphones and tablets, faculty need to take advantage by devising curriculum that incorporates mobile video production as a means of contributing to the discourse of the university and the world at large. Projects where students use mobile devices to make videos create active learning environments where they are more likely to build and connect their classroom learning with what they already know. These types of projects also develop student digital composing skills while navigating several issues pertinent to a 21st century participatory culture. These assignments engage students with themes and issues that not only promote success in higher education but throughout their careers.

Preface

All the world's a video,
And all the men and women have their players:
They have their Hulus, Rokus, and their YouTubes;
And one man in his time can watch the world.[1]

We live in a video era surrounded by flat-screen televisions, myriads of monitors, and collections of mobile devices. Media flows everywhere, inescapable – it's in our restaurants, in our cars, and even in our doctors' offices. One video at a time is no longer enough to entertain as "consumers are turning to the so-called second screen like never before" (Hanas, 2012).

With video all around us, it seems natural to bring the screen into the classroom, but is it really valuable? Do students benefit from moving media? Can video improve learning?

LIGHTS: ILLUMINATIONS OF NEED

Students at Austin Peay State University certainly believe that video can improve instruction, as evidenced in our online statistics course. In response to a discussion board question about what is most and least helpful, students have said:

I love these videos and wish all online classes would have this.
I don't miss a beat, and if I do, I can just rewind or pause to work a problem.
There aren't words to describe my happiness with having these videos accompany the text.

Salmon Khan, who single-handedly created the most viewed educational video library on YouTube, explains, "There is a deep hunger for this type of thing." Khan receives hundreds of emails daily from students around the world who are thrilled to have access to his videos. After watching Khan's videos for a single summer, one student previously considered mathematically deficient earned a perfect score on a mathematics placement exam. He wrote to Khan, "I can say without a doubt that you changed my life and the lives of everyone in my family" (Khan, 2010).

Sebastian Thrun, already famous for the Google Glass project and designing a driverless car, became inspired by Khan to teach the masses for free. Along with his Stanford colleague Peter Norvig, Thrun hosted the most massive of Massive Open Online Courses (MOOCs) at the time: 160,000 students enrolled in one artificial intelligence course. Of these, 23,000 graduated from the course at Stanford level quality and 410 of whom surpassed even the best Stanford student that term.

How did Thrun and Norvig do it? One of the biggest obstacles to online learning, especially on this scale, is motivating and engaging the online learner throughout the course. Thrun and Norvig did just that by creating a gaming atmosphere where students would only advance to the next level after completing truly complex and provocative tasks. To implement this game-like atmosphere, they designed their own system of interactive video content embedded with questions that were both interesting and extremely challenging. Even though other technologies were used in the course, this video- and exercise-based learning platform was the primary tool driving the learning forward (Thrun, 2012).

Though these cases are impressive, they do not embody the rigor of scholarly research. What do empirical studies say about the value of video technologies in education?

CAMERA: EMPIRICAL EVIDENCE FOR CAMERAS IN THE CLASSROOM

According to a comprehensive review of 47 journal articles published between 2005 and 2011, an overwhelming majority of students claim *lecture capturing* – a video recording of classroom lectures for on-demand consumption – improves their learning experience. Most studies indicate that over 80% of students prefer courses with a lecture-capturing component. Lecture capture is generally found to have a positive effect on grades and course performance, to compensate for absenteeism, and to improve the learning experience and make learning easier (Pursel and Fang, 2011).

Zhang, Zhou, Briggs, and Nunamaker (2006) found that online students using *interactive video* content were more satisfied and demonstrated significantly improved learning (as measured by pre- and post-tests) than both online students without interactive video and, more impressively, students in a traditional classroom.

Rath and Gunter (2012) researched large-scale classrooms to see which Web 2.0 tools could be used to establish presence and help students succeed, even in classes as large as 900 students. Of the tools in this study – including an online discussion tool, Twitter, and Second Life – two tools emerged as clearly the most helpful for both learning and establishing presence: lecture capture and instructional video.

ACTION: RESHAPING EDUCATION

As evidence of the benefits of instructional video grows, the market for integrating this media ripens while classrooms are flipped and educational technologies are redesigned around visual media. Desire2Learn announced at their most recent users' conference that they are introducing *native video* in their Learning Management System (LMS). Depending upon institutional settings, this native video feature allows both faculty and students to record video content directly through the LMS, without the intermediate step of saving video to the hard drive first and uploading later. Native video is available in almost every part of the course, including the discussions, email, content, and assessment feedback areas (Desire2Learn, 2012).

TED (Technology, Entertainment, Design) has stretched its tentacles into the education arena by introducing TED-Ed in early 2012. TED-Ed allows educators to take a TED Talk – or *any* educational YouTube video – and create a lesson by adding interactive content and probing questions. Educators can then use TED-Ed to track which students watched which videos, for how long, and what students learned as a result.

Similar to what Thrun and other educational philanthropists before him have done, MOOCs are cropping up everywhere, delivering educational video to the masses. After successfully launching his artificial intelligence course, Thrun broke away from Stanford to build a set of MOOCs called Udacity. Massachusetts Institute of Technology (MIT) and Harvard fused their influence to create edX, and other prestigious universities jumped aboard the edX train. Coursera forms an even larger conglomerate of MOOCs with contributions from Johns Hopkins, Stanford, Rice, Princeton, Columbia, and twenty-seven other elite universities to stream top lecture videos for all to see and for all to learn.

Desire2Learn's native video feature, TED-Ed's tool, and the MOOC movement are each mere puddles in the pond of what is happening to education through video technologies. To better explore the changing shape of education, this book will lead the reader through a series of scholarly chapters on how visual media is being used to remold the classroom.

CUT: A MONTAGE OVERVIEW

We intend for this book to be a balance between the scholarly and the practical – a guide for educators that, through research, establishes trust and shares practical applications for improving instruction within the higher education classroom, whether that classroom is face-to-face, online, or a blend of both. We aim the book toward an audience of higher education faculty, faculty development staff, instructional designers and technologists, and administrators, though most of the chapters have applications outside higher education as well.

We suspect many of our readers will want to pick and choose the chapters that appeal specifically to their needs, but we arranged this book in a natural order so that readers may, if they prefer, read from cover to cover to first be introduced to the tools and techniques for basic recording and then progressively learn more complex ways to design visual media experiences to maximize learning. The book is organized into five sections. We start with a vision of a future university environment where lecture capturing is the norm and then introduce the knowledge and tools that educators need before hitting the record button. Next, we dedicate one section of the book exclusively to lecture capturing and another section exclusively for the short instructional video. We follow these sections up with a section dedicated to pedagogy – chapters covering research-based best practices in using video technology. We end with a section of chapters dedicated to our students, emphasizing student-centered learning and student-created videos.

Section 1: Setting the Stage, as the title implies, provides background to prepare instructors for video and lecture capturing. We open with a vision of how a future university might function when lecture capturing has become a well-established norm. We move on to explore ways to find existing educational video resources so time is not wasted duplicating the efforts of another. For those who will create their own video content, we talk about the tools available for video and lecture capturing.

We open with *The Digital Lectern,* a chapter that, though grounded by research, is much more visionary than scholarly. This introductory chapter was penned by the authors of the annual Mindset Lists, as featured on the *Today* show, in the *New York Times,* in the *Wall Street Journal,* and in many other prominent news media. The Mindset Lists use recent history and trends to put into perspective the mindset of traditional incoming freshmen, especially as that mindset might contrast with their professors. In this chapter, the authors analyze current trends in lecture capturing and use these trends as a basis for their vision of what college could look like in 2020 when lecture capturing has become a universal university experience. How will lecture capturing change the roles of homework and classwork? How will pedagogy be altered? What are the possibilities?

In *Navigating Multimedia: How to Find Internet Video Resources for Teaching, Learning, & Research,* we take quite a practical look at questions every educator should examine before spending thousands of dollars and hundreds of hours creating video content: Does the video I want already exist? The web provides an astonishing selection of educational resources. Search engines contain tools to mine *visual* content, but finding *video* content creates different challenges. This chapter, which goes far beyond Google, will guide the reader in how to search for multimedia content and will provide a showcase of innovative collections and resources.

To round out our Getting Started section, we spend two chapters highlighting the video technology tools that educators need to consider before beginning the video creation process. The first chapter focuses on three specific tools which can be integrated into classrooms to improve learning, while the second chapter provides a much broader overview of the tools available.

In *Integrating Video Lecture Tools in Online and Hybrid Classrooms,* the reader will explore a popular lecture capturing tool (Tegrity), a popular web conferencing tool (Adobe Connect), and a popular video streaming website (YouTube). This chapter focuses on how these three tools, as well as similar competitor's products, can enrich online instruction. For each tool, the chapter dedicates a section to describing an overview, basic features, the pros and cons, typical costs, and tips for effectively integrating the tool into the online and hybrid classroom.

The *Tools of the Trade* chapter investigates and compares a much wider cross section of educational video tools – both hardware and software, both enterprise systems and desktop applications. Specifically, this chapter explores tools for screen capturing, video editing, video conferencing, video recording, and lecture capturing. While this chapter does not attempt the impossible feat of covering all of the video creation tools available, it does give an overview of tools for creating, editing, and delivering digital media content to enhance instruction.

Section 2: Lecture Capturing includes three chapters describing specific applications for *lecture capturing technologies* – software and hardware tools designed to record classroom lectures. One chapter will look at a traditional application of lecture capturing in delivering business courses, while the other two chapters examine nontraditional applications such as recording intimate counseling sessions and recording lessons that address the individual online learner instead of an entire face-to-face classroom.

In *Using Presentation Capture in Counselor Education Programs,* we examine how Emporia State University recently implemented a lecture capture tool for their counselor education program. Even though lecture capturing was designed to capture the classroom, Emporia State saw an opportunity to turn this tool to their own purpose: recording counseling sessions led by students for evaluation, review, and feedback from their instructors. This chapter will explore exactly how Emporia State's program implemented lecture capture, including special measures to ensure that all Health Insurance Privacy and Accountability Act (HIPAA) requirements were satisfied. Most impressively, this chapter will detail an empirical research study that Emporia conducted to gauge the effectiveness of capturing client sessions via lecture capture. Results indicate that both students and faculty found the tools quite easy to use and credited these tools for significantly enhancing the quality of their counseling education program.

Student Performance and Perceptions of Business Courses Delivered Using Lecture Capture assesses a traditional lecture capturing approach in the College of Business Administration at the University of Central Florida. Within undergraduate business courses, this assessment compares performance and withdrawal rates for students taught with lecture capture to students taught using face-to-face instruction. Results indicate no statistically significant difference in performance between these two groups. Freshman and sophomores showed higher withdrawal rates while using lecture capture than face-to-face, while upperclassmen showed no significant differences. This chapter also examines student perceptions of lecture capture, most of which were quite positive.

The final chapter for lecture capturing section, *Toward* LessonCapture*: A New Approach to Screencasting and Lecture Capture*, serves as a segue to our next section on short instructional videos. This practical chapter advises faculty of methods in optimizing quality while recording either lecture captures or short instructional videos. The author uses the term *LessonCapture* to describe an approach to designing and creating educational video content using proven public speaking principles, presentation design ideals, and instructional multimedia fundamentals to improve learning and ensure content reusability.

Section 3: Short Instructional Video examines two unique applications for short video content – one for grading and feedback and another as an online tutoring resource – as well as a chapter on the pedagogy behind using humorous short videos in the classroom.

We begin with *Video Capture for Grading: Multimodal Feedback and the Millennial Student.* Here, the author uses a screencasting tool to record a short video as she critiques each student's paper. As the instructor scrolls through and discusses the different parts of the paper, her screen, mouse movements, and voice are all recorded and made available to the student for playback. This chapter evaluates qualitative research on student sentiments toward this type of feedback. Results indicate that students prefer screencasting assessment to traditional written commentary. With video feedback, students gain deeper insight into the instructor's thought processes through more detailed explanations of why each part was graded the way it was. Students also gain a better sense of the instructor's tone with access to the voice behind the words.

Creating and Implementing a Virtual Math Tutoring Lab for Undergraduate Students describes how mathematics faculty at the University of Tennessee at Martin teamed together to build an online, on-demand tutoring resource for their undergraduate students using short, instructional videos to convey content and demonstrate examples. The faculty exclusively used the Livescribe SmartPen to very simply record their voices along with everything being written or drawn by this pen on special paper. The author found this technology to be so simple that any faculty member could record with the pen, regardless of technological prowess, and then someone with sufficient savvy could collect the pens and upload the video content.

In *Videagogy: Using Humor and Videos to Enhance Student Learning*, video technologies merge with pedagogy to form *videagogy* – a technique using short, humorous, educational videos to improve learning. Research tells us that, when content-related humor is employed, we learn more effectively and enjoyably. Humor can also relieve stress by lowering cortisol and epinephrine levels and by releasing endorphins. This chapter connects research with practical ways of integrating humorous video content into the classroom.

Section 4: Research-Based Best Practices will delve even deeper into the pedagogies behind using video technologies in the classroom. Two chapters advocate specific video-related practices through which research suggests we can improve learning and foster social, teaching, and cognitive presence in the online classroom. We'll wrap up this section with a *mediafesto* calling attention to the need for better screen media literacy in today's society.

The chapter on *Using Video and Web Conferencing Tools to Support Online Learning* delineates between *video conferencing*, which networks together non-Internet-based interactive television systems to communicate, and *web conferencing*, which includes any sort of online, synchronous meeting and which may include video. The authors explore how these two conferencing tools can influence learning and establish a sense of presence as described by the Community of Inquiry teaching model. This chapter also describes both teaching-centered and student-centered approaches to conferencing.

Similar to the previous chapter, *Using Video to Foster Presence in an Online Course* explores how the short instructional video, rather than conferencing, can establish a sense of presence – social presence, teaching presence, and cognitive presence – in online courses, making individuals feel connected and part of a community. Within this chapter, the author describes her online course design with four types of video content:

1. A personal introduction,
2. Introductory videos for each content module,
3. On-the-fly video check-ins at the end of each module to address student questions and concerns, and
4. *Cool Tools* videos for demonstrating content-related technology.

This chapter then analyzes evidence from the course on whether videos can establish presence within an online classroom.

In *Media and the Moving Image: Creating Screen Media Literacy*, the author pulls from his experience managing the *Rosebud Institute* – an organization dedicated to promoting screen media literacy – to pen a chapter introducing the reader to screen media literacy and its growing importance in our screen-obsessed society. The chapter presents sound arguments for why a course on creating video content should be added to core curricula. We have taught reading and writing for centuries and more recently public speaking, not just to students seeking degrees in these fields but to all students because, for centuries and millennia, this has been how we communicate across all professions. Now, with video streaming sites like YouTube and Vimeo that empower everyone to convey information via video, there is a new kid on the communication block who cannot be ignored.

In Section 5: *Student-Centered Learning and Student-Created Videos*, four chapters share ideas for creating student-centered learning environments through *student-created* video – one chapter encouraging students to take charge of their tales by becoming digital storytellers, one on the value of mobile media projects in which students whip out their phones and record, one chapter exploring the pedagogical power behind students creating the content, and one advocating for student-generated digital media portfolios. Another chapter in this section explains how face-to-face classes can put the spotlight on students by covering content outside class via *instructor-created* video while reserving class time for more student-centric activities.

Digital Story-Making in Support of Student Meaning-Making examines what storytelling is and how it can build connections and motivate learners. This chapter reviews two separate video-creation projects in which undergraduate students tell video stories. With the first assignment, the *Boston Story Map*, students explore the greater university community and complete significant background research and journaling before telling their own story of the area. With a final, culminating assignment, *Digital Stories of Service Learning*, students complete a service-learning project, further connecting themselves with the community. This chapter analyzes evidence for how these two student-led video projects affect learning.

Video Projects: Integrating Project-Based Learning, Universal Design for Learning, and Bloom's Taxonomy describes projects where students group together to create videos related to course content. The authors demonstrate how such projects support an alloy of three instructional theories (Project-Based Learning, Universal Design for Learning, and Bloom's Taxonomy) that is much stronger than each theory individually. This chapter describes how each theory is supported and then explains the synergistic effect these three have on each other. To put the theories into practice, the reader is introduced to the five Rs of multimedia projects: rationale, roles, resources, rubrics, and readiness.

Putting Me in Media: Communicating and Creating Screen Media with a Purpose, another chapter from an author associated with the *Rosebud Institute*, describes the process for students creating their own multimedia portfolios as digital representations of themselves. This chapter advises students to start by identifying a focus, a purpose, and an audience; to organize what they want to showcase; to create the digital self; and to reflect, revise, and collaborate. The chapter also offers several solutions for how to handle issues ranging from tech support to matters of privacy, accessibility, and copyright.

With *Flipped or Inverted Learning Strategies for Course Design*, the author explores one of the biggest trends in face-to-face and hybrid classes, the *flipped* classroom, which is sometimes called the *inverted* classroom – where the traditional classroom is flip-flopped so lectures, typically recorded on video, become homework while homework-styled problems and activities become classwork. This chapter describes the components of an inverted course, provides detailed design strategies, and summarizes research in this field.

With *Making Learning Reel: Student-Made Videos on Mobile Devices*, we have saved one of the best reads for the very end. This chapter presents fascinating background material and research into the value of using student-created video assignments in the classroom. The authors share their own innovative ideas for video assignments and explore a variety of logistical concerns.

Ellen G. Smyth
Austin Peay State University, USA

John X. Volker
Austin Peay State University, USA

REFERENCES

Desire2Learn. (2012). *Product update*. FUSION 2012: 9th Annual Desire2Learn Users' Conference. Retrieved October 26, 2012, from http://www.desire2learn.com/resources/announcements/2012/fusion/highlights-and-announcements-from-fusion-2012/

Hanas, J. (2012, February). The race for the second screen: 5 apps that are shaping social TV. *Fast Company*. Retrieved October 16, 2012, from http://www.fastcocreate.com/1679561/the-race-for-the-second-screen-5-apps-that-are-shaping-social-tv

Khan, S. (2010). *Salman Khan speaks at GEL (Good Experience Live) Conference*. Retrieved October 19, 2012, from http://www.youtube.com/watch?v=yTXKCzrFh3c

Pursel, B., & Fang, H. (2011). *Lecture capture: Current research and future directions*. The Shreyer Institute for Teaching Excellence. Retrieved October 18, 2012, from http://www.psu.edu/dept/site/pursel_lecture_capture_2012v1.pdf

Rath, V., & Gunter, G. (2012, October). *Online tools for creating teaching, social, and cognitive presence in large blended classes*. Presented at the 18th Annual Sloan Consortium International Conference on Online Learning, Orlando, FL.

Thrun, S. (2012, October). *Democratizing higher education*. Presented at the 18th Annual Sloan Consortium International Conference on Online Learning, Orlando, FL.

Zhang, D., Zhou, L., Briggs, O., & Nunamaker, J. (2006). Instructional video in e-learning: Assessing the impact of interactive video on learning effectiveness. *Information & Management, 43*(1). doi:10.1016/j.im.2005.01.004

ENDNOTES

1.   With apologies to Shakespeare (As You Like It, II.vii.139-42).

Acknowledgment

This book is, by and large, a collection of contributions where credit lies with the collective rather than any individual. First and foremost, we recognize our impressive set of authors who regularly present at top international conferences on teaching and learning with technology. These scholars take direction with surprising eagerness and humility. Thank you for sharing your expertise.

Second, we wish to sing of our unsung heroes, those reviewers who have enhanced this book immeasurably. Your insight and improvements amaze us. Thank you for the hours you gave each chapter. We especially want to thank our Editorial Advisory Board for their guidance and for reviewing both the chapters and chapter proposals.

Last but not least, we would like to thank our families, friends, and our colleagues. Over and over, we asked our Austin Peay comrades for assistance. Thank you for stepping up. To friends serving as unofficial reviewers, Peggy Russell and Mike Weinstein, we owe special thanks. We have also been blessed with two wonderfully supportive spouses, Diann Volker and Thomas Smyth, who make our work on this book possible. Thank you for starting where we stop, beginning where we end.

Ellen G. Smyth
Austin Peay State University, USA

John X. Volker
Austin Peay State University, USA

Section 1
Setting the Stage

Chapter 1
The Digital Lectern

Tom McBride
Beloit College, USA

Ron Nief
Beloit College, USA

ABSTRACT

This chapter projects how higher education will be systematically transformed once the practice of capturing lectures is widespread and common: in particular how the practice will affect the lecture format itself, bring about a reversal of homework and class work, influence the dialectic of interdisciplinary education, transform the communications ontology of the lecture, and affect small liberal arts colleges, for whom in-person pedagogy has been a hallmark—and to which captured lectures would appear to be alien.

INTRODUCTION

Colleges and universities have always been 'capturing' their lectures. --a prospective item on The Mindset List for the Class of 2042 (born 2020).

In this chapter we offer speculation about how a single technological change in American higher education—the captured lecture—will transform educational practices and possibly redefine best practices regarding the subject of pedagogy. Our perspective is that of two authors who have been studying the impact of technological change as it affects the mindsets of succeeding generations of young persons. In our past studies we have focused on how different generations absorb what appears to be novelty and quickly make it a normal part of their everyday lives. We approach the subject of captured lectures in the same way: once they become a routine part of the mindset of higher education, what else will seem *always* to have been true? Our objective is to stir imaginative discussion about the pros and cons of this almost inevitable technological change in higher education.

DOI: 10.4018/978-1-4666-3962-1.ch001

BACKGROUND

Last year in the New Yorker Adam Gopnik neatly summarized major attitudes about digital technology. He said there were three major points of view: those who thought such technology had fostered a paradise of vast information and individual choice; those who thought it had unleashed a dystopia of diminished concentration and fragmented knowledge; and those who shrugged and said that every new technology was a blend of good and bad that required lots of adjustment. (Gopnik, 2011)

As authors of The Mindset Lists of American History (McBride & Nief, 2011), which traces what was normal for ten generations of Americans from 1880, count us as mostly in the third category. In our research we discovered that every older generation regards the technology that marks the new one as having caused a great decline and loss. Thus automobiles brought unwelcome strangers into town and allowed youngsters to get away from home and do Lord-Knows-What. Telephones would end house visits (just as text messages, it might be feared, will end phone calls). Radio would destroy conversation around the fireplace. Television would ruin viewers' eyes. Besides that, by 1961 Newton Minow, former head of the Federal Communications Commission, called TV "a vast wasteland" (Minow, 1961) of culture: this after a decade that is now regarded as TV's golden age with its many live theatrical performances. If we go back long enough we discover that even the lowly zipper was thought to have been a threat to civilized values. Buttoning up was thought central to a virtuous and industrious life. The microphone that made crooners like Bing Crosby possible was regarded as the ruination of American music, which had depended upon more full-throated tenors and baritones who required no mic and performed on a live stage.

At the same time, new technology has also brought with it no shortage of theorists to explain what it meant. The most famous of these was the Canadian English professor Marshall McLuhan, who wrote about how television had created an electronic global village and punished politicians whose stentorian gifts may have once been appropriate to the sweaty convention hall but utterly inappropriate, and even scarily off-putting, on the cool medium of the Tube. (McLuhan, 1964) Meanwhile, in an earlier era the microphone had made possible a more intimate form of singing, and while no theorist of McLuhan's stature was around to say so, it just became obvious after a while. What is equally apparent is that new technology is frightening. It brings with it new ways of presenting and organizing information, new consumer habits, and new words. No wonder the public, especially the older public, craves an explanation of what seems to be a new, and not necessarily brave, world. Theorists who can say What It All Means will often find an audience: hence, Mr. Gopnik's categorization of today's theorists in three slots.

This theorizing has been especially true of the digital age, so thinkers as diverse as MIT's Sherry Turkle and the editors of Wired Magazine (such as Christopher Harris) have developed followings. But is the digital age overrated in importance? The social theorist Claude Fischer suggests that we are inaccurately sentimental about the American past and claim a false nostalgia for a less violent and mobile, more religious, US of A. (Fisher, 2010) If we follow this line of thought, perhaps the current epoch is less disturbing when compared to the technological revolutions of yore, when the telegram, the railroad, the phonograph, the movies, the auto, and the radio all succeeded each other in rapid order. Of their revolutionary importance there should be no doubt. Without them mass culture would have been impossible, yet as late as the 1880s there was no mass culture of the sort we take for granted today in the United States. In this sense all these inventions founded new ways of organizing information. Even the auto was an instrument of communications, bringing people of vast distances together face to face for the first time. Yes, the car was on the information highway, and a servant of it, before there even was…an information highway.

Still, it is unlikely that the significance of the digital revolution has been overestimated. Take just one example of the profound difference it has brought. Once upon a time, not all that long ago, there was constant worry about the effects of mass culture on conformity. We all listened to the same programs (I Love Lucy), read the same news (Associated Press), and shopped at the same chain stores (Sears). In time there developed pushback, especially around 1960, when the kids started listening to their own music and stopped listening to the same big bands that Mom and Dad adored. A separate youth culture developed. Cable television offered a seemingly infinite variety, despite Bruce Springsteen's complaint that "there's 57 channels and nothing on."

Even so, culture remained pretty massive—until the Internet. Now it is virtually custom-made for everyone. You can surf onto millions and millions of websites, including your own. You can get your news and opinions from dozens of journals on line every day. You could spend the rest of your life, and that of your kids and grand-kids too, watching youtube. The fretting about mass culture and conformity has been stood on its head. Now those who are anxious about the loss of any national identity pray for a return to mass culture. A little conformity wouldn't hurt anyone. Better that than an out of control atomism. Once there was information that *everyone* (who was anyone) knew; now information is so abundant that it drives out other information. There is only so much room for it in our brains. The philosopher Daniel Dennett says that price of remembering the Beatles may be forgetting about Berlioz (Dennett,, 2007) It is very hard to speak hyperbolically about the importance of a revolution like this turn of the worm seems to be.

About twenty-five years ago, before this worm turned, the child of one of us was enrolled in a Washington, DC grammar school. His teacher thought it was a good thing for the kids to watch the launch of the Challenger Space Shuttle. She forgot to bring her portable TV and after the Challenger exploded glad she had forgotten it. She used television so little in the classroom that she wasn't used to having to pack it in her car. Radio and television have had scant educational impact—unless you count the often-made assertion that TV has reduced everything to image (a declaration that cannot be proved). Most classrooms look much as they did one hundred years ago, with movable desks and perhaps an electronic board being the major innovations.

But will digital technology—like other new technologies in the past, feared and theorized about, an innovation about which revolutionary claims are made—at last become the technology that changes the old classroom forever?

In answering this question, our aim is to be as constructively provocative and speculative as possible.

Issues and Controversies

Imagine the following conversation between university students in 2020:

John: *Mary, where are you off to?*
Mary: *Off to a lecture*
John: *Live or captured?*

Today the term *lecture capture*—the pod-casting and archiving of class room lectures for general access--is known mostly as the argot of a relatively few educators, mainly those who are vitally interested in the role of new technology in the process of instruction. But within a decade or less it may well become a term of common and ordinary use on campus. In 1900 not much of anyone would have thought *ignition* would become a part of the American lexicon soon to be known by nearly everyone. The same would have been said about such terms as *rabbit ears*, *VHS*, or *mouse* in future years. Here is a cautionary tale. *Rabbit ears*, the nickname for indoor TV antennae, have long been forgotten—so some new technology becomes old and buried except in the memories of more elderly people. But another aspect of this story of caution is that we must not blind ourselves to any possibility, as who would have predicted in 1980 that *mouse* would cease to become known mostly as a rodent? Why not the same for the term *captured lecture*?

Here is a pertinent backstory, both historical and conceptual. In many colleges and universities the lecture has become a somewhat outmoded instructional art form, having given away in many schools, if not all, to a mode of discussion and collaborative learning known as "guide on the side," in which the professor is no longer a centralized source of information ("a sage upon a stage") but a helpful facilitator of conversation and joint student projects. Such modes of instruction have been praised as more democratic and egalitarian, and as an excellent preparation for the work actually done beyond the campus walls, especially the intensive labor of collaborative work teams in both the public and private sectors.

Yet we have learned in our research for The Mindset Lists of American History a striking trend: the more things change, the more they stay the same. Call this the "Eternal Return" theory of history, captured by the famous French expression about constancy amid change. And so we predict that new technology will make the lecture return as a dominant method of instruction in American higher education, just as text messages brought back telegrams in a new key. Once lectures become captured by digital technology, there will be no turning back from them any time soon. The lecture shall return in a new key.

Why is this likely to be so?

One answer is because the Internet has already changed the name of the game from process to information. Creative, collaborative solutions are still at a premium, but they must now operate against the significant danger that such solutions may still be information-poor (or poorly informed) and thus of lower quality. Thus the efficient, well-modulated delivery of information is already on the way to becoming a senior partner in the enterprise. Discussion courses will become LECTURE-Discussion simply because more information can be offered in an hour by lecture than by discussion.

Another answer is because lectures, especially those delivered on podcast, are cheaper. They can reach vastly larger audiences. Students can access them anywhere. They can live at home and do so at a time when the cost of tuition in higher education seems almost doomed to increase.

Still, there seems something a little tawdry about both these reasons, especially for an enterprise as seemingly noble as higher education. A gusher of information and a better-balanced checkbook would seem to be rather inadequate rationales. Isn't education about the discovery and mastery of first principles, not simply an access to innumerable facts? As for money: isn't a cheap education likely to be a cheap product? Don't' students get what they pay for?

But something more is afoot. What is it? The answer is that captured lectures will be enhanced lectures. They will be vastly improved ways of transmitting information and fostering learning. Students can play the lectures over and over if they need to. They can go back to hard-to-understand passages and have a better chance of getting them. Professors, meanwhile, can expose their charges to other professors. Professor of English: "Hamlet is an early modern example of alienation, a concept especially developed by Karl Marx. For an excellent introduction to Marx's concept please consult Professor Davis's fine lecture in Sociology 100. You can find it in our archives (exact coordinate follows)." Captured lectures actually promote an intellectual community in ways far more difficult before their advent.

Professors sometimes long to pair courses, but they are logistical nightmares, as students must find room in their schedules for both courses, and since professors can't be at two places at once, it is especially hard to get the two course sections together at once. Captured lectures solve this scheduling problem in a flash. Students need only view the podcast of lectures in the first course (let us call it "The Psychology of Religion" instructed by Professor Smith) and then view the podcast of lectures in the second (let us call it "Major Cognitive Errors" taught by Professor Jones). Thus the two professors need not worry about their students needing to make sure they have room at both 9 AM on Mondays, Wednesdays and Fridays and 2 PM on Tuesdays and Thursdays, for students are now freed of such shackles. On their own time they can hear Professor Smith discuss the cognition of religious persons as emotionally rich and Professor Jones discuss the cognition of religious persons as typical mistakes in logical thinking. They can also view Professor Smith and Professor Jones encountering one another's rather conflicting viewpoints in a separate podcast.

Please note that captured lectures so conceived reject the false choice between education as absorbing a deluge of information and education as travel into the realm of first principles. Both Professor Smith and Professor Jones in our example are fact and information rich—they are experts—but both also come at their subjects from different first principles and thus view the same phenomena through different lenses. Students' perception of this dialectic is possible without the technology of captured lectures. But it is much more logistically daunting and therefore much less likely to occur.

Yet this is hardly all. Think of other possibilities. Professors can capture their lectures with other features as well. Professor Wilson can lecture on the subject of the evolution of the extendable thumb while flashing on the screen questions for further inquiry at various points of her presentation. "What would have been the course of human evolution without such an adaptation? Which would have been the more salient adaptation: the extendable thumb or walking upright?" Students may stop these lectures at any point and research answers to these questions before continuing with the presentation. Sometimes a more in-depth un-

derstanding of one point makes understanding of subsequent points both richer and easier. Lectures tend to be linear in format, but with this *stop-and research* feature students may convert them into a more webbed learning experience.

Once a great many lectures are captured, then a great many lectures become archived. Prospective students and their parents can consult such archives as they search for quality and appropriateness in a future college or university. Current students could even self-design their own fields of study based on approved reading lists and a great variety of lectures from different areas of inquiry. *Homework* can be done as *class work*, as students get the major principles on captured lectures listened to on podcasts while heading to class to do collaborative work based on these principles. In fact, the word *lab*, thanks to captured lectures, may come to be a common term in all fields of study. In the captured lecture you get the principle of the subjunctive in Spanish; in the classroom lab you meet with your peers and exchange fantastic stories in the Spanish subjunctive mood. In the captured lecture you learn about discourses of explanation. In your homework you go into the larger community and ask people from various walks of life to explain why something happened. That would be half of your lab; the other half is when you go to class to discuss your findings with your peers, and when they discuss theirs with you. Time for this is freed up simply because you didn't have to attend the lecture at a set time.

Therefore terms such as *captured lecture*, *lab* and *homework* may come to have profound new meanings. Like the terms *windows* and *spam* and *text*, these ordinary words will come to wear clothes so new that an older generation would barely recognized them.

To all this innovation we might add: "And students can use summer evenings after work to access lectures, do readings, and take courses from their home universities without having to be at their home universities." Or: "Bright and enterprising high school students may begin their college courses early by 'taking' them, via captured lectures, at night and on weekends." Scheduling, in the sense of being at a certain place at a certain time, is no longer a problem. Flexibility reigns.

But at this point we should stop, for always at our back we hear, hurrying near, the ancient adage: If it seems too good to be true, that's because it is. Is the purported beneficial revolution to be brought by lecture capture too good to be true?

Problems

In answering such a question we should ask what problems such an innovation cannot solve. It cannot solve the problem of students with learning difficulties of all sorts, of students who are unmotivated, or professors who are boring or disorganized, and of reading materials that are poorly linked to lectures and discussions. (It may, nonetheless, make professors more embarrassed about recycling the same lectures year after year, as the very ambience of digital technology leans towards constant updating.) It will cause no end of transitional challenges for the professoriate, which will have to practice its lecture skills—perhaps rusty in an age of "guide on the side." Some professors will quit rather than go along.

Meanwhile, graduate preparation for new faculty and their progress towards tenure will probably include instruction and practice in how to capture lectures. It may be easier for students to skip lectures if they don't have to show up in a particular place at a particular time. After all, one reason students attend classes is to see their friends there. Then there is the question of the amount of academic credit, if labs are added to three captured lectures a week in such traditional non-lab disciplines as French, political science, and philosophy; will and should students earn added credit for these courses? Finally, there are many professors for whom in-person attendance is a holy grail—points taken off if you aren't

there—and who insist on live classroom audience feedback.

This is not to say that some of these difficulties—and there are many more not yet contemplated—cannot be ironed out. If professors miss the live audience when podcasting their presentations, they may, however, not have to miss it in whole, for students can decide whether or not they want to get the lecture live or captured. As for whether or not students are there for professors' lectures, this is an uncertainty that teachers will have to become accustomed to: the evaluation of the papers and quizzes will have to become the sole basis for final grades.

But here again we should stop, for the process is less likely to be a matter of problems solved than adjustments made. Those who thought the telephone would end forever and always the glory of house calls were not right but they were not wrong either. People these days would rather ring your phone than ring your doorbell. Yet folks still drop over from time to time. We have learned how to visit on the telephone. We have adjusted. Professors and students will adjust. In time there will be a generation for whom captured lectures are normal. There will be grandparents who will come to say to their grandchildren not "When I was your age I had to walk three miles in the snow to go to the little country schoolhouse," but "When I was your age I actually how to show up a set time for lecture."

The transition may be especially painful for small liberal arts colleges, such as the one from which we hail. Our own college proved nearly half a century ago that one reformulation of time and space can lead to huge and improved innovation, as when Beloit College installed its then famous Beloit Plan. Students went to school year round—a true trimester system—and were thus free to do such life-changing things as four to eight month *field terms*, challenging experiences off campus that superbly matured them. Captured lectures are a similarly creative redefinition of time and space. But what will liberal arts colleges, which specialize in small classes and live professors who are available nearly 24/7 for extra help, do in such a digital lecture atmosphere?

The answer, we predict, is that they will thrive. Such colleges were once known for their great lecturers, and this tradition will return, as more and more professors will be hired for their capacity to deliver captivating captured lectures. But this will hardly be all, for the small college will become an especially keen laboratory for reversing homework and class work. Twelve hours a week per class will be freed up for enrollees to gather together and discover practical applications for the platinum-encased principles podcasted to them at their convenience. We would predict some marvelous collaborative investigations by students and faculty alike. Some may well be publishable, and they may center around such topics as the process of aging as seen partly through regular visits to nursing homes, or the conundrums of small city governments as seen through participant-observation at city hall, or the application of rhetorical theory as found by visits to advertising agencies or even the campus public relations office. Small liberal arts colleges, with their emphasis on a constant and collaborative learning environment, will be ideally suited to make this reversal of homework and class work become both novel and effective. The professors and the students, and the students and the students, will not stop seeing one another in person after all.

Therefore the advanced technology of lecture capture will usher in a brave new world. (We have said nothing about its capacity for letting whole classes visit academic conferences on a particular subject without having to board so much as a bus to the airport.) But it is not a world that will happen all at once, just as there were still big banks of pay phones in airports as late as 2001. Students still buy textbooks made from pulp, though less

and less often all the time. Lectures will not be captured all at once, but we would not be surprised to find that they become a regular option for students by 2020.

Is it a brave new world? Yes. But it will not become new overnight. And we don't have to be all that brave to enter it, as we will do so gradually—and more or less together. But here is a prediction that enter it we will. It will not bring with it an educational Nirvana, but it should transform the milieu in which learning occurs, and, not infrequently, for the better.

Understanding the nature of the lecture itself will lead to an even better case for such a positive prediction. Indeed, another approach to the potential excellence of lecture capture is to consider the problems posed by the lecture itself as a mode of education, and to examine how lecture capture may well mitigate such difficulties. Here we refer especially to the lecture's present status, by which we mean its *communication ontology*. What sort of communication is the lecture—and how might its technological *capture* change it? Let us review some thinking about the sort of communication the lecture is, its pros and cons, and the potential transformation of its communication ontology when captured.

One may trace the lecture back to medieval universities, but colleges and universities have obviously favored the lecture a pedagogical form ever since it began to educate students in critically large numbers. While tutorials and seminars may be ideal pedagogical arrangements for small numbers of students, the lecture proves to be a quick, cheap and efficient method of imparting knowledge. Anyone who champions the lecture as an antidote to the "waste of time" or "pooled ignorance" of the classroom discussion should not overlook the economic element—affordability--in the lecture itself for tens or hundreds of students. It is as much an economic arrangement as it is a logical one.

In the past two or three decades the lecture has come under sustained critique as promoting passive learning. In this indictment the lecturer talks while the students listen. As Donald A. Bligh has archly put the matter, lectures "represent a conception of education in which teachers who know give knowledge to students who do not and are therefore supposed to have nothing worth contributing." (Bligh, 2011) Leaving aside for the moment the question of whether or not the charge made against the lecture—excessive student passivity—is fair and accurate, we might state with greater neutrality that Marshall McLuhan, whose work is now encountering a revival of interest because of the Internet, assigned the lecture to the category of being a *hot* medium, which calls for little audience participation. (McLuhan, 1964) It is a communication that prizes linear logic and predictable sequences. It may even announce a journey in advance and then take its listeners on it, precisely as promised at the start. There are no surprises or distracting side trips. The lecture here is rather like a Protestant sermon of the traditional (but dying) churches (e.g., Presbyterian, Congregational): first the minister tells the congregation what he or she is about to say; then the minister tells the congregation; and finally the minister tells the congregation what he or she has told them. The congregation, satisfied with this predictable format of beginning, middle and end, says nothing! This is as classical an illustration of Aristotle's beginning, middle, and end as one is likely to find. It should be noted, however, that McLuhan did not necessarily equate passivity of reception with passivity of thought. People still think, even in lectures and during films, another hot medium.

Another insight into the communications ontology of the lecture comes more indirectly from Roland Barthes, who distinguished between two types of texts: *writerly* and *readerly*. (Barthes, 1974) The former is by far the more common; it is one in which the meaning of the text is in the hands of its producer, who makes sure the text does not depart from common sense as defined by prevailing conventions and who assures that the principle of non-contradiction will always prevail. The writer makes sure the dear reader knows what to think and how to react. The latter, the readerly text, is one in which the usual consumer of the meaning becomes the producer of it. A readerly text has much greater potential for an unconventional hermeneutics, as readers do not so much read against the grain and organize their own grain. The readerly text is rather parallel to McLuhan's notion of the *cool* medium, such as the seminar, the newspaper cartoon, and (most famously) television, where active participation in the communications process is not only common but may even be required for the production of meaning. For our purposes, think especially of the discussion encouraged by the readerly seminars.

Thus the lecture is plausibly located as a hot medium and a writerly text. While it is fashionable today to aver, with some justification, that students' intellectual lives are changed mostly by the self-discovery of their own journals or through independent or collaborative projects, there is no good reason to exclude the possibility that lives have been changed by lectures, as students rush from the classroom enlightened by the principles they have heard and eager to try them for themselves. We should not conflate the behavioral passivity of students in the lecture classroom with what may well be a fermenting intellectual activity at the same time, which will lead to seminal results in the library or even in a future career.

When the lecture is captured, however, these point and counterpoints may well disappear as irrelevant. To take a small but pertinent example, one knock against the lecture is that it almost asks for flagging attention. Bligh cites research showing that student concentration is highest during the first twenty-five or so minutes and declines quickly after that. (Bligh, 2000) But students have nowhere else to go and must thus sit it out. Captured lectures make this problem vanish, as the student can stop at any point where she feels her attention is diminishing.

Captured lectures, furthermore, can combine hot and cool media, writerly and readerly texts, into one package. A seventy-five minute captured lecture may consist of three twenty-five minute parts, with each part followed by an interactive exercise of some sort. For instance, after the lecturer has offered a disquisition on various ways to define emotions (neurological, behavioral, functional and subjective), the lecture may stop and ask students to pause at this point in the podcast to write a paragraph in their journals about the manifestation of these four notions of emotions in their own lives during the previous week. This can be a marvelous opportunity to go from passive (but not thoughtless) listening to active self-discovery. Or, to take another hypothetical example, after the lecturer has discoursed on the limits of relativism as a philosophical doctrine, students could be asked to write a paragraph in their journals about one thing in their own lives about which they are comfortable taking a relativist approach and one thing about which they are uncomfortable—and to account for the difference. Both of these are examples of how, from a student's point of experience, the more passive lecture can be packaged with the more active *writing to learn*, (Zinsser, 1993) with the latter possibly sparking the student to begin writing the lecture for herself, with added, more personal, or even opposing viewpoints. It can help turn a writerly lecture (to use Barthes' terms) into a more readerly one. When one writes for oneself, possibilities of clarification and dialectic are launched.

These are ways by which the captured lecture can become neither a cool nor hot medium but a *cot* or *hool* one, or by which it can become a (w)readerly text: combining the best of both types of communication. The point, however, is to make sure the technology is the servant of the goals and not the master of such goals. There are, to be sure jazzier things that can be done with the captured lecture format (such as Power Point or graphs), but

Edward Tufte, an expert on visual communication, has argued that Power Point presentations are not only distracting and overly bulleted but also bury the story that is central to every good presentation or report. (Tufte, 2012) In any event, the main advantage of the captured lecture is temporal, not graphic. The major advantage is the way by which it can reformulate the learning time, and therefore pace, of the student. If the classroom is *flipped*, so that the lecture occurs at home while the collaboration occurs on campus, then the captured lecture has a novel impact on space as well.

RECOMMENDATIONS

Capture the Future: Assume as a top academic administrator in your institution that lecture capture is inevitable and begin to experiment with it on a limited basis.

Put Professors on Podcasts: Request or assign a limited number of professors to have themselves videoed and view the results. What are the differences between how they appeared to themselves and how they appear on video? Is their lecture better on video or in person? How might they change their styles and approaches if their primary medium were podcasts? How might they change their courses and content if they knew that students could stop viewing their lectures for purposes of reflection or clarification, and if they knew their students could play back sections of the lecture for purposes of more precise understanding?

Kick It Around: Assign a campus committee to study the issues, controversies and problems of lecture capture, to host faculty discussions of the subject, and to make recommendations about future practices.

REFERENCES

Barthes, R. (1974). *S/Z* (Miller, R., Trans.). New York, NY: Hill and Wang.

Bligh, D. A. (2000). *What's the use of lectures?* San Francisco, CA: Jossey-Bass.

Dennett, D. (2007). There aren't enough minds to house the population explosion of memes. In Brockman, J. (Ed.), *What is your dangerous idea?* New York, NY: Harper Perennial.

Fischer, C. (2010). *Made in America: A social history of American culture and character.* Chicago, IL: University of Chicago Press.

Gopnik, A. (2011, February 14 and 21). The information. New Yorker, (pp. 124-30).

McBride, T., & Nief, R. (2011). *The mindset lists of American history.* Hoboken, NJ: John Wiley and Sons.

McLuhan, M. (1964). *Understanding media.* New York, NY: McGraw-Hill.

Minow, N. (1961, May 9). *Speech to the National Association of Broadcasters.* Retrieved August 5, 2012, from http://www.terramedia.co.uk/reference/documents/vast_wasteland.htm

Tufte, E. (2012). PowerPoint does rocket science. Retrieved August 5, 2012, from http://www.edwardtufte.com/bboard/q-and-a-fetch-msg?msg_id=0001yB

Zinsser, W. (1993). *Writing to learn.* New York, NY: Harper Perennial.

Chapter 2
Navigating Multimedia:
How to Find Internet Video Resources for Teaching, Learning, and Research

Julie A. DeCesare
Providence College, USA

ABSTRACT

The Web has quickly become a resource for multimedia and video content. Search engines have tools to mine for visual content, but finding video content creates different challenges than searching for text. This chapter presents a detailed guide on searching for visual multimedia content and provides a showcase of innovative collections and resources. The reader will learn research strategies, gain specific skills in navigating multimedia, and receive a list of resources for finding subject-specific and interdisciplinary video content. Resources are reviewed based on content quality, partnerships, technical specifications, and overall usability.

INTRODUCTION

In 2010, the Pew Internet & American Life Project, an initiative of the Pew Research Center, published "The State of Online Video." The study reported that educational videos have experienced considerable growth, from 22% of online adults watching educational video content in 2007 to 38% in 2009 (Purcell, 2010). Even before this study, it was very clear that video content on the Web was expanding

at rapid paces. In addition to many born-digital resources, there are multiple initiatives to digitize analog video and audio content. How can these resources be discovered? How can a needle be found in the haystack? Search engines have tools to help narrow and expand our searches. Programmers and developers are also improving search technologies at rapid paces – facial recognition, shape and color recognition, and audio search are available in some cases, but these advancements

DOI: 10.4018/978-1-4666-3962-1.ch002

Copyright © 2013, IGI Global. Copying or distributing in print or electronic forms without written permission of IGI Global is prohibited.

are in their infancy. Finding video content creates a new set of challenges compared to the more classic research methods involving text. How videos are labeled, categorized, and tagged will determine the end results. Think about searching for an image of a women putting on a red shoe. How many different ways can this be imagined? How many different ways can this be found in a search engine? Each word has a variety of representations and personal interpretations that will lead to a new set of results - women, female, mother, lady, woman, gender - red, crimson, scarlet, burgundy, rose, rouge, maroon, merlot - shoe, sandal, heels, flats, sneaker.

Using the research strategies and specific skills outlined in this chapter, instructors, students, teachers, faculty, instructional technologists, and librarians will be able to navigate the wealth of multimedia available online for teaching, learning, and research. This chapter also provides an opportunity to learn about some innovative collections, reliable resources, and a variety of subject-specific and interdisciplinary multimedia content that is available online.

BACKGROUND

From transparencies and filmstrips to streaming video, visual content has always been an important learning tool used in a variety of class environments. Currently, an immense amount of multimedia is available on the Web for educators, but how can professors get to what they need? A brief inquiry on a search engine just scratches the surface. Many websites strive to showcase historical, cultural, or educational video content and yet never top the results list in an initial search engine keyword entry. Copyright, accessibility, proprietary software and hardware, and metadata all add to the complexity of multimedia searching.

Additional complexities lie in understanding licensing, accommodating mobile devices, and using consumer streaming products such as

Netflix, Amazon Instant, iTunes, Hulu Plus and cable company websites. These products are designed for individual consumers and do not offer institutional subscriptions or licensing.

Educators need to look deeper than YouTube, Vimeo, and iTunes U. The larger video-sharing sites have hours of worthwhile and interesting content, but there is a growing collection of mostly free, educational content from libraries, museums, content producers, and distributors on the Web. Web 2.0 tools and social networks help collections expand to more users and continue discussion. In some cases there are video annotation tools that allow users to perform close viewing and technical analysis of the presented media.

Multimedia content can be found through subscription databases for libraries and institutions, but the market is uneven and inconsistent in regards to price, licensing, and format. Companies like Alexander Street Press, Annenberg Learner, and Films Media Group are creating innovative products for educators and are providing high quality content for a fair price.

Some websites and online collections are proprietary, corporate, or commercial, while others are library, archival, museum, and educational initiatives. Video researchers and educators need to recognize the differences. Many sites are free but include advertisements, fees for premier subscription services, or paywalls for accessing additional content.

MAIN FOCUS

Multimedia and in particular video streaming allow for flexibility and adaptability in curriculum and learning environments. Media as a term in education and pedagogy is a massive topic, as is the critical viewing, analysis, and manipulation of media forms. Analysis of a multimodal form - video, audio, text (digital or analog) - should be approached as a critical literacy. Ultimately, the educator decides why and what content will be used to convey lessons, lectures, interactions, and assignments.

In regards to how educators should use multimedia and video, we should first acknowledge the how-not. In the 2006 article "Non-optimal Uses of Video in the Classroom," Renee Hobbs addresses key findings in a survey of 130 secondary level teachers and their use of various media in the physical classroom. In brief summary, non-optimal uses of video are:

- As time-fillers;
- As substitute teachers;
- With no use of pause, rewind, or review;
- As class breaks or rewards instead of requirements;
- When educators ignore video while expecting students to give attention;
- Solely as an attention hook;
- To quiet or settle the class;
- Touting video as fun or easy work while reading and writing are hard work.

Dr. Hobbs argues that these passive forms of viewing in the classroom replicates how media is used in the home, more as entertainment or casual enjoyment. Use of video without critical perspective and interaction can discourage administrators, colleagues, students, parents, and other educators, and can reduce the educational value of videos as learning objects and tools (Hobbs, 2006).

Dr. Hobbs' article was written when media was hardware and location specific - VHS and DVDs were the most accessible formats. Students were tethered to the classroom and the audiovisual machines. Non-optimal use should be recognized and avoided regardless of technology and format, but new technologies and the influx of digital, streamed video have given educators more options. So, how can educators make optimal use of video?

- Educators should determine their educational goals and objectives for using multimedia materials.

- Context and discussion should surround the viewing experience.
- When appropriate, multimedia should be examined critically as a scholarly work, as much as text.
- Educators can encourage students to actively search for these materials and contribute findings as learning objects for the class.
- Physical audiovisual equipment in the classroom should be abandoned in lieu of virtual options. Embedded or linked videos in courseware management systems, with discussion and discourse available in the forum tools, allow for flexibility while making the best use of class time. Students control the pace of learning with guidance from their instructor.
- Embedded tools and functionality within the content itself assist educators in controlling the context and use of the video. For example, by creating an account on YouTube, a user can create playlists of clips, as well as add annotation to the videos. Another useful, and recently developed, tool is TEDEd (http://ed.ted.com/videos), which allows instructors to *flip* a YouTube video, by adding supplemental materials, and the ability to share the lessons with your students.
- Professors should explore free online multimedia resource options.
- Faculty can use multimedia to address multiple learning styles, especially in online and hybrid courses.
- Educators can use video to mediate translation and language barriers.

Armed with the optimal uses of video, how do educators go about finding the perfect multimedia resources to support their learning objectives? Before we dive into the individual sites, it is important to cover some basics about multimedia searches. As search engines develop and become more advanced, the search functions become more intuitive for users, and the results more streamlined. It is best to be as specific as possible when selecting a query term for the search box. Here are some recommendations to keep in mind while hunting for multimedia items hidden in the World Wide Web.

Keyword Search

As mentioned earlier, it is important to think of your visual search in as many specific keyword terms as possible. In addition to a reliable Thesaurus, there are tools that can help you evaluate your topic. A tool like Notre Dame's Hesburg Library Keyword Generator (http://wwwtest.library.nd.edu/reference/keyword_generator/) can help you think critically about your topic and build useful terms ("Keyword Generator," 2012). Adding terms such as *video*, *multimedia*, *film*, or *movie* can shape your results more efficiently as well.

Search Engines

Rather than settling on just one search engine, try a variety of engines. Google, Bing, Yahoo, or even lesser known sites, like Carrot2 (http://search.carrot2.org/stable/search), Yippy (http://yippy.com/), Ixquick (https://www.ixquick.com/), and Gigablast (http://www.gigablast.com/), can provide different top hits to your keywords. There are many search engines out there, and using several can help expand your results list effortlessly.

Look for *Advanced Search* interfaces that include additional fields to narrow and focus your search criteria. For example, date, format (video, image, and sometimes as specific as file format), duration, author, and sources are often options. Each search engine is unique, and many offer their own lists of specific tips for searching multimedia content. Check the Help or FAQs links for keyboard shortcuts and useful query formats.

Some sites and search engines give an option for a *Family Filter* or *Safe Search* to weed out adult content. These options are often available in the preferences or settings menu of the search engine. Use of these options will depend on the situation: research, audience, and personal sensibilities.

Browsers and Software

Web browsers can certainly influence and adjust your multimedia experience. Something as simple as permitting pop-up windows on the browser platform (e.g., Firefox, Safari, Chrome, Internet Explorer) can alleviate initial viewing issues. Switching browsers or refreshing the page can help troubleshoot content when a video is not playing.

Certain requirements may affect how well you can view or listen to content on your computer or mobile device. Requirements that can affect the quality of the sound or image include operating systems, file formats, software requirements, browser limitations, and network robustness or speed. Most likely, an error message will appear, if there is an issue. *About* and *FAQ* sections of websites often contain multimedia technical requirements and specifications. Since the web is a moving target, search functionality on sites can change, and content or entire websites can disappear. When bookmarking, use permalinks if possible. Permalinks remain unchanged indefinitely.

Copyright

Copyright is a complicated area in multimedia and visual content. Most video hosting websites that allow uploaded content are protected by the Online Copyright Infringement Liability Limitation Act (OCILLA), a provision of the Digital Millennium Copyright Act Section 512. These provisions are designed to shelter service providers from the infringing activities of their customers, such as the upload of full-length feature films to YouTube. The

Internet service is required to delete any infringing content, if notified and requested to do so by the copyright holder (OCILLA 1998, 2012). It is important that researchers and instructors know that multimedia content can be fluid and is often not a permanent resource.

For aid in navigating copyright and fair use law, there are several sites that can help. The Center for Social Media at American University published a "Code of Best Practices in Fair Use for Online Video" (http://www.centerforsocialmedia.org/fair-use/best-practices/online-video). This document helps creators, distributors, and educators interpret the copyright guidelines surrounding fair use and online video content.

Many of the born digital (i.e., media created in the digital form) or public domain content websites also adhere to Creative Commons (CC) licensing, an initiative that allows content creators to share freely and openly. From their mission statement, "Creative Commons develops, supports, and stewards legal and technical infrastructure that maximizes digital creativity, sharing, and innovation" (CC, 2012). The creator can choose a license that best suits their needs. CC gives creative owners control of how their content can be used: commercial, open access, limited use, etc.

Google Tips

As mentioned earlier, there are many search engines, and most have search shortcuts and options. One of the benefits to using Google is the range of search options it provides, especially for multimedia. As many searchers do not venture past Google's first 10 results, there are ways to refine searches for more accurate results. Google provides a full listing at Google Inside Search (http://www.google.com/insidesearch/tipstricks/) (Google, 2012). By setting up a Google Account (http://www.google.com/intl/en/policies/), users will get more functionality and options when searching Google via enhanced search features visible only when logged in. Users concerned about privacy should proceed carefully and read the account agreement in its entirety.

Google has both an Advanced Search portal and a Google Video Search portal. Either can be very helpful when hunting for multimedia content. However, Advanced Search provides more control over the results of a search. To directly access Advanced Search, visit http://www.google.com/advanced_search. It is important to note that Google search portals and interfaces can change depending on the browser version and compatibility.

Once on the Google Advanced Search page, there are several fields useful to the multimedia researcher. They are *site or domain* (a shortcut to a domain or specific website), *Safe Search* (adult content filter), *file type* (short cut to specific file type), and *usage rights* (search by copyright information about the content). As mentioned earlier, another option is Google Video Search interface (http://www.google.com/videohp), which allows you to filter the search by duration, date posted, and source.

The following Google shortcuts are particularly helpful for multimedia searches and will work on all Google search interfaces, including YouTube.

- Adding *and* in Google is unnecessary since Google automatically searches for all words.
- Quotation marks are using when searching for a specific phrase or name. For example, "art therapy" will return only websites where the word *art* is immediately followed by *therapy*. Without quotes, Google will retrieve all websites that contain the words *art* and *therapy* anywhere on the page, which broadens the results considerably.
- The word *OR* can be used when looking for at least one match among a list of pos-

sibilities. For example, searching for *dog OR dogs OR puppy OR puppies* will return all websites that contain any one of these four terms.

- A minus sign (-) will exclude the word following the minus, with no space before the excluded term. For example, *terriers -rat* will return all websites that contain the word *terrier* but not the word *rat*.
- An asterisk (*) following a search term acts as a wildcard. For example, *dog** will retrieve dog, dogs, doggie, doggone, dogma, and so on.
- An asterisk (*) can also be included to complete a phrase: "ken burns * war" retrieves video results on Ken Burns' documentaries "The War" and "The Civil War."
- An **intitle:** Command searches for words in a title. For example, *intitle:superman*, with no space before or after the colon, will provide results where *superman* is in the title of the website.
- The **site:** Command searches for a specific website or a specific domain extension (e.g., .com, .edu, .gov, .mil, .org). For example, *autism site:pbs.org* will retrieve pages on the pbs.org website that contain the word *autism*, whereas *autism site:.edu* will return results from any .edu sites containing the word *autism*. Again, note the lack of a space before or after the colon.
- The **filetype:** Command will only bring back the requested file extension and format. There are dozens of file types (e.g., doc, pdf, swf, mp3, mp4, wmv, mov, jpg) for images, audio, and video. For example, *filetype:png cat* returns any PNG files with *cat* in the name.
- Shortcuts can be combined to make a very precise search. For example, *intitle:ARKive site:youtube.com* will return YouTube pages with *ARKive* in the title.

Search skills and techniques become habit. By incorporating just a few of these shortcuts, searches become more efficient and yield a greater amount of quality content that accurately meets search expectations.

MULTIMEDIA RESOURCES

In addition to being more specific in search engine queries, below are several great sites dedicated solely to multimedia and video content. These collections range in subject, technical requirements, and technical options. Organizations representing a wide range of expertise and partners (e.g., grant, legal, technical, subject, categorization) maintain these valuable and complicated web resources.

News and Archival

Collections focusing on archival news footage include NewsFilm Online (http://newsfilm.bufvc.ac.uk/) from the British Universities Film and Video Council and the Moving Image Archive (http://www.archive.org/details/movies) from the Internet Archive (http://www.archive.org).

NewsFilm Online has produced 67 news stories and associated clips from British news journalists and sources. Much of the content is freely accessible and may be browsed by decade or theme. They offer subscription access to over 3,000 hours of digitized news stories spanning the 1910s to the present day, including some primary research materials, as well as television news and cinema newsreels (NewsFilm, 2012).

The Internet Archive (IA), a non-profit organization founded to build and maintains an Internet library, might be best known for the Wayback Machine, a historical web archive of preserved webpages. Through the Wayback Machine users can view the progression of websites from 1996 (IA, 2010). In addition to the Wayback Machine, the IA includes texts, audio, moving images, and software. The IA's Moving Image collection contains full length feature films (now in the public domain), newsreel and commercial footage, user uploaded content, and subject-specific collections from a range of donors.

The IA is making great strides to preserve and catalog the Internet as a medium, though that is only a small part of the initiatives they support. The IA partners with the Smithsonian and the Library of Congress to provide a platform to archive born digital material, as well as digitize and preserve unique cultural collections and artifacts. In addition to the library and museum collections, users are able to upload content. Some interesting collections in the Internet Archive Moving Image Archive include the following.

- The Khan Academy (http://archive.org/details/khanacademy), a non-profit educational organization created in 2006 by Bangladeshi-American educator Salman Khan, comprises an online collection of academic, instructional micro-lectures in video format on a variety of subjects. A great example of a multimedia collection that utilizes different avenues, not only are Khan Academy lectures available through IA, but also through YouTube, iTunes U, and a stand alone site, http://www.khanacademy.org/. Khan Academy videos also provide subtitles in multiple languages through the help of volunteers (http://www.khanacademy.org/contribute).
- The Prelinger Archives (http://archive.org/details/prelinger) - a collection of over 60,000 ephemeral films including vintage educational films, advertisements, and home movies - was founded in 1983 by Rick Prelinger and then acquired by the Library of Congress Motion Picture, Broadcasting, and Recorded Sound Division in 2002. All

films in the public domain are available through IA, and filmmakers can showcase mash-ups they create from the Prelinger Archive.
- A large collection of full length, vintage Hollywood films, which are now in the public domain can be found here, http://archive.org/details/moviesandfilms.
- One subject-specific example would be the television news archive, documenting the media events surrounding 9/11. "Understanding 9/11: A Television News Archive" grew out of a conference held at NYU in August 2011 (http://archive.org/details/911).
- AdViews (http://archive.org/details/adviews), a digital archive of vintage television commercials from the 1950s to 1980s, provides a unique collection about the American culture, advertising, and consumerism. Kraft, Proctor & Gamble, Post, Beech-Nut, and Alphabits are just a few of the brands represented. The commercials are a part of the D'Arcy Masius Benton & Bowles Archives found at the John W. Hartman Center for Sales, Advertising & Marketing History in Duke University's David M. Rubenstein Rare Book & Manuscript Library (IA, 2011).

The default video player is Adobe Flash, but most videos are available for free download in a variety of formats, such as HTML5, mpeg4, and ogg. Using the available player, there are options to embed and share the videos (via email, Facebook, and Twitter), as well as basic player controls.

How Tos

One of the most interesting digital video trends that have been popping up online is How To tutorial sites.

Pertaining to online research and technology, the In Plain English series from CommonCraft (http://www.commoncraft.com/) provides simple explanations of Web 2.0 technology and associated online tools. *Not sure what RSS is? How about phishing? Wonder how and why people use Twitter or other social networking sites?* In Plain English showcases a variety of topics such as plagiarism, compounding interest, and online reputation. CommonCraft offers fee-based subscriptions and memberships for the ability to download, embed, or use for corporate training; however, branded and streaming videos are are available to anonymous surfers for free.

eHow, HowCast, and HowStuffWorks are three other video sites that connect self-directed learners with instructions on an array of topics. *Have you ever wanted to repair your own garbage disposal? Learn Yoga, or to play a guitar? Want to start a grassroots movement? Need to make chocolate covered strawberries?* These sites show you how it is done, but like everything else on the web, it is important to be critical. Only a handful of these sites are closely monitored and controlled for accurate, useful, and appropriate content. All three of these sites rely on advertisement for income.

eHow (http://www.ehow.com/) provides how-to videos and articles from acknowledged experts in a variety of fields. Video topics range from pet training to home repairs to cooking. The company pairs freelance videographers with experts described as having professional credentials, training, or established work experience. Both parties complete an application process and make their credentials available. Videos are streamed via an embedded Adobe Flash player with abundant advertising.

Howcast (http://www.howcast.com/) is designed to bridge the gap between user-generated and professionally-produced videos. "Howcast brings together the personality of user-generated content with the quality of a professional video studio to create engaging, informative, and free how-to videos for consumers. It also offers

emerging filmmakers an opportunity to gain experience, exposure, and income." (Howcast, 2012). Alongside videos are well written essays and additional tips. "How to Write Essays and Research Papers" can aid a struggling student, tutorials on a new video game can push a user to the next level, and "How to Make a Raised Bed Garden" can spark interest in a new hobby. Like eHow, Howcast provides embed code, so content can be easily shared by users and added to other websites, blogs, and social networking sites.

HowStuffWorks (http://www.howstuffworks.com/) was started in 1998 by Marshall Brain as a website and a book series geared towards students and teachers. "Our premise is simple: Demystify the world and do it in a simple, clear-cut way that anyone can understand." (HowStuffWorks, 2012) HSW is now owned by the Discovery Channel (of Discovery Communications, Inc.) and the video center is just a small corner of the overall website (HowStuffWorks, 2012). The site is advertisement heavy but can act as a content aggregator to other video sites and resources.

Nature and Environment

Several multimedia collections available online are designed as teaching and learning resources about the environment, the Earth, and wildlife diversity. The web provides a platform for animal lovers, conservationists, zoologists, scientists, environmentalists, photographers, photojournalists, academics, instructors, and videographers to reach a wide demographic and make nature studies and documentation collaborative and cooperative.

One of the top sites for educators due to their content, quality, and partnerships is ARKive: Images of Life on Earth (http://www.arkive.org). Because of its usability and content, this site servers as an excellent, reliable resource for teachers, lecturers, librarians, students, and instructional technologists. ARKive's overall mission is to include all of the world's most threatened species on the International Union for Conservation of Nature (IUCN) Red List of Endangered Species and promote their conservation (Wildscreen, 2012). Created by the Wildscreen Trust, a charitable foundation based in the UK and US, ARKive's initiative relies on partnerships and sponsorships to create, maintain, and publish its content. The principal sponsor is the Environmental Agency of Abu Dhabi. Other notable sponsors are HSBC, Bank of America, Merrill Lynch, and the British Council. Technical and media partnerships include Hewlett Packard, the Smithsonian Institution, London Natural History Museum, World Wildlife Fund, and the BBC. ARKive provides over 70,000 high quality images and videos, from more than 5,000 media donors (including BBC, National Geographic, and Discovery Communications). Their impressive list of content and research partners includes the Smithsonian and the Natural History Museum, London (Wildscreen, 2012).

Options to share the resources with various Web 2.0 and social media tools are available, but they do not provide embed code to cut and paste the video into personal websites. Google Earth established a technical partnership with Arkive to place the species and its associated multimedia in a geographical context (Wildscreen, 2012). The streamed video files are mp4 format, which works on mobile and touch devices. Videos can be downloaded in QuickTime and Windows Media formats. All content – images, video, text, and audio – is hosted by ARKive's servers.

Hewlett Packard Labs collaborated with Wildscreen Trust to design and develop ARKive. HP developed a Media Production system for digitizing, cataloging, and tracking media assets and a Media Vault with storage capacity around 74 Terabytes (Nelson n.d.). Committed to preserving media assets for long term use, ARKive offers a high level of reliability for educators.

In an email to the author, Andrew Nelson of Hewlett Packard explained that Wildscreen relies on a staff of media researchers and biology experts to catalog and create descriptive metadata regarding the content, subject, and provenance

of the media. By consulting with natural history and subject matter experts, all content is verified while Wildscreen defines the cataloging structure. Some technical metadata is captured automatically during import or edit of the media asset by the systems HP Labs created. Wildscreen recently received funding to create "ARKive in your pocket," a mobile complement to the site (University of Bristol - School of Biological Sciences News, 2011). In an email to the author, Lucie Muir of Wildscreen stated that QR codes (strategically placed 2D barcodes) are being tested at the Field Museum to work with their mobile site, and Wildscreen is currently redesigning the entire site to improve usability for mobile and touch devices. Other avenues are being explored such as second screen technology, where viewers use mobile devices to interact with secondary material while a larger screen plays primary content.

ARKive contributes to the Encyclopedia of Life (EOL) (http://eol.org/), an ongoing and ambitious project to organize and make available via the Internet virtually all information about life on Earth - animals, plants, fungi, microorganisms, and bacteria. The content on EOL is open, freely available, and a trusted global resource. EOL is a series of webpages—one for each of the approximately 1.8 million known species. Each species site is constantly evolving and features dynamically synthesized content ranging from historical literature and biological descriptions to quality images, videos, and distribution maps. After an initial search, searchers can filter by image or video, and from trusted or unreviewed sources. The EOL allows you to create an account so users can save videos and images to their collection.

The history of EOL begins when biologist E. O. Wilson announces a dream for a networked encyclopedia focused on the biosphere and based on the world's knowledge of life. This announcement came during Wilson's March 2007 Technology, Entertainment, and Design (TED) Prize speaking engagement, a yearly forum where important, innovative, and luminary speakers are given the opportunity to ask for a dream prize (TED Talks, 2007). E.O Wilson's dream was realized two months later when cornerstone institutions and two foundations announced an initial 50 million dollar grant to get the project started. The grants were from the John D. and Catherine T. MacArthur Foundation and the Alfred P. Sloan Foundation, and the cornerstone institutions include the Biodiversity Heritage Library, The Field Museum of Natural History, Harvard University, Missouri Botanical Garden, Smithsonian Institution and Marine Biological Laboratory (EOL n.d.).

Art and Culture

The TED Conference began in 1984 to bring together the best thinkers from technology, entertainment, and design. TED's scope has become far broader over the years, as the quality of the videos, speakers, and content advances along with its increased popularity. Over 1300 of the best recorded presentations from the annual conference are made freely available online as TED Talks (http://www.ted.com/talks). Videos can be browsed by length, spoken language or written subtitles, dates, subject, or overall sentiment (inspiring, thought provoking, challenging, funny, etc.). Because TED Talks are released under a Creative Commons license, they can be freely shared and embedded. Closed captioning is available for TED using Google's speech recognition technology for, but this technology is still fairly primitive.

A multimedia site dedicated to art, Art Babble (http://www.artbabble.org/) was created in 2009 at the Indianapolis Museum of Art (IMA) with a mission to provide a high quality showcase of video content about art and the issues around it. ArtBabble provides a great resource to learn more about art, artists, and technique, as well as information about some of the most famous museums in the world.

Funded through the Ball Brothers Foundation (ArtBabble, 2012), ArtBabble and has many partners for content including the Smithsonian American Art Museum, the Metropolitan Museum of Art, the Museum of Modern Art, and the National Gallery of Art, as well as international partners such as the Van Gogh Museum (Amsterdam) and the Prado Museum (Spain). Each individual video is credited and branded by the institution that produced them, and each partner has its own channel or group of videos that can be referenced.

The site is organized by the subheadings Series, Channels, Artists, and Partners. Series are specific exhibits, programs, or workshops at the individual institutions. Channels consist of portals that allow users to browse the site based on a chosen genre or topic. The Artists subheading provides an alphabetic listing of the artists themselves. The Partner subheading lists the institutions and provides direct links to their video collections and productions. Though the site has basic keyword search box, an advanced search box would be a welcome addition to this website.

The available tools offered alongside the content make ArtBabble unique. All videos have a Creative Commons license, regardless of the partner institution. The videos are high-definition h.264 with options to download (to an iPod), embed, comment on, rate, or share. One of the most interesting features on the home page is a section called Video Quotes -- these are clips and quotes, usually very pointed and interesting, that pull you into the video. It will be interesting to see how the site is developed for mobile devices. Based on a brief survey available on the site, they are working towards providing live streaming art events and expanding their content to a variety of formats (blogs, images, micro-sites, and articles).

UbuWeb (http://www.ubuweb.com/) is a resource dedicated to creative writing and poetry. Founded in 1996, UbuWeb was initially created as a repository of vanguard visual, text, and sound poetry, but has grown into a resource for the progressive, obscure, and avant-garde art in all formats (Goldsmith, 2011). Videos are streamed in Adobe Flash and can be shared via web link, though not embedded. Audio is available in mp3 format or through the iPhone ubuRadio app (http://itunes.apple.com/us/app/wfmu-radio/id324175340?mt=8). Volunteers along with some technical and strategic partners run UbuWeb. According to their FAQ page, their only cost is a $50 hosting fee for the site. Content on the site ranges from the famous to the obscure. Poets like Charles Bukowski, Samuel Beckett, Bertolt Brecht, Maya Deren, and John Cage feature prominently, though lesser known works and artists are also showcased.

UbuWeb's technical and content partners include Anthology Film Archives, PennSound, and WFMU. Even though it has been stable, growing, and evolving over the past 15 years, Ubu Web says the site was never created as a permanent archive and could vanish at any time (Goldsmith, 2011). UbuWeb works with content directly from donors, items in the public domain, or items that are out of print. UbuWeb is a huge proponent of open access, fair use, and access as preservation. While copyright infringement issues have surfaced, Ubu is making content accessible that is not otherwise currently for sale, online, or available in a digitized format (Goldsmith, 2011). Unlike some of the other sites mentioned, no content from the site is purchasable and the site does not allow advertisements.

At the crossroads of culture and history is Folkstreams (http://www.folkstreams.net/), an interesting and unique resource for full-length independent documentaries about American culture and anthropology. Among Folkstreams' partners to host and maintain the site are several divisions of the University of North Carolina at Chapel Hill, including the Public's Library and Digital Archive initiative (ibiblio.org) and the Southern Folklife Collection. Funding is achieved through grants by the National Endowments, the Institute for Museum and Library Services, as well as several state arts and humanities organizations.

By creating an online database of streaming films, Folkstreams accomplishes two goals: build a national repository of hard-to-find documentary films about American folk or roots culture *and* give films new life by streaming them on the internet. The Folkstreams films begin in the 1960s and focus on the culture, struggles, and arts of Americans from many different and very often unnoticed regions and communities. The site includes transcriptions, study and teaching guides, suggested readings, and links to related websites. Film facts are provided for each title, including distribution, creation, and copyright credits. An advanced search interface (http://www.folkstreams.net/pub/searchindex.php) as well as bookmarking and sharing capabilities make the site easy to navigate. Streamed videos are available for download in multiple file formats (e.g., Adobe Flash, mpeg-4, and Real Media), and some can be purchased on DVD.

History

One of several historical multimedia collections available online is The Living Room Candidate (http://www.livingroomcandidate.org/) from the American Museum of the Moving Image. The Living Room Candidate hosts an innovative online exhibition of more than 250 television presidential campaign commercials from every election year beginning in 1952 and ending with our most recent election. Users can watch nearly four hours of TV commercials and explore the expanding world of web-based political advertising. The site includes a searchable database featuring commentary, historical background and context, election results, and navigation organized by year, by theme (e.g., taxes, civil rights, change, etc.), and by commercial type (e.g., fear, background, biographical).

Though not as well designed and organized as The Living Room Candidate, another great site is American Rhetoric (http://www.americanrhetoric.com) from Speech Bank. American Rhetoric features original audio recordings (and supporting text and video) of the most important speeches delivered throughout the 20th Century and into the present day. Content is freely available via streaming or download. Most of the speeches are political in nature, by presidents such as John F. Kennedy, Richard M. Nixon, Franklin D. Roosevelt, and Barack Obama. The site also includes speeches from Democratic and Republican National Conventions, commencements, legal proceedings, and famous orators such as Martin Luther King, Jr. and Malcolm X. From the list of most accessed speeches, one can hear a wide range of historical topics. Video available is often linked out to YouTube, and speech entries can include additional resources, such as related books and content for sale. American Rhetoric has commercial advertisements on all pages of the site which can make it a challenge to navigate. The quality content and site search box positively outweigh the negative aspects of site layout.

The American Memory Collection (http://memory.loc.gov/ammem/index.html) from the Library of Congress incorporates written and spoken words, sound recordings, still and moving images, prints, maps, and sheet music into an online module to document the American experience. American Memory is an open-access digital record of American history and creativity. These materials and collections, from the Library of Congress and other institutions, serve the public as a resource for education and lifelong learning. American Memory can be browsed by geographic location, time period, subject, collection, or format (e.g., maps, motion picture, audio recordings, print, image). Certain collections and titles contain video and sound recordings in a variety of formats.

The multimedia resources outlined in this chapter represent many different subjects. These collections can supplement or provide learning objects for educators, students, and technologists to analyze, distribute, critique, or absorb. News and archival multimedia can be a great resource in showing the context of a historical event. Footage from a specific event can assist in a talk about environmental, societal, or cultural implications (such as Internet Archive's Understanding 9/11).

Vintage advertisements (such as AdViews and Library of Congress's American Memory) and training films are a great way to breach the subject of gender, class, or product marketing. Tutorials and How-Tos can give students new perspectives on careers and promote self-directed learning on topics they know little about. Nature and environmental multimedia collections give students high quality access to written text, references, video, and audio about biological and environmental issues. These sites also provide a context on how these species are thriving, or are endangered, in their environment. Arkive provides an entire section of teacher resources, complete with lesson plans, presentations, and assignments. Art and Culture collections, such as, Ubu, ArtBabble, and TED, provide opportunities for educators and students to do close analysis of creative works and theories around those works. An anthropological resource like Folkstreams provides glimpses into lifestyles and local histories about craft, work, and community. The Living Room Candidate can introduce the theories of foreign policy, our government, and the perspectives of democracy. These collections, and those like them, will continue to expand and develop as multimedia search becomes more sophisticated and as digital media continues to evolve.

FUTURE RESEARCH

The Institute for the Future released the report "The Future of the Video: Becoming People of the Screen" in 2009 as part of their Technology Horizons Program. This report points out that multimedia resources and video collections are building communities around content. Mainstream education is swiftly moving towards incorporating media literacies both in screening and in creating content in all levels of education. Video is now global and can capture attention from anywhere in the world. Video culture is participatory and theories of ownership and copyright implications are shifting. As a format itself, multimedia addresses multiple learning styles by engaging sight, sound, and sometimes touch (such as user manipulation of the media and technology available) (Dunagan, Harris 2009).

Multimedia websites and initiatives face many current and future challenges. For example, born digital or digitally converted multimedia collections often require vast partnerships and collaboration. Whether from libraries, archives, corporations, or the users themselves, these sites would not exist without contributions of time, money, and materials. Very often researchers, metadata specialists, technologists, lawyers, and content consultants are the core professional roles needed to pull together the specialized content necessary in a streamlined search interface.

In addition to funding and maintaining core content, multimedia sites are challenges by rapid developments in technology and file formats. Certainly mobile devices and the constant evolution of file types and standards are changing how we access the web. Many video collections that have been converted from an analog medium were done so using Adobe Flash, Windows Media, Real, and QuickTime streaming formats. Video formats are constantly becoming outdated and are quickly being replaced by more efficient, detailed means. Video on mobile devices is just truly starting to gain momentum. Stand alone apps are replacing the wide reach of the web. Devices are proprietary, as is the software to load content on the devices. Due to funding and organization constraints, mobile accessibility will be another layer of complexity to these multimedia sites, though a necessary one for institutions and their partners to tackle.

CONCLUSION

Searching for media can be adventuresome and at times frustrating but with practice can be skillfully done. Personal search and research habits should be modified and changed as the technology and advancement of search engines adapts to multimedia formats. The wealth of multimedia on the web is growing exponentially and the sites listed here just scratch the surface of what is available. Finding, recognizing, evaluating, and understanding multimedia resources for teaching, learning, and research is a critical literacy.

REFERENCES

About HowStuffWorks. (2012). *HowStuffWorks*. Retrieved May 17, 2012, from http://www.howstuffworks.com/about-hsw.htm

ArtBabble. (n.d.). *Home*. Retrieved May 17, 2012, from http://www.artbabble.org/

British Universities Film & Video Council. (2006). *The Newsfilm online digitization project*. Retrieved May 17, 2012, from http://newsfilm.bufvc.ac.uk/

Creative Commons. (n.d.). *About*. Retrieved May 17, 2012, from Creative Commons: http://creativecommons.org/about

Eidenmuller, M. E. (2012). *American rhetoric*. Retrieved May 17, 2012, from http://www.americanrhetoric.com/

Encyclopedia of Life Learning + Education Group. (n.d.). *What is EOL?* Retrieved May 17, 2012, from http://education.eol.org/who/what_is_eol

Goldsmith, K. (2011). *About UbuWeb*. Retrieved May 17, 2012, from http://www.ubu.com/resources/

Google. (n.d.). *Google | Inside search: Tips & tricks*. Retrieved May 17, 2012, from http://www.google.com/insidesearch/tipstricks/

Hesburgh Libraries University of Notre Dame. (n.d.). *Keyword generator*. Retrieved May 17, 2012, from http://wwwtest.library.nd.edu/reference/keyword_generator/

Hobbs, R. (2006). Non-optimal uses of video in the classroom. *Learning, Media and Technology, 31*(1), 35–50. doi:10.1080/17439880500515457

Institute for the Future. (2012). *The future of video: Becoming people of the screen.* Retrieved May 24, 2012, from http://www.iftf.org/node/3584

Internet Archive. (2010). *Wayback machine beta FAQs.* Retrieved April 30, 2012, from http://faq.web.archive.org/what-is-the-wayback-machine/

Nelson, A. (2009). *ARKive.* Retrieved May 17, 2012, from HP Labs: http://www.hpl.hp.com/research/ssrc/services/publishing/arkive/

Purcell, K. (2010). *The state of online video.* Retrieved from http://pewinternet.org/~/media//Files/Reports/2010/PIP-The-State-of-Online-Video.pdf

University of Bristol - School of Biological Sciences News Item. (2011, March 11). *£680K for "ARKive in your pocket" audiovisual wildlife experience.* Retrieved April 3, 2012, from http://www.bristol.ac.uk/biology/news/2011/106.html

17USC § 512 - *Limitations on liability relating to material online.* (2009). Cornell University Law School, Legal Information Institute. Retrieved from http://www.law.cornell.edu/uscode/text/17/512

Wildscreen. (2011). *ARKive: Images of life on Earth information sheet.* Retrieved from http://www.wildscreen.org.uk/downloads/ARKive.pdf

Wilson, E. O. (2007, March). *E.O. Wilson on saving life on Earth.* Retrieved May 17, 2012 from http://www.ted.com/talks/e_o_wilson_on_saving_life_on_earth.html

ADDITIONAL READING

Alexander Street Press. (2012). *Alexander Street Press.* Retrieved May 17, 2012, from http://alexanderstreet.com/

Amazon.com. (2012). *Amazon instant video.* Retrieved May 17, 2012, from Amazon.com: http://www.amazon.com/Instant-Video/b?ie=UTF8&node=2858778011

Annenberg Foundation. (2012). *About Annenberg learner.* Retrieved May 17, 2012, from http://www.learner.org/about/

Apple Inc. (2012). *iTunes.* Retrieved May 17, 2012, from http://www.apple.com/itunes/

Apple, Inc. (2012). *Apple in education.* Retrieved May 17, 2012, from http://www.apple.com/education/itunes-u/

Apple, Inc. (2012). *iTunes preview: WFMU radio.* Retrieved May 17, 2012, from http://itunes.apple.com/us/app/wfmu-radio/id324175340?mt=8

Center for Social Media. (2012). *Online video.* Retrieved May 17, 2012, from http://www.centerforsocialmedia.org/fair-use/best-practices/online-video

Columbia Center for New Media Teaching and Learning. (n.d.). *MediaThread.* Retrieved May 17, 2012, from http://ccnmtl.columbia.edu/portfolio/custom_software_applications_and_tools/mediathread.html

Creative Commons. (n.d.). *Choose a license.* Retrieved May 17, 2012, from http://creativecommons.org/choose/

Social Science Computing, University of California, Los Angeles. (2010). *Video annotation tools.* Retrieved May 24, 2012, from http://kb.ucla.edu/articles/video-annotation-tools

Electronic Frontier Foundation. (n.d.). *Electronic Frontier Foundation: Defending your rights in the digital world*. Retrieved May 17, 2012, from https://www.eff.org/

Films Media Group. (n.d.). *Films for the humanities & sciences*. Retrieved May 17, 2012, from http://ffh.films.com/

Geelhoed, E. (2002, September 16). *Wild wild web: Wildlife enthusiasts' use of the Internet*. Retrieved from http://www.hpl.hp.com/techreports/2002/HPL-2002-248.pdf

Gigablast. (n.d.). *Gigablast: The search engine*. Retrieved May 17, 2012, from http://www.gigablast.com/

Google. (n.d.). *Google*. Retrieved May 17, 2012, from https://www.google.com/

Hulu. (n.d.). *Hulu plus*. Retrieved May 17, 2012, from http://www.hulu.com/plus-

Institute for the Future Tech Horizons. (2011). *The future of video* [Prezi presentation]. Retrieved from http://prezi.com/nk6yv4atvm1u/the-future-of-video/

Intelligent Television. Copyright Clearance Center, & New York University (2009, June). *Video use and higher education: Options for the future*. Retrieved from http://library.nyu.edu/about/Video_Use_in_Higher_Education.pdf

Intelligent Television. (2012). *Intelligent television: Video for culture & education*. Retrieved May 23, 2012, from http://www.intelligenttelevision.com/

Ixquick. (2012). *Ixquick*. Retrieved May 17, 2012, from Ixquick: https://www.ixquick.com/

Khan Academy. (2012). *Khan Academy*. Retrieved May 17, 2012, from http://www.khanacademy.org/

Microsoft. (2012). *Bing*. Retrieved May 17, 2012, from Microsoft: http://www.bing.com/

Museum of the Moving Image. (2012). *Museum of the Moving Image*. Retrieved May 23, 2012, from http://www.movingimage.us/

Netflix. (2012). *How Netflix works*. Retrieved May 17, 2012, from https://signup.netflix.com/MediaCenter/HowNetflixWorks

Open Culture, L. L. C. (2012). *475 free movies online: Great classics, indies, noir, westerns, etc.* Retrieved May 23, 2012, from http://www.openculture.com/freemoviesonline

Open Culture, L. L. C. (2012). *Intelligent video: The top cultural & educational video sites*. Retrieved May 23, 2012, from http://www.openculture.com/intelligentvideo

Oskinski, S., & Weiss, D. (2012). *Carrot2 clustering engine*. Retrieved May 17, 2012, from http://search.carrot2.org/stable/search

Partners, A. I. Y. P. (2011). *About us*. Retrieved May 23, 2012, from AIYP: http://www.aiyponline.org/

Vimeo, L. L. C. (2012). *Vimeo*. Retrieved May 17, 2012, from http://vimeo.com/

Wildscreen. (2012). *Wildscreen > home*. Retrieved May 23, 2012, from http://www.wildscreen.org.uk/

World Wildlife Fund. (2012). *World Wildlife Fund*. Retrieved May 23, 2012, from http://www.worldwildlife.org/home-full.html

Yahoo. Inc. (2012). *Yahoo!* Retrieved May 17, 2012, from http://www.yahoo.com/

Yippy, Inc. (2012). *Yippy*. Retrieved May 17, 2012, from http://yippy.com/

YouTube. LLC. (2012). *YouTube*. Retrieved May 17, 2012, from http://www.youtube.com/

KEY TERMS AND DEFINITIONS

Copyright: Legal right, given to a creator to print, publish, perform, film, or record literary, artistic, or musical material, and to authorize others to do the same.

Creative Commons: An organization that offers a flexible range of protections and freedoms for authors and artists. CC was developed as an option to, or in conjunction with, traditional copyright law and focuses on digital mediums.

Embed: To fix an object within another system (ex. webpage).

Fair Use: A provision of copyright law that outlines how copyrighted work can be used without seeking permission.

Metadata: Data that describes or gives information about other data.

Multimedia: Using more than one medium or material (audio, video, text, animation, etc.) in expression or communication via web pages and web browsers.

Open Access: A movement which aims to make scholarly literature and creations freely available on the public web. For example, by open access journal publishing, author self-archiving in institutional repositories, or personal websites. Open access extends to non-text formats as well.

Video: Moving visual images.

Chapter 3
Integrating Video Lecture Tools in Online and Hybrid Classrooms

Patricia Desrosiers
Western Kentucky University, USA

ABSTRACT

Use of technological resources can greatly enhance the effectiveness of online instruction. Developing familiarity with these new resources can be time consuming and difficult for professors already overburdened with high class sizes and course load assignments. This chapter introduces the basic components of three general types of video lecture tools: lecture capturing tools, web conferencing tools, and video hosting and streaming tools by providing details of three specific software platforms: Tegrity™, Adobe^R Connect™, and YouTube. Suggestions for their effective use in both online and hybrid classrooms are given.

INTRODUCTION

There has been a definitive trend in many universities and colleges over the last decade embracing E-learning and moving towards more online based instruction (Kim & Bonk, 2006; Ko & Rossen, 2010). In an increasingly technologically dependent and proficient world, and given the rapid growth of distance education, the ability to effectively teach online is thus becoming more important for instructors to master. In response to this rapidly shifting education milieu, there have been a host of dynamic programs developed to assist instructors in effectively conveying material online. The purpose of this chapter will be to afford readers a beginning familiarity with three of the most cutting edge and promising modalities: lecture capturing tools, web conferencing tools and video hosting and streaming tools. By utilizing these tools (separately or in tandem), instructors

DOI: 10.4018/978-1-4666-3962-1.ch003

can stay ahead of the technology curve and enhance the overall quality of their online classes. A method for integration of these software tools into course design will be provided.

INTEGRATION OF VIDEO SOFTWARE INTO HYBRID AND ONLINE COURSES

Using synchronous and asynchronous software platforms in both hybrid and completely online courses can be challenging. It is advisable to avoid simply putting a face-to-face course online because the learning activities won't be appropriate (Simonson, Smaldino, Albright, & Zvacek, 2009). By using Bloom's Taxonomy (1956) and determining the content type required by the learning objectives (Clark, 1999), it is possible to determine which format would be better suited for the delivery of selected content. Consequently, components of course design related to choosing video technology formats will be discussed in this section, using case examples. By taking advantage of the strengths of both environments, students become more engaged in their learning, resulting in better learning outcomes.

Bloom's Taxonomy

A revision to Bloom's Taxonomy (Krathwohl, 2002) is used here to begin the discussion of a method of software tool selection. By adding a second dimension, the knowledge dimension, to Bloom's six cognitive processes, Krathwohl (2002) designed a useful grid. The knowledge dimension includes factual, conceptual, procedural and metacognitive types of knowledge, and this dimension is on the vertical axis of the grid. The cognitive processes of remembering, understanding, applying, analyzing, evaluating and creating make up the horizontal axis.

By placing each of the learning activities for a course within the grid, it is easy to determine

which dimensions are emphasized or underutilized. Depending upon the level of learner expertise and the learning objectives for the course, it may be appropriate to emphasize certain types of knowledge over others or to minimize certain types of knowledge.

For example, a course on professional ethics included the following learning objectives: (1) Students will analyze and evaluate current ethical practices in their workplace environment; (2) Students will successfully recall, interpret and apply a professional code of ethics to an ethical dilemma; (3) Students will identify personal biases and the influence of those biases upon their ethical decision making practices and (4) Students will produce a plan for the reduction of the influence of personal ethics upon their professional practice. Each of these learning objectives can be placed within the Taxonomy Table as described by Krathwohl (2002) as shown in Table 1.

This ethics course is a combined 4th year Bachelor's/1st year Master's level course, and as you can see the objectives lean toward the lower right quadrant of the grid which would be appropriate. If your course was a first year introductory course, your objectives would most likely cluster towards the upper left quadrant although there are frequently objectives that would be found appropriately out of that quadrant. It is not necessary to fill all of the quadrants to plan a successful course, and it is typical that some learning objectives would fit into multiple categories. It is most important to make sure the learning objectives lean towards the expected quadrant of the table. Use of Table 1 in the planning stage will ensure that your objectives are appropriate for your course.

Method of Tool Selection

After applying the course grid to your course's particular learning objectives, you will need to choose appropriate learning activities to meet these objectives. It is important at this point to

Table 1. Application of Krathwohl's (2002) revision of Bloom's taxonomy

	Remember (recognizing; recalling)	Understanding (interpreting; exemplifying; classifying; summarizing; inferring; comparing; explaining)	Apply (executing; implementing)	Analyze (differentiating; organizing; attributing)	Evaluate (checking; critiquing)	Create (generating; planning; producing)
Factual Knowledge (terminology/specific details and elements)	Learning Objective 2	Learning Objective 2				
Conceptual Knowledge (classifications and categories; principles and generalizations; theories, models and structures)				Learning Objective 3	Learning Objective 1	
Procedural Knowledge (subject-specific skills and algorithms, subject-specific techniques and methods; criteria for determining when to use appropriate procedures)			Learning Objective 2	Learning Objective 1		Learning Objective 4
Integrative Knowledge (strategic knowledge; cognitive tasks including appropriate contextual and conditional knowledge; self-knowledge)	Learning Objective 3			Learning Objective 3	Learning Objective 3	Learning Objective 3

determine whether or not utilizing hybrid or online contexts would be appropriate based on the required learning activities. If your school utilizes a hybrid format, the best of both worlds are available. As long as you have enough face-to-face time to complete the learning activities requiring a face-to-face environment, you simply schedule those activities for face-to-face class time and use online hours for other activities. If your course is completely online, you may be able to utilize a web conferencing tool such as Adobe®Connect™ to complete those learning activities requiring real time feedback or interaction for success.

Continuing with the ethics course example, Learning Objective 3 (Students will identify personal biases and the influence of those biases upon their ethical decision making practices) is a very important component of the course. More than one learning activity will be used to work on this objective, but they needn't all be completed face-to-face. This particular course was taught in a hybrid format with 8 face-to-face hours and 29.5 asynchronous online hours, so each of those face-to-face hours are precious. Learning activities to work on Learning Objective 3 included an emotive video about research ethics surrounding the Tuskegee Experiments, discussion of reactions to the video, reaction papers on articles discussing ethical issues, and an ethics docket exercise where students are required to verbally support an assigned stance based on their professional code of ethical conduct. As you can see from the list of learning activities only one –the ethics docket exercise—must be completed face-to-face since it requires practicing verbal support of an argument. Since in the profession of social work, the ability to verbally support one's decision making processes based on the professional code of ethical conduct is often required and you cannot assess this skill easily in a videotaped session where there is the ability to do retakes, prepare for the session well ahead of time, and edit out inappropriate comments or reactions, this exercise would only be able to be completed face-to-face.

Next, match your learning activities with the appropriate and available technologies. The ethics docket exercise mentioned above could easily be completed using a web conferencing tool such as Adobe®Connect™Pro 8, as well, however, not all colleges and universities have that software available. Even if available it may be very difficult or impossible for students to utilize the tool due to technological challenges in some rural areas. Students living in indigenous settings may have limited access to computers or internet (Rao, 2007). These students would not do well if held to the same learning activities as students with full access to the necessary technologies. They may need some alternative assignments. With some forethought, those challenges can sometimes be overcome, however you need to consider the availability of technology within your school and within your student population. We will discuss how to use web conferencing tools such as Adobe®Connect™ to facilitate this exercise as an example in that section.

Several aspects need to be considered when deciding whether a technology or tool is appropriate for the learning activity or the course. Manning and Johnson (2011) recommend evaluating technologically based teaching tools using a set matrix including several factors such as cost, level of user expertise, the problems this technology will solve, and any cautions among others. Through assessing technologies, decisions can be made ahead of time about availability and appropriateness.

Remember, all professors and students are not equally savvy when it comes to technology use. Additional training or expertise may be needed prior to use of certain technology tools such as lecture capturing, web conferencing, and video hosting and streaming. Extra time will need to be allowed. If learning new technologies becomes too difficult for students or instructors, then they will not be able to focus on learning the content of the course. Consider that time spent learning new technologies could be spent learning new course concepts, and minimize time by choosing only a few new technologies or none to use in a course. Make sure to offer online training in the form of a recorded video lecture or an assigned online tutorial as an early assignment. Many video lecture tools have available online training

videos that are very useful in this regard for both instructors and students.

It is imperative to maintain "flow" between in class activities and asynchronous online activities especially when utilizing a hybrid format (Caulfield, 2011). Flow refers to the connections between learning activities of a course that facilitate greater student understanding of content. Carefully timed learning activities as well as a variety of activities lead to greater student engagement with the learning community and ultimately the course content (Palloff & Pratt, 2007). The concrete example given in the lecture capturing example demonstrates this concept clearly.

Student variables need to be considered in the tool selection process. Students may learn in many different styles. Technology can allow for the use of a variety of learning activities to facilitate learning among many types of learners. In the example of Learning Objective 3 above, you can see how the four activities to meet that particular objective appeal to a variety of learners ranging from auditory and visual to kinesthetic or tactile learners (Fleming & Baume, 2006). The movie and reaction papers would appeal to auditory and visual learners the most, while the ethics docket exercise with its costuming and active role plays would appeal most to the kinesthetic learners. Technology can allow for self-directed learner activity choices. For example, it is possible to allow discussion assignments to be submitted via a video, written, or a podcast recording format when using a virtual classroom. This would allow learners to capitalize on their strengths for high stakes assignments while allowing them practice on their weaknesses during low stakes ones.

Students with different learning rates can benefit from a variety of learning activities. Slow and deliberate learners can study at their own pace or repeatedly review materials continually available online (Johnson, 2005). Students with disabilities can access some technology tools easier than others, however, instructors can increase accessibility by displaying information in flexible online formats so that perceptual features such as text or image size, sound or speech amplitude, contrast between background and text or image, color of text, speed or timing of video, and the layout of visual elements can be varied by the student user (Coombs, 2010). While this is required in the face-to-face classroom, it must be implemented in the virtual classroom by law, as well. It benefits all students, not just those with documented learning difficulties.

Beginning with learning objectives development, progressing to developing learning activities based on those objectives and then finally determining the appropriate technology for each activity is the basic three step process of technology selection. Figure 1 depicts a visual representation of these steps.

The rest of this chapter will focus on three video lecture tools: lecture capturing tools, web conferencing tools, and video hosting and streaming tools. Basics elements and features, challenges and benefits, costs, and tips for effective instructor use will be provided for each tool. The specific software platforms of Tegrity™, Adobe®Connect™ and YouTube will be used to exemplify each category.

Figure 1. Steps of technology selection

Technology Selection

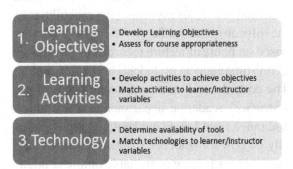

LECTURE CAPTURING TOOLS

Overview

Lecture capturing tools as a general category include software applications that enable instructors to record video and audio simultaneously as a way to deliver course content that students can access via internet. This category includes tools such as Echo 360, Elluminate, and Screenr.

Tegrity™ version 2.0 is the preeminent lecture capture software on the market today and can significantly enhance online and hybrid courses through the addition of an online lecture platform. It can be employed in real time or on-demand formats, according to instructor preferences. The software affords instructors the ability to present material in a dynamic way by enabling them to show Powerpoint slides, websites, and brief videos to students while they are lecturing on screen. It also allows students the ability to record lectures, has a function for remotely proctoring exams, and can be used to hold virtual office hours. This section will give an overview of some of its basic elements and features, discuss some challenges and benefits of using it, and review pertinent costs.

Basic Elements and Features

Lecture capturing tools generally include the elements of simultaneous video and audio display of course content recorded by instructors at a point in time to be accessed by students at a later time. It is typically asynchronous, but some software platforms allow for synchronous applications. Often there is a feature of screen sharing or document sharing and the ability to add text to the video feed at selected points.

Specifically while using Tegrity™ instructors can record a lecture while simultaneously displaying whatever is on the computer screen which may include Powerpoint presentations, websites, brief videos, and Word documents. Other tools like

Bamboo can be used in tandem to draw pictures, equations, or models on the screen. There is a function to remotely proctor exams and to hold virtual office hours. Tegrity™ includes edit capabilities so that after a lecture is recorded an instructor can go back into the video to remove poor sections or to add lecture notes and bookmarks.

There are specific features for students. Students can record videos to share with others. There is a chat feature that allows students to chat with other online students about course material. A search feature allows students to search all Tegrity™ lectures in a course for key words. They can bookmark material for review or to ask clarification about later. Students can download podcasts, audio recordings, of your lectures on their iPad, iPhone, MP3 player or computer for review at a convenient time such as during a long commute or while washing dishes. All of these features are very useful for students.

See Figure 2 for a screenshot of a Tegrity™ Lecture page recorded by the author.

Challenges and Benefits

There are many benefits for lecture capture tools, in general. In an age of easy mobile access to internet service students can download instructional content 24/7 using their smartphone or other mobile device. Students can watch and listen to lectures/classes they have missed and review content repeatedly for clarification or in order to increase understanding of the material. Instructors can review their lectures to make sure that all content is covered appropriately, can record in class lectures for use in online courses, and can reuse lectures from one course to the next if applicable.

Students like Tegrity™ which was used as the case example here. Western Kentucky University has had great success using Tegrity™ increasing online enrollments over 1,000 percent in 7 years in the midst of student outcry for Tegrity™ use across campus (Wyatt, 2012). Professors like Tegrity™ because it is user friendly. It takes a moderate level of technological skill to use this tool; most instructors will need to complete a video tutorial to be able to start using Tegrity™. It is accessible in that all lectures are automatically prepared a written transcript to accompany the auditory and visual recording. As long as instructors follow the rules mentioned previously for accessibility, Tegrity™ will be accessible to those with disabilities. Tegrity™ solves the problem of creating a sense of presence in online courses. Students can hear from the instructor on topics related to the course. I often use Tegrity™ to respond to student questions about course content so that all students can access my answer. It is often helpful to have a visual aid available for clarification, too, and Tegrity allows for that where a phone call does not.

Challenges are that this is usually an asynchronous video lecture software meaning that the instructor ability to read student nonverbal behaviors and respond accordingly is missing. The students and the instructor are not interacting at the same time. Student questions require interaction. In the context of Tegrity™ immediate feedback is minimal. In short, real time teaching skills to check understanding and elicit instruction are not appropriate, so instructors must develop new strategies to facilitate student participation.

Costs

Much like cost of your time to learn a new software tool, the monetary cost of lecture capturing tools vary from free to a few hundred dollars per month or year. Costs depend upon the features offered and synchronous versus asynchronous capabilities of the software platform Tegrity™ can be purchased based on hours of lecture recorded or on number of full-time equivalent students in your institution. The costs depend on the particular needs of the instructor, academic department, or institution and range from low to moderate. There is generally no cost for students. Contact information is available for pricing is available online at http://www.tegrity.com/

Figure 2. Tegrity™ screen from video lecture with PowerPoint (© 2012, Tegrity™: used with permission)

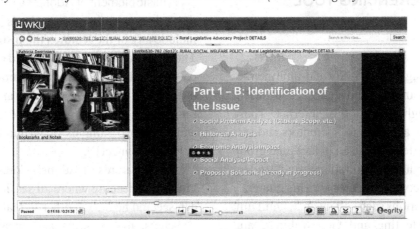

Tips for Effective Use

In an effort to engage students, it is possible to make your lecture capturing video somewhat enjoyable with a few simple tips. Keep your video lectures short—under 30 minutes. While students have on occasion reported listening to a lecture podcast on their MP3 player a dozen times or more, most students do not have an interest in spending hours listening to lectures. Additionally, there is research demonstrating that learners need material to be "chunked" due to the inability of the brain to process more than 4-5 ideas at one time (Malamed, 2012). Good instructional design incorporates short lectures into a learning plan interspersed with active components such as brief writing assignments for maximum effectiveness (Conaway, 2011).

In the case example of the ethics course, using lecture capturing can free up in class time for more active learning exercises. The assignment of watching an emotive video about research ethics can be done outside of class, and the instructor can then give a short video lecture (the focus of this section) further clarifying important points of research ethics. During the lecture the instructor can assign questions to be answered in a discussion board posting or other written assignment. In class time is then available for a discussion about the video and the lecture with clarification of confusing points and application of the concepts to other current research dilemmas to check for understanding. Learning objective 3 is then covered in multiple ways that appeal to the many different learning styles of students.

Use humor and background or clothing changes to lighten the mood. Wear your green hat on St. Patrick's Day or your Santa cap near Christmas. Move your camera to record different areas of your office or record your lecture on location at some local event relevant to your course or just some fun place you are going like the lake or the local baseball stadium. Students will appreciate the variety, and they will comment that the extra effort made your lectures more enjoyable.

It is advisable to do a brief lecture to orient your students on the features of your course management site and demonstrate accessing the lecture capturing tool for the maximum student benefit. Lecture capturing tools allow instructors to show anything on their screen and that includes the browser view showing demonstration of the course management site. A fun instructor information video is easy to do, and you can use it for all of your courses in the semester. If you can make it personal by doing it on location or including your family pet, it will make increase student comfort levels in approaching you when needed.

WEB CONFERENCING TOOLS

Overview

Web conferencing tools allow for real-time interaction between instructors and students at different locations through utilization of internet. These tools are readily available to instructors and students, and are effectively used to facilitate group projects, individual consultations, and student discussions of complex material. This category includes applications such as Tinychat, DimDim, Citrix's GotoMeeting and GotoWebinar, and Cisco's WebEx.

Adobe[R] Connect™ Pro 8 is a synchronous learning software platform that creates a virtual classroom for instructors and students. It allows real time interactivity between students and instructors (and between students) via the use of webcams, microphones, speakers, and headsets. The discussion of Adobe[R] Connect™ Pro 8 in this section will focus on some of its basic features, student satisfaction with the software, research on its effectiveness, and its costs. Also, tips for effective use by instructors will be provided, as some unexpected challenges were encountered when the author and a colleague employed this software (Cappiccie & Desrosiers, 2011).

Basic Elements and Features

Basic elements of web conferencing tools include full audio and video interactivity and typed chat. Some tools feature whiteboard, polling, screen and document sharing, and session recordings. These tools accommodate from 12 to 1,000 participants allowing from 1 to 50 participants to share at a time. There is generally a host of the room that decides who can share their screens, webcam feeds, and microphones. Features such as smartphone and mobile device access and electronic hand raising are more rare.

A basic element of Adobe®Connect™ Pro 8 is the pod organization system. Pods (or blocks) can include any of the features the instructor prefers. The pods can be resized, removed or added based on the needs of the course. Several pods can fit on your virtual classroom site, and you can arrange them however you choose. See Figures 3 and 4 for two samples of virtual classrooms in Adobe®Connect™.

Basic features of Adobe®Connect™ include videoconferencing where all session participants can see and hear each other in real time by using webcams, microphones and speakers or headphones. There is a screenshare feature allowing all participants to view websites, Powerpoint or Word documents provided by students or instructors. There is a file sharing feature, a polling or quiz feature and a notes feature. The small group rooms called breakout rooms are easily used to assign small group discussion, role play, or skills practice.

Instructors are called hosts and have certain privileges that participants and presenters do not have. As a host, the discussion can be controlled through the ability to call on those who use the "raise hand" button and grant them microphone rights. A host may choose to grant everyone microphone rights, but that can result in chaos. Grant microphone and webcam rights wisely. Hosts can change pod configurations. Presenters may upload files or share their computer screen. Participants can only use microphone and webcams when granted permission.

There is the capability to record lectures for later review. Participants may be invited in from outside of the course management system if you would like to have an online guest lecturer or allow others into the virtual classroom for whatever reason. It is a private courseware product in that it is not public. The instructor (host) must invite those not registered through the course management system.

Figure 3. Screenshot of Adobe®Connect™ configuration with 2 webcams and a poll (© 2012, Adobe®Connect™: used with permission)

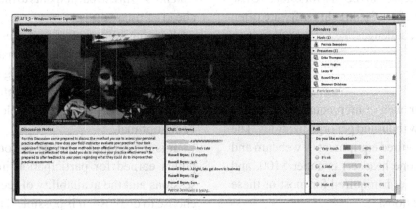

Figure 4. Screenshot of Adobe®Connect™ configuration with 18 webcams (© 2012, Adobe®Connect™: used with permission)

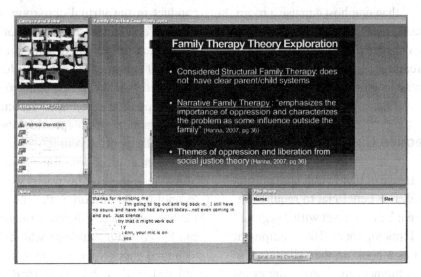

Challenges and Benefits

Web conferencing tools solve the problem of students feeling disconnected from their classmates and instructors because it is real-time interactive video and audio communication (Manning & Johnson, 2011). It is as close as you can get to a face-to-face live classroom while being online. Synchronous software leads to increased motivation to participate (Chen, Ko, Kinshuk & Lin, 2005).

A challenge with web conferencing tools is the requirement for a certain level of bandwidth and a high speed internet connection (Manning & Johnson, 2011). If one user on this application doesn't meet the required levels, it affects the entire online classroom. The video feed may stop working or become unrecognizable or audio could cut in and out. Students with older computers or those residing in rural areas might have difficulty maintaining their connection.

Scheduling is a difficulty with synchronous software. Getting adult learners to find a coordinated time to meet is sometimes difficult. This challenge is addressed in the tips for effective use section. The benefits of using this software often outweigh these challenges.

Costs

Yearly costs for web conferencing tools range from free to a few thousand per organizations. The cost for basic required equipment (a webcam and a USB microphone headset) is under $100, and high speed internet is required for most of these software applications.

Adobe®Connect™Pro 8 costs a less than $500 per year per host, but these rates depend on how many hosts are enrolled. There is a lower rate for a university. More than one host can use a room, but not at the same time. Adobe®Connect™ is free for students, but a plug in download and installation is required. Visit www.adobe.com/products/acrobatconnectpro/ to get more details about costs.

Tips for Effective Use

To solve the challenge of bandwidth and internet connection speed, it is beneficial to require students to purchase a USB headset with integrated headphones and microphone. This equipment should be listed as a book on the syllabus. Use of this specific equipment maximizes the available bandwidth also reduces feedback that can occur when using speakers and a microphone. It is important that students are aware of these requirements in order to choose the best location to attend the scheduled course events (Cappiccie & Desrosiers, 2011).

It is important that students are aware that there will be required online meeting times. Putting the dates in your syllabus as well as the published class schedule is advantageous so that students can plan to meet online during those dates and times. If you do not specifically state the online meeting dates and times, students think the online

course is asynchronous. You may also use Outlook Calendar to invite participants to the class sessions ahead of time.

Keeping web conferencing sessions below 2 hours in length is optimal. Past that, and students get inattentive and tired. Such long sessions cause eye strain and physical discomfort. It is also advisable to keep class sizes below 20 with 10 being optimal.

It is important to specify in your syllabus the points earned for participation in these online sessions and the availability of recordings if you choose to do those. It is possible that students can view a recording of the online session and then report on that at a later time, however that is not optimal. It is important to explicitly state that conduct in the virtual classroom should be the same as conduct in the face-to-face classrooms. That means fully clothed (some students take their shirts off at home), no eating (it looks really bad on camera) and keep side chats to a minimum.

Completing a preclass "technical check" is good practice. Also, provide the number for technical support at your university and set limits on student interruptions for technical difficulties. Some students struggle greatly with learning new technology. It is important that they lean on experts for that assistance. Valuable virtual classroom time can be wasted on students who didn't attend the technical check yet can't get started. They must call the help desk. It is helpful to display help desk information on your course site and in the virtual classroom, as well.

Instructional design with web conferencing software is very similar to a face-to-face course design. Depending on your purpose, Adobe®Connect™Pro 8 might be the best choice. As described in Table 2, if you want to host a small group discussion, field chat questions, demonstrate a step wise process or complex equations, models, or diagrams (or have students demonstrate), or engage students through quick opinion polls, then Adobe®Connect™ will meet you pedagogical needs in a way that other video

Table 2. Tools and suggested pedagogical uses

Tools	Suggested Pedagogical Use	TEGRITY™	ADOBE® CONNECT™	YOUTUBE
		Availability of Tool in Application		
Powerpoint sharing	Delivery of factual and conceptual knowledge	X	X	
Asynchronous video lecture	Introductory videos, brief videos to introduce a topic or concept, clarification of difficult concepts or assignments	X	X	X
Synchronous chat feature	Alternative to text discussion boards, useful in fielding questions about course content		X	
Collaborative web space	Small group tools for collaborative discussions		X	
Synchronous videoconferencing	Demonstration of steps in solving problems in relation to real-time learner questions		X	
Screen sharing	Share documents, videos and websites	X	X	
Video sharing with comment capabilities	Upload student videos as an alternative to text based discussion boards, assessment of student process skills			X
Synchronous Polling/Quiz	Engage students through quick opinion polls		X	
Closed Captioning	Allow students with perceptual difficulties to have equal access	X	X	X
Voice capture through microphone	Use for podcast and discussions if synchronous	X	X	X
Whiteboard	Use for demonstration of complex equations, drawing models or diagrams		X	

lecture tools cannot. Allowing for student questions and participation makes web conferencing tools uniquely suited to completely online courses that require a real time interaction component for optimum success.

VIDEO HOSTING AND STREAMING TOOLS

Overview

Video hosting and streaming tools are web-based depositories for uploaded videos that can be either publicly or privately shared with others. PlayStream®, Adobe®Flash Video Streaming Service, and vzaar are a few of these tools.

YouTube is a popular video sharing site visited 3 billion times per month by people from all walks of life (http://www.youtube.com/t/press_statistics). In addition to music videos (its most popular feature), it also contains numerous clips that capture key aspects of the human condition and that portray social problems. These can include video blogs of an intimate and personal nature and video lectures and newscasts of a more general nature. The discussion of YouTube in this section will focus on its potential utility in the higher education classroom. Personal examples of the incorporation of this technology into both all online and hybrid format courses by both instructors and students will be given. As well, the potential benefits and limitations of using YouTube will be discussed and research on the effectiveness of YouTube will be presented.

Basic Elements and Features

Video hosting and streaming tools give credence to the old adage: a picture is worth a thousand words. Some concepts are best shown in real time to be fully appreciated or understood (Manning & Johnson, 2011). It is difficult to demonstrate a clinical social work intervention technique, explain a difficult mathematical concept, or demonstrate an intricate model without showing it. Demonstrating process is often necessary for learning objectives to be met.

Figure 5. Screenshot of a YouTube channel (© 2012, YouTube, used with permission)

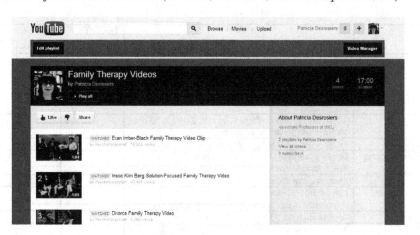

Most video hosting and streaming tools allow access via mobile devices such as iPads and smart phones which is convenient for many students. The typical smart phone can record and view short video clips on site upon demand making it easy to use.

As a subscriber to YouTube you can upload short videos less than 15 minutes in length to share with others. Sharing can be done privately or publicly. Due to privacy laws protecting students, it is always best to share privately among class members only. YouTube allows comments to be posted about the video content that has been shared. This feature makes it useful for stimulating discussion and interest using a resource that will be available upon graduation.

Figure 5 depicts a screenshot of a YouTube playlist used by this professor in a social work with families' course. As an example assignment, students watch the video of their choice, and then they critique it and describe how they could or could not use the techniques in their practice. Other students are then directed to respond to other critiques in a discussion format. This is an asynchronous application, therefore, you must keep in mind that students may require additional discussion regarding questions about complex material or applications.

Benefits and Challenges

A benefit is that recording and sharing simple videos through video hosting and streaming can be done by novices. Elaborate videos including subtitles and transitions require intermediate or expert level skills. Windows Movie Maker and Mac's iMovie are video editing software that allows even a beginner to edit like a pro (Manning & Johnson, 2011). Students in my courses have used them with great success.

YouTube offers a free closed-captioning service for videos that you distribute on their site. Some students may need a text-based alternative to produce videos, so make sure you make those accommodations as needed.

A big challenge is the time it takes to create a demonstration video. It is important to consider the preparation time required for students to complete their video project when planning the learning activities for your semester (Manning & Johnson, 2011).

Costs

Video hosting and streaming tools vary in cost from free to $30-$200 per month depending on features and the amount of storage required by the user. YouTube is free to instructors and students.

The only cost is the time to set up your account. The cost for basic recording equipment (a webcam and a USB microphone headset) is under $100. Go to YouTube at www.youtube.com to set up your account today.

Tips for Effective Use

Video length of less than 30 minutes is best for demonstration projects. Students can upload videos of their skill demonstrations and even produce a second video critiquing it. Instructors can then respond with comments within the video website. It is easier to get your students to upload onto a video streaming website than to use specified file formats.

YouTube is great as an alternative to written discussion boards. Depending on the learning objectives of the course it may add some variety and interest for students, particularly students in a completely online course, to meet each other and see each other talking on video. When attempting to build an online community, it is very useful to increase face time with other students even if it is asynchronous. Controversial videos are often found on YouTube. These can be posted to your private channel for students to comment on. Funny videos can be shared to lighten the mood during stressful points in the semester.

It is useful to use professional's videos to demonstrate skills or process. Students benefit from seeing other practitioners at work. It gives them permission to develop their own style and to try doing things a little different than their faculty mentors. YouTube is a great place to find vignettes from other practitioners in your discipline.

FUTURE RESEARCH DIRECTIONS

Given the rapid growth of distance education, it is evident that new tools will frequently be developed and touted as better, faster, more advanced, and easier to use. This chapter has provided you with a framework for use as you begin making logical and informed decisions about the use of technological tools. In an effort to keep up with the Jones', many academic institutions have quickly developed online learning programs with phenomenal growth rates. Simultaneous advances in technology and educational practiced coupled with a tech savvy generation of students are making print and lecture based courses obsolete. (Bates, 2006). The value computers and the World Wide Web bring to education cannot be denied.

Looking toward the future it is going to be imperative that instructors don't allow the tools to drive our course content or learning objectives. Instructors need to carefully select tools that work for us and our students. Three such tools have been presented in this chapter. Tegrity™, Adobe®Connect™ and YouTube are all video lecture tools that have been used with great success by this author. It is important to note that great technical training and support for online learning is present in the author's academic institution. This support has facilitated the professional growth and development of pedagogical strategies necessary to successfully implement these tools. Without administrative support, it is doubtful that learning outcomes for students would be as great.

While online learning has repeatedly demonstrated comparable learning outcomes for students (Madoc-Jones & Parrott, 2005) and students like them (Jackson & Helms, 2008), this mode of education can be very isolating. Building successful online learning communities (Palloff & Pratt, 2007) and creating a sense of presence in online teaching (Lehman & Conceicao, 2010) are two ways to increase student engagement and decrease isolation inherent in being offsite during the education process.

CONCLUSION

Table 2 summarizes the three technologies discussed in this chapter and their suggested pedagogical uses. Do not allow Table 2 to limit your ideas about appropriate utilization of these tools. Their uses are as varied as the professors that use them in their teaching. Use your creativity to develop exciting online assignments that will make learning memorable for your students. Allow your students the virtual space to creatively use the resources available. If students are using their creativity, they are indeed engaged. If they are engaged, they are indeed learning.

REFERENCES

Bates, T. (2006). *Technology, e-learning and distance education.* New York, NY: Abingdon.

Cappicie, A., & Desrosiers, P. (2011). Lessons learned from using Adobe Acrobat Connect in the social work classroom. *Journal of Technology in Human Services, 29*(4), 296–302. doi:10.1080/15228835.2011.638239

Caulfield, J. (2011). *How to design and teach a hybrid course.* Sterling, VA: Stylus Publishing.

Chen, N., & Ko, H., Kinshuk, & Lin, T. (2005). A model for synchronous learning using the Internet. *Innovations in Education and Teaching International, 42*(2), 181–194. doi:10.1080/14703290500062599

Conoway, T. (2011, June 15). Lecture capture can change classroom dynamics for the better. *Faculty Focus: Focused on Today's Higher Education Professional.*

Fleming, N., & Baume, D. (2006). Learning styles again: VARKing up the right tree! *Educational Developments, 7*(4), 4–7.

Gabbard, J., & Desrosiers, P. (2012, June). *Effective pedagogical strategies for engaging students in online learning.* Paper presented at the meeting of the Teaching Professor Conference, Washington, DC.

Jackson, M. J., & Helms, M. M. (2008). Student perceptions of hybrid courses: Measuring and interpreting quality. *Journal of Education for Business, 84*(1), 7–12. doi:10.3200/JOEB.84.1.7-12

Johnson, C. G. (2005). Lessons learned from teaching web-based courses: The 7-year itch. *Nursing Forum, 40*(1), 11–17. doi:10.1111/j.1744-6198.2005.00002.x

Krathwohl, D. R. (2002). A revision of Bloom's taxonomy: An overview. *Theory into Practice, 41*(4), 212–220. doi:10.1207/s15430421tip4104_2

Lehman, R. M., & Conceicao, S. C. (2010). *Creating a sense of presence in online teaching: How to "be there" for distance learners.* San Francisco, CA: Jossey-Bass.

Madoc-Jones, I., & Parrott, L. (2005). Virtual social work education—Theory and experience. *Social Work Education, 24*(7), 755–768. doi:10.1080/02615470500238678

Malamud, C. (2012). *Chunking information for instructional design.* Retrieved from http://thee-learningcoach.com/elearning_design/chunking-information/

Manning, S., & Johnson, K. E. (2011). *Technology toolbelt for teaching.* San Francisco, CA: Jossey-Bass.

Palloff, R. M., & Pratt, K. (2007). *Building online learning communities: Effective strategies for the virtual classroom.* San Francisco, CA: Jossey-Bass.

Simonson, M., Smaldino, S., Albright, M., & Zvacek, S. (2009). *Teaching and learning at a distance: Foundations of distance education* (4th ed.). New York, NY: Pearson.

Wyatt, R. (2012). *Tegrity case study: Western Kentucky University.* Retrieved June 1, 2012, from http://www.tegrity.com/sites/default/files/WKU.pdf

ADDITIONAL READING

Allen, I. E., & Seaman, J. (2010). *Learning on demand: Online education in the United States, 2009*. Retrieved from www.sloan-c.org/publications/survey/pdf/learningondemand.pdf

Bloom, B. S., Engelhart, M. D., Furst, E. J., Hill, W. H., & Krathwohl, D. R. (1956). *Taxonomy of educational objectives: The classification of educational goals (Handbook I: Cognitive domain)*. New York, NY: David McKay Company, Inc.

Blumberg, P. (2009). *Developing learner-centered teaching: A practical guide for faculty*. San Francisco, CA: Jossey-Bass.

Boeetcher, J. V., & Conrad, R. (2010). *The online teaching survival guide: Simple and practical pedagogical tips*. San Francisco, CA: Jossey-Bass.

Bourne, J., & Burstein, D. (2008). *Web video: Making it great, getting it noticed*. Berkeley, CA: Peachpit Press.

Conrad, R., & Donaldson, J. A. (2011). *Engaging the online learner: Activities and resources for creative instruction*. San Francisco, CA: Jossey-Bass.

Coombs, N. (2010). *Making online teaching accessible: Inclusive course design for students with disabilities*. San Francisco, CA: Jossey-Bass.

Doyle, T. (2008). *Helping students learn in a learner-centered environment: A guide to facilitating learning in higher education*. Sterling, VA: Stylus.

Hastie, M., Chen, N., & Kuo, Y. (2001). Instructional design for best practice in the synchronous cyber classroom. *Journal of Educational Technology & Society, 10*(4), 281–294.

Jonassen, D., Howland, J., Marra, R., & Crismond, D. (2008). *Meaningful learning with technology* (3rd ed.). Upper Saddle River, NJ: Pearson.

Kim, K. J., & Bonk, C. J. (2006). The future of online teaching and learning in higher education. The survey says…. *EDUCAUSE Quarterly, 4,* 22–30.

Ko, S., & Rossen, S. (2010). *Teaching online: A practical guide* (3rd ed.). New York, NY: Routledge/Taylor & Francis.

Moore, B. (2005). Faculty perceptions of the effectiveness of web-based instruction in social work education: A national study. *Journal of Technology in Human Services, 23*(1), 53–66. doi:10.1300/J017v23n01_04

Morrison, G. R., Ross, S. M., & Kemp, J. E. (2007). *Designing effective instruction*. Hoboken, NJ: Wiley.

Norris, D., Mason, J., & Lefrere, P. (2003). *Transforming e-knowledge*. Ann Arbor, MI: Society for College and University Planning.

Schneider, S., & Evans, M. (2008). Transforming e-learning into e-learning: The centrality of sociocultural participation. *Innovate, 5*(1). Retrieved from http://www.innovateonline.info/index.php?view=article&id=511

Smaldino, S. E., & Lowther, D. L. (2007). *Instructional technology and media for learning* (9th ed.). Upper Saddle River, NJ: Prentice Hall.

Suduc, A. M., Bizoi, M., & Filip, G. (2009). Exploring multimedia web conferencing. *Informatica Economica, 13*(3), 5–17.

Wang, H., Gould, L., & King, D. (2009). Positioning faculty support as a strategy in assuring quality online education. *Innovate, 5*(6). Retrieved from http://www.innovateonline.info/index.php?view=article&id=626

KEY TERMS AND DEFINITIONS

Asynchronous: The interactions of teacher and students or students and other students occur at different times.

Chat Feature: Typed communication that can be either synchronous or asynchronous in nature.

Screen Sharing: Showing others a duplicate image of your computer screen.

Synchronous: The interactions between teacher and students or students and other students occur in real time.

Videoconferencing: Two way video and audio communication that can occur between 2 people or many.

Webcam: A video recorder attached to a computer.

Whiteboard: An online space where conference attendees can write directly on a virtual screen.

Chapter 4
Tools of the Trade

Terri Gustafson
Michigan State University, USA

ABSTRACT

Visual media can be created using a plethora of software and hardware tools, including enterprise-wide deployed lecture capture system. Tools can be as simple as single click record software or require extensive knowledge of options, formats, or end-user devices. While this chapter does not cover all of the visual media creation tools available, it does give a brief overview of the tools for creating, editing, and delivering digital media content to enhance instruction.

INTRODUCTION

The constructivist learning theory maintains that the purpose of learning is to construct knowledge and meaning from experience, such that the instructor's role is to facilitate and negotiate meaning-making with the learner. The classroom, whether face-to-face or virtual becomes learner-centered instead of teacher-centered (Merriam & Caffarella, 1999). Bruce and Levin (as cited in Burbules & Callister, 2000) build on the definition of the learner-centered classroom by borrowing four categories from Dewey to categorize information technologies and their many uses: inquiry, communication, construction, and expression.

They go on to explain that for Dewey, these represented "four basic interests of the learner, human inclinations that motivate the activities that make learning possible" (p.4). In the digital age, there has been a shift from the print culture to the digital culture making learning a more visible process, where knowledge is co-created through sharing experiences (Batson & Bass, 1996). Digital media, such as video, is a learning tool that can be used to co-create learning experiences and make learning a more visible process for the learner-centered face-to-face classroom or distance learning environment. Zhang (2005), in a study of the effectiveness of interactive multimedia based e-learning, found that the lectures that included interactive

DOI: 10.4018/978-1-4666-3962-1.ch004

multimedia, including videos, resulted in greater learning performance and learner satisfaction over those that experienced the learning content in the face-to-face traditional classroom groups. In a similar study, it was found that video can be a more effective medium than text to present real-life situations through problem-based instruction to enhance learner satisfaction, comprehension, and retention (Hee Jun Choi & Johnson, 2007). Hee Jun Choi and Johnson (2005), in an earlier study, found that context-based video instruction was more memorable than the traditional text-based instruction in an online learning situation.

In a world that is always on and ready to disseminate information twenty-four hours a day, seven days a week, multimedia is the vehicle that delivers the deluge of content consumed every day. The generation of students filling universities and colleges in present time is considered to be part of the Net Generation or Millennials, defined by the year they were born somewhere between 1977 and 1997. They have been described as the generation that has grown up in the age of fast advancing technologies in computing, communication, social networking, and mobile devices. As they enter post-secondary education, the expectations to have grown up digital follows them into their coursework and they are expected to have a level of digital media literacy knowledge not previously set forth to earlier generations. As stated by Brown (2006), "In today's Internet environment, learning to be literate in multiple media, is an important tool in learning to be" (p.20). For those that teach in higher education, incorporating multimedia into course materials or assignments to grow student digital media literacy often leads one down the road to confusion over what tools are available for content creation. This chapter will give an overview of software, hardware, and Internet tools available for multimedia creation and delivery for faculty, instructors, graduate assistants and students.

BACKGROUND

Long before online learning and consumer digital video equipment became available during the 1980's, enhancing instruction with visual media started out as showing a filmstrip during a class period or using a 35 mm slide deck. Faculty could go to the library on campus and check out a film to use as instructional material, the same way they could assign a book or course pack for reading materials. Technology in classrooms often meant an overhead projector and a slide deck for faculty to show 35 mm slides. Outside of students bringing their own cassette recorders to class, recording the visual and audio content of a class for later playback was unheard of until instructional television units popped up on college campuses. Even then, viewing and playback of courses was limited to local cable access channels or university cable systems. If students missed class, there was no way to watch the lecture when you returned unless an archive was produced and filed at the library media center. All of that changed with the emergence of personal computers, the Internet, and personal video recording devices like the camcorder.

Early lecture capture systems required a manual process of synchronizing Microsoft PowerPoint slides with recorded lecture video. Screen capture programs were flakey, at best, and often bogged down the early computer processors, rendering the other functions of a computer frozen until the capture was processed into an end-user format. As the technology of video recording and personal computers rapidly advance, cameras started producing better quality videos and computers became the vehicle for distribution as processor technology improved. Also key to the advancement of visual media distribution was the increase in the speed that data could be transferred over the Internet and eventually, the creation of high-speed broadband networks. Without this improvement, large video files could not be transferred between content creators, servers, and eventually end users. During the late 1990's and early 2000's though, video content that used to be broadcast over satellite or cable systems started showing up in web browsers. As more people started buying laptops instead of desktop computers, the demand for content on the go grew, and as Apple and Microsoft released consumer friendly video editing software, the possibility of individual creation of content became a reality.

Fast forward to 2008, three years after the creation of YouTube by three former employees of PayPal, and enhancing instruction with visual media was well on its way. No longer did instructors have to order a TV/VCR cart to show a video in their classroom because they could stream it through an Internet browser on their laptop, which was connected to the data projector hanging from the ceiling of the classroom. Students taking online courses could view a course introduction recorded by their instructor using a pocket digital video camera and uploaded to a course management system. And as lecture capture started to find its way into classroom technology, medical students could review content from their classes instead of furiously trying to take notes during the live lecture and missing key content.

In the current decade, the options for enhancing instruction with visual media are endless. Just when it seemed that pocket-sized cameras would be the next best thing, smart phones added HD quality recording features, expanded memory to handle large file sizes, and instant upload to content sharing sites or learning management systems. What used to only come with a steep price can now be done with free open source tools. Access to course content captured as part of a live class lecture or recorded as learning modules by a faculty member in their office is available anyplace, anytime, and on almost any mobile device. Determining where the future will

take us is not clear, but if the last 30 years are any indication, visual media will be created, shared, and available for all learners on any device, no matter where they are in the world, and at speeds hardly imagined when the world was connecting with a modem just two decades ago.

MULTIMEDIA SOFTWARE: CREATING ORIGINAL CONTENT

Screen Capture Tools

Software tools available to create multimedia content using the technique called screen capture varies in price, features, and availability for Windows and Mac OS X computers. In the free category for content creation is Jing, by TechSmith (www. techsmith.com). Jing can be downloaded for Mac OS X or Windows computers from the TechSmith website. It can be used to grab still shots or create screen capture videos up to 5 minutes in length. Screenshots can be annotated with highlights, arrows, word bubbles, and simple shapes to draw attention to specific areas of the screenshot. Screen capture videos can include a voiceover or users can mute the microphone. Similar to other TechSmith screen capture products, users are presented with an onscreen ready countdown of "3 – 2 – 1" before the software begins the capture process. Once the recording is completed, they can preview the video before saving it locally, uploading to YouTube, or uploading to TechSmith's video hosting and sharing service, Screencast.com. Anyone that installs Jing gets a free account to Screencast.com, with 2 GB of storage and 2 GB of monthly bandwidth. (TechSmith, 2012a).

Another screen capture product that features a free account and subscription service is Screenr. com by Articulate Network (http://www.screenr. com). It also has a 5-minute time limit for screencasting videos but unlike Jing, is completely web-based with no software to download. Users have the option to login via Facebook, Twitter, Google, Yahoo, LinkedIn, or WindowsLive ID before publishing their finished product, thus prompting the "Allow Access" prompt from those accounts to link Screenr publishing. All screencasts created using the free option are published publicly. Once the screencast is finished publishing, options include sharing the URL, embedding the video on a website, download the .mp4 file, publishing to YouTube, or sharing the video to Twitter. If a more private option is desired, Screenr has a business version with a monthly subscription cost at four price levels, depending on the number of screencasts stored and added features like an embedded recorder, analytics, player branding, and unlimited users. All four subscriptions include private sharing (Articulate Network, 2012).

For creating content with more features, editing options, and sharing formats there are several software packages that range in price just under $100 up to $300. Most are available for both Windows and Mac OS users and have education pricing. Available from TechSmith are Camtasia Studio 8 for Windows, Camtasia for Mac 2.2, and Snag-it. All three software packages offer a multitude of screen capture options, editing capabilities, and output formats. While Camtasia Studio 8 and Camtasia for Mac 2.2 share a similar name, the look and feel of both products are comparatively different and the features vary depending on the computer platform you are using. Both specialize in video screen capture of the screen, mouse movements, system audio and voiceovers, but once the process of the capture is done, the look of the editor and features are somewhat different between the Windows and Mac OS X platforms.

Both Camtasia for Mac 2.2 and Camtasia Studio 8 feature the ability for precise editing of video and audio tracks, insertion of callouts on top of the video to draw the end users attention to a specific area of the screen, cursor highlights, picture-in-picture to overlay your image from a web camera, the option to add title clips, audio adjustments, transitions, and TechSmith's exclusive SmartFocus technology. SmartFocus keeps track of where the action happens during the recording and produces a video that zooms in on the parts that you want to show and zooms back out to full screen mode after the action ends. Features exclusive to Camtasia for Mac 2.2 include a chroma key or green screen feature to put content creators in front of their video (think weather person standing in front of the forecast map) and clip speed to adjust videos to the exact length needed. Exclusive features of Camtasia Studio 8 include a Microsoft PowerPoint Add-In, a library of professionally designed assets, enhanced captioning through speech-to-text, quizzing, and creating searchable videos. Sharing of completed videos in both platforms can be done through various file formats, including formats specific to Apple's iOS devices like the iPad and iPhone. In addition, videos can be shared to YouTube, Apple's iTunes, and Screencast.com (TechSmith, 2012).

SnagIt, also by TechSmith, is primarily a static screen shot capture tool that offers a robust set a features to annotate, highlight, and capture menu actions in a variety of still formats. SnagIt can also capture MPEG4 videos that can be shared using social media sites and Screencast.com. While there is no limit to the maximum length of video captures, TechSmith encourages users to limit recordings to shorter lengths and save longer recordings for Camtasia Studio 8 and Camtasia for Mac 2.2. SnagIt is primarily a still capture workhorse and a step between Jing and Camtasia Studio for screen capture videos. As the step up from Jing, it offers you more editing options, sharing options, and compatibility with TechSmith products like Camtasia for Mac and other software tools like Evernote (TechSmith, 2012). There are two other software packages that focus exclusively on creating videos of screen captures, instead of serving the dual purpose of still capture and video creation.

Screenflow (http://www.telestream.net/screen-flow/overview.htm), by Telestream, Inc., is a Mac exclusive software package for OS X Snow Leopard 10.6.6 and higher, including Mountain Lion. With Screenflow, content creators can record the entire area of their screen while capturing system audio, a web camera, and a voice over. It also has Keynote and PowerPoint support and HD capture, optimized for the highest resolution possible. Similar to its main competitor, Camtasia for Mac 2.2, Screenflow allows you to add call-outs, video annotations, text overlays, advanced audio controls, clip speed changes, video actions to zoom, pan, and add motion, and full screen preview. New additions to Screenflow 3 include the ability to add movement and transitions to annotations, the ability to reorder, delete, and resize the height of tracks, group clips, insert gaps, and select and remove gaps in the timeline. In addition, a nice new audio feature lets the user view audio waveforms and clipped audio peaks to see the effects of volume changes. Finally, exports options include the new iPad format or directly to Vimeo, an alternative video sharing site to YouTube that specializes in hosting HD videos. Other export options for Screenflow are QuickTime, Windows Media movie, YouTube, or an all-in-one Flash video presentation (Telestream, 2012).

The final screen casting software tool that will be covered is Adobe Captivate (http://www.adobe.com/products/captivate.html). Captivate captures all screens and applications that are opened and accessed and creates sequential slides that can be manipulated and edited before the final project is published. It is available for Windows and Mac OS. Editing features include adding text captions, animation effects, zooming by object (similar to TechSmith's SmartFocus feature of Camtasia), custom skinning, quizzing, audio editing, and the importing image and video files to add to the captured project. Also similar to all of the TechSmith products, you can preview your project before initiating the publish process. In addition to creating a project from a screen capture event, users can create a project from Microsoft PowerPoint slides or blank slides to build a project by using a combination of PowerPoint slides, images, and recordings of applications. All project types can add objects like text captions afterward or adjust the timing of the project. Projects can be published as a SWF file or to an FTP server. More advanced publishing options include formats such as EXE, APP, MP4, PDF, or uploading the project to YouTube from within the Adobe Captivate menu system. For users that want to explore the more advanced features, Captivate offers the ability to make slides more robust and creative with the addition of gradients and shadows. Finally, mouse-over actions can be added to display images, text, audio, and videos. Adobe Captivate is by far, the most feature-rich screen casting software package available, thus increasing the learning curve and the time needed to become familiar with all of the features.

Video Editing

Choosing a software program to edit video and audio files can be confusing and tricky. There are many options available for both Mac OS X and Windows, however the options for Mac OS X outnumber the Windows options and Macs are just better at handling the heavy lifting of editing and exporting finished projects. In addition, the programs for Mac OS X offer the flexibility to export to more formats, including the industry standard MPEG4 format, and sharing to sites like YouTube. This does not mean that efficient editing cannot be done on a Windows PC, but for instructors that want an easy solution and small learning curve, the choices available for Mac users outnumber those for Windows users.

Apple's all-in-one suite, iLife (www.apple.com/ilife/), includes one of the more popular editing software choices, iMovie. iLife is available from Apple's App Store. iMovie can import video directly from a camera, import files that were created with other packages or cameras that record directly to a hard drive, or can record projects using Apple's built-in iSight web camera ("Apple," 2012). File formats that iMovie can import include MOV, MPEG-2, AVCHD, DV, HDV, and MPEG-4. For other formats (AVI, FLV, MPG), an extra step is needed to convert the files to MPEG-4 with another software package.

iMovie provides even novice video editors the ability to make creative videos that include titles, transitions, Ken Burns effects, and dual audio tracks. Adding video clips from the Events bins creates Projects. In addition, because iMovie is part of the iLife suite, music from the iTunes playlist and pictures from iPhoto albums can be added to video projects with a simple click or two on the effects bin. Once a music track or photo is found, the drag-n-drop action adds it on the project timeline. The same action is needed for adding titles, transitions between clips, and to add iMovie's included maps, backgrounds, and animatics. Ken Burns effects and cropping of clips is done by selecting a clip or still photo in the project timeline and clicking on the crop icon in the middle of the iMovie toolbar. Audio adjustments available in iMovie include volume adjustment, adding a fade in or fade out to the beginning and end of the audio track, background noise reduction, clip normalization, and ducking which reduces the volume of other tracks by a user-selected percentage. For example, ducking is useful for projects that include voiceover and a song that plays along in the background of the entire project. Setting a ducking level reduces the volume of the song, thus making it easier for viewers to concentrate the voiceover. Once all of the elements are added to the project, iMovie's share options include iTunes, iDVD (for creating DVD projects), MobileMe gallery, YouTube, Facebook, Vimeo, CNN iReporter, and Podcast Producer. Exporting a file that can be uploaded to a local video hosting solution or an LMS is

accomplished by choosing the "Export using QuickTime" option from the Share drop-down menu. Using the "Export to QuickTime" option also provides more experienced users advanced export options to control compression settings, video size, filters, audio formats, and streaming settings.

Apple's Final Cut Pro X is one of the preferred choices for the truly advanced video creators and editors. Not only does it feature advanced editing effects and functions that are not available in iMovie or other "amateur" software packages, it is one of the most used editing packages used in the movie and broadcast industries. Novices with high expectations of easy to use features and a quick learning timeframe should not approach this software. In addition to being available on Mac OS X, Adobe Premier Pro CS6 is available for Windows as part of Adobe's Creative Suite 6 package. Similar to Final Cut Pro X, Premiere is aimed at professional editors. For the novice that wants some of the features of Premiere without the steep cost and learning curve, there is Premiere Elements, with similar features as iMovie and sharing ability to YouTube, DVD and Blue-ray, or mobile device formats. Another limited feature option for Windows users is Windows Live Movie Maker.

Bundled as part of Windows Live Essentials (windows.microsoft.com/en-US/windows-live/essentials-home), Movie Maker will import photos and video footage from an external storage device (USB thumb drive, hard drive) or camera to edit and create a finished project sharable on video sharing sites or other websites. It supports 14 available video formats. Webcam recording is also supported in Movie Maker, as well as drag-n-drop of elements. Similar to the previously mentioned consumer grade software editing programs, Movie Maker comes with several visual effects and animations that can be applied to single video clips or the entire project. Advanced settings for the effects will change the timings for transitions, background color, font size and color, and audio adjustments. Unique to Movie Maker is the one-click feature for users that don't want to spend a lot of time tweaking and fine tuning a project. The user selects the video files, images and music that they want to include in the movie and with one-click, the Movie Maker pre-set themes add a title, transitions, and credits. Regardless of how the finished movie is created, sharing it to popular social networking sites can be accomplished by clicking on the site logo on the "Publish movie to the web" menu. To publish the finished movie for delivery to other devices or delivery methods, Movie Maker features common settings for high-definition displays, computers, email, Windows Phones, and the Zune HD. Custom save settings can also be created, but the end file format for this feature and the common settings for computer and email is WMV. So while Movie Maker will import several formats, the output is tied to Microsoft's Windows Media Video format ("Windows Live Essentials - Download Windows Live Essentials," 2012).

If instructors are looking for free options for editing video on both Mac OS X and Windows, MPEG Streamclip (http://www.squared5.com/) is a basic video editing solution that saves files in various formats, include MPEG-4, MOV, AVI, and DV. The export function features the ability to adjust the compression CODEC, frame rate and size, rotation, zooming, cropping, and quality. By default, the quality scaler is set at 50%, so if you want a higher quality end file you will need to adjust the scaler. This is a handy tool to compress larger files so that they comply with the file size limits of some sharing sites like Vimeo, YouTube, or Facebook. The downside to compressing video files is that the end product quality can be compromised to fit the standards of those sharing sites. However, a little adjustment here and there of the settings in MPEG Streamclip can still result in an acceptable end product. Finally, those that want to use this solution on Windows will have to install

QuickTime Alternative 1.81 and uninstall their current version of QuickTime to access the full functionality of MPEG Streamclip. QuickTime Alternative 1.81 can be also be downloaded from the Squared 5 website (Squared 5, n.d.).

Desktop Videoconferencing

The multimedia toolkit also includes software for desktop video and audio conferencing with students taking distance-learning courses, for collaboration among students between face-to-face class meetings, or for virtual office hours. Adobe Connect, Blackboard Collaborate, Vidyo, Fuze Meeting, and GoToMeeting all fall under the category of desktop multimedia video conferencing and include features such as application sharing, chat, a virtual whiteboard, document sharing, and breakout rooms for group collaboration. All five options usually require institutional contract pricing based on either the number of users, meeting "rooms" required, or full time enrollment. Adobe Acrobat and Blackboard Connect (created after the Blackboard purchase of Wimba Classroom and Elluminate *Live!*) have a specific focus on use in higher education for distance learning. Vidyo, Fuze Meeting, and GoToMeeting have a higher use cases in the business sector, but do have a place in higher education applications.

Adobe Connect (http://www.adobe.com/products/adobeconnect.html) enables organizations to collaborate anytime, anywhere with wide a range of group sizes on many different delivery platforms. It supports use on Windows, Mac OS X, Linux, Solaris, and iOS, Android, and Blackberry mobile devices. In addition, Adobe licensing includes the option for hosted or on-premise licensed deployments for clients. The hosted deployment option enables clients to use Connect while Adobe handles all of the hardware and software set-up and maintenance with available support. An on-premise deployment is set-up behind an institutional firewall and integrates with existing IT architecture, including Single Sign-On authentication. Also, the on-premise solution features customizable capabilities, control over usage, and integration with existing LDAP directory servers, Jabber, or VoIP applications. Each institution should evaluate both deployment options before making the investment to evaluate the best deployment path for management scalability and educational applications.

Available features for each meeting room created by hosts include pods for the broadcast of webcams, live chat, content sharing (whiteboard, application, and document), notes, polling, Q&A, and breakout rooms for collaboration between teams during a live conference. Audio can be managed using Connect's built-in VoIP feature or using an external phone conferencing system for toll-free access. Included in the latest version of Adobe Connect is the two-way Universal Voice feature that bridges the audio between audio conferencing providers and VoIP to deliver a blended audio experience. For meetings using VoIP as the primary audio delivery method, all participants should be advised to complete the Audio Setup Wizard to train the system to their individual microphone and speaker equipment and environment ambient sounds. This step will balance the audio input and output for each participant and make for a better (no echo) experience for all those attending the meeting. Finally, hosts can passcode-protect meeting rooms to protect sensitive information and record sessions for future viewings by participants that could not attend the live meeting room ("Web conferencing software - Conference services | Adobe Connect," 2012).

Similar to Adobe Connect, Blackboard Collaborate features different licensing models for enterprise, departmental, or single room deployments. Enterprise or departmental licensing includes the most features like integration with industry leading LMS platforms, simultaneous rooms, and the largest number of participants in any one session. Collaborate can also be integrated with custom interfaces and homegrown content

management systems using a comprehensive set of Standard Application Programming Interfaces (APIs). In addition, Microsoft Windows, Mac OS, Linux, and Ubuntu are supported for end-user delivery. Interactivity features include audio, video, an interactive whiteboard, desktop and application sharing, breakout rooms, multimedia content delivery, instant polling, file transfer, and session recording. These features are available for all licensing levels. Similarly, communication features such as full-duplex VoIP, text chat, and integrated teleconferencing are also available.

Unique to Blackboard Collaborate is the voice-authoring feature; previously a component of Wimba Classroom called Wimba Voice. Instructors can create feedback recordings or lectures for distance students or setup threaded voice boards, voice-enabled email, embed voice within course pages, as well as live group discussions. The Voice Podcaster feature gives instructors the power to create and upload podcasts for student subscription. Finally, the voice authoring feature can be a pathway to help with accessibility of course content for visually impaired students, providing an alternative method of course content delivery and feedback on assignments ("Blackboard Collaborate | Online Collaboration Software for Engaging, Collaborative Learning," 2012).

The final two desktop video conferencing products that require a contract for services at various levels of price and features are GoToMeeting by Citrix Online LLC (http://www.gotomeeting.com/fec/) and Fuze Meeting (https://www.fuzebox.com/). Web conferencing products by Citrix scale up by attendee capacity from up to 15 attendees for GoToMeeting to up to 1,000 attendees at the upper level contract for GoToWebinar. The third product, GoToTraining, which includes GoToMeeting, is marketed to those that want for-fee training and employee education, including interactive training features such as tests and materials, a timer, and online course catalogs. All three products include basic features such as desktop and application sharing, one-click recording, drawing tools, audio conferencing (both VoIP or teleconference), and keyboard and mouse sharing. One downside to GoToMeeting is that not all features, such as application sharing or drawing tools, are available for Mac OS users. So while hosting sessions is available across platforms, a webinar with multiple presenters is limited by their computer operating system and the feature restrictions of GoToMeeting ("Online Meeting | GoToMeeting," 2012).

While the earlier products featured in this section on desktop conferencing are primarily hardware/server-based products, FuzeMeeting is a software only platform that operates on a cloud-based architecture. FuzeMeeting places a heavy focus on its ability to open up conferencing between mobile devices and legacy platforms like Windows, Mac OS, and Linux computers. Apps are available for both iOS and Android phones and tablets with HD content sharing in full resolution. Also, it features real-time markups, sticky notes, and pointers. For those concerned with the security of cloud-based products, FuzeMeeting uses SSL Session Encryption for all web and mobile clients and SAS70 Type II Audited Data Storage. Similar to Citrix, FuzeBox.com has a 30-day free trial before any purchase of one of the four contract levels. Each price level has limits on web and audio attendees, storage space and HD videoconference streams ("Welcome to FuzeBox — FuzeBox," 2012).

One of the newest entrants into the web conferencing market is Vidyo (http://www.vidyo.com/). Vidyo features compatibility with Windows and Mac OS operating system, mobile devices, and is the only desktop conferencing system to work with traditional H.323 and SIP endpoints using the VidyoGateway. VidyoMobile has apps for iOS and Android mobile devices and features HD-quality video connections. Application sharing is also available for all Vidyo products. Similar to products featured in earlier sections on desktop conferencing VidyoGateway is a hardware-based solution that requires the installation of Vidyo-Desktop or VidyoMobile to connect users. Costs include the purchase of the Gateway server and licenses for an institutionally determined number of users and licenses of VidyoDesktop ("Video Conferencing and Personal Telepresence Solutions – Vidyo," 2012). As for features, it does not include many of those mentioned for Adobe Connect and Blackboard Collaborate, such as a whiteboard, chat, notes, and breakout rooms.

Finally, for no-cost or low-cost desktop conferencing, Skype, ooVoo, and Google+ Hangouts offer viable options for enhancing instruction with visual media. All three feature one-to-one or group video conferencing or chats and Skype and ooVoo feature the ability to screen share with participants. Skype (http://www.skype.com/) charges subscribers under its Skype Business or Premium banner for group video calling. Group video calls can be between three or more people and up to a maximum of 10. For the best quality, Skype recommends a high-speed broadband connection and the latest version of Skype installed on all participants computers. Only one person participating in the video call needs to have a subscription to Skype Premium. Skype is available for Windows, Mac OS, iOS and Android operating systems and features instant messaging on all devices and screen sharing on computers ("Video Chat - Free Online Video Calls - Video Calling - Skype," 2012). Recording of Skype calls is available by purchasing additional software from third party software sites.

ooVoo (http://www.oovoo.com/home.aspx) features video chat with up to 12 people. It is available on Windows and Mac operating systems and some iOS and Android mobile devices. The free version does not include screen sharing, but does include instant messaging and call recording. ooVoo also offers a University Partner Program with academic pricing based on institution size and enrollment ("Free Video Chat and Video Conferencing from ooVoo," 2012). Unlike Skype and Google+ Hangouts, updates to ooVoo for Mac OS upgrades has been slow to keep up and some features will not work consistently. Institutions with a high percentage of Mac OS users will want to touch base with the ooVoo higher education sales team to confirm updates before purchasing.

Lastly, Google+ Hangouts is a quick method to do video chats with groups or individuals that have an existing Google account. Hangouts do require the installation of Google Voice. Once installed, a hangout can be started from within Google+, Gmail chat, or Orkut. Participants just need a webcam and microphone. Video chats can be done with up to 10 people and started by clicking on the "Invite" button on the photo of a contact or entering names. Users can also invite groups to a Hangout by selecting your Google+ circles from a dropdown menu. For existing Google users, Hangouts can be a quick, easy, free way to communicate with individuals for office hours or with distance education students for group work or small class sessions. Hangouts are also available on phones with Android 2.3+ with front facing cameras and iOS 4.3 or later devices.

MULTIMEDIA HARDWARE: FROM HANDHELD TO LECTURE CAPTURE

Cameras and Smartphones

Hardware tools available for creating multimedia content have come a long way since the first camcorders were released for public use in the mid-1980's. Today, most cell phones and smart phones will take still pictures and have the ability to record video in some format and for varying lengths of time. In addition, the weighty camcorders of the past have been replaced by smaller and lighter handheld cameras that fit in a shirt pocket or take up no more space than a couple of decks of playing cards held together with a rubber band. Until the spring of 2011, the Flip Video camera by Cisco dominated the market of pocket size video cameras, only to be discontinued by Cisco at the peak of market dominance. The next best camera on the market was the line of Playsport cameras by

Kodak, Inc. The cameras were small, easy to use, produced a consumer friendly end format (MP4), and many of the cameras were also waterproof. But in early 2012, Kodak announced it was getting out of the dedicated capture devices business altogether, thus phasing out the production of pocket video cameras. With the two biggest sellers out of the market, what is left for educators to use for creating visual media to enhance instruction are a few familiar names in audio and video creation, smart phones, and tablets.

Sony (http://www.sony.com/index.php), a name that has been associated with multimedia creation for over three decades, sells the Bloggie Touch pocketsize camera that records in 1080p full HD and 12-megapixel still captures with the ability to grab pictures while filming. It has a 3-inch touch screen that auto-rotates for portrait and landscape viewing. It is compatible with both Macs (it works with iMovie) and PCs ("Sony Handycam Camcorders | Sony Store USA," 2012). The Sanyo Xacti VPC-PD2BK also records in full HD video, captures 10 – megapixel stills, and saves videos on either SD or SDXC memory cards up to 64GB. Like the Sony Bloggie Touch, it's compatible with both Macs and PCs ("SANYO:: Dual Cameras:: VPC-PD2BK Full HD 1080 Pocket Movie Dual Camera with 10MP Digital Photos and 3X Optical Zoom," 2012). Two other pocket-sized cameras on the market are Creative's Vado and the Samsung HMX-U20. Both cameras record in HD, but do not offer as many options as the Sony and Sanyo cameras, and the quality of video and audio is limited ("Creative Vado HD Pocket Video Cameras - Capture & share moments," 2012, "HD Ultra Compact Digital Video Camcorder | Samsung HMX-U20 - Camcorders," 2012). The market life of pocket sized video cameras may be slowing though, as more and more smart phones and tablets can record, edit, and share video.

The iPhone and iPad, both by Apple (http://www.apple.com/) have the capability to record HD quality video and in some cases, depending on the model of the iPhone or iPad, can edit the video and share it within minutes of finishing a final version. Smart phones running the Android operating system also record HD quality video and have apps that will edit and share the finished video. In addition, with expandable memory card slots, the Android phones can record for the same length of time as many pocket video cameras. Whether using an iPhone or an Android phone, video recorded on either device can be imported from the Smartphone to a software solution like iMovie or MPEG Streamclip for further editing or to use in a larger compilation of videos for a class project or to share with students as part of the digital media content of a course.

Lecture Capture

In recent years, lecture capture has enjoyed a steady adoption growth by higher education institutions (Ramaswami, 2009) and has been touted by some as an ideal solution for blended learning programs (Phillips et al., 2010). However, lecture capture can also be a significant financial investment for institutions depending on the pricing structure of the lecture capture company and the initial investment in hardware such as servers, classroom podium modifications, infrastructure upgrades, and training for staff and faculty. Some systems require the installation of hardware in a classroom to capture everything that gets sent to the projector and some systems only require access to software on a USB memory stick. Also, some lecture capture systems need to run on locally managed servers while others only require the bandwidth to upload content to a cloud-based service. Regardless of the set-up and content capture requirements, lecture capture is a continually growing service that institutions are willing to invest in for blended courses and student review of face-to-face lectures.

Echo360 (www.echo360.com), the marriage of Lectopia and Apresso, boasts three options for the creation of capture files: SafeCapture HD, Classroom Capture, and Personal Capture. All three send raw capture files (AAC audio, H.264 video, and VGA sources) to the Echo System Server (ESS) for processing into user or system administrator designated end formats such as the multimedia rich EchoPlayer, vodcast format, or audio podcast (Phillips et al., 2010). Captures can be scheduled to automatically start and stop or can be manually controlled using the Ad-hoc login feature via an Internet browser. Once the end formats have completed processing, the ESS auto publishes links to files to the EchoCenter, a designated LMS/CMS/VLE, email, RSS feeds, or iTunes U. Files can be viewed on a browser, smart phone, tablet, or MP3 player. SafeCapture HD is a hardware appliance that gets integrated into existing podium systems and includes live streaming of lectures. Classroom Capture is a software-only solution that gets installed onto classroom podium PCs (Windows operating system only), and Personal Capture is a software solution that can be installed on personal computers to create learning modules or mini-lectures by recording their voice, webcam video, and computer screen. The Echo360 ESS will also import and host multimedia created by third-party cameras and software products, delivering content using the Echo360 system player. Finally, there is a simple cuts-only editor that allows instructors to cut out unwanted content or create custom segments.

Similar to Echo360, Mediasite, by Sonic Foundry (http://www.sonicfoundry.com/), offers hardware appliances for lecture capture that are integrated into existing classroom podiums. The RL Recorder integrates with existing room technology, including Crestron and AMX control systems, and captures in HD or SD quality. In addition, the Mediasite ML Recorder is a portable recorder for single-use recordings, symposiums, or other special events outside of the classroom setting. Both the RL Recorder and ML Recorder feature live webcasting and content capture from multiple sources. Combined with the Mediasite EX Server (on-premise solution) or Mediasite Hosting (off-site hosting within Sonic Foundry's

SaaS datacenter) both recorders provide a video content-management platform to record, edit, manage, and archive captured lectures and events. Captures can be scheduled ahead of time or started, paused, and stopped on the fly. In addition, the Mediasite architecture integrates with LMS/CMS systems, videoconference systems, and enterprise directories for secure delivery of content based on course enrollment. Finished captures served up by either the Mediasite EX Server or Mediasite Hosting can be viewed on a PC, Mac, or Linux computer and mobile devices ("Mediasite by Sonic Foundry - Create Online Multimedia Presentations, Briefings and Courses Automatically I Sonic Foundry," 2012).

Camtasia Relay 2 by TechSmith, integrates a Windows server to ingest and produce finished videos for viewing, with front end software to start, pause, stop, and upload recordings for creation into pre-determined video profiles. Camtasia Relay software can be installed on Mac OS and Windows computers or it can be installed on a USB memory stick. Relay operates from the USB memory stick to create the screen-captured lecture and save the raw files on the same drive. When the instructor returns to their main computer and plugs in the drive, they are prompted to upload the saved lecture to the Relay server for processing. Profiles are predetermined by system administrators and presented to users as a drop down menu on the Relay software interface. With limited options, the user interface is designed to keep things simple for instructors. Features include profile selection, presentation title and description, audio input level monitoring and adjustment, a "test" button to do a test recording, and finally a large, red record button. Other features at the top of the user interface include menu options to turn on/turn off webcam video, change which display screen will be captured, select a different audio input, and a menu option to log into the Camtasia Relay server if not prompted to do so right after launching the program. Relay operates on the

same concepts as other TechSmith products like Camtasia Studio or SnagIt; creating content with screen capture. However, instead of the computer doing the heavy lifting to create a finished product, the Relay server does the work to produce a finished product and provide a link via email or direct publishing to an LMS/CMS, iTunes U, Screncast.com, or other media delivery services. If instructors want to trim the front and back end of a recording to eliminate software launches or other mouse movements, Relay has a simple cuts-only editor option for simple trimming before uploading for processing. The one thing that Relay cannot do is automatically start and stop a recording. Instructors still have to remember to click on the red "REC" button to get things rolling and remember to hit "Stop Recording" at the end. The limited options of Relay may not be appealing to everyone and if that's the case, then Panopto might be the better software only choice.

Developed at the Carnegie Mellon University School of Computer Science, Panopto (http://www.panopto.com/) is a video and screen capture software solution that can record any type of input, with any equipment, on a laptop or smartphone. Panopto's three products are Focus, Unison, and Mobile. Available for Windows or Mac OS users, Focus, like the previously mentioned products, uses screen capture to create videos of content in HD or SD streams. In addition, live streaming of events is available while recording for archival purposes. After the event or class has ended, a link is automatically sent to an LMS/CMS or other video content distribution system. However unlike Camtasia Relay, the user interface of Panopto presents instructors with broader controls over video and audio inputs, instant live streaming, and session recording destination folder. Panopto also features the option to designate a Microsoft PowerPoint presentation so that it will create a searchable index based on the text of the slides. Panopto for the Mac OS also includes the integration of Keynote slides to create the searchable index. Unique to Panopto is the Panopto Mobile app for recording on iOS devices, in addition to the broad support of viewing recorded video files on mobile devices. Panopto also features live notes to take time-stamped notes while a recording is in progress or while viewing a presentation on-demand. Similar to Camtasia Relay, login to the server is required to load recording profiles and authenticate the final destination of the files on the server and make the connection to an LMS or other media distribution system. The enterprise media library and database can be a Windows-based server located on-premise or Panopto will contract for their cloud-based system ("Video Capture and Management Software Company | Panopto," 2012).

INTERNET TOOLS: EDITING AND SHARING

Distribution and Sharing

Internet tools available for the distribution or sharing of completed videos range from the most well know sites, like YouTube, to Google Drive. While some may cringe at the thought of using YouTube to share video content for a course because of the public nature and search ability of YouTube, there are privacy restrictions that can be placed on videos to block video from public searches or only share the video links with designated contacts. Not as well know as YouTube, Vimeo is another site for sharing videos that specializes in HD quality videos and provides users with privacy options like password protection and restrictions on downloads of the original video. The caveat with Vimeo is that the free membership restricts users to a 500 megabyte per week upload limit and longer wait times for video processing and access to links and embed codes. However, the Vimeo Plus membership increases that upload limit to a 5 gigabyte per week upload limit, priority upload-

ing, HD embedding, unlimited group and channel creation, and player customization. Google Drive can be used to create collections for courses to be shared with students who have Google accounts. Sharing content with Google Drive adds another layer of privacy since instructors have to designate the sharing contacts, but it also eliminates the ability to share a link to a multimedia file on a course page, blog, or wiki since students must log into Google Drive to view the files. Finally, iTunes U is a distribution resource that over 1,000 higher education and K-12 institutions use to distribute podcasts and videos of courses for their students and sometimes, the public at large. It is also a plentiful resource to find lectures, video, books, and other resources related to a particular subject matter to share with students, and all of it for free.

Editing

For those that do not want to use a dedicated software package on their laptop or desktop to edit video, there are a few resources available for simple online editing. The first is Stroome, a free service that allows users to upload video footage, edit it online, and then share the finished project through social media, blogs, or course sites. Stroome also allows for collaboration on a project with other Stroome members. WeVideo, similar to Stroome, features a full editor and collaboration, plus music mixing, support for all file formats, and a mobile version to upload video from a smart phone for editing later on. The free version includes 1 gigabyte of storage, 15 export minutes per month, and export to Facebook, Twitter, YouTube, or Vimeo. For more storage, HD capability, and export minutes, WeVideo offers various price plans. For an option that is institutionally supported, Kaltura offers a hosted solution that has many of the same feature of the previously mentioned online options, but also offers Mediaspace, which can be branded as the "YouTube" for an institution and offers authentication and API's to work with the institution's LMS and other campus learning services. However the cost of Kaltura, like many other institutional based contracts, varies depending on the size of the institution and the features included in the purchase agreement.

FUTURE RESEARCH DIRECTIONS

As the use of visual media and lecture capture continues to grow, future research could investigate the end-user experience of students as learners. Or explore their expectations of a course delivered using lecture capture and how their experiences during a semester or term compared to those expectations. Research could also investigate how delivery of content to mobile devices changed the perspective of students on what it means to be in a classroom; has the method of delivery of the content changed the value of the educational material? Research could also explore how the advent of pocket video cameras and the expansion of the video recording capabilities of smart phones has changed the way we look at video content; from expert created to everyone can create content and share it. Does the technology enable learning in new ways or just give a voice to all content, good or bad? Finally, research could explore the subject matter retention by students who review material recorded with lecture capture technology compared with students who do not review course material with lecture capture technology and rely on notes taken during the live face-to-face class.

CONCLUSION

As the current generation of students and future generations come to rely more and more on digital media for content consumption and they are expected by employers to obtain a certain level of digital media literacy, the need to enhance instruction with visual media could become as routine as

assigning readings. To meet this growing demand, the tools available to create original content or connect instructors with distance students using video technology needs to continually evolve to make the processes easy, convenient, and seamless. Mobile technology will continue to be available to a greater number of students and with that growth, the ability to create original video content will be in the palm of their hand. Institutions must evaluate the best tools to reach out to students and how to create content available to students anywhere, anyplace, and anytime. The tools of the trade for creating, editing, and sharing original video content and lecture captures are many, but deciding what tool to use to match the desired outcome and goals of a program, school, or institution can be the toughest test yet with little room for failure considering the financial investment required to implement some solutions. For those that teach in higher education, incorporating multimedia into course materials or assignments to grow student digital media literacy will become the next great challenge that touches almost every discipline.

REFERENCES

Apple. (2012). Retrieved May 29, 2012, from http://www.apple.com/

Articulate Network. (2012). Screenr | Instant screencasts: Just click record. *Screenr*. Retrieved May 14, 2012, from http://www.screenr.com/

Batson, T., & Bass, R. (1996). Primacy of process: Teaching and learning in the computer age. *Change*, *28*(2), 42–47. doi:10.1080/00091383.1996.9937750

Blackboard Collaborate | Online Collaboration Software for Engaging, Collaborative Learning. (2012). *Blackboard Collaborate*. Retrieved May 29, 2012, from http://www.blackboard.com/platforms/collaborate/overview.aspx

Brown, J. S. (2006). New learning environments for the 21st century: Exploring the edge. *Change, 38*(5), 18–24. doi:10.3200/CHNG.38.5.18-24

Burbules, N. C., & Callister, T. A. (2000). *The risky promises and promising risks on new information technologies for education. Watch IT: The risks and promises of information technologies for education.* Boulder, CO: Westview Press.

Creative Vado HD Pocket Video Cameras - Capture & share moments. (n.d.). Retrieved May 29, 2012, from http://www.creative.com/myvado/

Free Video Chat and Video Conferencing from ooVoo. (2012).*University partner program.* Retrieved May 29, 2012, from http://www.oovoo.com/edu/

HD Ultra Compact Digital Video Camcorder | Samsung HMX-U20 - Camcorders. (n.d.). Retrieved May 29, 2012, from http://www.samsung.com/us/photography/camcorders/HMX-U20BN/XAA

Hee Jun, C., & Johnson, S. D. (2005). The effect of context-based video instruction on learning and motivation in online courses. *American Journal of Distance Education, 19*(4), 215–227. doi:10.1207/s15389286ajde1904_3

Hee Jun, C., & Johnson, S. D. (2007). The effect of problem-based video instruction on learner satisfaction, comprehension and retention in college courses. *British Journal of Educational Technology, 38*(5), 885–895. doi:10.1111/j.1467-8535.2006.00676.x

Mediasite by Sonic Foundry - Create Online Multimedia Presentations, Briefings and Courses Automatically | Sonic Foundry. (2012). Retrieved May 29, 2012, from http://www.sonicfoundry.com/mediasite

Merriam, S. B., & Caffarella, R. S. (1999). *Learning in adulthood: A comprehensive guide.* San Francisco, CA: Jossey-Bass.

Online Meeting | GoToMeeting. (2012).*Citrix online GoToMeeting.* Retrieved May 29, 2012, from http://www.gotomeeting.com/fec/online_meeting

Phillips, R., Preston, G., Roberts, P., Cummins-Potvin, W., Herrington, J., Maor, D., & Gosper, M. (2010). Using academic analytic tools to investigate studying behaviours in technology-supported learning environments. *Curriculum, Technology & Transformation for an Unknown Future: Proceedings ASCILITE Sydney 2010* (pp. 761–771). Sydney, Australia.

Ramaswami, R. (2009, June 1). Capturing the market. *Campus Technology.* News. Retrieved August 23, 2012, from http://campustechnology.com/Articles/2009/06/01/Lecture-Capture.aspx

SANYO: Dual Cameras: VPC-PD2BK Full HD 1080 Pocket Movie Dual Camera with 10MP Digital Photos and 3X Optical Zoom. (2012). Retrieved May 29, 2012, from http://us.sanyo.com/Dual-Cameras/VPC-PD2BK-Full-HD-1080-Pocket-Movie-Dual-Camera-with-10MP-Digital-Photos-and-3X-Optical-Zoom

Sony Handycam Camcorders | Sony Store USA. (2012). Retrieved May 28, 2012, from http://store.sony.com/webapp/wcs/stores/servlet/CategoryDisplay?catalogId=10551&storeId=10151&langId=-1&identifier=S_Video_Camcorders&SR=nav:electronics:cameras_camcorders:video_cameras_camcorders:shop_compare:ss

Squared 5. (n.d.). *Squared 5: MPEG Streamclip for Mac and Windows and more...* Retrieved May 29, 2012, from http://www.squared5.com/

TechSmith. (2012a). *Jing, record and share videos on your computer, by TechSmith.* Retrieved May 14, 2012, from http://www.techsmith.com/jing-features.html

TechSmith. (2012b). *Snagit, screen grab for Mac and Windows by TechSmith.* Retrieved May 14, 2012, from http://www.techsmith.com/snagit-features.html

TechSmith. (n.d.). *Camtasia video recording and editing software by TechSmith.* Retrieved May 14, 2012, from http://www.techsmith.com/camtasia-features.html

Telestream. (2012). *Screencasting software - ScreenFlow overview - Telestream.* Retrieved May 14, 2012, from http://www.telestream.net/screen-flow/

Video Capture and Management Software Company | Panopto. (2012). Retrieved May 29, 2012, from http://www.panopto.com/video-capture-and-management-software-company

Video Chat - Free Online Video Calls - Video Calling - Skype. (2012). Retrieved May 29, 2012, from http://www.skype.com/intl/en-us/features/allfeatures/video-call/

Video Conferencing and Personal Telepresence Solutions – Vidyo. (2012).*Vidyo personal telepresence.* Retrieved May 29, 2012, from http://www.vidyo.com/

Web conferencing software - Conference services | Adobe Connect. (2012). *Adobe Connect.* Retrieved May 29, 2012, from http://www.adobe.com/products/adobeconnect.html

Welcome to FuzeBox — FuzeBox. (2012). *Fuze Box.* Retrieved May 29, 2012, from https://www.fuzebox.com/

Windows Live Essentials - Download Windows Live Essentials. (2012). *Windows live essentials.* Retrieved May 29, 2012, from http://windows.microsoft.com/en-US/windows-live/essentials-home

Zhang, D. (2005). Interactive multimedia-based e-learning: A study of effectiveness. *American Journal of Distance Education, 19*(3), 149–162. doi:10.1207/s15389286ajde1903_3

ADDITIONAL READING

Bates, A. W., & Sangra, A. (2011). *Managing technology in higher education: Strategies for transforming teaching and learning* (1st ed.). San Francisco, CA: Jossey-Bass.

Bell, P. (2008). An instructional design approach for integrating digital storytelling into the classroom using iMovie. In K. McFerrin et al. (Eds.), *Proceedings of Society for Information Technology & Teacher Education International Conference,* (pp. 883–888). Chesapeake, VA.

Blevins, A., & Elton, C. W. (2009). An evaluation of three tutorial-creating software programs: Camtasia, PowerPoint, and MediaSite. *Journal of Electronic Resources in Medical Libraries, 6*(1), 1–7. doi:10.1080/15424060802705095

Burt, J. (2011). Vidyo challenges Cisco, Polycom with telepresence offering - VOIP and telephony. *eWeek.com.* Retrieved May 29, 2012, from http://www.eweek.com/c/a/VOIP-and-Telephony/Vidyo-Challenges-Cisco-Polycom-with-Telepresence-Offering-227601/

Carlson, J. (2011). *The iMovie 11 project book.* Berkeley, CA: Peachpit Press. Retrieved from www.peachpit.com

Cooke, M., Watson, B., Blacklock, E., Mansah, M., Howard, M., & Johnston, A. (2012). Lecture capture: First year student nurses' experiences of a web-based lecture technology. *The Australian Journal of Advanced Nursing, 29*(3), 14–21.

Educause Learning Initiative. (2005, 2012). *7 things you should know about...* Retrieved May 30, 2012, from http://www.educause.edu/ELI7Things

Fenton, W. (2011). Adobe Connect Review & Rating | PCMag.com. *PC Mag.* Retrieved May 29, 2012, from http://www.pcmag.com/article2/0,2817,2387818,00.asp

Green, K. C. (2010). 2010 campus computing survey: IT budgets cuts slowing; Campus LMS strategies in transition. *The Campus Computing Project*. Retrieved from http://www.campuscomputing.net/

Keegwe, J., & Georgina, D. (2012). The digital course training workshop for online learning and teaching. *Education and Information Technologies, 17*(4), 365–379. doi:10.1007/s10639-011-9164-x

Lifehacker, tips and downloads for getting things done. (2012). *Lifehacker*. Retrieved May 29, 2012, from http://lifehacker.com/

Mark, K. P., Vogel, D. R., & Wong, E. Y. W. (2010). Developing learning system continuance with teachers and students: Case study of the Echo360 lecture capturing system. *PACIS 2010 Proceedings*. Retrieved from http://aisel.aisnet.org/pacis2010/170

Nelson, F. (2011). FuzeBox brings iPad 2, Android 3.0 tablets into video meetings. *Informationweek*. Retrieved May 29, 2012, from http://www.informationweek.com/news/mobility/messaging/229400560

ooVoo Video Conferencing Review. (2010). Retrieved May 29, 2012, from http://www.notebookreview.com/default.asp?newsID=5489&review=ooVoo+Video+Conferencing+Review

Osterman, M. D. (2012). Digital literacy: Definition, theoretical framework, and competencies. In M. S. Plakhotnik, S. M. Nielsen, & D. M. Pane (Eds.), *Proceedings of the 11th Annual College of Education & GSN Research Conference*, Miami: Florida International University, (pp. 135–141).

Owston, R., Lupshenyuk, D., & Wideman, H. (2011). Lecture capture in large undergraduate classes: Student perceptions and academic performance. *The Internet and Higher Education, 14*(4), 262–268. doi:10.1016/j.iheduc.2011.05.006

Perkins, S., & Casdorph, M. (2011). The digital Swiss army knife. *EDUCAUSE Review, 46*(2). Retrieved from http://www.educause.edu/er/PerkinsCasdorph

Pilarski, P. P., Johnstone, D. A., Pettepher, C. C., & Osheroff, N. (2008). From music to macromolecules: Using rich media/podcast lecture recordings to enhance the preclinical educational experience. *Medical Teacher, 30*(6), 630–632. doi:10.1080/01421590802144302

ProfHacker - Tips about teaching, technology, and productivity. (2012). *The Chronicle of Higher Education*. News. Retrieved May 29, 2012, from http://chronicle.com/blogs/profhacker/

Rahman Syed, M. (2008). *Strategic applications of distance learning technologies: Advances in distance education technologies*. Hershey, PA: IGI Global. doi:10.4018/978-1-59904-480-4

Review: Desktop and Laptop HD Video conferencing products 2011. (2012). Retrieved May 29, 2012, from http://www.vcinsight.com/118/HDVideoConferencingEquipment/662/ReviewDesktopandLaptopHDVideoconferencingproducts2011

Schubert, P. (2011). Grasping the realities of educating in the digital age. *EDUCAUSE Review, 46*(2). Retrieved from http://www.educause.edu/EDUCAUSE+Review/EDUCAUSEReviewMagazineVolume46/GraspingtheRealitiesofEducatin/226177

Sloan, C., & Ray, C. (2009). Tegrity: Successes and failures of a pilot program introducing lecture capture to campus. *SIDLIT*. Presented at the The Summer Institute on Distance Learning and Instructional Technology, Overland Park, Kansas: ScholarSpace @ JCCC.

Stern, Z. (2010). Fuze box fuze meeting web service review. *MacWorld*. Information. Retrieved May 29, 2012, from http://www.macworld.com/article/1153775/fuzemeetingreview.html

Tamarkin, M., & Rodrigo, S. (2011). Evolving technologies: A view to tomorrow. *EDUCAUSE Review*, *46*(6). Retrieved from http://www. educause.edu/EDUCAUSE+Review/EDU-CAUSEReviewMagazineVolume46/Evolving-TechnologiesAViewtoTom/238392

The New Media Consortium and Educause Learning Initiative. (2012). *2012 horizon report.* Retrieved from http://www.educause.edu/Resour ces/2012HorizonReport/246056

Walsh, T., & Bowen, W. G. (2010). *Unlocking the gates: How and why leading universities are opening up access to their courses.* Princeton University Press.

Web Conferencing Review 2012 | Best Web Conference Services | Online Meeting Services – TopTenREVIEWS. (2012). Retrieved May 29, 2012, from http://web-conferencing services. toptenreviews.com/

KEY TERMS AND DEFINITIONS

Desktop Video Conferencing: Communication between two or more locations using computer hardware and/or software or mobile devices to share voice, video, applications, content, whiteboard collaboration, or questions via live chat.

H.264/MPEG-4: Advance Video Encoding is a standard for video compression and currently one of the most commonly used video formats.

Lecture Capture: The use of video, audio, and display systems to capture and synchronize the content of a lecture and make a browser-based or mobile technology accessible asynchronous video or audio file.

Multimedia: Media and content that uses different combinations of video and audio technology to create deliverable content over the Internet or other information technology.

Screen Capture: The action of grabbing a still capture of whatever is displayed on a computer screen.

Screencasting: The action of recording a video of all of the applications and actions occurring during a specific period of time on a computer screen.

Visual Media Hardware: Computers, servers, or physical cameras.

Visual Media Software: Applications installed on computers or servers to create original content.

Section 2
Lecture Capturing

Chapter 5
Using Presentation Capture in Counselor Education Programs

Robert Gibson
Emporia State University, USA

Ann Miller
Emporia State University, USA

ABSTRACT

Emporia State University recently implemented a web-based presentation capture application for use in both a graduate and undergraduate counselor education program. Presentation capture, sometimes referred to as course capture or lecture capture, is most often used in traditional classrooms to record lectures by faculty for playback and review by students following class. However, in this educational scenario the students record sessions with assigned clients from the Emporia, Kansas community that are later played back by the faculty for review and evaluation – most often in a classroom environment where all the students gather to review and discuss the client recordings. The faculty critique the interview techniques, interview questions, and client engagement with the students as part of their training, research, and coursework. One of the unique needs of this approach is that the recordings conform to Health Insurance Privacy and Accountability Act (HIPAA) requirements and thus can only be replayed outside the counseling facility using an encrypted Virtual Private Network (VPN) access. Although this is a very small academic program at a modest-sized university, an empirical research study was conducted to gauge the effectiveness of capturing client sessions using a presentation capture application. Results from that study indicate that both students and faculty found the software and hardware to be very easy to use, and believed it significantly enhanced the quality of the counseling program.

DOI: 10.4018/978-1-4666-3962-1.ch005

INTRODUCTION

The use of presentation capture applications in counselor education programs is actually quite common. Schaefle, Smaby, and Liu (2006) found that 93% of the Counsel for Accreditation of Counseling and Related Educational Programs (CACREP) regularly utilize some type of digital software and hardware system to encode student-client sessions in their academic programs (e.g., counselor education, mental health counseling, school counseling, substance abuse counseling, marriage and family therapy). Specifically, Auburn University's Family and Marriage Therapy program has utilized digital video capture for various research and training purposes for many years (Melton, 2007). Web-based presentation capture in counseling is most often a replacement for earlier generations of analog-based recording systems. Earlier generations of recording systems suffer from a number of technical limitations. Videocassette tapes, for example, are considered an obsolete technology that is difficult to purchase in retail stores. Both Best Buy and Wal-Mart discontinued sales of VHS tapes as early as 2006 (Library Copyright Alliance, 2008). In addition, most forms of transportable media do not conform to rigid *Health Insurance Portability and Accountability Act* (HIPAA) requirements for storing and retrieving client/patient data (Retrieved from: http://www.hhs.gov/ocr/privacy/). Tapes, disks, thumb drives, and other forms of portable media can easily find their way into the wrong hands outside of a controlled environment. Furthermore, they are somewhat clumsy and difficult to operate. For example, locating a specific point in a 90-minute taped session can take several minutes of searching using a videocassette player, whereas using a web-based digital recorder the student or faculty member can insert bookmarks or placeholders into key locations for near-instantaneous access. Also, web-based systems do not require a larger physical storage area for the recorded media. A thousand hours of semester recordings

using VHS would consume at least 200 tapes, as opposed to one modest-sized server hard drive.

However, not all colleges and universities have adopted an academic presentation capture solution to replace their aging analog system. Several have leveraged digital recording systems intended for athletic game review. These systems also provide digital capture and playback of client sessions; however, they tend to be quite expensive; are normally stand-alone appliances that do not easily scale across the institution; are specifically designed for athletics; and do not afford many of the features required of academic programs. For example, many of these products do not provide closed captioning or include the ability to insert student or faculty notations into the recordings at key points. Rather, they are specifically designed so that athletes and coaches can analyze sports plays during or at the conclusion of games. Therefore, these athletic game review systems are often poor substitutes for presentation capture products intended for academics.

In this chapter we discuss the effectiveness of web-based presentation capture systems in the context of a counselor education program. The American Counseling Association (ACA) defines counseling as:

… a professional relationship that empowers diverse individuals, families, and groups to accomplish mental health, wellness, education, and career goals. (American Counseling Association, n.d.)

At Emporia State University the presentation capture technology is used to support a variety of academic disciplines that fall under the umbrella of counseling education including Mental Health Counseling, Rehabilitation Counseling, School Counseling, Art Therapy Counseling, Crime and Delinquency Studies, and Rehabilitation Services Education, which includes alcohol and drug abuse counseling, student services, corrections, and child and family services. When the program faculty and staff initially embarked on selecting a replacement for the aging VHS system, several products and solutions were entertained based on specific academic requirements, including the ability to do the following.

- **Add and exchange notations between students and faculty:** These notations needed to be private between the individual student and faculty.
- **Support two captures cameras:** This was required in the larger counseling rooms that were installed with cameras at opposing ends of the room.
- **Easily use the system:** Some students using the system were not technologically adept, so the system needed to be turn-key.
- **Automatically backup recordings:** This system had to include an automatic backup in the event the server recording was lost. Student grades were dependent upon a reliable system.
- **Record in high fidelity:** Faculty and students required clear video images captured at high frame rates. The audio also had to be very high-fidelity in order to provide accurate observational information.
- **View full-screen video playback:** Faculty desired seeing video playback in full-screen as opposed to small window.
- **Create unique, privatized folders for each student:** Unless authorized, the student-client recordings should not be visible to other students.
- **Easily administer student folders:** Since the program director would be assigning students to clients through the software, the system needed to be easy to manage.
- **Have faculty see all student recordings:** Using the administrative functions, faculty must be able to see all the recordings for their students.
- **Include captioning:** Americans with Disabilities Act (ADA) standards require that software products be equally accessible to individuals with a variety of physical or learning impairments.
- **See a live stream in classroom within the Counseling Center:** At least two program faculty members review live, mock student-client recordings from outside client counseling rooms. The former system provided closed-circuit viewing capabilities. The web-based system needed to support something similar.
- **Have distance students record and upload videos:** Many students do not reside in Emporia. They record client sessions in alternative locations and must be able to upload those sessions to the instructors.
- **Do scheduling:** The new system needs the ability to trigger recorders to turn themselves on at prescribed times and days.
- **Do editing:** Faculty and students must be able to perform minor editing of the recordings if necessary.

In addition to the programmatic requirements, a technical team was empanelled to review product options from the vantage of support and integration with existing enterprise systems. This panel included individuals from server operations, client services, academic technology, security, and network operations. Some of the technical requirements included the ability to do the following.

- **Virtualize the servers:** The new system needed to run the system using virtualized rather than physical servers.
- **Integrate with the existing database:** Support for enterprise database schema.
- **Store content on a SAN:** Ability to store recordings on a separate storage array (SAN) rather than local hard drives.
- **Support Single Sign-On:** Integration with the campus' Active Directory schema and Single Sign-On (SSO) authentication.

- **Scale across the enterprise:** The product needed to run on PCs or Macintoshes as opposed to appliance-based systems, which are more expensive to purchase and maintain and which do not scale easily.

- **Provision student accounts:** The ability to provision student accounts/folders with unique permissions is a critical component. Each student will require a unique folder with express access permission to upload recordings. "Bulk" folders where all students share the same virtual space is not acceptable.

- **Support reporting and diagnostics:** Ease in server administration; provide excellent reporting and diagnostics features that assist in troubleshooting problems as they arise.

- **Privatize content to conform with HIPAA:** Ability to access recordings using a virtual private network (VPN) connection from outside the counseling facility. This is particularly important to ensure the recordings are digitally protected and privatized.

- **Integrate with the Learning Management System Integration:** Although the counseling program would not be integrating the product with the LMS, the university envisioned that traditional faculty on campus would require that functionality if the product were mainstreamed.

- **Reach technical support personnel when issues arose:** Solid technical support is required for a system of this complexity. Students and faculty utilize this system very rigorously. If and when technical problems arise, it is critical to have reliable support.

Ultimately, a product was selected that meets all of the criteria from both the faculty stakeholders and the technical team. Projecting forward, once successfully introduced within the counseling program, presentation capture was believed to have the capacity to quickly spread across campus. In order to support that likelihood, a second instance of the product was installed on separated server architecture, intended for traditional campus applications.

BACKGROUND

In 2008, Dr. Ann Miller – an Emporia State University Associate Professor and Director of Emporia Community Counseling Services (CCS) – approached the university's Technology and Computing Services (TCS) regarding replacement of an aging VHS recording and viewing system installed in the Counseling Center in the late 1990s. CCS provides counseling for individuals, couples, families, and groups throughout the community of Emporia, Kansas, as part of graduate and undergraduate training for ESU students seeking degrees in mental health, rehabilitation, and school counseling. Counseling students consult with assigned community clients on a weekly basis in one of ten counseling rooms specifically designed for this activity. Eight of the rooms are intended for individual, couple, or parental consultation. A larger room is intended for group therapy, which often includes sessions with extended family members. A second larger room is designated as a play therapy room to be used in conjunction with children's therapy. All participants sign a consent form that permits recording of the sessions as part of the program.

In order to accommodate the Counseling Center's video recording needs, the goal of the project was to replace the old analog system with a more sophisticated digital presentation capture application. In its broadest sense, *lecture (presentation) capture* is a set of technologies used to record or capture classroom lecture to be replayed later by students for review (EDUCAUSE, 2008). Presentation capture can include video, audio, graphics, whiteboard or document camera capture, or a combination of mediums. There are several empirical studies that substantiate the relevance of recorded lectures in higher education. In a study by McKinney, Dyck, and Luber (2008) at the State University in New York, students who listened to lectures plus lecture podcasts - as opposed to lecture-only or lecture plus slide notes - did significantly better on examinations. A similar study conducted by Neil Morris (2006) at the University of Leeds in the UK found that students expressed an improved learning experience, improved interactions with co-students and faculty, and improved productivity following the introduction of podcast recordings. A meta-analysis of lecture capture conducted by Pursel and Fang (2011) found that students leveraged lecture capture for a variety of reasons.

- Lecture supplements (Settle, Dettori, & Davidson, 2011)
- Convenience (Akiyama, Teramoto & Kozono, 2008; Mark, Vogel & Wong, 2010)
- Examination prep (Brotherton & Abowd, 2004; Craig, Hyde, & Burn 2009; Engstrand & Hall, 2011; Preston, Phillips, Gosper, McNeill, Woo, & Green, 2010; Settle & Davidson, 2011)
- Enhancing lecture concepts (Brecht & Ogilby, 2008; Gosper, Green, McNeill, Phillips, Preston, & Woo, 2010)
- Note-taking (Collie, Shah, & Sheridan, 2009)
- Reviewing missed materials (Settle, Dettori, & Davidson 2011)

Although presentation capture technology as we know it is only about ten years old, its roots go back to the days when lecture was recorded on tapes and later distributed to students for review. For example, starting in the 1980s and throughout much of the 1990s, institutions with substantial outreach educational programs, such as Colorado State University's Mechanical and Civil Engineer-ing, would record hundreds of hours of classroom didactic lectures on VHS tape and distribute them to students via mail on a weekly basis (Powell, 2012). However, it wasn't until high-quality video became widely available over the Internet a few years ago that digital presentation capture began to piqué the interest of colleges and universities. A research effort conducted in 2008 at the University of Wisconsin-Madison involving 7,500 undergraduate and graduate students found that 82% of the students preferred courses that included lecture capture over those that did not (Nagel, 2008). Much of what has driven this interest of late is the rise in mobile computing that provides ubiquitous access to high-quality video content (McClure, 2008).

According to Zhu and Bergom (2010), presentation capture can be used for much more than simply capturing and replaying didactic content. They suggest that it can also be used to support the following academic activities.

- Provide additional resources, including tutorials for lab work, demonstrations of difficult concepts and complex procedures like printmaking or CPR, and presentations by guest speakers.
- Allow students to review material at their own pace and convenience (Coghlan, E., Futey, D., Little, J., Lomas, C., Oblinger, D., & Windham, C. 2007).
- Offer students more flexibility in note-taking.
- Make time for active learning during class by having the lecture available for viewing before the class meetings (Lund, 2008).
- Allow students to catch up with a missed lecture.
- Offer another tool for student learning projects (e.g., student-generated podcasts for interviewing locals and sharing with peers in a study-abroad program).

Engaging the students in presentation capture *prior* to formal class time with the faculty is particularly empowering. This methodology, made popular through the Khan Academy, is often termed "flipping" the classroom (The Economist, 2011). That is, the bulk of the didactic coursework is actually composed or viewed by the students outside of the weekly class meetings. The scheduled weekly meetings are instead used to review and discuss the lectures, providing a better use of time, a deeper transfer of knowledge, and more content coverage. This type of emerging didactic model is becoming more common as presentation capture becomes mainstreamed (Pursel & Fang, 2011).

Perhaps what makes the student-led counseling application somewhat unique is that this technology is really intended for classroom-based capture. For example, presentation capture includes the ability to integrate PowerPoint and desktop application capture along with the video and audio. In fact, the interface is designed to seamlessly blend PowerPoint with the lecture video. Thumbnails and hyperlinked bookmarks of the PowerPoint are automatically generated as the lecture is composed. However, in this setting, the tables are turned. Rather than the faculty recording lectures and students replaying them on demand, the students – both graduate and undergraduate – record themselves in controlled environments along with assigned clients from the local community or among co-students when in undergraduate training. The *faculty* then watch the recordings in classroom settings along with all the co-students.

Every student is provided a 30-minute training session as a precursor to using the system – an approach that has proven to be more than adequate. Once the students begin using the product with clients, it normally takes between 1 and 2 minutes to initiate a recording. Students turn off the PowerPoint and desktop capture features – concentrating on the video and audio only. An advantage of the product is that the preferences are retained for each

student, so they only are required to make modifications to the interface options once. The next time they log into the application, the preferences are preset. The students are trained to perform the following activation sequence.

1. Log into the capture station.
2. Start the capture product.
3. Ensure the PowerPoint and desktop capture features are disabled (only required once).
4. Ensure video and audio are enabled and functional (only required once).
5. Ensure the correct destination folder is selected (only required once).
6. Begin the recorder and turn the monitor off to prevent client distraction.
7. Turn the recorder off at the conclusion of the session and log off.

At the conclusion of each session, the capture product will begin upload to the servers automatically. Normally, it takes about 60 minutes to encode and upload every 30 minutes of video recording. However, students do not need to wait. As long as the computer is powered on, the capture application will continue to encode and upload the video even after the student logs off and leaves. Furthermore, another student can use the workstation immediately following the first student's session without interfering with the upload. Or the first student can record back-to-back sessions without interfering with the first session upload. In a typical semester, students compose more than 1,000 hours of student-client recordings. Since the system was installed in 2009, only one session has ever been lost – the result of a PC malfunction.

Issues, Controversies, Problems

One of the biggest challenges of implementing a digital capture system for this type of application was security and privacy. As part of any technology adoption process, the university Internet Security

Officer (ISO) was engaged in a thorough analysis as various products were entertained. The primary concern expressed by the ISO was ensuring that the data complied with federal regulations – primarily HIPAA. In addition to the need for discrete video capture of counseling sessions, the students, many of whom live in remote locations, required access to the recordings through their computers while still maintaining client confidentiality. These recordings had to be treated with the same care and concern as any private patient medical information. According to Health and Human Services, the presentation capture system needed to comply with:

...the HIPAA Privacy Rule, which protects the privacy of individually identifiable health information; the HIPAA Security Rule, which sets national standards for the security of electronic protected health information; and the confidentiality provisions of the Patient Safety Rule, which protect identifiable information being used to analyze patient safety events and improve patient safety (Retrieved from hhs.gov May, 2012).

When the ESU counseling program faculty were engaged in the product review process, some initially resisted the move to a web-based capture solution. The familiarity and reliability of VHS tape was a difficult obstacle to overcome, despite its technological obsolescence, and its security and regulatory concerns. Additionally, accessing web-based client recordings from the main campus classrooms, where the classes often take place, required certain security measures. For some faculty accustomed to simply inserting a VHS tape into a deck and pushing *play*, the steps required to access the recordings were considered cumbersome. Briefly, those steps are as follows.

1. Open a web browser and type an encrypted (SSL) address to invoke the Virtual Private Network (VPN) client.

2. Allow the client to initiate establish a secure connection (can be up to 1 minute).
3. Open another browser tab and type a specific secure URL to access the capture product.
4. Log in and access the recordings.

Although arguably an unwieldy access protocol that can take several minutes to invoke, these steps are nonetheless required to ensure a secure transmission from any location outside the counseling facility. (When accessing recordings from classrooms located inside the Counseling Center, faculty only need to type the name of the server in a browser.) Using a VPN client and a privatized VLAN (Virtual Local Access Network) significantly reduces the chance of breach through a rogue attack.

Accrediting bodies, such as the Council for the Accreditation of Counseling and Related Educational Programs (CACREP), the Council on Rehabilitation Education (CORE) and the American Psychological Association (APA), increasingly require safeguards to ensure HIPAA standards are being met when recordings are composed and distributed (American Counseling Association, Retrieved May, 2012). Streamed recordings significantly reduce the likelihood that sessions can be viewed by non-authorized individuals from outside of the program. However, it is still possible to capture a streamed recording. There are a number of readily available software products that can be used to re-record streamed video and audio, although the likelihood of this occurring is remote.

Another unique challenge of the program has been finding a solution to assist students in uploading videos that they record from outside of the Counseling Center. Since many students live in remote locations, they are often required to record clients wherever they reside. To date, it has been challenging to upload these videos, which are often recorded in a format that is incompatible with the native presentation system, into their assigned client folders. However, recent advances in the technology should help to mitigate this concern. Students can now be assigned a special folder in the system that provides a convenient option for uploading and transcoding video from nearly any location. In addition, new advances in mobile recording systems using smart phone technology will provide students the ability to record in otherwise difficult locations, such as detention and detoxification centers.

Finally, locating a solution to accommodate students with disabilities has been challenging, but is nonetheless extremely important. Some studies have found that one in ten undergraduate students presents with at least some form of disability (Henderson, 1999). Newest advances in speech-to-text software applications have helped to mitigate some of the issues, but their accuracy remains somewhat subpar. Other product advances that have been recently introduced include the ability to slow down the captured recordings to half-speed, which helps those students with learning or language barriers.

Solutions and Recommendations

Using much of the existing audio-visual infrastructure, the university was able to reduce the presentation capture installation expense. Older VHS decks were replaced with a PC installed with a video capture card. However, much of the audio system was deemed salvageable and was

repurposed. In rooms with two cameras, dual capture cards were installed in the PC (Figure 1).

The network was architected so that it runs on a segregated virtual LAN (VLAN) outside normal IP traffic on campus. The workstations can only be used to record client sessions using the capture software. Students cannot access any external web sites, nor can outside sites reach the workstations. A dedicated switch was installed in the Counseling Center building and network connections added to each of the counseling rooms and classrooms. Since the building is located two blocks off-campus, a fiber trunk was activated that sends the video and data back to the data center, where two servers store and serve the content. Additional hardware firewalls were also added within the network schema. Faculty access the recordings within the Counseling Center using laptops connected directly to the switch. LCD monitors were installed in each classroom that are also connected, via the laptops, so that the faculty can review and discuss the archived recordings with the students (Figure 2). Since the presentation capture product supports streaming, faculty can also view live sessions from any of the ten rooms in order to evaluate a student's counseling skills.

Study Methodology

In order to study the efficacy of the presentation capture system, we surveyed several students and faculty in the counseling program regarding their

Figure 1. An original VHS capture station (left) and an updated presentation capture station (right)

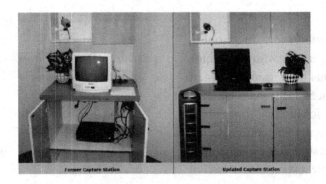

Figure 2. Typical classroom with laptop and plasma screen for reviewing client sessions

perceptions of the technology. This is a small program at the university, so the study group size was very limited.

Participants

ESU is considered a rural university with a student population of approximately 5,900 students, situated in Emporia, Kansas (Pop. ~26,000). The Community Counseling Services Center is the only counseling facility of its type in the community. The next nearest counseling center is located in Topeka, 45 miles northeast.

Twenty-nine students (80% response rate) and four faculty members (66% response rate) participated in a survey regarding the efficacy of presentation capture in counseling education. The students were enrolled in a variety of majors, both graduate and undergraduate (Table 1).

Study Procedure

Participants agreed to complete a short online survey regarding their experience with the technology. Many of the students have used the system since it was first introduced last year, while others are using the system for the first time. Those that used the system initially encountered a few technical issues as the system was launched that may have influenced their responses.

Results and Discussion

Students Participants

Generally, the students expressed a high degree of satisfaction with the capture technology (Figure 3). This may be a result of a sustained training campaign conducted at the beginning of every semester for all the students who use the technology. On average, the students collectively record approximately 1000 hours of interviews each semester.

Students also indicated that the technology improved their skills as counselors (82%); made access to learning activities more convenient (79%); and improved their overall learning (76%). The majority of students are using the system to capture approximately 1-2 hours of client sessions per week. Much of the usage is contingent upon whether or not the student was assigned a community client that is able to travel to the facility (Figure 4).

Regardless of whether or not the students are recording sessions with clients, they all participate in reviewing a certain number of sessions on a weekly basis. These sessions are recorded by other students who are assigned clients, and then analyzed collectively by the entire class along with the instructor (Figures 5 and 6).

Since reviewing the archival sessions from off-campus requires a unique login procedure where-

Table 1. Student majors

Students	Major
1	School Psychology
2	Rehabilitation Services Education
13	Mental Health Counseling
2	Sociology
8	Rehabilitation Counseling
1	Art Therapy
1	Crime and Delinquency Studies

Figure 3. Student satisfaction with the presentation capture system (= 4.03 = 0.87)

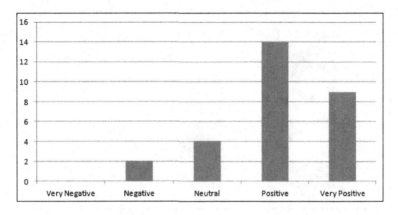

Figure 4. Number of student-led recordings/week (= 2.29 = 1.21)

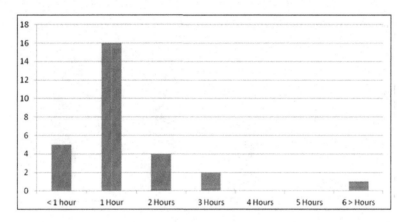

Figure 5. Number of student hours/week reviewing sessions (= 2.04 = 0.94)

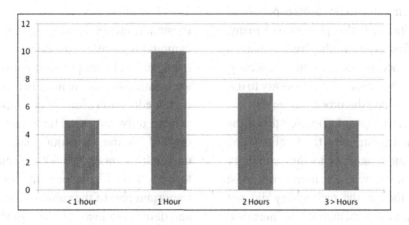

Figure 6. Primary student viewing location

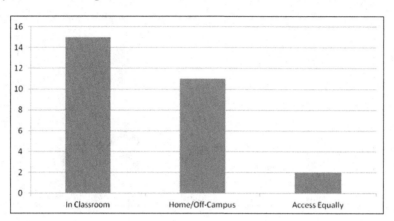

Figure 7. Potential client distraction created by presence of presentation technology (= 3.14 = 0.88)

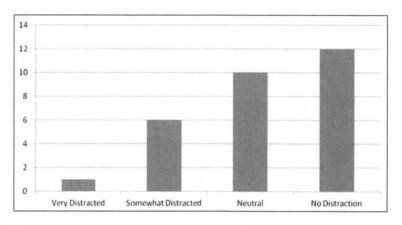

by a VPN software client product is activated, the researchers were curious if the students experienced technical difficulties with this process. For many, this may be the first exposure they've had using a VPN product to access secure data. Generally, students found the VPN access process easy to use (50%). Only 27% found the process onerous.

The researchers also wanted to ascertain if the technology created a distraction for the client (i.e., the interviewee) and whether or not the technology influenced the interview itself. In general, most students felt as though the technology did not create a distraction nor influence the interview (Figures 7 and 8).

FUTURE RESEARCH DIRECTIONS

Presentation capture is rapidly becoming a critical campus infrastructure resource. According to data from the 2011 Campus Computing Project, there are significant gains in interest across nearly every higher education sector (e.g., public universities, private universities). Those gains have trended upward for the past four years. Among public universities, more than 80% of senior technology leaders believe that presentation capture is an important part of the campus plan for developing and delivering instructional content. Still, actual deployment rates hover at a modest 5% (Campus

Figure 8. Potential for technology to influence client responses (= 2.28 = 0.70)

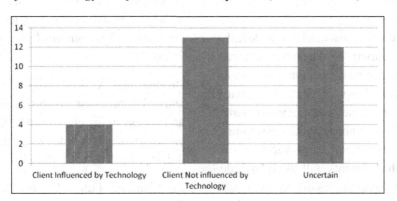

Computing Project, 2011). This will undoubtedly increase as campuses find utility in the software for a variety of applications – including medical and counseling education.

The companies that develop and support presentation capture systems continue to offer increasingly sophisticated features to satisfy a variety of academic applications. For example, several companies now support the ability to capture video using Internet-enabled phones and tablets – which may assist students who are conducting mobile field research and activities. This may also provide an easier option for students to conduct interviews in locations that are currently difficult, if not impossible, to work with clients and patients. Other product improvements will likely target captioning systems so that the audio will automatically be converted to text for students with visual impairments. One area companies are also leveraging is cloud-based solutions. Using the cloud, presentation capture systems can be made available to students 24/7 and from nearly any locale. For the institution, the cloud could potentially lower the total cost of ownership. These improvements will provide even more features and functionality for a variety of applications.

Emporia State intends to continue this research effort by collecting student and faculty data annually, providing longitudinal support regarding the efficacy of presentation capture in counseling scenarios. We also believe it will be important to collect data from the clients themselves regarding the influence of the technology on their responses. Often referred to as the *Hawthorne Effect*, this research effort attempts to determine if the presence of the technology in the counseling rooms in any way influences the responses of the clients (Shuttleworth, 2009). In the current installation, the camera and computer are in plain view of the clients. We believe these devices should be obscured as much as possible to reduce distraction and possible influence on the clients.

The researchers also believe there may be opportunities to extend the product and research into some other academic areas that may be less commonplace. For example, the system could be used in capturing pre-service teacher interactions with K-12 students as they are conducting student teaching rotations in various school districts throughout the state. Student teachers might be able to capture themselves in actual classroom environments using mobile devices, and later upload these interactions to the faculty preceptors through the application. Similarly, nursing and medical students may be able to utilize this technology in their training as they visit patients in various medical facilities. These options open an entirely new area of exciting research opportunities.

CONCLUSION

Presentation capture systems can be successfully repurposed for a variety of academic applications – beyond traditional classroom instruction. Survey results from Emporia State University clearly indicate that counselor education students and faculty find the technology both easy-to-use and academically beneficial in its various programs. Future enhancements will likely include installation of various esthetics that suppress the technology from the view of the client and product upgrades that will improve universal access, such as automatic captioning. We also believe there is significant potential to leverage the technology in a variety of other academic disciplines, including teacher and nursing education.

Although a variety of systems exist in the lecture capture spectrum, institutions will need to determine the specific criteria they require before making a product selection. No singular product yet has amassed every desired feature along with an aggressive price point that can be scaled across the institution. In addition, consideration should be given as to whether the selected product will be used beyond niche programs and how that product will match the needs of the traditional classroom instructors.

Clearly, presentation capture is a technology that academic programs can easily leverage in their curriculum. Furthermore, it can be repurposed to extend beyond simply capturing lecture but also be used a tool for students to capture and upload video.

REFERENCES

American Counseling Association. (n.d.). *Resources*. Retrieved April 1, 2012, from http://www.counseling.org/resources/

Brecth, H. D., & Ogilby, S. M. (2008). Enabling a comprehensive teaching strategy: Video lecture. *Journal of Information Technology Education*, 7, 71–86.

Brotherton, J. A., & Abowd, G. D. (2004). Lessons learned from eClass: Assessing automated capture and access in the classroom. *ACM Transactions on Computer-Human Interaction, 11*(2), 121–155. doi:10.1145/1005361.1005362

Coghlan, E., Futey, D., Little, J., Lomas, C., Oblinger, D., & Windham, C. (2007). *ELI discovery tool: Guide to podcasting*. Retrieved April, 2012 from http://www.educause.edu/Guideto-podcasting/12830

Collie, L., Shah, V., & Sheridan, D. (2009). *An end-user evaluation of a lecture archiving system*. Paper presented at the 10th International Conference NZ Chapter of the ACM's Special Interest Groupon Human-Computer Interaction.

Economist. (2011). *Flipping the classroom: Hopes that the internet can improve teaching may at last be bearing fruit*. September, 2011. Retrieved May 1, 2012 from http://www.economist.com/node/21529062

EDUCAUSE. (2008). *Seven things you should know about lecture capture*. Retrieved April 1, 2012, from http://net.educause.edu/ir/library/pdf/ELI7044.pdf

Engstrand, S., & Hall, S. (2011). The use of streamed lecture recordings: Patterns of use, student experience and effects on learning outcomes. *Practitioner Research in Higher Education, 5*(1), 9–15.

Gosper, M., Green, D., McNeill, M., Phillips, R., Preston, G., & Woo, K. (2008). The impact of web-based lecture technologies on current and future practices in learning and teaching. *ALT-J, 16*(2), 81–93.

Green, K. C. (2011). *2011 campus computing project*. Retrieved May 1, 2012, from http://www.campuscomputing.net/sites/www.campuscomputing.net/files/Green-CampusComputing2011_4.pdf

Henderson, C. (1999). *College freshmen with disabilities: Statistical year 1998*. Washington, DC: American Council on Education. Retrieved May 1, 2012, from http://www.answers.com/topic/college-students-with-disabilities-accommodating#ixzz1wAhcakla

Library Copyright Alliance. (2008). *Comments of the library copyright alliance and the music library association on proposed exemptions*. Retrieved May 1, 2012, from http://www.ftc.gov/os/comments/drmtechnologies/539814-00705.pdf

Lund, C. R. F. (2008). *Moving lectures out of the classroom to make room for learning* [PowerPoint slides]. Retrieved May, 2012 from http://www.ubtlc.buffalo.edu/workshops/handout.asp?titleID=170&eventID = 639

Mark, K. P., Vogel, D. R., & Wong, E. Y. W. (2010). *Developing learning system continuance with teachers and students: Case study of the Echo360 lecture capture system*. Paper presented at the PACIS.

McClure, A. (2008). Lecture capture: A fresh look. *University Business, 77*. Retrieved April 1, 2012, from http://www.universitybusiness.com/article/lecture-capture-fresh-look

McKinney, D., Dyck, J. L., & Luber, E. S. (2008). iTunes University and the classroom: Can podcasts replace professors? *Journal of Computers & Education, 52*(3). Retrieved from http://www.fredonia.edu/department/psychology/pdf/CAE1263.pdf

Melton, M. (2007). *An investigation of the relationship between supervision quality, quantity, and type with client outcomes in therapy*. Graduate thesis. Retrieved April, 2012 from: http://etd.auburn.edu/etd/bitstream/handle/10415/924/MELTON_MICHELE_53.pdf?sequence=1

Morris, N. (2006). *Using technology to enhance the quality of the student experience*. Bioscience Education Research Group. Faculty of Biological Sciences. Retrieved April 1, 2012, from http://www.sddu.leeds.ac.uk/uploaded/hotf/HOTF_morris_2012_no_video.pdf

Nagel, D. (2008, September). Lecture capture: No longer optional? *Campus Technology*. Retrieved May 1, 2012, from http://campustechnology.com/articles/2008/09/lecture-capture-no-longer-optional.aspx

Powell, A. (2012). *Why online courses matter*. Retrieved April 1, 2012, from http://www.online.colostate.edu/blog/posts/why-online-courses-matter

Pursel, B., & Fang, H. N. (2012). *Lecture capture: Current research and future directions*. Retrieved April 1, 2012, from http://www.psu.edu/dept/site/pursel_lecture_capture_2012v1.pdf

Schaefle, S., Smaby, M., & Liu, Li Ping (2006). Counselors attitudes toward video editing technology. *American Counseling Association Vistas*. Retrieved May, 2012 from: http://counselingoutfitters.com/Schaefle.htm

Settle, A., Dettori, L., & Davidson, M. J. (2011). *Does lecture capture make a difference for students in traditional classrooms?* Paper presented at the 16th Annual Joint Conference on Innovation and Technology in Computer Science Education, Germany.

Shuttleworth, M. (2009). *Hawthorne effect*. Retrieved May, 2012 from: http://www.experiment-resources.com/hawthorne-effect.html

U.S. Department of Health and Human Services. (n.d.). *Health information privacy*. Retrieved April 1, 2012, from http://www.hhs.gov/ocr/privacy/

Zhu, E., & Bergom, I. (2010). *Lecture capture: A guide for effective use*. CRLT Occasional Papers. N. 27. University of Michigan. Retrieved from http://www.crlt.umich.edu/publinks/CRLT_no27.pdf

ADDITIONAL READING

Economist (2011). *Flipping the classroom: Hopes that the internet can improve teaching may at last be bearing fruit*. Retrieved May, 2012 from: http://www.economist.com/node/21529062

EDUCAUSE. (2008). *Seven things you should know about lecture capture*. Retrieved from http://net.educause.edu/ir/library/pdf/ELI7044.pdf

Lund, C. R. F. (2008). *Moving lectures out of the classroom to make room for learning* [PowerPoint slides]. http://www.ubtlc.buffalo.edu/workshops/handout.asp?titleID =170&eventID = 639

Mark, K. P., Vogel, D. R., & Wong, E. Y. W. (2010). *Developing learning system continuance with teachers and students: case study of the Echo360 lecture capture system*. Paper presented at the PACIS.

Nagel, D. (September, 2008). *Lecture capture: No longer optional?* Campus Technology. http://campustechnology.com/articles/2008/09/lecture-capture-no-longer-optional.aspx

Chapter 6
Student Performance and Perceptions of Business Courses Delivered Using Lecture Capture

Patrick Moskal
University of Central Florida, USA

Patsy Moskal
University of Central Florida, USA

Patricia Euzent
University of Central Florida, USA

Thomas Martin
University of Central Florida, USA

ABSTRACT

This research compared student performance and withdrawal rates in undergraduate business courses taught using lecture capture and face-to-face. Student perceptions of lecture capture are also described. Lecture capture refers to storing videos of live course lectures, which students may view at their convenience from anywhere with an Internet connection. Results indicate no significant difference in student performance between the lecture capture and face-to-face conditions. Withdrawal rates also were similar, although freshman and sophomores had higher withdrawal rates in lecture capture than in face-to-face. Student perceptions of lecture capture were quite positive. Students were satisfied with the video instruction they received, they liked having more control over their learning, they liked the convenience that lecture capture provided, and about 70% said they would take another course that used lecture capture. However, the majority of students did not feel that lecture capture enhanced their performance or their interest in the course.

INTRODUCTION

Increasing student enrolments combined with funding cuts have resulted in stretched resources and larger class sizes, especially for lower level undergraduate courses. This environment has brought to the forefront the challenge of how best to deliver quality instruction, while still providing access to students. The use of lecture capture with video-streaming of instruction offers a cost-effective approach which eliminates the constraint of physical classroom space, while still maintain-

DOI: 10.4018/978-1-4666-3962-1.ch006

ing quality. Lecture capture takes advantage of economies of scale in providing course instruction, but also gives students more flexibility in when and where to receive the instruction, while also allowing them the opportunity to review content as they need to. With the growth of lecture capture technology, more research is needed to examine the effectiveness of this instructional delivery approach and issues surrounding its adoption into the culture of higher education.

This chapter describes research that examined both performance and perceptions of undergraduate business administration students at the University of Central Florida who took courses using lecture capture. As college enrollment and individual class sizes increased, the College of Business Administration (CBA) examined ways to provide quality instruction and assessment for its students, including those who may be employed or who are enrolled at one of eleven regional campuses. With the recent advances in computer technology, the CBA decided to move to lecture capture for its undergraduate core and other large course offerings. In this case, lecture capture refers to storing videos of actual course lectures on a UCF computer server, which are then made available to students on demand from course websites. Students may view these videos at their convenience, as often as they wish, and without the need to download the lectures onto their computers.

LECTURE CAPTURE IN THE CBA

CBA lecture capture course sections are digitally captured in one of two large multimedia classrooms. The multimedia classrooms use three cameras, including two broadcast quality television cameras to record the lecture, and a document camera. A portable microphone system that allows up to eight individuals to speak at the same time is used to capture audio throughout the classroom so the live class questions and discussion can be recorded.

The lectures (both audio and video components) are captured and streamed during the lecture (with about a 30-second delay). The lectures are archived for later viewing on the course websites. Students have unlimited viewing opportunities during the semester. The videos have standard controls, such as pause, replay, and fast forward, as well as varied playback speeds, and can be downloaded to portable devices such as MP3 players.

This lecture capture system does not change the classroom teaching arrangement and is quite unobtrusive for both the instructors and the students. Because the instructors conduct their lectures in front of students in a live classroom, course content is presented as if it were a face-to-face class.

At present, the CBA is offering 17 course sections that use lecture capture. These courses are in the undergraduate core curriculum and most have enrollments of over 480 students. Because of the large number of students involved, the college wanted to ensure that student performance and student attitudes about these courses were comparable to those same courses taught with live, face-to-face instruction.

The research described here includes two studies. They both provided data on student performance in lecture capture and corresponding face-to-face courses, and student perceptions of the lecture capture delivery medium. The first study examined student performance and perceptions between lecture capture and face-to-face sections in an undergraduate macroeconomics course. The second study inspected the overall general success and withdrawal rates of students across all CBA lecture capture course sections that had corresponding face-to-face sections. Data on general CBA student perceptions of lecture capture were also obtained.

Courses taught using lecture capture may be more challenging for students who choose not to attend a similar face-to-face course, because students have to be motivated and disciplined to view the videos and complete the assignments on their own time. Withdrawal rates are one gauge of students' difficulty completing the course. If a large percentage of students withdrew from the lecture capture sections compared to those in face-to-face sections, then this could indicate a problem that may not be reflected if student success rates alone were examined (e.g., Navarro, 2000; McLaren, 2004).

Data on student grades, including withdrawals, are readily available from institutional records. Because student grade distributions are likely to vary across departments, and even across faculty within a department, Moskal et al. (2006) and Dziuban, et al. (2005) reduced student grades into binary success or non-success categories in order to increase the reliability in examining student performance. Success is defined as a student achieving a course grade of C or higher. Because higher education institutions generally consider a C to be passing, this grade was chosen as the cut point for success. Other grades, such as C-, D, F, and I (incomplete) were defined as non-success. Students who withdrew from a course were also identified; a withdrawal is also considered to be a non-success. Students who withdrew for medical reasons were excluded from the analysis.

STUDENT PERFORMANCE

Study One

The first study reported examined student performance between two sections of an undergraduate Principles of Macroeconomics course, using a quasi-experimental design with data collected over the spring and fall semesters of 2011. During registration, students could choose between the lecture capture course section and the face-to-face section. However, random assignment to sections

was not possible. The two course sections were equivalent in all other ways, with the exception of course delivery format. The same instructor taught all four course sections (one face-to-face section and one lecture capture section each semester). Finally, students in the lecture capture sections were asked for their perceptions of the course.

Both lecture capture and face-to-face course sections used the same instructional materials, homework assignments, and exams. The instructor presented course information in a standard lecture format, supplemented with PowerPoint slides. During the semester, four exams were given, which accounted for 75% of the students' grade. *Aplia* was used for online homework assignments, and these comprised the other 25% of the grade. Identical Aplia assignments were required by students in both lecture capture and face-to-face sections, to be completed on their own time, and each assignment had a specific due date.

The face-to-face and lecture capture classes each met three hours per week. The instructional content and pacing was the same for both groups. The lecture capture sections were recorded during a live session, in essence a "face-to-face" class, with fresh lectures given and recorded each semester. The instructor gave her lectures in a 280-seat origination classroom, and these lectures were recorded and made available online. Lecture capture students were given the option to attend the live origination sessions and/or they could watch the videos from wherever they had an Internet connection. Given that course enrollment was larger than the classroom, students could attend the live session on a first-come, first-served basis, but only about eight percent of students regularly attended these classes. The remainder of the students used the recorded lectures to review course content.

The lecture capture section enrollments were 547 and 399 students, respectively, for the two semesters. There were 317 and 324 students enrolled in the face-to-face sections for the two semesters. The face-to-face students did not have access to the lecture capture videos in their course, although it is possible that some may have gained access through friends in the lecture capture sections. However, as the lecture capture course is password protected through UCF's learning management system, it is unlikely that students in the face-to-face section accessed these videos.

The mean age for the face-to-face students who responded to the survey was 19.4 years (standard deviation=1.7, N=437), and the mean age for the lecture capture students was 21.6 (standard deviation=4.7, N=547). Thus, the lecture capture students were approximately two years older, on average, than the face-to-face students. Table 1 provides a summary of the demographic data obtained for the two course delivery groups.

Gender and employment status also provided some interesting results. For the face-to-face students, there was an approximate 50-50 split in females to males, but there were more females in the lecture capture sections (56% vs. 44%). In addition, many more students were employed, either part or full time, in the lecture capture sections (63%) than in the face-to-face (39%) sections. Moreover, almost five times more lecture capture students were employed full-time (21.3%) compared to face-to-face students (4.6%). These findings tend to support earlier distance learning research which found the students who chose distance or online education tended to be older, more independent and employed (Moore & Kearsley, 1996, Diaz, 2002, Sitzmann, et al., 2006).

A multivariate analysis of variance was used to examine the student performance results. Dependent variables were the four exam scores (each based on a maximum of 100%) and the Aplia homework score. Instructional delivery condition (face-to-face vs. lecture capture) was the independent variable. The Manova results showed no significant differences across the two conditions (F (Pillai) $_{5, 998}$ = 12020.895, p=.000). Table 2 provides the summary of the performance results.

We also looked at student withdrawal data across the two course delivery conditions. For the two face-to-face sections, 16 students withdrew out of a sample size of 641 (2.5%). For the lecture capture sections, 55 out of 946 students withdrew (5.8%). Thus, the lecture capture withdrawal rate was a little more than twice as high as the face-to-face withdrawal rate. A higher withdrawal rate in lecture capture courses is consistent with earlier research (e.g., Navarro, 2000; McLaren, 2004).

Study Two

Previous research on student performance in online instruction at UCF has focused on success and withdrawal rates in fully online courses (Moskal, et al., 2006) and in blended learning courses (Dziuban, et al., 2005). In general, these studies found that student performance in online and blended courses was comparable to face-to-face instruction. This evaluation of the CBA's lecture capture courses was based on the approach that Dziuban and Moskal used in their research.

Student performance was examined for two consecutive academic years (six semesters) from summer 2007 through spring 2009. During this period, 67,737 CBA success and withdrawal records were obtained and analyzed from 15 courses.

Table 3 provides a summary of the major demographic data that were collected with the success and withdrawal data, student survey data, as well as the distribution for UCF undergraduate students as a whole. The mean age for the success and withdrawal data was 22.6 years (SD=4.46), and 23.6 years for the student survey data (SD=5.09). Based on the observed frequencies, the two samples appear to be fairly similar to each other, and representative of the university population. The proportion of lower and upper level undergraduate students was similar in both groups.

Table 4 shows the overall CBA lecture capture and face-to-face success and withdrawal rates over the two year period. These data are averaged over the 15 courses that employed both lecture capture and face-to-face delivery. The success and withdrawal rates were very similar, with the lecture

Table 1. Study one demographic data by course delivery condition

Demographic Category	Course Delivery Mode	Attribute	Percent Selected	Sample Size
Gender	Face-to-Face	Female	50.4	210
		Male	49.6	207
	Lecture Capture	Female	55.7	284
		Male	44.3	226
Employment	Face-to-Face	Full-Time	4.6	20
		Part-Time	34.6	151
		Not Employed	60.8	266
	Lecture Capture	Full-Time	21.3	117
		Part-Time	41.8	230
		Not Employed	36.9	203
Ethnicity	Face-to-Face	Asian	5.1	22
		Black/African American	13.8	60
		Hispanic/ Latino	18.9	82
		White	61.8	268
		Other	<1	2
	Lecture Capture	Asian	8.7	48
		Black/African American	8.5	47
		Hispanic/ Latino	18.0	99
		White	58.2	320
		Other	6.5	36

Table 2. Student performance results by course delivery for study one

Measure	Face-to-Face		Lecture Capture	
	Mean (N)	Standard Deviation	Mean (N)	Standard Deviation
Exam 1	71.9 (614)	11.9	70.8 (844)	13.2
Exam 2	75.3 (603)	12.4	73.1 (825)	13.8
Exam 3	73.0 (605)	12.2	72.3 (780)	13.4
Final Exam	73.8 (615)	11.9	72.6 (833)	12.6
Aplia Online Homework	84.3 (317)	11.7	81.1 (882)	15.5

Table 3. Demographic results for success and withdrawal data, student survey data, and all UCF un-dergraduates

Demographic	Success & Withdrawal		Student Survey		UCF Undergraduates Percent
	N	%	N	%	
Class year	66,942		5,742		
Freshman	5,719	9	304	5	17
Sophomore	12,627	19	1,071	19	16
Junior	26,374	39	3,142	55	28
Senior	22,222	33	1,157	20	39
Gender	67,886		5,713		
Females	28,560	42	2,739	48	55
Males	39,326	58	2,974	52	45
Ethnicity	67,890		5,698		
Am. Indian/AK Native	275	0.4	37	1	0.4
Asian	4,432	7	410	7	5
Black/African American	5,982	9	489	9	9
Hispanic/Latino	9,947	15	937	16	14
White	45,223	67	3,747	66	68
Other	2,031	3	78	1	3
Employment Status			5,736		
Employed full-time		--	1,236	22	--
Employed part-time		--	2,488	43	--
Not employed		--	2,012	35	--

capture courses showing a slightly higher percentage of students succeeding (A, B, or C grade). The success percentage was significantly different over the two conditions ($\chi^2(1)$=13.83, p<.0001), but the withdrawal percentage was not ($\chi^2(1)$=0.02, p=.883).

Next, we looked at these data by academic standing (i.e., freshmen, sophomores, juniors, and seniors) in an effort to see if this grouping affected success and withdrawal rates (Table 5). For freshmen and sophomores, both the success and withdrawal rates were worse for the lecture capture group than for the face-to-face group, but particularly the withdrawal rates. For upperclassmen, the two groups performed equivalently, although the lecture capture group performed slightly better. Comparing success rates between the lecture capture and face-to-face groups, chi-square tests of success were significantly different between the two delivery modalities within each class year (Freshman: $\chi^2(1)$=4.12, p=.045; Sophomore: $\chi^2(1)$=8.59, p=.004; Junior: $\chi^2(1)$=15.78, p=.000; Senior: $\chi^2(1)$=10.75, p=.001).

For withdrawal rates, chi-square tests showed that the lecture capture and face-to-face groups were significantly different for both the freshman and sophomore classes, but they were not significantly different within the junior and senior classes (Freshman: $\chi^2(1)$=37.50, p=.000; Sopho-

more: $\chi^2(1)$=28.55, p=.000; Junior: $\chi^2(1)$=0.13, p=.716 Senior: $\chi^2(1)$=2.50, p=.113). Both success and withdrawal rates improved as students moved up in academic standing, for both delivery conditions.

During 2010-11, the face-to-face sections of the large lecture capture courses were discontinued on the main campus for all but the Principles of Economics classes (Micro and Macroeconomics). However, in an effort to continue to monitor the effectiveness of lecture capture courses, success and withdrawal data were collected during the 2009-10 and 2010-11 academic years (excluding summer terms) for lecture capture students. The data showed that the success rates were 80.6 percent (N=20,041) and 82.4 percent (N=20,504), respectively. Withdrawal rates have actually improved, with 3.5 percent of the students withdrawing in 2009-10 (N=24,801), and 3.6 percent in 2010-11 (N=21,747).

STUDENT PERCEPTIONS OF LECTURE CAPTURE

The online student perceptions surveys (Study Two) were administered from fall 2008 through spring 2010 (four semesters; summer terms excluded). The survey was administered in a total

Table 4. Success and withdrawal rates for lecture capture and face-to-face courses

Delivery Medium	N	Overall	
		Success %	Withdrawal %
Face-to-Face	27,863	80	6
Lecture Capture	39,874	83	6

Table 5. Success and withdrawal rates by class year for lecture capture and face-to-face courses

Class year	Success			Withdrawal		
	N	Face-to-Face %	Lecture Capture %	N	Face-to-Face %	Lecture Capture %
Freshman	5,705	73	70	5,705	7	13
Sophomore	12,593	80	78	12,593	6	8
Junior	26,318	80	82	26,323	6.2	6
Senior	22,179	84	86	22,182	5	5

of 11 of the lecture capture course sections during this time period, although the number varied each semester depending on faculty willingness to participate. Faculty were encouraged to give extra credit in their courses for students to participate in the survey, but they were not required to do so, and many chose not to because of the logistical difficulty of awarding extra credit points with large classes. Some students were also enrolled in several of these courses at the same time, in which case they likely only completed the survey once. Overall, 5,811 survey responses were obtained out of a sample size of 33,041, yielding a response rate of 18%. Although more responses was certainly desirable, 5,811 responses is a considerable number. The lecture capture surveys used in both studies were very similar. Thus, we have combined the student perceptions results, and a summary of the pertinent findings is provided in Table 6.

First, the majority of students in both samples responded that they watched the lectures from their home, apartment, or dormitory room. Watching the videos at an on-campus location with Internet access was the second highest response.

The next question concerned if the students were keeping pace with the course. We wanted to know if students were waiting to watch the videos until later, and hence, falling behind in the course. However, it appears that the majority of lecture capture students (52%) watched the videos in the same week as the lecture, and approximately 75% did so at least some of the time.

We also wanted to know how often students watched the videos, since that is one of the potential benefits of lecture capture. We expected a high percentage of students would watch the videos multiple times, but this did not occur; we found that students typically watched the video lectures only once. We were also surprised to find that the approximately 30% of the Study One students reported that they rarely or never watched the videos at all (this question was not asked in the Study Two survey).

Table 6. Summary of student perceptions of lecture capture attributes

Question	Study One (Macroeconomics) Response Percent (Frequency)	Study Two (CBA LC) Response Percent (Frequency)
What was the primary location that you watched the videos?	N=673	N=5,655
• Home/apartment/dorm:	85 (572)	68 (3,826)
• On campus location with Internet:	7 (44)	27 (1,525)
• Job:	1 (9)	2 (87)
• Other:	7 (48)	4 (217)
Did you watch videos in the same week as the lecture?	N=674	N=5,774
• Always:	18 (119)	17 (982)
• Most of the time:	34 (226)	35 (2,021)
• Sometimes:	20 (134)	24 (1,386)
• Rarely:	15 (102)	16 (924)
• Never:	14 (93)	8 (461)
Did you watch videos for the first time close to exams?	N=674	N=5,775
• Always:	3 (19)	4 (231)
• Most of the time:	12 (83)	16 (924)
• Sometimes:	25 (169)	23 (1,328)
• Rarely:	25 (171)	25 (1,444)
• Never:	34 (232)	32 (1,848)
On average, how many times did you watch each video?	N=671	Question Not Asked
• Rarely or never watched the videos:	30 (119)	
• Usually watched each lecture 1 time:	65 (436)	
• Tried to watch each lecture 2 times:	5 (31)	
• Tried to watch each lecture 3 times:	1 (6)	
Do you feel like you have more control over your learning in LC courses compared to a similar course taught face-to-face?	N=643	N=5,767
• Definitely Yes:	39 (248)	29 (1,682)
• Probably Yes:	34 (216)	32 (1,853)
• Not Sure:	11 (70)	16 (897)
• Probably Not:	11 (70)	14 (786)
• Definitely Not:	6 (39)	10 (549)

Question	Study One (Macroeconomics) Response Percent (Frequency)	Study Two (CBA LC Courses) Response Percent (Frequency)
Do you feel like lecture capture enhanced your performance compared to a similar course taught face-to-face?	N=642	N=5,760
• Definitely Yes:	16 (104)	19 (1,094)
• Probably Yes:	27 (174)	24 (1,383)
• Not Sure:	29 (186)	24 (1,382)
• Probably Not:	20 (130)	21 (1,210)
• Definitely Not:	8 (48)	12 (691)
Do you feel like lecture capture enhanced your interest compared to a similar course taught face-to-face?	N=643	N=5,760
• Definitely Yes:	13 (84)	16 (921)
• Probably Yes:	25 (161)	21 (1,210)
• Not Sure:	21 (135)	20 (1,152)
• Probably Not:	27 (176)	26 (1,498)
• Definitely Not:	14 (87)	17 (979)
Please enter your overall rating of this course compared to a similar course taught face-to-face.	N=642	N=5,730
• Much Better: 19.2 (123)	19 (123)	17 (982)
• Somewhat Better: 26.9 (173)	27 (173)	26 (1,512)
• About The Same: 34.9 (224)	35 (224)	33 (1,862)
• Somewhat Worse: 15.1 (97)	15 (97)	17 (956)
• Much Worse: 3.9 (25)	4 (25)	7 (418)
If you have the opportunity, will you take another course that uses lecture capture?	N=643	N=5,764
• Definitely Yes:	39 (250)	41 (2,381)
• Probably Yes:	34 (221)	29 (1,652)
• Not Sure:	12 (80)	12 (716)
• Probably Not:	10 (66)	10 (602)
• Definitely Not:	4 (26)	7 (413)

Students could attend the live session, but only about eight percent did so consistently (discussed below). A fairly large number of students chose to complete the course simply by reading the textbook and other materials, and completing the online homework assignments. The nature of this course apparently made it possible for a large number of students to bypass the videos entirely. There was no significant correlation between course grade and the number of times the videos were viewed.

A majority of students in both studies believed that they had more control over their learning with lecture capture than they would in a similar course taught face-to-face (73% and 61%, respectively, reported definitely or probably yes). In addition, 43 percent of students in both studies believed that lecture capture enhanced their performance in the course, compared to approximately 25% who were not sure, and 30% who said that it did not improve their performance. Students who felt that lecture capture improved their performance may have felt this way because of being able to watch the videos on demand, as often as they wished. This finding agrees with previous research regarding the benefits of being able to access archived videos (e.g. Cascaval et al., 2008; Nicholson et al., 2010). However, students did not feel that lecture capture enhanced their interest in the course compared to a similar face-to-face course. This finding may have been because the CBA lecture capture courses are presented very much like a traditional face-to-face course, and also because interest level in lower level undergraduate courses may not be high in general.

Concerning the students' lecture capture experience, 81% in Study One and 76% in Study Two reported that it was as good as or better than in a large lecture class taught face-to-face. Over 62% of the students (both studies) commented that the flexibility and convenience of lecture capture were what they liked the most. These responses also corresponded to what has been found in previous research (e.g., Cascaval, et al., 2008; Craig, et al., 2009; and Nicholson & Nicholson, 2010).

Moreover, 70% percent of the students in both studies reported that they would choose to take another lecture capture course. The following are some representative quotes indicating what students preferred about lecture capture:

- "Being able to watch class when I wanted to. Most of the time it was after work."
- "I liked that I could pause the video if I need to write notes down. I also liked that I'm not bound by the class schedule, if I need to do something, I don't feel guilty that I missed a lecture."
- "The fact that one does not have to be on campus to engage in the lectures."
- "Being able to do the class on my own time."
- "I like that I don't usually have the pressure to go on campus. I commute … so if I'm feeling ill one day, I'm not stuck having to go to school because I don't want to miss class. With the video streaming, I can stay home … and watch the video."

Responses concerning what students liked least about lecture capture were more diverse. The primary negative comment, with 43% of the responses, was the lack of interaction with others. Technical difficulties affected 15% of the students. The remainder of the items showed small response rates. Interestingly, three of the primary negative responses were about student attributes rather than the delivery modality (lack of student discipline, procrastination, and lack of motivation), and these agree with the findings of Vamosi, et al. (2004). These attributes have also been shown in the distance learning literature to be important factors in whether students are successful in this medium (e.g., Moore & Kearsley, 1996). Thus, although a large majority of students were happy with lecture capture, there is a certain percentage that definitely does not like it, and it was probably not the right mode of instruction for them.

Because students could attend the initial, live presentation of the lectures (on a first-come, first-served basis), we were interested in learning how often they chose to attend this session, and would high attendance confound the lecture capture performance results? Fifty-five percent of the students (N=5,767, combined over both studies) who responded to this question said that they never attended a live session. Another 19% said that they only attended a few times during the semester, and approximately 10% said they attended the live lectures weekly. Thus, given the class sizes, only about 25-30 students were consistently attending the live session, which was confirmed by the instructor. The only time the classroom was full was during the first week of classes. Thus, the live session was a nice feature for a small number of students, but with the low attendance, we do not feel that the lecture capture group was more like the face-to-face group; thus, we do not feel it is a cause for concern in interpreting the results.

CONCLUSION

This research was conducted to determine if student performance in lecture capture courses was comparable to similar courses taught face-to-face, and to learn about student perceptions of lecture capture. The results indicate that students did perform as well in the lecture capture conditions, and that their perceptions of these courses were quite high, suggesting that this delivery approach is feasible and may be used to improve course access for students. Student withdrawal rates did vary by course delivery, with lecture capture showing higher withdrawal rates. However, these withdrawal rates were still very low.

In Study Two, the examination of the results by academic class year revealed interesting, but not surprising, results. Success rates increased each academic year for both lecture capture and face-to-face groups, but success rates in the lecture capture modality were lower than face-to-face until students reached their junior year (Table 5). Then, success in the lecture capture course sections was basically equivalent for the last two years. Student performance increased each year for both groups, suggesting that maturation and experience increased over time, as one would hope, but this change was more pronounced for the lecture capture students. Other factors may also play a role, including course requirements, instructors, student preferences for the medium, and the least successful students across both groups may have changed majors by this time, and thus, would not be included in the population.

In Study One, withdrawal rates were higher in the lecture capture sections (5.8%) compared to the face-to-face sections (2.5%). In Study Two, withdrawal rates were also higher for freshman and sophomores in both course delivery modalities, but they were significantly higher for the lecture capture courses than the face-to-face courses (13% to 7% for freshman, 8% to 6% for sophomores; see Table 5). The withdrawal results in both studies support Navarro (2000) and McClaren (2004).

The withdrawal data appear to indicate that some undergraduate students in lower level, introductory type courses have more difficulty in lecture capture or other distance learning type courses than do their counterparts in face-to-face courses. These results could be due to students being on their own for the first time, needing to learn how to function successfully in college, having less experience with distance learning course formats, and so forth. Our findings support previous research in distance learning which observed that successful students in these courses typically were older, more independent, and more intrinsically motivated (e.g., Moore & Kearsley, 1996; Diaz & Cartnal, 1999; Diaz, 2002; Sitzmann, et al., 2006). These courses require more discipline to be successful, and this is something that younger students may not have learned to the extent that the upperclassmen have, as well as simply adapting to college life. The results also suggest that our faculty may need to provide more training in how to manage a lecture capture course, and emphasize the outside-of-class requirements that are involved, so that students can make accurate judgments about whether they should take these courses.

Unfortunately, random assignment of students to delivery condition was not possible, which could have biased the results. And students who selected lecture capture may have been more likely to be positive about their experience. However, given that student performance was equivalent in the two delivery conditions, and the fact that the demographic data were similar on many attributes, we believe that this is not an appreciable problem.

The majority of lecture capture respondents preferred the convenience and flexibility of this delivery format over traditional face-to-face instruction, largely because they could watch lectures on demand and as often as they wished. Students taking lecture capture courses have more opportunities to learn the material.

Students liked the flexibility of receiving instruction when they wanted, and not having to come to campus at a specific time. This flexibility also can allow an institution to increase its student enrollment for a particular course, program, or college, and it can improve access to college courses for students who have family commitments, full-time employment, or who are disabled (Bell, Cockburn, McKenzie, and Vargo, 2001).

According to Gratton-Lavoie and Stanley (2009), institutions that offer online course instruction may be able to register regional, national, and even international students. Increasing class size

is feasible if course management systems and/or graduate assistants are available for faculty support. Moskal, Caldwell, and Ellis (2009) describe a large testing lab that is used to support CBA course exams.

One area of future research that would be very valuable is to be able to document how often students actually watch the course lectures, and how many times they watch them. This information would allow the one to measure the relationships between course grades and withdrawal rates with video viewing frequency. This technological capability is now becoming more available with newer lecture capture delivery systems, and may provide significant research opportunities.

The training of students and faculty also should be addressed for this medium. The results for freshman and sophomores indicate that students new to lecture capture courses may benefit from additional support to be more successful in these courses, and may need encouragement and reminding to remain engaged.

A true experimental design that examines student performance and perceptions in face-to-face only and lecture capture only courses would be valuable, if it could be conducted with appropriate controls. A longitudinal study of student performance and perceptions may also be worthwhile. Once the novelty of lecture capture and/or video streaming wears off, how will it affect students' performance and their perceptions?

In closing, we believe that higher education institutions may successfully utilize well-designed, non-traditional forms of instruction, such as lecture capture, in an effort to cope with fiscal constraints, increased student enrollment, and to increase access for students. Lecture capture does not appear to be harming students, although there is a certain percentage, particularly the younger students, who do not like it, and who should take traditional instruction where possible.

REFERENCES

Bell, T., Cockburn, A., McKenzie, B., & Vargo, J. (2001). Flexible delivery damaging to learning? Lessons from the Canterbury Digital Lectures project. In the *13th Proceedings of the ED-MEDIA 2001 World Conference on Education Multimedia & Telecoummunications,* Tampere, Finland.

Cascaval, R. C., Fogler, K. A., Abrams, G. D., & Durham, R. L. (2008). Evaluating the benefits of providing archived online lectures to in-class math students. *Journal of Asynchronous Learning Networks, 12*(3-4), 61–70.

Craig, J., Gregory, S., El Haggan, A., Braha, H., & Brittan-Powell, C. (November, 2009). *Lecture capture systems: Are they worth it?* Paper presented at the Educause Mid-Atlantic Regional Conference, Philadelphia, PA.

Diaz, D. P. (May/June 2002). Online drop rates revisited. *The Technology Source.* Retrieved from http://technologysource.org/article/online_drop_rates_revisited/.

Diaz, D. P., & Cartnal, R. B. (1999). Students' learning styles in two classes: Online distance learning and equivalent on-campus. *College Teaching, 47*(4), 130–135. doi:10.1080/87567559909595802

Dziuban, C., Hartman, J., Juge, F., Moskal, P., & Sorg, S. (2005). Blended learning: Online learning enters the mainstream. In Bonk, C. J., & Graham, C. (Eds.), *Handbook of blended learning environments: Global perspectives, local designs.* Hoboken, NJ: Pfeiffer Publications, a division of John Wiley and Sons.

Gratton-Lavoie, C., & Stanley, D. (2009, Winter). Teaching and learning principles of microeconomics online: An empirical assessment. *The Journal of Economic Education, 40*(1), 3–25. doi:10.3200/JECE.40.1.003-025

McLaren, C. H. (2004). A comparison of student persistence and performance in online and classroom business statistics experiences. *Decision Sciences Journal of Innovative Education, 2*(1), 1–10. doi:10.1111/j.0011-7315.2004.00015.x

Moore, M. G., & Kearsley, G. (1996). *Distance education: A systems view.* Belmont, CA: Wadsworth Publishing Company.

Moskal, P., Caldwell, R., & Ellis, T. (2009). Evolution of a computer-based testing laboratory. *Innovate: Journal of Online Education, 5*(6). Retrieved from http://www.innovateonline.info/index.php?view=article&id=672

Moskal, P.D., Dziuban, C., Upchurch, R., Hartman, J., & Truman, B. (Fall, 2006). Assessing online learning: What one university learned about student success, persistence, and satisfaction. *peerReview, 8*(4), 26-29.

Navarro, P. (2000). Economics in the cyber classroom. *The Journal of Economic Perspectives, 14,* 119–132. doi:10.1257/jep.14.2.119

Nicholson, J., & Nicolson, D. B. (2010). A stream runs through IT: using streaming video to teach information technology. *Campus-Wide Information Systems, 27*(1), 17–24. doi:10.1108/10650741011011255

Sitzmann, T., Kraiger, K., Stewart, D., & Wisher, R. (2006). The comparative effectiveness of web-based and classroom instruction: A meta-analysis. *Personnel Psychology, 59,* 623–664. doi:10.1111/j.1744-6570.2006.00049.x

Vamosi, A. R., Pierce, B. G., & Slotkin, M. H. (2004). Distance learning in an accounting principles course—student satisfaction and perceptions of efficacy. *Journal of Education for Business, 79,* 360–366. doi:10.3200/JOEB.79.6.360-366

ADDITIONAL READING

Arbaugh, J. B., Godfrey, M. R., Johnson, M., Pollack, B. L., Niendorf, B., & Wresch, W. (2009). Research in online and blended learning in the business disciplines: Key findings and possible future directions. *The Internet and Higher Education, 12*, 71–87. doi:10.1016/j.iheduc.2009.06.006

Dey, E. L., Burn, H. E., & Gerdes, D. (2009). Bringing the classroom to the web: Effects of using new technologies to capture and deliver lectures. *Research in Higher Education, 50*, 377–393. doi:10.1007/s11162-009-9124-0

Euzent, P., Martin, T., Moskal, P. J., & Moskal, P. D. (2011). Assessing student performance and perceptions in lecture capture vs. face-to-face course delivery. *Journal of Information Technology Education: Research, 10*(1), 295–307.

Kozma, R. B. (1994). A reply: Media and methods. *Educational Technology Research and Development, 42*, 11–14. doi:10.1007/BF02298091

McFarland, D., & Hamilton, D. (2005). Factors affecting student performance and satisfaction: Online vs. traditional course delivery. *Journal of Computer Information Systems, 46*(2), 25–33.

Means, B., Toyama, Y., Murphy, R., Bakia, M., & Jones, K. (2009). *Evaluation of evidence-based practices in online learning: A meta-analysis and review of online learning studies*. Prepared by the Center for Technology in Learning for the U.S. Department of Education, Office of Planning, Evaluation, and Policy Development Policy and Program Studies Service. Retrieved from www.ed.gov/about/offices/list/opepd/ppss/reports.html

Sanders, D. W., & Morrison-Shetlar, A. I. (2001). Student attitudes toward Web-enhanced instruction in an introductory biology course. *Journal of Research on Computing in Education, 33*, 251–262.

KEY TERMS AND DEFINITIONS

Lecture Capture: An instructional method where lectures are "captured" on video for playback at a later date, usually on a PC over the Internet, although they may be downloaded to portable devices like MP3 players. They are available to students on demand.

Student Perceptions: Student perceptions about the quality of the lecture capture experience, obtained via online surveys.

Success and Withdrawal: The proportion of students who have achieved success (on our campus a grade of A, B, or C) or have withdrawn from a lecture capture course before its completion.

Chapter 7
Toward *LessonCapture*:
A New Approach to Screencasting and Lecture Capture

Steve Garwood
Rutgers University, USA

ABSTRACT

LessonCapture is an approach to the creation and recording of presentation content (course lecture or demonstration), delivered either face-to-face or via screen-recording, and based on effective public speaking, presentation design, and multimedia learning principles. The combination of these principles with particular procedures and practices helps to ensure effective learning and reusability of content. The field of education faces many challenges: budgets, time limitations, new delivery approaches, and effectiveness. LessonCapture is one way to help maximize the return on the financial investment in recording technology and the instructor time needed to create high quality instructional materials.

INTRODUCTION

Through years serving as an instructor, qualitative course feedback was collected from regarding advice they would give to future students taking the course. The comments below apply to screencasting and lecture recording.

The [screencasts] that Steve put together were invaluable!!! Review them, take notes, and review them again. The picture was worth a thousand words - and the added words made it all the more clear.

Watch the [recorded] lectures first thing. Then use them again, as you need to. Within a few minutes of seeing and hearing Steve go through steps you get an idea of what the whole unit or week is about.

Listen to the [recorded] lectures first as they are very helpful. I could hear Steve teaching, and something about his voice makes it evident that

DOI: 10.4018/978-1-4666-3962-1.ch007

he is enjoying this class and that he really wants you to enjoy it as well.

I found the video lectures one of the most helpful parts of this class. Reading alone does not always make technology concepts clear, but seeing someone else using the different applications is indispensable. In an online course it can be nice to hear a human being on the other side of the computer.

With few exceptions, every instructor using screencasting, lecture capture, and podcasting to deliver instructional materials to their students has a similar set of comments. We know anecdotally and via the literature that students appreciate having these types of materials available for face-to-face, online, or blended courses.

Being involved with the lecture recording process as a full-time instructor, a human resources trainer, and an instructional technology designer has provided ample opportunity to evaluate a wide variety of recordings and to assess the direct and indirect impact on those who view them. New developments in instructional delivery, educational initiatives, instructor responsibilities, and approaches to instructional video technology point to the need for analyzing how we design and record these lessons in a more critical way -- beyond the idea of recording instruction as a single event.

LessonCapture approaches the creation and recording process that will have a beneficial impact on recorded presentations, whether lectures or screencasts. By combining present best practices, lessons from public speaking and presentation design, and principles of multimedia learning, sessions can be recorded that capture the attention of our learners, better enable them to retain the material presented, and offer developers of the material possibilities to scale usage.

BACKGROUND

Definitions and Approaches to Capturing Content

There are many tools used to educate students in face-to-face, online, and blended learning classrooms. In order to achieve course objectives, instructors may lecture, provide demonstrations, assign readings, display videos, facilitate discussions, conduct quizzes and exams, assign projects, and have students write papers.

One of the core tools of instruction is the lecture (Jones, 2007). Although often maligned in education literature for being neither efficient nor effective (Anderson & Garrison, 1998), the lecture is a robust tool that "persists as a pedagogical form not simply as a matter of inertia and tradition but due to its flexibility and adaptability in response to changes in media and technology" (Friesen, 2011). Instructors frequently include demonstrations in lectures to show a process or procedure, which may be either screen-based if related to computer software and programming techniques or physical in nature to demonstrate a process in chemistry or kinesiology, for instance. For the consistency within this chapter, course lectures and demonstrations will be broadly referred to as *presentations*.

The concept of capturing a presentation is not new -- captured content has been available for generations via correspondence courses using audio cassettes and VHS tapes. Lecture capture is "an umbrella term describing any technology that allows instructors to record what happens in their classrooms and make it available digitally" in the form of a presentation (ELI, 2007).

A preponderance of sites and services such as iTunesU, college and university YouTube channels, TED, Udacity and Coursera, have brought lecture capture presentations to the forefront of educational listservs and conferences. Some examples of popular lecture capture systems are Sonic Foundry's Mediasite, McGraw Hill's Tegrity, TechSmith's Camtasia Relay, and Panopto's Focus. Lecture capture can also be accomplished by simple video-recording as well; a longer list of lecture capture systems is available in Table 1.

Screencasting is another method of capturing presentations, used by both face-to-face and online instructors to record brief lessons, tutorials, demonstrations and lecture-based content. The term screencast, coined by columnist Jon Udell (2005) when he solicited names for the screencast process from his readers, is a "digital movie in which the setting is partly or wholly a computer screen, and in which audio narration describes the on-screen action." Screencasts have been used to deliver content as wide ranging as mathematical modeling (Ellington & Hardin, 2008) and information literacy (Williams, 2010).

One of the most popular educational websites, Khan Academy (www.khanacademy.org), makes extensive use of screencasting software, as does the very popular computer-based training site lynda. com. Some examples of popular screencasting programs and services are TechSmith's Camtasia, Telestream's Screenflow, and Adobe Captivate; a longer list of screencasting programs is available in Table 1.

Rapid eLearning programs are feature-rich presentation applications. Depending on the particular application, a rapid eLearning program can record PowerPoint with narration or screencast actions for different types of content, and also create learning objects incorporating quizzes, games, and other interactive elements.

Examples of popular rapid eLearning programs and services are Articulate Presenter, Adobe Presenter, iSpring Pro, Lectora Inspire, and Softchalk; a longer list of programs is available in Table 1. Online learning object repository sites, such as MERLOT or SOPHIA, can provide examples of the advantages of developing content using more advanced applications.

Lecture capture, screencasting, and the use of rapid eLearning tools focus on the *process* of recording and delivering presentation content.

Table 1. Popular programs for capturing content

Popular Lecture Capture Programs

Product	Company	URL
Mediasite	Sonic Foundry	http://www.sonicfoundry.com/mediasite
Tegrity	McGraw Hill	http://www.tegrity.com/
Focus	Panopto	http://www.panopto.com/video-capture-platform
Echo360	Echo360 Inc.	http://echo360.com/
Camtasia Relay	Techsmith	http://www.techsmith.com/camtasia-relay.html
Matterhorn	Opencast	http://opencast.org/matterhorn/

Popular Screencasting Programs

Product	Company	URL
Screencast-O-Matic	Screencast-O-Matic	http://screencast-o-matic.com/
Screenr	Articulate Global	http://www.screenr.com/
Snagit	TechSmith	http://www.techsmith.com/snagit.html
Screenflow	TeleStream	http://www.telestream.net/screen-flow/
Captivate	Adobe	http://www.adobe.com/products/captivate.html
Camtasia	TechSmith	http://www.techsmith.com/camtasia.html

Popular Rapid e-learning Programs

Product	Company	URL
Proform Learning Studio	Rapid Intake	http://rapidintake.com/proform-rapid-elearning-studio
Lectora Inspire	Trivantis	http://www.trivantis.com/e-learning-software
Softchalk	Softchalk LLC	http://softchalk.com/
Adobe Presenter	Adobe	http://www.adobe.com/products/presenter.html
iSpring Pro	iSpring	http://www.ispringsolutions.com/ispring-pro
Articulate Presenter	Articulate Global	http://www.articulate.com/products/presenter.php

However, at the core of any presentation, regardless of recording method, is the lesson, or the *product*. Defined by Merriam-Webster's dictionary as "a piece of instruction," a *lesson* is a key point or set of points delivered as a presentation. Instructors need to consider both the process and the product -- the lesson's purpose and lifecycle -- when creating recordings of presentations for original and future audiences.

LessonCapture is a holistic approach that combines current best practices of lecture capture, screencasting and rapid eLearning tool use, with lessons from public speaking, presentation design, and multimedia learning principles, to create presentations that are effective for both learning and reusability of content.

- **Presentation:** A course lecture or demonstration.
- **Lesson:** A piece of instruction delivered as a presentation (lecture or demonstration).
- **LessonCapture:** A recorded lesson, created to be effective for student learning and reuse.

Strengths and Weaknesses of Current Approaches to Capturing and Recording Content

As with all processes and technologies there are both strengths and weaknesses inherent in the process as a whole and within any particular method chosen.

The multitude of recording options available is both the greatest strength and the greatest weakness to be found in the capture of lessons. While an instructor has a vast range of approaches and applications to choose from, the particulars of the recording process, delivery products, costs, and learning curve within each application can become overwhelming. How capture software is used by instructors, programs, and departments can be very different, as well, often resulting in one application

being used for a myriad of purposes. Such wide-ranging usage accommodation can cause the process of creation to be indicated by the software rather than the lesson objectives.

The following is a list of the strengths and weaknesses of technologies and approaches used to capture lesson content. This list is general in nature; specific applications may be included for descriptive purposes, and not necessarily for any inherent strengths or weaknesses.

Lecture Capture

Strengths

- Lecture captures provide high quality recordings with multiple recording options and views (i.e., instructor, lecture slides, screen content, and second camera).
- These tools have a fairly low learning curve for instructor as production usually done on server rather than local machine.
- Recordings can be viewed on personal computers and mobile devices.
- Systems provide additional features such as search (indexes text from PowerPoint) and note-taking.
- Analytics are available to instructor (who watched when, for how long, and how many times).

Weaknesses

- Lecture capture systems are generally cost-prohibitive -- these systems are designed at the program, department, or school level and often require an administrator to set-up. Costs can be by license, FTE, or other arrangement.
- To get the best results, a camera operator may be required.
- If screen capture rather than video camera capture is used to record video streaming

on the PC, the content may not display properly as online video tends to play at 30 frames-per-second (fps) and screen recorders in lecture capture systems capture at 15 fps.

- Editing features are not very robust.

Screencasting

Strengths

- These recordings are convenient to make -- software is generally installed on a local computer so recordings can be made anywhere the instructor is.
- Screencasts are flexible-- if something can be shown on a computer screen it can generally be recorded.
- Screen-based capture can easily accommodate 30fps with most programs.
- Recordings can usually be viewed on personal computers and mobile devices (if produced properly).
- Costs are affordable at $15 to $300 per license (some free with limitations like 5-15 minute maximum recording times).
- Screencasting technologies contain fairly comprehensive editing and easy to add features like captioning, call-outs, and cursor highlighting.

Weaknesses

- These tools have a moderate learning curve as the instructor often does production (easier for some applications than others).
- While lecture capture systems automatically store recordings on a server, screencasts are created locally and need to be uploaded to a server or service to be viewed.

- Screencasting can be a challenge to administrate across an entire program, department or school as each installation is licensed separately.

Rapid eLearning Development (Learning Objects)

Strengths

- Learning objects tend to be very easy to use and produce files with simple narration over PowerPoint.
- Software is conveniently installed on a local machine.
- It's easy to add elements like multimedia, quizzing, games, and branching.
- Tools contain built-in professional and attractive templates.
- These objects are cost effective; the more basic programs are around $99 per license.

Weaknesses

- Most applications are only for Windows.
- For interactivity, files generally need to be produced as Flash which limits mobile viewing possibilities.
- Some of the more full-featured programs can cost $1000+ per license.
- These systems can be a challenge to administrate, as most licenses are local.

Direct and Indirect Strengths and Weaknesses of Capturing and Delivering Presentation Content

Strengths

Students find them useful and like having them: Numerous studies indicate that students like to have recorded sessions available and find them useful (Dey, Burn, & Gerdes, 2007; Gosper, McNeill, & Woo; Owston, Lupshenyuk, & Wideman, 2011; Soong, Chan, & Cheers, 2006; Traphagan, Kucsera, & Kishi, 2009). In particular, students appreciated the ability to:

- View the recording when they had to miss class.
- Take notes without worrying about missing anything since the presentation was being recorded.
- Watch the presentation repeatedly at their convenience.
- Review materials at their own pace, starting and stopping when they needed to. This was particularly indicated by students who spoke English as a second language.

Students learn from them: Not only do students like having the recordings available, but research indicates that they learn from them as well (Dey, Burn, & Gerdes, 2007; Traphagan, Kucsera, & Kishi, 2009). For example, Dey et. al (2007), found that students in video presentation groups (both neutral and personalized) had significantly higher test scores on transfer questions than control groups observing the presentation directly.

Further, how recordings are used in a course significantly influences whether they impact students learning. If recordings are aligned with course objectives, activities, and student needs, then they can effectively support learning (Owston, Lupshenyuk & Wideman, 2011)

Recordings are reusable and re-purposeable: Capturing lessons offers multiple affordances such as the ability to use recordings over multiple course semesters, for different courses, or to quickly answer an urgent student request for assistance.

Personality and a human voice are added: When students experience a recorded lesson, the personality and voice in the video can create a powerful connection to someone out there. In situations where the students view a recording following a face-to-face presentation, a familiar voice can act as a powerful reminder of the classroom experience.

Credibility and tech savviness are demonstrated: Younger students have a certain level of expectation regarding technology use. An instructor, program, department, or school, can enhance their credibility by making captured content available to students.

Long-term time saving is achieved: While the preparation and capture process can take longer for creating captured lessons than the preparation of face-to-face lessons, the ability to re-use a recording to teach students, acclimate new instructors, and handle frequently asked questions, can result in significant time savings.

Improvement of instructional skills: Most instructors have never seen nor heard themselves teach. The ability of instructors to view recordings can provide insight on their verbal quirks, pacing, and presentation. For instructors who teach online and face-to-face courses, any time spent preparing materials for recorded delivery will also improve their face-to-face presentations as well.

Easier on-boarding of adjuncts or part-time lecturers: Adjunct lecturers who receive recordings are rapidly able to assimilate how to present and conduct their new course. Without such information, new adjuncts could have a much greater learning curve.

Increased course consistency, especially across multiple sections: An extension to the benefit of rapid adjunct preparation, having sets of lesson-based recordings can ensure clear and consistent presentation across multiple sections. While keeping the core course information constant, this approach allows for instructor customization related to delivery and course activities.

Analytics are available for course management: While some recording systems have built-in analytics, having students access files via a course management system or virtual learning environment allows instructors to see if students are making use of them.

Weaknesses

Possible negative effect on attendance: Attendance issues are often an instructor's principal concern related to capturing content (Taylor, 2007). Research shows, however, that students attend live lectures when learning content is expected to be difficult (Basili, 2008). Attendance is also improved when students feel the lecturer adds value, the lectures are motivating, they like to meet their friends, or they wouldn't have listened to the lecture recording anyway (Gosper, McNeill, & Woo, n.d).

The impact of captured content on attendance related to the quality of the original lecture has not been well researched. One might ask: If the lecture itself was improved would attendance rates be higher? If yes, would recording the lecture have any impact?

Significant time to create, produce, and distribute recordings: The amount of time needed to prepare, rehearse, record, produce, and distribute content can be significant. While experience and the establishment of new habits and procedures reduces time spent, the approach used and amount of control desired also has an impact. Most lecture capture systems are fairly easy to use with server-based processing and various options for embedded links. Recording control is the trade-off for this ease of use; lecture capture systems record only on the computer desktop rather than a window or specified region. Screencasting programs offer a finer level of recording control and file production but at the cost of more set-up and production time.

Finally, one of the greatest influencers on time spent is the perceived level of quality the instructor wants to achieve. This is often more about the instructor's opinion of their performance than the quality of the recording. While a high level of recording quality is optimal, research indicates that a clear, concise delivery method has more impact on learning, with a conversational style found to be more effective than a formal style (Mayer, 2009).

Learning curve can be a challenge: Recording systems are becoming easier to learn, as large communities of practice continue to develop and share resources. While an instructor's learning curve depends on the approach used and the requirements of the final product, in this author's experience an average of 1-2 hours of active training and 1 hour of follow-up support is sufficient for an instructor to effectively utilize a Lecture Capture system.

Things change and updates will need to be made: Keeping materials up-to-date is one of the more frustrating aspects of capturing recorded material. There will always be new research developments, even for lessons on well-established theories or practice, requiring lectures to be recorded again. Online systems or services may also make significant interface changes necessitating file format updates or even the rerecording of new lectures.

Other Considerations

Compliance with Section 508 of the Rehabilitation Act of 1973 (Equal Access): Making recorded content accessible can be time-consuming, costly, and challenging. To facilitate compliance, every instructor and school should include the development of transcripts or captions in their planning process. Note: Disability offices can assist faculty with issues related to the accessibility of captured presentations in face-to-face courses, and, more importantly, the use of captured lecture in a fully online setting.

Recognition of Digital Divide issues: Recorded content can disadvantage those with no computer or Internet access, or slow access, outside of the physical classroom. Such considerations should be part of the discussion when determining how content should be recorded and delivered.

Best Practices for Capturing and Delivering Presentation Content

Plan for what's being recorded: Just like staging a photo or video shoot, staging your recording is important to achieve the best quality possible and limit retakes.

Consider how your presentation will be recorded: A computer screen, a particular window, multiple windows, or even multiple monitors? What should be recorded: the instructor only, any co-instructors, your PowerPoint presentation, what you write on a chalkboard, dry erase board, or Smart board, just an object in your hands, or some combination of all of these?

Weigh the strengths and weaknesses of scripting: Screencasts allow for scripting and reading aloud as you proceed, although rehearsal is needed to keep your words from sounding flat. A major advantage to scripting is the ability to add the script to your PowerPoint presentation, or create a separate transcript or caption for screen recording, ensuring compliance with the Americans with Disabilities Act.

Reading a script in front of a live class is not ideal; at the other extreme, *winging it* or loosely preparing can cause instructors to inadvertently get off topic and forget to include key points. This can result in repeatedly recording the same lecture, spending too much time editing, or the release of an inferior lesson. While speaking extemporaneously can be appropriate for answering a student's immediate help question, it is not recommended for longer recordings.

The best approach for recording while presenting to a live class is to use a speaker's outline. Instructors prepare a one-page outline of what will be covered in the lesson, in what order, and how each topic will be introduced and concluded, which is then referred to as needed while recording.

Establish a work-flow: Whether recording during a face-to-face course or in your office, establishing a standardized work-flow can make the recording and production process easier. Workflow items can include setting up the work area in a quiet location, ensuring water availability, establishing how bumpers or title cards will be set up and incorporated into the recording, post-production and editing work, and how the recording will be shared – via email, course management systems, or other online services.

Record for remix, repurposing, and long-term use: If recordings will be used across multiple-sections, courses, semesters, or even years, it is best to avoid any indication of time frame in the recording. Bumpers or title cards should limit information to the presentation title and *Recorded by:* credit while leaving out any reference to course name, semester, and so on. In the content of the recording, leave out statements such as "as we did last week" or "in the last video," which will allow independent use of the recordings.

In working with online instructors, both lesson videos and procedural or personal videos for their course sites will be beneficial to students. The lesson videos are specific to the course content, while procedural and personal videos allow the instructor to provide procedural direction and create a personal connection. This type of delivery can be beneficial in face-to-face classroom settings as well; students tend to *perk up* when it's lesson time and relax during procedural and personal time.

Segment or chunk recordings: Student attention spans are short and working memory can only handle so much, so recording lessons in segmented sections of 15 minutes or less is a helpful best practice. There are process and production gains to this approach as well; it is much easier to re-record a short video due to quality issues or *flubs* than a long video. Segmenting (chunking) will be discussed further in the section on LessonCapture.

Accept yourself and overcome imperfection: Instructors must overcome the desire for a *perfect take*, completely free of *ums*, *ohs*, or the occasional misstep. We all want to represent ourselves as professionally as possible; however, the more perfect the video, the less natural it is. It is acceptable to have some verbal filler, mirroring the actual classroom experience -- warts and all.

The desire to create a good recording can also improve the quality of the instructor's face-to-face teaching. And, as painful as it can be to watch and listen to yourself on video, it is a great way to review your performance.

Invest in good equipment: The choice of equipment, particularly microphones, determines the technical quality of the final product. Using a quality microphone is important to help students connect positively with their instructor's voice. A $30-$100 headset or tabletop USB microphone is sufficient for a single user; classroom audio-setups should be determined by an audio recording professional.

Invest time in rehearsal: The process of rehearsing content delivery improves the instructor's confidence and comfort level, helps avoid rushing or rambling, and roots out problems prior to recording. Assuming the lesson content is already well-organized, nothing improves the recorded content delivery quality more than rehearsing.

Restrict the amount of editing you do: If you follow the best practice of keeping your videos short, it is usually easier to re-record a video than to edit. For most recorded content, the only editing needed is to chop off any dead time at the beginning or end of the recording.

TOWARD LESSONCAPTURE FOR EFFECTIVE LEARNING AND EDUCATIONAL GROWTH AND FLEXIBILITY

While using best practices makes the recording process easier and more productive, the Lesson-Capture approach also seeks to raise the bar on the overall instructional quality of recorded presentations, improving an educational setting's options for growth and flexibility by creating recordings for effective use beyond the original instructor or course.

This section explores current happenings in society and educational settings require moving beyond simple content capture. Additionally, in two particular areas, in public speaking and presentation and in multimedia learning, additions to best practices will support the design of effective lessons.

Need for Scale and Flexibility Afforded by LessonCapture: Current Happenings in Education and Instruction

This is an interesting and challenging time for time instructors in college and university settings. Rapid developments in society and education indicate a need for highly effective and impactful video based lessons.

Watching videos is now a mainstream activity in American society. According to the Pew Center's Internet and the American Life project, 71% of online adults use video-sharing sites like YouTube and Vimeo, up 38% from five years ago (Moore, 2011). On YouTube alone, over 4 billion videos are viewed daily (Press Room Statistics, n.d.).

Fueled by Americans' increasing comfort with video, there has been an explosion of video-based educational materials and services available on internet sites such as Khan Academy, iTunes U, Coursera, and Udacity. These new approaches to education and learning are influencing how instruction is delivered on a broad scale. Elite institutions of higher learning now offer free or inexpensive learning opportunities via Massive Open Online Courses (MOOCs) to thousands of students worldwide; some institutions even provide certificates of completion.

Along with the rising demand for educational video, Americans view access to higher education as a precursor to success. According to the Whitehouse.gov site, all Americans "should be prepared to enroll in at least one year of higher education or job training to better prepare our workforce for a 21st century economy" (2012). Many of these enrollments will be in face-to-face courses utilizing technologies like lecture capture at an increasing rate (Techsmith, n.d.; Waters, 2011).

This demand for education cannot be met entirely by face-to-face courses; most students want the flexibility of online courses. According to Going the Distance: Online Education in the United States (2011), "31% of the enrollments in higher education in 2010 are online, a number that has been growing since the report started in 2002." As more online courses are offered, face-to-face instructors must learn to effectively transfer their courses to an online format. The rise in blended learning and the rapid *flipping* of courses can also muddy the idea of what it means to teach a course.

In order to be successful, instructors will need training in the significant differences between teaching and learning in face-to-face, blended, and online courses. As well, the full-time faculty tasked with the creation of new online courses and overseeing curricula face increasing demands for time-consuming research and administrative duties. These demands come at a time when the number of full-time instructional faculty has declined from 77.8% in 1970 to 50.7% in 2009 (NCES, 2011, Table 263).

Traditional instructional roles are shifting, impacted by Americans' desire for educational attainment, changes in how education is delivered, and the reduction in available faculty time for teaching. Expectations of what happens in the classroom are changing and must change. Instructors may find themselves becoming *course coordinators* as they supervise other instructors teaching the same course in multiple settings. Other faculty may become *executive producers* as they create captured lessons that accommodate various delivery approaches and develop course materials with the help of a team of instructors, instructional designers, and instructional technologists.

The popularity of educational video necessitates that lessons are recorded for use beyond a single instructor-led course for a particular session or semester. The next two sections will detail particular approaches to the creation of lessons, that when combined with best practices, result in effective, efficient, and scalable recordings or LessonCapture.

Beyond Best Practices: Utilizing Lessons from the Field of Public Speaking

When preparing theoretical or technical content lessons, it's not just how but what you present. A poorly constructed lesson is not effective for either face-to-face or recorded delivery. Incorporating principles and practices, in this example from the field of public speaking, can create a presentation that is attention-grabbing, interesting, and truly informative. Therefore, the LessonCapture approach starts with a solid theoretical foundation that provides a framework for lesson development.

Focus on the audience: In LessonCapture, the focus of an instructor's development and delivery of a presentation to an audience needs to change from "What do I want to present?" to "What do students and viewers need to know ?" Instructors sometimes forget that at one time they were also students learning new material. And, while a full audience analysis is not required, considering content learning requirements can result in a more direct and interesting presentation.

Instructors teach courses because of their experience, mastery and interest in a subject; students enroll in courses for a variety of reasons with mixed interest in the topic. A course may fit a student's schedule, be part of a general education requirement, or be suggested by their academic counselor. Instructors need to recognize this potential lack of interest and accept the challenge of creating student interest in the material.

Construct and deliver a thesis statement: Adult learners want to know why they are being taught new information. A thesis statement introduces the "What's in it for me?" in a single sentence that conveys the topic, focus, and purpose of the lesson. While most are good at conveying the topic, they don't always provide a concise thesis statement clearly indicating the purpose or context of the lesson.

Structure the delivery of content: An excellent approach to presenting information is the "tell them what you're going to tell them, tell them, and then tell them what you told them" model. By setting the stage, informing while staying consistent to your main points, and then reminding students of what they learned by summarizing the main points and purpose, instructors provide a student with a framework for paying attention. While this repetition might seem banal, it's important to creating a memory of the lesson (Medina, 2008, p. 97).

A general structural model from public speaking courses that incorporates well in recordings is: Attention Getter > Preview > Main and Sub-Points (where transitions to tie each point together) > Summary > Conclusion (clincher to cue attention).

Another model to consider is Monroe's Motivated Sequence, which focuses on getting the audience to *do* something with a *call to arms*. The sequence is broken down into five stages: attention, need, satisfaction, visualization, and action. Lessons are presented as "There's a problem," "Here's more information about the problem," "Here's a solution," "This is how the solution fixes the problem," and finally, "This is what you can do about the problem." Monroe's model works well for explaining how questions are addressed by theory or to provide solutions to difficult technical problems. This approach can be powerful for adult learners who tend to like the idea of solving a problem.

Outside of the field of public speaking, Sugar, Brown and Luterbach (2010) have developed a screencast framework checklist that identifies common structural components and instructional strategies. While not focused on effective-

ness, this framework checklist inspires much of the LessonCapture approach.

Use rhetorical questions: A good rhetorical question focuses attention on the specific *problem* in the lesson and primes students to make active sense of the presentation within a known context; by asking questions an instructor prompts students to think in a way that relates to the lesson. Rhetorical questions are perfectly suited for recordings and can be as well for other instructional elements such as discussions and written assignments.

Consider methods of persuasion – ethos, logos, pathos: While many instructors believe we are informing students, we are instead persuading students to consider new explanations, theories, and approaches. By focusing on the act of persuasion, instructors can cultivate a higher level of interest and attention, thereby leading to greater retention.

Ethos establishes credibility and can be achieved quickly by utilizing strong, reputable evidence, connecting information to the student, and even speaking confidently.

Logos is the evidence and reasoning behind a lesson: How does an approach fix a problem? How does theory explain a phenomenon? Has the instructor's reasoning conveyed the point of the lesson? Does this reasoning make sense to students?

Pathos, the use of emotional appeal, is especially powerful. Creating an emotional response that connects students to the material is especially helpful for keeping them interested and attentive (Medina, 2008).

Repeat and reiterate (to aid retention): Instructors often overlook the importance of repetition when creating materials for face-to-face audiences and recordings. Repeating words, phrases, and ideas helps show their importance and aids retention. Reiterating and rewording within a lesson supports students' understanding of the topic in relation to the context presented at the time of the repetition.

Use your voice: The primary course feedback received from students outside of comments on lesson content relates to the effect of voice. Students have remarked on how voice creates a personal connection for them as they sense the instructor's passion for the topic and belief in their ability. Voice volume, tone, rate of delivery, and articulation can go a long way towards connecting with students and achieving the goal of the lesson. As well, mastering the art of the well placed pause can trigger students to pay greater attention and let them know something important is about to happen.

Beyond Best Practices: Utilizing Lessons from Principles of Design for Multimedia Learning

Multimedia instruction refers to presentations involving words (printed or spoken text) and pictures (static – illustrations, graphs, photos, maps or dynamic – animations or video) that are intended to foster learning (Mayer, 2009). The purpose behind the LessonCapture approach is to prepare multimedia lessons for recorded delivery with the expectation they will work just as well for standalone recordings as for review after a face-to-face lesson. It is anticipated that LessonCapture preparation process will also improve the effectiveness of direct face-to-face delivery.

The work of commercial presentation designers, such as Nancy Duarte and Garr Reynolds, offers excellent guidance on designing and preparing a presentation for a live audience. The research on cognitive load theory in multimedia learning, however, particularly by John Sweller and Richard Mayer, provides a wealth of additional information to consider when preparing recorded lessons.

A primary focus of cognitive load theory-based instruction is to ensure a learner's working memory is not overloaded by poorly designed instructional materials that contain extraneous material (Paas, van Gog, & Sweller, 2010). Extraneous cognitive processing can negatively impact a student's ability to create a schema while

viewing a presentation; therefore, when using the LessonCapture approach, lessons should be clear, purposeful, and without extraneous information.

The findings of Dey, Burn, and Gerdes' (2009) research with instructional staff developing multimedia presentations incorporating Mayer's design principles also informs the approach of LessonCapture.

Participants who viewed the presentation online uniformly rated the presentation as of high quality, agreed that the information presented in the slides was clear, and disagreed that there was too much information presented in the slides. Moreover, the regression showed that the quality variable was the most significant predictor of retention scores. It should, of course, be noted that the students in the live presentation enjoyed the benefits of the effort to create a well-designed presentation intended for the video formats.

So what does an effective computer-based multimedia presentation look like? According to Mayer (2009): first, the presentation should consist of both words and pictures (narration and image rather than narration alone); second, corresponding portions of the image and narration should appear together; third, only core explanations should be presented without extraneous words, sounds, or pictures; and fourth, the words should be presented as speech (narration), rather than text or speech and text (words to the auditory channel and pictures to the visual).

In respect to the LessonCapture process, nine out of Mayer's (2009) twelve multimedia design principles stand out:

- **Coherence Principle:** People learn better when extraneous words, pictures and sounds are excluded rather than included.
- **Signaling Principle:** People learn better when cues that highlight the organization of the essential material are added.

- **Redundancy Principle:** People learn better from graphics and narration than from graphics, narration and on-screen text.
- **Temporal Contiguity Principle:** People learn better when corresponding words and pictures are presented simultaneously rather than successively.
- **Segmenting Principle:** People learn better when a multimedia lesson is presented in user-based segments rather than as a continuous unit.
- **Modality Principle:** People learn better from graphics and narration than animation and on-screen text.
- **Multimedia Principle:** People learn better from words and pictures than from words alone.
- **Personalization Principle:** People learn better from multimedia presentations when words are in a conversational style rather than a formal style.
- **Image Principle:** People do not necessarily learn better from a multimedia lesson when the speaker's image is added to the screen.

LessonCapture incorporates these principles into the lesson recording process to ensure the most effective use of these learning tools possible.

FUTURE RESEARCH DIRECTIONS

This chapter attempts to address issues of student learning and the growth of educational offerings and delivery methods; however, to truly enhance instruction we must look past the technologies to the root of our educational efforts by considering past and present research, emerging trends and practices, and feedback from educators and learners alike.

LessonCapture is an approach to creating and capturing effective content that focuses careful attention on a key method used for instruction – presentation (lecture or demonstration), whether video-based or face-to-face. It is also this author's proposition that the LessonCapture approach provides substantial administrative benefits, such as improvements in course consistency, as well as significant time savings for instructors and course coordinators.

Development and research in several new arenas will be needed to ascertain the accuracy of these propositions:

- The creation of frameworks, checklists, and other support material to implement and capitalize on the LessonCapture approach.
- Kirkpatrick-style evaluations of instructional and institutional improvements following the implementation of LessonCapture.
- Measures of the effects of using LessonCapture for course presentations, including the impact of individual recordings as well as recordings made available throughout the semester.
- Analysis of the effects of course attendance when LessonCapture techniques are incorporated.

CONCLUSION

The path to LessonCapture has been challenging, enjoyable, and a deep learning experience on various topics of interest, including attention, retention, instructional methodology, educational administration, presentation design delivery, and multimedia learning design. While much of this path was an exploration of relevant topical research, this more formal approach was complemented with describing the process of learning what worked and didn't work. Readers are encouraged to try this as well while exploring LessonCapture.

This chapter is intended serve as a starting point for how to create and record effective content while enjoying the prospects and challenges of different recording processes, multiple course delivery methods, various instructional methods, and the inevitable administrative issues.

REFERENCES

Allen, I. E., & Seaman, J. Babson Survey Research Group. (2011). *Going the distance: Online education in the United States, 2011*. Babson Park, MA: Babson Survey Research Group.

Anderson, T. D., & Garrison, D. R. (1998). Learning in a networked world: New roles and responsibilities. In Gibson, C. C. (Ed.), *Distance learners in higher education: Institutional responses for quality outcomes* (pp. 97–112). Madison, WI: Atwood Publishing.

Basili, J. N. (2008). Media richness and social norms in the choice to attend lectures or to watch them online. *Journal of Educational Multimedia and Hypermedia, 17*(4), 453–475.

Bligh, D. A. (2000). *What's the use of lectures?* San Francisco, CA: Jossey-Bass.

Burns, R. A. (1985, May). *Information impact and factors affecting recall*. Paper presented at Annual National Conference on Teaching Excellent and Conference of Administrators, Austin TX. (ERIC Document Reproduction Service No. ED 258 639)

Dey, E. L., Burn, H. E., & Gerdes, D. (2009). Bringing the classroom to the web: Effects of using new technologies to capture and deliver lectures. *Research in Higher Education, 50*(4), 377–393. doi:10.1007/s11162-009-9124-0

Educause Learning Initiative (ELI). (2006). *7 things you should know about lecture capture*. Retrieved May 21, 2012, from http://net.educause.edu/ir/library/pdf/ELI7044.pdf

Ellington, A. J., & Hardin, J. R. (2008). The use of video tutorials in a mathematical modeling course. *Mathematics and Computer Education, 42*(2), 109–117.

Gosper, M., McNeill, M., & Woo, K. (n.d.). *Web-based lecture recording technologies: Do students learn from them?* Retrieved May 29, 2012, from http://www.caudit.edu.au/educauseaustralasia07/authors_papers/Gosper.pdf

Johnstone, A. H., & Percival, F. (1976, March 01). Attention breaks in lectures. *Education in Chemistry, 13*(2), 49–50.

Mayer, R. E. (2009). *Multimedia learning*. Cambridge, UK: Cambridge University Press. doi:10.1017/CBO9780511811678

Medina, J. (2008). *Brain rules: 12 principles for surviving and thriving at work, home, and school*. Seattle, WA: Pear Press.

Middendorf, J., & Kalish, A. (1995). *The "change-up" in lectures*. Retrieved May 26, 2012, from http://www.iub.edu/~tchsotl/part3/Middendorf%20&%20Kalish.pdf

Moore, K. (2011). *71% of online adults now use video-sharing sites*. Retrieved May 28, 2012, from http://pewinternet.org/Reports/2011/Video-sharing-sites/Report.aspx

National Center for Education Statistics (NCES). (2008). *Digest of education statistics*. Washington, DC: U.S. Department of Education.

Owston, R., Lupshenyuk, D., & Wideman, H. (2011). *Lecture capture in large undergraduate classes: What is the impact on the teaching and learning environment?* Retrieved May 29, 2012, from http://www.yorku.ca/rowston/AERA2011final.pdf

Paas, F., van Gog, T., & Sweller, J. (2010). Cognitive load theory: New conceptualizations, specifications, and integrated research perspectives. *Educational Psychology Review, 22*(2), 115–121. doi:10.1007/s10648-010-9133-8

Soong, S. K. A., Chan, L. K., & Cheers, C. (2006). Impact of video recorded lectures among students. *Proceedings of the 23rd Annual ASCILITE Conference: Who's Learning? Whose Technology?* Retrieved May 29, 2012, from http://www.ascilite.org.au/conferences/sydney06/proceeding/pdf_papers/p179.pdf

Stuart, J., & Rutgersford, R. J. D. (1978, September 2). Medical student concentration during lectures. *Lancet*, 514–516. doi:10.1016/S0140-6736(78)92233-X

Sugar, W., Brown, A., & Luterbach, K. (2010). Examining the anatomy of a screencast: Uncovering common elements and instructional strategies. *International Review of Research in Open and Distance Learning, 11*(3), 1–20.

Taylor, D. M. (2007, November 5). *Let's not kill the classroom experience.* University Affairs. Retrieved May 29, 2012, from http://www.universityaffairs.ca/lets-not-kill-the-classroom-experience.aspx

Techsmith (n.d.). *The student demand for lecture capture solutions.* Techsmith Corporation. Retrieved May 30, 2012, from http://download.techsmith.com/relay/docs/CampusTech_white-paper.pdf

Traphagan, T., Kucsera, J. V., & Kishi, K. (2010, February 01). Impact of class lecture webcasting on attendance and learning. *Educational Technology Research and Development, 58*(1), 19–37. doi:10.1007/s11423-009-9128-7

Udell, J. (2005). *What is screencasting?* Retrieved from http://www.oreillynet.com/pub/a/oreilly/digitalmedia/2005/11/16/what-is-screencasting.html

Waters, J. K. (2011, June 01). Lights! Camera! Action! *Campus Technology, 24*(10), 22.

WhiteHouse.gov. (n.d.). *Education.* Retrieved from http://www.whitehouse.gov/issues/education

Williams, S. (2010, April 01). New tools for online information literacy instruction. *The Reference Librarian, 51*(2), 148–162. doi:10.1080/02763870903579802

YouTube. (n.d.). *Press room statistics.* Retrieved from http://www.youtube.com/t/press_statistics

ADDITIONAL READING

Atkinson, M. (2004). *Lend me your ears: All you need to know about making speeches and presentations.* London, UK: Vermilion.

Bransford, J., & the National Research Council. (U.S.)., & National Research Council (U.S.). (2000). *How people learn: Brain, mind, experience, and school.* Washington, DC: National Academy Press.

Brown, A., Luterbach, K., & Sugar, W. (2009, January 01). The current state of screencast technology and what is known about its instructional effectiveness. *Technology and Teacher Education Annual, 3*, 1748–1753.

Clark, R. C., & Mayer, R. E. (2008). *E-learning and the science of instruction: Proven guidelines for consumers and designers of multimedia learning.* San Francisco, CA: Pfeiffer.

Duarte, N. (2008). *Slide:ology: The art and science of creating great presentations.* Sebastopol, CA: O'Reilly Media.

Educause Learning Initiative (ELI). (2006). *7 things you should know about lecture capture.* Retreived May 21, 2012, from http://net.educause.edu/ir/library/pdf/ELI7044.pdf

Educause Learning Initiative (ELI). (2008). *7 things you should know about screencasting.* Retreived May 21, 2012, from http://net.educause.edu/ir/library/pdf/ELI7012.pdf

Farha, N. W. (2009). An exploratory study into the efficacy of learning objects. *Journal of Educators Online, 6*(2).

Garwood, S. (2009). Screencasting: Extending your educational environment. In Cvetkovic, V., & Lackie, R. (Eds.), *Teaching generation M: A handbook for librarians and educators* (pp. 277–297). New York, NY: Neal-Schuman Publishers.

Holbrook, J., & Dupont, C. (2011). Making the decision to provide enhanced podcasts to post-secondary science students. *Journal of Science Education and Technology, 20*(3), 233–245. doi:10.1007/s10956-010-9248-1

Horton, W. K. (2006). *E-learning by design*. San Francisco, CA: Pfeiffer. Retreived May 21, 2012, from http://www.mq.edu.au/ltc/altc/wblt/index.htm

Mayer, R. E. (2005). *The Cambridge handbook of multimedia learning*. Cambridge, UK: Cambridge University Press. doi:10.1017/CBO9780511816819

Mayer, R. E. (2011). *Applying the science of learning*. Boston, MA: Pearson/Allyn & Bacon.

McCord, S. A., & Drummond, W. H. (2010). Lecture capture: Technologies and practices. In Song, H. (Ed.), *Distance learning technology, current instruction, and the future of education: Applications of today, practices of tomorrow* (pp. 113–131). Hershey, PA: Information Science Reference.

Osborn, M., Osborn, S., & Osborn, R. (2012). *Public speaking: Finding your voice*. Boston, MA: Allyn & Bacon.

Peterson, E. (n.d.). Incorporating screencasts in online teaching. *International Review of Research in Open & Distance Learning, 8*(3).

Preston, G., Phillips, R., Gosper, M., McNeill, M., Woo, K., & Green, D. (2010). Web-based lecture technologies: Highlighting the changing nature of teaching and learning. *Australasian Journal of Educational Technology, 26*(6), 717–728.

Reynolds, G. (2008). *Presentation zen: Simple ideas on presentation design and delivery*. Berkeley, CA: New Riders Pub.

Shaw, G. P., & Molnar, D. (2011). Non-native English language speakers benefit most from the use of lecture capture in medical school. *Biochemistry and Molecular Biology Education, 39*(6), 416–420. doi:10.1002/bmb.20552

Smithers, M. (2011). *Is lecture capture the worst educational technology?* Retrieved from http://www.masmithers.com/2011/03/11/is-lecture-capture-the-worst-educational-technology/

Traphagan, T., Kucsera, J. V., & Kishi, K. (2010, February 01). Impact of class lecture webcasting on attendance and learning. *Educational Technology Research and Development, 58*(1), 19–37. doi:10.1007/s11423-009-9128-7

Vajoczki, S., Watt, S., Marquis, N., Liao, R., & Vine, M. (2011). Students approach to learning and their use of lecture capture. *Journal of Educational Multimedia and Hypermedia, 20*(2), 195–214.

Woo, K., Gosper, M., McNeill, M., Preston, G., Green, D., & Phillips, R. (2008). Web-based lecture technologies: Blurring the boundaries between face-to-face and distance learning. *ALT-J: Research In Learning Technology, 16*(2), 81–93. doi:10.1080/09687760802315895

KEY TERMS AND DEFINITIONS

Learning Object: A reusable content item, usually in multimedia form, that can be used alone or together with other material for instructional purposes. A learning object is very similar in purpose to the idea of LessonCapture. The terms learning object and LessonCapture can be distinguished as follows: while a recorded lecture or demonstration can be considered a type of learning object, learning objects can also take on many other forms (i.e., animations, PowerPoint decks, handouts, user guides) and have other value added elements (i.e., quizzes, games).

Lecture Capture: Process of recording content that is delivered via a lecture method, generally with audio and video of the presenter or a recording of the lecture materials (e.g., PowerPoint slides or content written on a chalkboard).

Lesson: In terms of LessonCapture, a lesson is instruction delivered via presentation (lecture or demonstration).

LessonCapture: An approach to the creation and recording of presentation content (lecture or demonstration; face-to-face or screen-recorded) based on effective public speaking, presentation design, and multimedia learning principles, which, when combined with particular procedures and practices ensure effective learning and reusability of the recording.

Presentation: Umbrella term for a lecture or demonstration.

Screencasting: A recording of computer screen content generally with narration. A screencast can demonstrate a process or be an approach to recording PowerPoint narration.

Section 3
Short Instructional Video

Chapter 8
Video Capture for Grading:
Multimodal Feedback and the Millennial Student

Elizabeth J. Vincelette
Old Dominion University, USA

ABSTRACT

This chapter addresses students' preference for screencast assessment over traditional paper or digital text-based comments. Screencast assessment allows for asynchronous audio and visual commenting on student papers using screencast software. A pilot study using a qualitative approach has indicated that students prefer screencast assessment because of its multimodality and its ability to make the instructor's thought process while grading transparent. Multimodality involves multisensory and multimedia approaches, which can broaden student understanding of teacher feedback. The screencast, because of its multimodality, enhances students' understanding of the instructor's thought process and reasoning. Because of the suggestion that students prefer this sort of feedback, the pilot study warrants a larger scale project in order to investigate the student preference for this feedback and whether the method leads to improvement in student performance.

INTRODUCTION

The objective of this chapter is to discuss one instructor's experience in piloting the use of screencasting to evaluate student papers, what will be referred to as *screencast assessment*. Screencast assessment allows for asynchronous audio and visual commenting on student papers using screencast software. Screencasting, a video form of screen capturing, records what is happening on the user's screen and includes the option of adding audio. With *screencast assessment*, an instructor can provide students with video captures of their papers being assessed so that students can see their papers from the vantage point of the instructor's monitor; with this view, students

DOI: 10.4018/978-1-4666-3962-1.ch008

also can see the instructor's cursor movements, scrolling, visits to any other page or websites outside the students' texts, and either pre-created or on-the-fly annotations—essentially anything occurring on the instructor's screen. At the same time, students can hear the instructor's voice commenting on their writing.[1] Because of the auditory and visual combination, a five-minute screencast allows more commentary than could reasonably be written on a student paper, whether by hand or electronically. Furthermore, in-depth explanations are augmented by the instructor's tone of voice, something impossible to provide to students with written comments alone.

This form of feedback improves upon traditional feedback by using aural and visual modalities, offering a multisensory approach unlike common methods of assessing student writing, which usually consist of handwritten comments (often editing marks with a narrative at the end); the Track Changes or Comments function in Microsoft Word; or a typed, memo-style narrative separate from the document. Although effective feedback can be demonstrated in written and digital comments, screencast assessment improves upon other forms of feedback by involving a wider variety of the student's senses. Text-based feedback, whether digital or paper-based offers a more limited form of feedback than screencast/ video of assessment, yet despite the availability of digital feedback methods, instructors often choose text-based assessment techniques.

Digital assessment is increasingly commonplace, and video is frequently used in social media and in the classroom, and often social media is used for learning. A number of today's college students were born "digital natives," and even for those who were not born into the digital world, many have adopted thoroughly mediated lives, with the Internet central to our lives and our daily routines. We conceptualize information as existing in a space of "open distribution and collabora-tion" (DeVoss & Porter, 2006, p. 182).[2] Students are accustomed to file sharing for classroom and personal use, and to video sharing sites like You-Tube for instruction and entertainment, as well as to working collaboratively online, whether via email, Google-docs®, or other sharing platforms. Therefore, the implication is that screencast assessment fits into students' daily experiences with technology, uses familiar interfaces, and can provide more effective feedback to students about their writing than can text-based feedback alone. In turn, the method could help students improve their writing.

Classroom instructors and students alike express frustration with the grading of papers, and for different reasons. Instructors typically bemoan the time consuming nature of grading and their inability to provide adequate feedback that will matter—that is, that will improve writing. Students often complain that it takes too long to get their work back, and when they do, they have too little information provided by the instructor to help them improve writing, or, worse yet, cannot read or understand handwritten comments. Furthermore, in an age in which multiple methods for digital assessment exist (including use of the aforementioned Track Changes and/ or the Comment function in Word, as well as the use of audio feedback using voice recording, or even pre-packaged assessment software), most of those methods still offer updated forms of existing paper-based technology, but do not offer a multi-sensory—nor a multimodal—approach. The literature on the use of screencasting in the classroom is sparse, such that research from a variety of disciplines proves beneficial for this study; in particular, literature from three main areas frame the background for this study: multimodality in writing assessment and transparency in teaching, and effective instructor feedback.

For the purpose of this study, screencasts were created using a free version of Jing® software because of its low cost and ease of use, along with free storage space on the website screencast.com (www.screencast.com) to store the screencasts for distribution to students. Other screencasting software programs like Camtasia®, CamStudio®, AdobeConnect®, and Snagit® can be purchased from anywhere from approximately fifty dollars to hundreds, and these programs offer more features than Jing®. (The author of this study has no affiliation with Jing®, nor suggests that any of the data serve as recommendations or reviews of the product.) A pilot study at Old Dominion University suggested that students have an overwhelmingly positive response to screencast assessment (Vincelette, 2011). The study focused on the efficacy, from the student's perspective, of screencasting assessment compared to more traditional written assessment, and this chapter reports upon the findings of this study, which used survey methodology in order to examine the use of screencast assessment methods in the classroom. The following research questions guided the study and will be addressed in this chapter: (1) To what degree is screencast assessment more beneficial than traditional text-based feedback?; (2) How do students perceive the effectiveness of screencast assessment?; (3) To what degree does screencast assessment help students improve writing?

BACKGROUND

The term "millennial students" refers to the generation born between 1982 and 2002 and is comprised of approximately 82-100 million U.S.-born and immigrant students (Strauss & Howe, 2000) who can be characterized by their inclination toward collaborative work and use of technology to learn (Pinder-Grover & Groscurth, 2009). Screencasting appeals to today's student's frequent use of technology, especially with the ubiquity of video in social media and in the classroom. After experimenting with the screencast assessment technique two years ago, the author of this chapter realized

the potential for this assessment method after receiving unsolicited praise for the method from students and hearing them talking about it excitedly before class. In particular, there was a level of enthusiasm that was not typical for students receiving a paper, from students reporting that they had watched their paper being graded three or more times, had spent anywhere from fifteen minutes to an hour watching their papers being graded, and had shared their screencasts with roommates, friends, and parents. In one case, a student reported that he had watched the video of himself receiving a "D" four times.

The positive student response was attributed to their response to the multimedia nature of screencast assessment and its appeal to a number of senses, and perhaps even its entertainment value. For the purposes of this chapter, the terms *multimedia*, *multisensory*, and *multimodal* will be differentiated. *Multimedia*, by definition, simply means being composed of a number of different media. *Multisensory* involves a number of different senses, from sight to hearing to feeling/tactile experience. *Multimodal* refers to having a number of modes of activity. Often, the terms multimedia and multimodal are conflated and overlap (Lauer, 2009).[3] According to Lauer (2009), the term *multimedia* is a gateway term related to the more scholarly term *multimodal*, which suggests design, process, and social and rhetorical situations. Ice, Curtis, Phillips, and Wells (2007) have examined the preference for *multimedia* feedback, following Bargeron, Brudin, Gupta, Sanocki, & Leetiernan's (2002) findings that online learners prefer multimedia texts over text-only content. In addition, studies indicate that students perceive *multisensory* feedback as flexible and effective (Ice, Swan, Diaz, Kupczynski, & Swan-Dagen, 2010; Crews and Wilkinson, 2009; Oomen-Early, Bold, Siginston, Gallien, & Anderson, 2008). This multisensory aspect reflects students' preference for *multimodality*, in particular the instructor's use of different forms of media to respond to student work (Ice, Swan, Diaz, Kupczynski, &

Swan-Dagen, 2010; Crews & Wilkinson, 2009; Greivenkamp, Stoll, & Johnston, 2009; Oomen-Early, Bold, Siginston, Gallien, & Anderson, 2008; Simonsson, Kupczynski, Ice, & Pankake, 2009). Kress and van Leeuwen (2001) defined multimodality as "the use of several semiotic modes in the design of a semiotic product or event, together with the particular way in which these modes are combined" (p. 20). Multimodal texts do not privilege alphabetic writing, but instead include a number of expressions, or modes, such as print, sound, and image. For the purposes of this study, the screencast serves as a multimodal form of feedback.

Feedback, multimodal or not, reflects particular characteristics as suggested in a study by Stern and Solomon (2006) conducted in order to determine characteristics of effective feedback in which Stern and Solomon (2006) examined 598 graded papers and coded teacher comments and noted three characteristics of effective feedback: (1) that the instructor provided both positive comments and corrections; (2) that the instructor narrowed feedback down to several select areas per assignment; (3) and that instructors pointed out patterns of strengths and weaknesses in the student writing (p. 25-26). Likewise, building on extensive theory in composition studies, Straub (2000) identified seven principles for effective teacher feedback, which can be read as advice or good practices: (1) turn your comments into a conversation; (2) resist taking control of the student's text; (3) prioritize giving comments on global concerns before addressing style and correctness; (4) limit the scope and number of comments; (5) focus the comments to reflect the stage or draft of the text; (6) individualize comments to fit each student; (7) praise writing often. With screencast assessment, providing effective feedback that reflects the above suggestions proves an easier task for an instructor than using text-based comments, while producing more detailed, useful observations for students.

Emergent scholarship suggests a burgeoning interest in the use of screen-capture technology in the classroom (Moore & Filling, 2012; Silva, 2012; Ice, Swan, Diaz, Kupczynski, & Swan-Dagen, 2010; Brick & Holmes, 2008; Stannard, 2008; Warnock, 2008; and Dean, 2007). Recent studies have examined feedback using screen capturing software (Moore & Filling, 2012; Silva, 2012; Ice, Swan, Diaz, Kupczynski, & Swan-Dagen, 2010; Brick & Holmes, 2008; Stannard, 2008; Warnock, 2008; and Dean, 2007). Moore and Filling (2012) examined how screencast feedback can be used effectively to respond to student writing in the college classroom. Silva (2012) studied students' responses to screencast feedback for college writing instruction. Ice, Swan, Diaz, Kupczynski, and Swan-Dagen (2010) examined students' perceptions of the effectiveness of screencast feedback. Brick and Holmes (2008) discussed trials of screen capturing use and students' responses to the method and practical issues. Stannard (2008) conducted a case study of the use of screen capture software for students in English Language Teaching (ELT) courses.

Viewed as an improvement over text-based feedback, screencast feedback reflects Yancey's (2004) discussion of the seductive nature of technologically-influenced or created assessment (see also Forbes, 1996; Whithaus, 2002). Furthermore, screencast assessment functions as a *remediation* (Bolter & Grusin, 2000) of print-based feedback. Bolter and Grusin (2000) defined *remediation* as the imitation, reinvention, and repurposing of older technologies; remediation is evident as each new technology borrows from and improves upon earlier forms of presentation and communication. Remediation involves the simultaneous destruction and adoption of an older media form—or at least its imaginary eradication; the process repurposes older technologies in an effort to achieve a close representation of reality. Screencast grading is not suggested to supplant text or paper-based grading, nor would it render it obsolete, but it presents an option for assessment and often can be combined with text-based grading techniques (to be discussed later in this chapter).[4]

Screencast assessment also can be viewed as a remediation of audio recorded feedback for students. A number of researchers have noted the effectiveness of audio feedback on student papers (Dagen, Mader, Rinehart, & Ice, 2008; Ice, Curtis, Phillips & Wells, 2007; LaFontana, 1996; Lunt & Curran, 2010; Mellen & Sommers, 2003; Merry, & Orsmond, 2007). Like audio feedback, screencast assessment is one-way, such that although it can reveal an instructor's thought process better than most written comments, it is still limited because the student cannot interact by talking back. Nevertheless, research suggests that students experience audio and audio-visual feedback as social. As Nass and Sundar (1996) asserted, users of technology must interact with media in order to respond to the technology as social and real, rather than as an artificial experience, and computer users respond to computers as social beings.

The social aspect of technology, along with transparent teaching strategies, increases the possibility for effective feedback. Arvidson and Huston (2008) illustrated how revealing what is otherwise concealed information can prove an effective strategy for teachers to improve student learning. In particular, Arvidson and Huston (2008) considered the "honesty and courage" of transparent teaching, which they defined as an intentional practice of encouraging openness between instructor and student through teaching practices (p. 4). Wisehart (2004) asserted the importance of teachers in training learning how to be passionate, transparent instructors. Transparency engenders trust (Brookfield, 2006; Bulach, 1993), and with trust, students are more likely to self-assess and follow other metacognitive strategies to monitor their own performance (Gillespie, 2002). A number of researchers have noted the importance of the perception of trust a student feels towards the instructor (Bain, 2004; Brookfield, 2006; Bulach, 1993; Curzon-Hobson, 2002).

The studies cited above have contributed to an understanding of multimodality, assessment, and student perception of feedback, especially in relation to transparency in teaching. This chapter contributes to the literature by investigating a small sample of student responses regarding their perception of screencast assessment used in a 200-level composition class. Although screencast assessment is a technique that could be applied to any course, the pilot study discussed here examined student reactions to the feedback method in a composition class order to develop a set of questions to inform a larger scale, future study.

STUDENT PREFERENCE FOR SCREENCAST ASSESSMENT

Students not only prefer a combination of visual mark-ups with audio feedback (Crews & Wilkinson, 2009; Greivenkamp, Stoll, & Johnston, 2009; Oomen et al., 2008; Simonsson et al., 2009), they consider electronic feedback as more valid and valuable than handwritten comments, as indicated in a case study by Denton, Madden, Roberts, and Rowe (2008). In particular, the popular grading technique of using Track Changes in Word has been found to hinder the learning process because of instructors' tendency to focus on editing instead of providing explanations (Deans, 2009). Furthermore, students often complain that comments are difficult to decipher, not specific enough, and vary greatly depending on the course (Beach & Friedrich, 2006). Frustration arises when students are neither able to read (a problem with handwritten comments) nor understand (a problem with both handwritten and typed or electronically rendered comments) an instructor's reasoning.

Beach and Friedrich (2006) have noted that most instructors use written comments more than any other form of feedback. Furthermore, students often complain that comments are difficult to decipher, not specific enough, and vary greatly depending on the course (Beach & Friedrich, 2006).

Students report needing more than comments and marks on papers to improve their writing and that they benefit most when they receive explanations for why certain comments are made (Beach, 1989). Students often have difficulty understanding the meaning behind instructors' comments (Thaiss and Zwacki, 2006), not to mention the difficulties they face reading handwriting. The use of screencasting allows the instructor to provide an in-depth explanation for why something is or is not working within the paper. A number of studies, including LaFontana (1996) and Bardine, Bardine, and Deegan (2000) have shown students' confusion because of instructor handwriting. Frustration arises when students are neither able to read (a problem with handwritten comments) nor understand (a problem with both handwritten and typed or electronically rendered comments) an instructor's reasoning. Again, screencasting helps eliminate this problem, though using a comment feature on a word processing program would, at least, address the ability to read the instructor's comments. Research also suggests that students prefer feedback on the content of their papers more than other types of comments such as those on grammar, mechanics, and structure, for example, and that audio feedback, because it tends to emphasize content, is therefore more valuable than other forms of feedback (Dagen, Mader, Rinehart, and Ice, 2008).

After using screencasting to assess student writing for two years and noting the overwhelmingly positive response to the technique, the author of this chapter developed a qualitative research methodology in order to more formally investigate why. For data collection, the research design consisted of a voluntary survey of nine open-ended questions administered in order to elicit participants' perspectives of screencast assessment. The remainder of this chapter will discuss the work flow, software, recommended practices (including suggested scripts for instructors), and other concerns, especially storage, dissemination of grades, and privacy.

Procedure

For the pilot study, after receiving approval of the research methodology from Old Dominion University's Human Subjects board, data was collected during the final week of the fall semester of 2011. The sample size is so limited (18 students, 9 of whom responded) that it cannot be claimed that results are neither generalizable nor statistically significant. To provide some background on the second year writing course at Old Dominion, English 211C is the second of two general education classes, with the first being English 110C. Instructors teaching English 211 are not required to follow standardized evaluation criteria or a standardized rubric for papers and have freedom in assessment techniques and design, although there are learning outcomes for the course that have been developed by the department.

During the course of the semester, screencast assessment was used three times. At the end of the semester, an anonymous survey was distributed.[5] The surveys provided illuminating, insightful data about screencast assessment, which was analyzed using qualitative analyses. Despite the small sample size, the sample presented findings that met the aim of this pilot study, in that a larger study is warranted in order to draw a representative sample that could be generalized back to a larger student population.[6]

Analysis

The inductive analysis for analyzing the survey results involved a coding process based upon grounded theory (Charmaz, 2006; Clarke, 2005; Dey, 1999; Glaser, 1978, 1998, 2001; Glaser & Strauss, 1967), in order to identify emergent themes regarding student perceptions of screencast assessment.[7] Overall, the recursive process of grounded theory coding involves valuing the researcher's interpretive strategies and acknowledging the relationship between methods and emergent theory. Furthermore, grounded theory underscores this author's belief in transparency in teaching, in that grounded theory supports transparency in research methods.

There were two phases of coding used. In the first phase, the survey results were copied into a word processing program. Second, the students' survey responses were placed into a two-column format, with the responses on the right and space for codings on the left. Third, using a line-by-line technique, chunks of the transcripts were named using gerunds in order to define, summarize, and categorize the data (Glaser, 1978; Charmaz, 2006). Fourth, the gerunds were organized into conceptual categories in order to determine what main themes were emerging from the student responses. Fifth, the information was classified further in several memo-writing codings, with focused coding used to synthesize data into conceptual clusters; from these codings, meanings emerged through the recursive process of sorting through the information. Gaps, questions, and analytic frames arose during the process (Charmaz, 2006), and core categories and subcore categories emerged (Glaser, 1998).

In the second phase of coding, the survey results were uploaded into a concordance program (concordancer) called Antconc (Anthony, 2012). Developed by corpus linguist Laurence Anthony, the Antconc program, like all concordance software, serves as a tool to explore patterns of language in a text or across more than one text. Anthony (2004) described Antconc as a freeware, multi-platform, multi-purpose corpus analysis toolkit intended for classroom use. Despite the robust capabilities of the program, only the Word List feature was used in order to sort words in the survey. The program was used to generate a word frequency list that provided the most frequently occurring words in the survey results along with the number of times each word occurred. It is worth noting that the word list cannot shed light on the importance of a word in a corpus, because near the top of the frequency list might be words that do not suggest much information; with the

results in this study, for example, there were the words *the, to, and, it, of, a,* and *is.*

An initial coding of the word frequency results by grouping the words into categories suggested by the data was then performed. First, words were grouped that denoted *action* by categorizing verbs and verb variants *actions.* Second, the remaining words were grouped into the categories of *place and movement, senses and experience, qualifiers and amounts, right and wrong,* and *time.* Third, these categories were developed from overlaps in meaning into five larger conceptual themes, including (1) self/other; (2) senses and experience/knowing and not knowing/ perception; (3) possibility and ability/utility/improving; (4) paper/writing/evaluating/process/organization; and (5) right and wrong/certainty and uncertainty/positive and negative.

One early coding involved locating the key words in the transcript. Using Antconc enabled identification of the top ten key words in the student surveys (see Figure 1).

The words *I/my* appear 84 times in the transcript and often overlap with the key words *paper, writing, mistakes,* and *you/your. You/your* occurs next in frequency, with 55 instances[8]. These word frequencies suggest that students associate themselves with their writing and their professors with grading. An "us/them" scenario emerges, with two "sides" to the assessment process. As one student responded about the use of screencast assessment, "I would learn what the professor is looking for in a paper and make sure that it is covered in the next one." Another explained, "Its [*sic*] a great way to see how the professor grades papers so you know what he or she is going to take points off for." It appears that students feel responsibility for their writing and recognize that grading is part of a process involving both students and instructors (with *writing, paper,* and *professor* in the next set of most-frequently occurring words). The following set of most-frequently occurring words included *improve/helpful/useful, screen-*

Figure 1. Top ten key terms and their word counts from student surveys

Key Terms	Frequency: number of times a word or its variants appear in the transcript
I/my	84
You/your	55
Writing	36
Paper	24
Professor	21
Improve/helpful/useful	19
Screencast	16
Mistakes/wrong/error	11
Watch	9
Listen	8

cast, and the word *mistakes* and its variants. These words revealed students' concern with learning from the assessment process, which they expect to help them identify problems; by using the screencast, students *watched* (nine occurrences) and *listened* (eight occurrences) for suggestions and critiques. In addition, the multisensory experience reveals three overarching implications emerged from the surveys: (1) multi-sensory assessment is an improvement over paper-based assessment ; (2) this assessment technique demonstrates/fosters transparency in the student/teacher dynamic ; (3) it reveals students' practices of how they use feedback (see Figure 2).

Along with comments discussing screencast assessment as an improvement over paper or text-based assessment, students associated assessment and writing with correction and students frequently commented on how papers are marked. Comments included:

- I just listened to it twice to understand where to improve.
- It's interactive. I look forward to hearing what my professor has to say about my paper. There is no mistake about what my professor is trying to say when screencast grading as opposed to scribble marks or extraneous question marks that do nothing

to explain what I did wrong or how I can correct my mistakes.

- I just listen to it twice to understand where to improve.
- Its [*sic*] very different it uses voice instead of pens.
- You get feedback that you can't get when a teacher marks your paper up with red pen. For example the teacher could say I would of [*sic*] put such and such here instead of what you put. Plus you can see your paper with the highlights and notes the professor has corrected in the background, so your [*sic*] seeing what the professor sees.
- It is much better than having to discern a professor's written words or symbols. I really like it. Because you get more feedback hearing what was wrong or good with your paper than just red lines drawn everywhere.

Students' focus on marking on papers reflects a concern with being correct and with understanding visual feedback, written or with video. A number of studies, including LaFontana (1996) and Bardine, Bardine, and Deegan (2000) have shown students' confusion because of instructor handwriting. Screencasting can eliminate the need for handwritten comments, but it is the combination

Figure 2. Expressions of student perceptions of screencast assessment

SENSORY	TRANSPARENCY	PRACTICES
<ul><li>watching</li><li>looking</li><li>seeing</li><li>viewing</li><li>hearing</li><li>listening</li><li>showing</li><li>feeling</li><li>sensing</li><li>being interactive</li></ul>	<ul><li>explaining</li><li>understanding</li><li>connecting</li><li>personalizing</li><li>revealing</li><li>understanding</li><li>helping</li><li>benefitting</li><li>enjoying</li><li>being useful</li><li>being "awesome"</li><li>being effective</li><li>being efficient</li><li>being "great"</li></ul>	<ul><li>correcting</li><li>deciphering</li><li>note-taking</li><li>re-watching</li><li>graduating</li></ul>

of the visual part of the video with the teacher's voice that students appeared to value most.

Survey data suggested that students perceive the visual aspect of screencast assessment as the most effective, followed by the auditory aspect, and then by a sense of feeling and interacting, which reflect their sense of virtual proximity. Students noted their perceptions of the screencasts, not only referring to sensory experience but larger feelings that emerged while watching their papers being graded. Below is a list of the most striking comments:

- [I]f I needed to understand something the professor said, in the screen cast, I would just watch it again.
- I look forward to hearing what my professor has to say about my paper.
- I think screencast grading should be mandated at my school. One, it saves paper because the assignment is submitted electronically. Two, it allows the professor to speak directly to the student compared to writing small words in the margins of papers that require the student to squint, use a magnifying glass, or employ the use of Rosetta Stone to interpret the professor's writing or meaning.
- It is better in the sense that it creates a personal relationship between the student and the teacher.
- I would compare it to actually sitting down with your professor and going over your paper line by line.

References to the "personal" aspect of screencast grading suggest that students perceived this form of grading as beneficial because it is not as impersonal as traditional text-based grading.

In classes after receiving their grades, students have reported that screencasting makes them feel as though they are with their instructor in a conference, and they often express a desire to talk back to the screen or request that they create their own screencasts to talk back to the instructor. They have perceived their instructor's presence, most likely due to the familiarity of the voice, and it appears that they perceive that the instructor has expended extra effort to help them. This perception of instructor presence reflects findings from studies on distance education and social and cognitive perceptions of presence conducted by Garrison (2007); Garrison, Anderson, and Archer (2001); and Rourke, Garrison, Anderson, and Archer (2001).

The multimodality of screencast assessment allows for the perception of presence and reflects the importance of what Ice, Swan, Diaz, Kupczynski, and Swan-Dagen (2010) have noted as students' perceptions of instructors' caring when students receive auditory and text-based feedback. In communication theory, Mehrabian (1969, 1981) examined the relationship between immediacy and a perception of proximity between communicators, whether physical or psychological closeness. Student responses in the survey reflect the feelings of immediacy, closeness, and proximity as related to trust. Immediacy may derive, in turn, from tone and enthusiasm (see Allen, Witt, & Wheeless, 2006). One student did, however, indicate that it made him or her "nervous." Although this comment is purely speculative, the author suspects that the intimacy of this grading process was overwhelming to that student, as might have been the amount of detail.

Most student remarks, however, indicated a preference for the level of detail provided by screencast assessment, again particularly in contrast to other forms of grading. Related to the detail is a theme of time, and as one student said, it can be "[t]ime comsuming in getting the grade out to the student"; another said, "I know it's time consuming for the teacher, but I think it's no less time consuming that grading a hard copy paper." The survey results are relevant to the problem that most feedback methods do not supply students with the same level of detail possible from screencasts and that students have expressed frustration with text-based grading.[9] For example, if one were to compare the amount of feedback possible using a screencast, the following formula could be applied: one double-spaced page of text typed with a 12-point font is approximately 250 words and takes two minutes to read aloud, so that a five-minute screencast can, theoretically, produce around 750 words of feedback, or 2.5 typed pages, depending on the pace of the speaker/instructor and number of pauses.

Although this chapter argues that screencast assessment is a useful pedagogic method for writing instruction in composition classes, there are limitations to the study, including that qualitative analysis of a small, pilot study of this type always presents problems, in that the data is not generalizable, and because a number of factors influence student performance and instructor assessment. It is also difficult, if not impossible, to state the degree to which students' writing could improve over the course of a semester based upon one survey questionnaire.

The findings of this study are intriguing, but with the sample size this small, generalizability cannot be achieved, such that a larger research project should be conducted with larger sample sizes in order to determine how and in what ways screencast feedback improves student writing. There was no survey given at the beginning of the semester, and a comparative analysis would have proven productive. Instead of comparing screencast assessment to text-based assessment in the class, students compared the screencasting method in this class to their knowledge of grading from past writing experiences in other classes, though not to specific classes or instructors. Nevertheless, this pilot study does suggest that screencasting is worth exploring as an assessment method and provides insight into students' preferences for how they receive feedback, as well as what the feedback contains.

As promising as screencast assessment sounds, instructors depend upon a number of factors in order to create screencasts, not the least of which might be financial. Although for this study a free version of Jing® was used, along with free storage space on screencast.com, there are a number of screencast software packages with better features that cost more.[10] In particular, a feature that would allow "glowing cursor" effect would to make it easier for the student to see where the cursor moves; the feature does not come with the free program used in this study and is often available only with higher-cost software. In addition, high-speed internet and a computer with a hard drive large enough to support it are both recommended, as well as a gamer headset with headphones for the ears and a microphone.

Limitations also include that on occasion, screencasting software can and does freeze. Also, using this sort of software requires a lack of fear to try technology on the part of the students and teachers, although both report the ease of use. For instructors, there is a portability problem, in that screencasting is not easy to do with an audience (your roommates, other people who live in one's house). Even with a script of sentence starters or preparatory notes such as written grading criteria or a rubric, the instructor's screencast is a performance. Overall, perhaps the most pressing concerns involve privacy for file sharing and dissemination and access to technology (to be discussed in further detail below).

Solutions and Recommendations

Before conducting screencast assessment, instructors should consider consulting with their university's attorneys to determine what types of file exchanges are allowed, as well as where and how the screencasts can be stored, because institutions vary widely in what is considered acceptable. The instructor must be sure to save files labeled by individual student if using protected online space and to share files directly with individual students to prevent students seeing other papers; this practice is no different than emailing papers saved on one's hard drive or flash drive back and forth. In addition, content management system such as Blackboard could facilitate file exchange. Because file size can be large, instructors may want to use storage space provided by their institutions, or, if allowed by their institution's rules, they may email links to files stored

online or create private YouTube® accounts with students. Students must be able to access email or have another way to exchange information electronically, such as a portal.

Most problems that students report can be addressed on the instructor's end, with practice and self-taught training. Instructors should watch online demonstrations or tutorials for the software they choose and then practice making a few mock assessments. After creating those mock-ups, one can watch the test captures and review one's performance, noting difficulties or problems. These trial runs will help instructors know how to adjust microphone or screen settings. Part of these practices involves setting up the work area where screencasting will be performed. Setting up a file management system for collecting papers electronically is essential for work flow. It also a good idea to have a rubric for the assignment that the students know well before they turn in their papers and to have a paper copy of the rubric available for reference. Using sticky notes or a scratch pad while talking can help with keeping track of what still needs to be said. Downloading and opening the set of documents one plans to screencast assess in one sitting also helps work flow. Furthermore, practice enables a more conversational tone because the instructor will feel more comfortable, reflecting Straub's (2000) first principle of effective feedback, which recommends comments appear as conversations. The very fact that screencast assessments are spoken lends the process a conversational feel, even though the process is one-sided.

Perhaps the most important step is pre-reading the paper. It is easier to screencast when one already has an idea of what grade the work will receive, and the instructor should consider before recording whether or not to speak the grade during the recording or to send the grade to the student separately. It is strongly recommended that instructors quickly read the paper beforehand and create a minimal cuing system to prepare for screencasting; this cuing system is for the instructor and the student, both helping instructors know what they want to say and leaving students visual markers. For example, one could use a two-color highlighting system in a word processing program or use a comment bubble at the end of each paragraph with one or two phrases or shorthand remarks. Separately from the screencast, an instructor can send the marked up document. Marks should be kept to a minimum so that the instructor does not grade the paper multiple times and generate extra work, and because excess markings both overload students and distract from the screencast's ability to provide auditory feedback. Pre-marking also allows for teachers to follow Straub's (2000) second suggestion to prioritize global or macro concerns over micro concerns such as style mechanics, or grammar; the fourth suggestion to limit the scope and number of comments; the fifth to focus comments to reflect the student's stage of writing; the sixth to individualize comments; and the seventh suggestion to praise writing often. By cuing the document beforehand, the teacher can achieve this focus.

For the actual recording, it is best to enlarge a document as much as possible before recording, and instructors should avoid too much scrolling and excessive motion. One should also test sound quality by doing microphone checks before starting to record for students. Screencasting software allows for pausing during recording (as well as pausing during viewing of the finished product). It can be useful to pause recording to re-read an upcoming section of a document or perform other necessary tasks. Furthermore, an instructor can suggest that a student pause the recording and take notes, again underscoring an instructor's ability to self-check against Straub's (2000) recommendations. While moving within a document, it is best to try not to scroll to fast nor speak too fast. Avoiding coughing, sniffing or sighing (the verbal equivalent of an "eye roll") maintains instructor ethos, although it is normal to make mistakes, and students not only do not mind when the instructor corrects him or herself, they seem to like the transparency. Also, one must watch time carefully, and it is best to limit recordings to a length of time appropriate for the length of the work being assessed. One should also keep in mind, as Dagen, Mader, Rinehart, and Ice (2008) note, that too much feedback can remove ownership or

Figure 3. Screencasting assessment example script

- Hi, ______, I'd like to begin by ________.
- Now, let's take a look at ___________.
- The introduction is ____________.
- I really like how you ___________.
- I noticed that ___________.
- The transitions paragraph to paragraph _________.
- The formatting is ________.
- Some of the strengths include _________.
- Here are some things you need to work on ___________.
- This is a difficult paper to grade, because_______.
- I'd like you to see me about _____ because _______.
- Taking all things into consideration, your grade is a ______; see the rubric we went over in class.

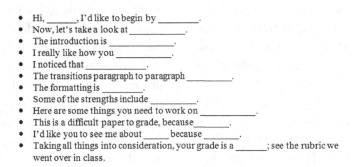

Figure 4. Screencasting assessment example email boilerplate

Dear _______,
Please click on the link below to access the evaluation of your paper. It has sound with my voice discussing parts of your paper, so you'll want to make sure you have the sound low or ear-buds if you're in public, etc.

Thank you,

marginalize student voices, a finding also reported by Straub (2000), who suggested that instructors avoid taking control of students' texts when grading. Following a script can help manage time (see Figure 3). Most recordings created for this study lasted for five minutes, and different software has different cut-offs for recording times. The longer the recording, the larger the file. Once this file is ready to be sent, keeping an email boilerplate (see Figure 4), is also efficient.

One final problem and solution to be discussed is the need to consider the use of this method in light of compliance with the Americans with Disabilities Act (ADA) of 1990, which requires equal access to public programs and services for people with disabilities; the ADA therefore prevents exclusion from participation or benefits from programs and services. The United States Department of Justice has noted that Internet use should follow the ADA. With this in mind, instructors are urged to consider the use of screencast assessment as an option for assessment, such that a student unable to access the resources because of a disability would have the option of *not* receiving feedback with this method. Furthermore, screencast assessment is done for individual students, and is not a full-class activity, and the instructor and student would be able to discuss alternatives to the standard screencast as needed.[11]

FUTURE RESEARCH DIRECTIONS

This pilot study as focused on how students perceive the efficacy of screencast assessment, and the following research questions emerged during the pilot study and would benefit from further exploration:

1. Do students find multi-modal assessment more effective than traditional written feedback?
2. Do instructors using Jing® (screencasting) as a method of multi-modal assessment believe

that the time it takes to learn is worthwhile in terms of providing effective feedback on writing assignments? Further, from their perspective, do they believe that their students' written works improved due to the use of a multi-modal assessment method? To what degree does screencast assessment save time or create more work?

3. Can screencast assessment provide a more robust platform for instructors to provide feedback beyond lower-order concerns, such as sentence-level grammatical or spelling errors?
4. What social contexts—personal and institutional—does screencast assessment involve?
5. How can the method be integrated into classroom lessons, portfolio assessment, or other assignments (intertwining assessment and teaching)?
6. How can screencast assessment be used for feedback on paper drafts or to reinforce classroom writing lessons?
7. How can screencast assessment be used for peer feedback?
8. How can screencast assessment support multiple learning styles?

CONCLUSION

Yancey (2004) argues that technology is not a villain but a tool "shaping and assessing the writers whose work we want to assess" (p. 93). The findings reported here suggest that instructors might want to consider screencast assessment as a useful pedagogical tool. As part of a desire to create a student-centered learning experience tailored to individual needs and learning styles, screencast assessment provides more relevant feedback for today's students because of its interpersonal feel, flexibility, and the portability of the technology. (A large number of this author's students have noted that they watch themselves getting a paper graded on their phones.) When integrated with existing teaching techniques, this form of assessment has the potential to improve student writing, especially at a time when "more students with weak verbal abilities are entering college" (Jameson, 2007, p. 17). Results of this pilot study suggest that screencast assessment pushes beyond exclusionary barriers associated with traditional paper grading; facilitates information exchange with students regarding their writing, particularly because the feedback is multimodal; provides more nuanced commenting; and promotes student interaction with assessment, thereby fostering participation and ownership, such that writing improves, particularly when this feedback is used within a larger context of transparent teaching.

REFERENCES

Allen, M., Witt, P. L., & Wheeless, L. P. (2006). The role of teacher immediacy as a motivational factor in student learning: Using meta-analysis to test a causal model. *Communication Education*, *55*(1), 21–31. doi:10.1080/03634520500343368

Anthony, L. (2004). AntConc: A learner and classroom friendly, multi-platform corpus analysis toolkit. *IWLeL 2004: An Interactive Workshop on Language e-Learning*, (pp. 7-13).

Anthony, L. (2012). AntConc (3.3.1w) [Computer Software]. Tokyo, Japan: Waseda University. Available from http://www.antlab.sci.waseda.ac.jp/

Arvidson, P. S., & Huston, T. A. (2008). Transparent teaching. *Currents in Teaching and Learning*, *1*(1), 4–16.

Bain, K. (2004). *What the best college teachers do*. Cambridge, MA: Harvard University Press.

Bardine, B., Bardine, M., & Deegan, E. (2000). Beyond the red pen: Clarifying our role in the response process. *English Journal*, *90*(1), 94–101. doi:10.2307/821738

Bargeron, D., Grudin, A., Gupta, E., Sanocki, F., & Leetiernan, S. (2002). Asynchronous collaboration around multimedia applied to on-demand education. *Journal of Management Information Systems*, *18*(4), 117–145.

Beach, R. (1989). Showing students how to assess: Demonstrating techniques for response in writing conferences. In Anson, C. (Ed.), *Writing and response: Theory, practice, and research* (pp. 127–148). Urbana, IL: National Council of Teachers of English.

Beach, R., & Friedrich, T. (2006). Response to writing. In MacArthur, C., Graham, S., & Fitzgerald, J. (Eds.), *Handbook of writing research* (pp. 222–234). New York, NY: Guilford.

Bolter, J., & Grusin, R. (2000). *Remediation: Understanding new media*. Cambridge, MA: MIT press.

Brent, R., & Felder, R. M. (1996). Navigating the bumpy road to student-centered instruction. *College Teaching*, *44*(2), 43–47. doi:10.1080/87567555.1996.9933425

Brookfield, S. D. (2006). *Skillful teacher: On techniques, trust, and responsiveness in the classroom*. San Francisco, CA: Wiley, John & Sons.

Bulach, C. (1993). A measure of openness and trust. *People and Education*, *1*, 382–392.

Charmaz, K. (2006). *Constructing grounded theory*. Thousand Oaks, CA: Sage.

Clarke, A. E. (2005). *Situational analysis: Grounded theory after the postmodern turn*. Thousand Oaks, CA: Sage.

Crews, T., & Wilkinson, K. (2010). Students perceived preference for visual and auditory assessment with e-handwritten feedback. *Business Communication Quarterly*, *73*, 399–412. doi:10.1177/1080569910385566

Curzon-Hobson, A. (2002). A pedagogy of trust in higher education. *Teaching in Higher Education*, 7, 265–276. doi:10.1080/13562510220144770

Cutliff, J. R. (2000). Methodological issues in grounded theory. *Journal of Advanced Nursing*, *31*(6), 1476–1484. doi:10.1046/j.1365-2648.2000.01430.x

Dagen, A., Matter, C., Rinehart, S., & Ice, P. (2008). Can you hear me now? Providing feedback using audio commenting technology. *College Reading Association Yearbook*, *29*, 152–166.

Dean, B. C. (2007). *Dynamic homework annotation*. First International Workshop on Pen-Based Learning Technologies. Retrieved July 15, 2012, from http://www.cs.clemson.edu/~bcdean/vgrade.pdf

Deans, T. (2009). *Requiring revision*. Retrieved March 15, 2012, from http://www.insidehighered.com/views/2009/06/25/deans

Denton, P., Madden, J., Roberts, M., & Rowe, P. (2008). Students' response to traditional and computer-assisted formative feedback: A comparative case study. *British Journal of Educational Technology*, *39*, 486–500. doi:10.1111/j.1467-8535.2007.00745.x

DeVoss, D., & Porter, J. (2006). Why Napster matters to writing: Filesharing as a new ethic of digital delivery. *Computers and Composition*, *23*(2), 178–210. doi:10.1016/j.compcom.2006.02.001

Dey, I. (1999). *Grounding grounded theory*. San Diego, CA: Academic Press.

Forbes, C. (1996). Cowriting, overwriting, and overriding in portfolio land online. *Computers and Composition*, *13*, 195–206. doi:10.1016/S8755-4615(96)90009-2

Garrison, D. R. (2007). Online community of inquiry7 review: Social, cognitive, and teaching presence issues. *Journal of Asynchronous Learning Networks*, *11*(1), 61–72.

Garrison, D. R., Anderson, T., & Archer, W. (2001). Critical thinking, cognitive presence, and computer conferencing in distance education. *American Journal of Distance Education*, *15*(1), 7–23. doi:10.1080/08923640109527071

Gillespie, M. K., & National Institute for Literacy, Washington, D. C. (2002). *EFF research principle: A contextualized approach to curriculum and instruction*. EFF Research to Practice note. Jessup, MD: Ed Pubs.

Glaser, B. G. (1978). *Theoretical sensitivity*. Mill Valley, CA: The Sociology Press.

Glaser, B. G. (1998). *Doing grounded theory: Issues and discussions*. Mill Valley, CA: The Sociology Press.

Glaser, B. G. (2001). *The grounded theory perspective: Conceptualization contrasted with description*. Mill Valley, CA: The Sociology Press.

Glaser, B. G., & Strauss, A. L. (1967). *The discovery of grounded theory*. Chicago, IL: Aldine.

Greivenkamp, D., Stoll, C., & Johnston, H. (2009, April 21). *Demystifying invisible processes using mediated feedback*. Paper presented at the 2009 Teaching and Learning with Technology Conference.

Ice, P., Curtis, R., Phillips, P., & Wells, J. (2007). Using asynchronous audio feedback to enhance teaching presence and students' sense of community. *Journal of Asynchronous Learning Networks*, *11*(2), 3–25.

Ice, P., Swan, K., Diaz, S., Kupczynski, L., & Swan-Dagen, A. (2010). An analysis of students' perceptions of the value and efficacy of instructors' auditory and text-based feedback modalities across multiple conceptual levels. *Journal of Educational Computing Research*, *43*(1), 113–134. doi:10.2190/EC.43.1.g

Jameson, D. A. (2007). Literacy in decline: Untangling the evidence. *Business Communication Quarterly, 70*, 16–33. doi:10.1177/1080569906297923

Kress, G., & van Leeuwen, T. (2001). *Multimodal discourse: The modes and media of contemporary communication.* New York, NY: Oxford University Press.

LaFontana, V. R. (1996). Throw away that correcting pen. *English Journal, 85*(6), 71–73. doi:10.2307/819831

Lauer, C. (2009). Contending with terms: 'Multimodal' and 'multimedia' in the academic and public spheres. *Computers and Composition, 26*, 225–239. doi:10.1016/j.compcom.2009.09.001

Lunt, T., & Curran, J. (2010). Are you listening please? The advantages of electronic audio feedback compared to written feedback. *Assessment & Evaluation in Higher Education, 35*(7). doi:10.1080/02602930902977772

Mehrabian, A. (1969). Some referents and measures of nonverbal behavior. *Behavior Research Methods and Instrumentation, 1*, 203–207. doi:10.3758/BF03208096

Mehrabian, A. (1981). *Silent messages* (2nd ed.). Belmont, CA: Wadsworth.

Mellen, C., & Sommers, J. (2003). Audio-taped responses and the two-year-campus writing classroom: The two-sided desk, the guy with the ax, and the chirping birds. *Teaching English in the Two-Year College, 31*, 25–39.

Merry, S., & Orsmond, P. (2007). *Students' responses to academic feedback provided via mp3 audio files.* Paper presented at the Science Learning and Teaching Conference in Stafford, UK. (accessed May 8, 2012).

Moore, N. S., & Filling, M. L. (2012). iFeedback: Using video technology for improving student writing. *Journal of College Literacy and Learning, 38*, 3–14.

Nass, C., & Sundar, S. S. (submitted). Is human-computer interaction social or para-social? *Human Communication Research.* Retrieved from http://www.stanford.edu/group/commdept/oldstuff/srct_pages/Social-Parasocial.html

Oomen-Early, J., Bold, M., Wiginton, K. L., Gallien, T. L., & Anderson, N. (2008). Using asynchronous audio communication (AAC) in the online classroom: A comparative study. *Journal of Online Learning and Teaching, 4*(3).

Pinder Grover, T., & Groscurth, C. R. (2009). Principles for teaching the millennial generation: Innovative practices of UM faculty. CRLT Occasional Papers. Center for Research on Learning and Teaching, University of Michigan, No. 26.

Rourke, L., Anderson, T., Garrison, D. R., & Archer, W. (2001). Assessing social presence in asynchronous text-based computer conferencing. *Journal of Distance Education, 14*(2), 50.

Silva, M. L. (2012). Camtasia in the classroom: Student attitudes and preferences for video commentary or Microsoft Word comments during the revision process. *Computers and Composition, 29*, 1–22. doi:10.1016/j.compcom.2011.12.001

Simonsson, M., Kupczynski, L., Ice, P., & Pankake, A. (2009, April). *The impact of asynchronous audio feedback in the dissertation advising process.* Paper presented at the American Educational Research Association Annual Meeting, San Diego, CA.

Stannard, R. (2007). Using screen capture software in student feedback. *The Higher Education Academy.* Retrieved July 15, 2012, from http://www.english.heacademy.ac.uk/explore/publications/casestudies/technology/camtasia.php

Stern, L., & Solomon, A. (2006). Effective faculty feedback: The road less traveled. *Assessing Writing, 11*, 22–41. doi:10.1016/j.asw.2005.12.001

Straub, R. (2000). The student, the text, and the classroom context: A case study of teacher response. *Assessing Writing, 7*(1), 23–55. doi:10.1016/S1075-2935(00)00017-9

Strauss, W., & Howe, N. (1992). *Generations: The history of America's future, 1584 to 2069.* New York, NY: Quill.

Thaiss, C., & Zawacki, T. M. (2006). *Engaged writers, dynamic disciplines: Research on the academic writing life.* Portsmouth, UK: Boynton/ Cook.

Vincelette, E. (2011). *Students' perception of multimodal screencast feedback in the writing classroom.* Unpublished raw data.

Warnock, S. (2008). Responding to student writing with audio-visual feedback. In Carter, T., & Clayton, M. A. (Eds.), *Writing and the iGeneration: Composition in the computer-mediated classroom* (pp. 201–227). Southlake, TX: Fountainhead Press.

Whithaus, C. (2002). Green squiggly lines: Evaluating student writing in computer-mediated environments. *Academic Writing, 3.* Retrieved April 1, 2012, from http://wac.colostate.edu/aw/ articles/whithaus2002/abstract.htm

Wisehart, R. (2004). Nurturing passionate teachers: Making our work transparent. *Teacher Education Quarterly*, 45–53.

Yancey, K. (2004). Looking for sources of coherence in a fragmented world: Notes toward a new assessment design. *Computers and Composition, 21*, 89–102. doi:10.1016/j.compcom.2003.08.024

ADDITIONAL READING

Anderson, T., Rourke, L., Archer, W., & Garrison, R. (2001). Assessing teaching presence in computer conferencing transcripts. *Journal of Asynchronous Learning Networks, 5*(2).

Anson, C. (1989). Response styles and ways of knowing. In Anson, C. (Ed.), *Writing and response: theory, practice, research* (pp. 332–366). Urbana, IL: NCTE.

Anson, C. (1997). In our own voices: using recorded commentary to respond to writing. In Sorcinelli, M. D., & Elbow, P. (Eds.), *Writing to learn: strategies for assigning and responding to writing across the disciplines* (pp. 105–113). San Francisco, CA: Jossey-Bass. doi:10.1002/tl.6909

Anson, C. (1998). Reflective reading: developing thoughtful ways to respond to students' writing. In Odell, L., & Cooper, C. (Eds.), *Evaluating writing: The role of teachers' knowledge about texts, learning, and culture* (pp. 302–324). Urbana, IL: NCTE.

Auten, J. G. (1998). Power and the teacher's pen: talking about teacher response to student writing. *CEA Forum, 28*, 1-4.

Bloxham, S., & Boyd, P. (2007). *Developing effective assessment in higher education: A practical guide.* Maidenhead, UK: Open University Press.

Brannon, L., & Knoblauch, C. H. (1982). On students' rights to their own texts: A model of teacher response. *College Composition and Communication, 33*, 157–166. doi:10.2307/357623

Brown, J. S. (2000, March/April). Growing up digital: How the Web changes work, education, and the ways people learn. *Change*, 10–20.

Connors, R., & Glenn, C. (1995). *Responding to and evaluating student essays. The St. Martin's guide to teaching writing* (3rd ed.). New York, NY: St. Martin's.

Connors, R., & Lunsford, A. (1993). Teachers' rhetorical comments on student papers. *College Composition and Communication, 44*, 200–224. doi:10.2307/358839

Danis, M. F. (1987). The voice in the margins: paper-marking as conversation. *Freshman English News, 15*, 18–20.

Dede, C. (2005). Planning for neomillennial learning styles: implications for investments in faculty and technology. In Oblinger, D., & Oblinger, J. (Eds.), *Educating the Net generation* (pp. 15.1–15.22).

Denton, P. (2003). Enhancing student learning using electronic feedback. *Exchange, 4*, 23–24.

Dragga, S. (1988). The effects of praiseworthy grading on students and teachers. *Journal of Teaching Writing, 7*, 41–50.

Elbow, P. (1993). Ranking, evaluating, liking: sorting out three forms of judgment. *College English, 55*, 187–206. doi:10.2307/378503

Fuller, D. (1988). A curious case of our responding habits: what do we respond to and why? *Journal of Advanced Composition, 8*, 88–96.

Gallien, T., & Oomen-Early, J. (2008). Personalized versus collective instructor feedback in the online courseroom: Does type of feedback affect student satisfaction, academic performance and perceived connectedness with the instructor? *International Journal on E-Learning, 7*(3).

Gorham, J. (1988). The relationship between verbal teacher immediacy behaviors and student learning. *Communication Education, 37*(1), 40–53. doi:10.1080/03634528809378702

Hackman, M. Z., & Walker, K. B. (1990). Instructional communication in the televised classroom: The effects of system design and teacher immediacy on student learning and satisfaction. *Communication Education, 39*, 196–206. doi:10.1080/03634529009378802

Haswell, R. (1983). Minimal marking. *College English, 45*, 600–604. doi:10.2307/377147

Jensen, G., & DiTiberio, J. (1984). *Personality and the teaching of composition.* Norwood, NJ: Ablex.

Jewitt, C., & Kress, G. (2003). Introduction. In Jewitt, C., & Kress, G. (Eds.), *Multimodal literacy* (pp. 1–18). New York, NY: Lang.

Journet, D. (2007). Inventing myself in multimodality: Encouraging senior faculty to use digital media. *Computers and Composition, 24*(2), 107–120. doi:10.1016/j.compcom.2007.03.001

Mutch, A. (2003). Exploring the practice of feedback to students. *Active Learning in Higher Education, 4*(1), 24–38. doi:10.1177/1469787403004001003

Richardson, J., & Swan, K. (2002). Examining social presence in online courses in relation to students' perceived learning and satisfaction. *Journal of Asynchronous Learning Networks, 6*(1), 68–88.

Selfe, C. (2007). *Multimodal composition: Resources for teachers.* New York, NY: Hampton Press.

Sommers, J. (1989). The effects of tape-recorded commentary on student revision: A case study. *Journal of Teaching Writing, 8*, 49–75.

Sommers, N. (1982). Responding to student writing. *College Composition and Communication, 33*, 148–156. doi:10.2307/357622

Straub, R., & Lunsford, R. F. (1995). *Twelve readers reading: Responding to college student writing.* Cresskill, NJ: Hampton Press.

Tapscott, D. (1998). *Growing up digital: The rise of the Net generation.* New York, NY: McGraw-Hill.

Tapscott, D. (1999). Educating the Net generation. *Educational Leadership, 56*(5), 6–11.

Thompson, T. (1995). Understanding attitudes toward assessment: the personality factor. *Assessing Writing, 2*, 191–206. doi:10.1016/1075-2935(95)90012-8

KEY TERMS AND DEFINITIONS

Grounded Theory: A method of qualitative analysis that privileges interpretive frameworks using a coding process to arrive a theory from data.

Millennial Student: Students born since the 1980s who show a preference for technological use in the classroom and who were born into the digital age.

Multimodal: Refers to composition that uses multiple modes of design, process, and social and rhetorical situations.

Remediation: The repurposing and reinventing of older technologies.

Screencast: A recording of the computer screen that captures what is on the monitor.

Screencast Assessment: A form of assessment that uses screencasts in order to provide feedback for students, often for a grade.

Transparency: Refers to a practice in teaching that encourages a teacher's revelation of reasoning and purposes for assigning activities, readings, questions, etc., and that fosters a sense of openness and trust.

ENDNOTES

1.   I should note here that screencasting is an *option* for feedback, such that a student with a disability may choose not to receive a screencast and instead opt for video only, audio only, or a different option altogether for receiving feedback on writing. Also, the instructor can easily control the size of the paper and magnify it before screencapturing, so it can be enlarged on the creator or user's end. The screencast is an individual form of feedback and not a whole class system.

2.   According to DeVoss and Porter (2006), the significance of this shift from a print-based culture to an online mediated culture is more significant than just switching from the printed page to the digital screen, leading them to conclude that we now live in a *post*-Napster era (p. 182). What we read/see/consume is different from previous generations and previous historical moments. Further, the way(s) we do understand and value information are different. Instead of reading this as merely a scientific or technological change, DeVoss and Porter argue that this shift is fundamentally cultural, constituting a new ethic for a new period - a "digital ethic" (p. 179).

3.   Lauer explains that the difference between the terms multimodal and multimedia is "largely a difference between 'modes' and 'media'" (p. 225). Kress and Van Leeuwen (2001) present modes as means of representation, the semiotics of textual composition, such as text/words, sound, images (still or moving), and color, whereas media are "tools and material resources" used in textual production and dissemination, including books, radio, television, computers, painting, and voices (p. 22).

4.   I am using considering the term "paper-based" loosely because Word and other word processing programs for most users tends to replicate paper use.

5.   See the Appendix for survey specifics.

6.   As Marshall (1996) maintained, small sample sizes are often undervalued, particularly by quantitative researchers, because of beliefs that generalizability should be the goal and main reason for all scholarly research. Furthermore, Marshall (1996) argues that appropriate sample sizes address the research question in a satisfactory manner, and in a study of grounded theory, Cutliff (2000) un-

derscores the need for purposeful sampling. In line with these assertions, the research questions for this pilot study outlined in the first section of this chapter guided my choice to use qualitative research.

7. Coding processes are rooted in what Cutliffe (2000) calls *symbolic interactionism*, which a researcher uses to elicit symbolic meaning from artifacts, in my case, the surveys (p. 1477). Therefore, I chose grounded theory for a number of reasons, including the following: theory emerges from interaction between researcher and text.

8. Note that the analysis did not account for instances in which students refer to themselves using "you."

9. For a sample screencast, please click here http://www.screencast.com/users/ejvincel/ folders/rakan/media/c2a3ed0b-2a4e-4fb4- a9ff-23f3b0fc699b. This screencast is an original and not edited in any way, which is evident by its roughness, some awkward pauses, and my difficulty moving around in the paper. It serves as a good example of the affordances screencasting permits, as well as the performance and workflow issues discussed in this chapter.

10. For example, there are programs like Camtasia, AdobeConnect, and Snagit that run from approximately fifty dollars to hundreds. Because of its ease of use and low cost, Jing has been selected as the screencasting software. Part of this chapter will discuss the use of Jing versus AdobeConnect and other programs. In particular, the "Pro" version of Jing lends itself to instructor and student use for screencast assessments of student writing; in my work, I have honed the work flow to a manageable, teachable number of steps that instructors find easy to learn.

11. I would suggest that students with certain disabilities can have modified screencasts, as well. A number of accommodation strategies can be developed. A student with visual impairments could opt for audio only or could use text-magnifying tools. The instructor could also enlarge the text simply by magnifying the student's paper on the screen, so that the screencast captures larger text. A student with a hearing impairment could opt for text captioning; the instructor could provide the cursor movements within the paper and insert comments or type inside the student's document on the screen. Or, if a student is hearing impaired but not deaf, the instructor could modify the pace of speaking to slow down, and the student has the option of turning the volume up, as well. A student with a disability that impacts the ability to process information may benefit from still shots of his or her paper captured and used in conjunction with the instructor's voice, rather than receiving a screencast with a lot of cursor movement and scrolling within the text. Students with mobility impairments could use alternative software or hardware to view and listen to their screencast. Screencast assessment can be modified to provide feedback for students with impairment and may, in fact, be an improvement over text or paper-based feedback for some students. In fact, screencasts may have benefits for students with mobility impairments who have difficulty participating in real-time communications online; they could benefit from the asynchronous nature of this feedback.

APPENDIX

The following information was given to students for the survey: Student participation was completely voluntary. Participation in the study is voluntary and that confidentiality is protected for all participants and all aspect of the study. Surveys will be distributed by Survey Monkey to maintain anonymity of participants. Anyone who does not wish to take the survey will not be required to do so.

I am working on a research project in which I am analyzing my own grading process and students' reactions to the feedback. You do not have to participate. I will not be recording your names, and when I will present my results, it will be in the aggregate, and I will not divulge your identities. If you would like to participate, simply fill out the survey you receive from Survey Monkey. The Survey Monkey program does not record your name or other information that identifies you. I will not ask you whether or not you participated and will not know whether or not you answered the survey.

These are the survey questions [that were] to be posted and distributed via Survey Monkey:

1. What is your reaction to screencast grading? Explain.
2. How many times did you watch your screencast? Explain.
3. Did you watch it on a computer, phone, or other device? Explain.
4. Did you take notes while watching the screencast? Explain.
5. How might you use your screencast in the future? Explain.
6. What are benefits of this type of grading? Explain.
7. What are detractions? Explain.
8. What could make the screencast more useful for students? Explain.
9. How would you compare screencasting to other forms of grading? Explain.

Chapter 9
Creating and Implementing a Virtual Math Tutoring Lab for Undergraduate Students

Curtis Kunkel
University of Tennessee Martin, USA

ABSTRACT

This chapter discusses the construction and implementation of a Virtual Math Lab for undergraduate students. The main technology used in the construction of the site was the Livescribe® SmartPen. Pros and cons of using this technology is discussed in detail. In addition, current usage numbers illustrate how the Virtual Math Lab has filled a need that this level of student desperately needed filled.

INTRODUCTION

From the beginning of the information age, when computers and the Internet began to demand more and more of our attention, there has been an increasing need for educational content on the World Wide Web. In particular, undergraduate students demand free educational resources in the areas of mathematics and the sciences. To this end, back in Fall 2009, The University of Tennessee at Martin (UT Martin or UTM) took it as their mission to create a Virtual Math Lab

(VML) specifically designed to help undergraduate students taking a college algebra course; not only the specific course offered at UTM but any such course offered around the world. This chapter will discuss the creation of the College Algebra Tutorials (CATs) wiki (see Figure 1), the first component of their VML. The main technology used in the CATs *wiki* – a website that allows its users to edit content collaboratively and simply within the browser itself – was the Livescribe® SmartPen system. As such, this technology will be discussed in great detail throughout the chapter.

DOI: 10.4018/978-1-4666-3962-1.ch009

BACKGROUND: IDENTIFIED NEED AND LITERATURE REVIEW

Each year, approximately one million students enroll in a college algebra or related course (Lutzer, et al., 2007). Despite years of pedagogical intervention in general education mathematics courses, nationwide failure and withdrawal rates remain high, typically ranging between 40% and 60% (Mayes, 2004; Katz, 2007). To try and combat this seeming disconnect between where this caliber of student is and where they should be, national mathematics organizations, including the Mathematical Association of America and the American Mathematical Society, have called for changes in lower division general education mathematics courses (Ganter and Barker, 2004; Piollatsek, et al., 2004). In recent years, various reform efforts have been tested, including the use of graphing calculators and other technology, writing assignments, group projects, and online resource systems (Lutzer, et al., 2007). Other recommended changes include the use of a modeling approach and the solicitation of input from certain *partner disciplines* whose content depends on mathematical literacy (Ganter and Barker, 2004). Most of these changes focus on classroom pedagogical approaches; few address the issue of student tutorials outside of the classroom.

UTM is typical of many colleges and universities that teach these lower division courses. Between the Fall 2008 and the Summer 2009, five of the top ten failed courses across the entire university included lower division, general education mathematics courses (Davis, 2010). A recent undergraduate research project on mathematics placement examined UT Martin student data over the ten-year period from Fall 1999 until Fall 2008. The ten-year failure and withdrawal rate (DFW) for College Algebra was 40%; for Pre-calculus, 35%; and for Elementary Probability and Statistics, 30% (Anthony, Sims, and McCullough, 2010).

The main campus of UTM offers tutoring in mathematics for all lower division undergraduate courses. However, UTM currently offers sections of mathematics courses at off-campus centers through dual enrollment at area high schools and online, with no access to one-on-one tutoring. Adjunct instructors, who generally have at most two office hours per week, teach most off-campus sections. Prior to Spring 2009, needs assessment surveys administered to students enrolled at the off-campus centers indicated that access to tutoring in mathematics was a top priority.

Prior to the creation of the CATs wiki, a search of available online mathematics tutoring yielded few results for college-level courses. These were usually course notes posted by an instructor (such as *Paul's Online Notes*), limited to review concepts or to only one method of delivery (*West Texas A&M University's Virtual Math Lab*), or embedded throughout a broader approach (*The Math Forum at Drexel*). The search did find a site that is strictly video lecture: KhanAcademy.org. There are no additional tutorials or supplements in addition to their videos. In the end, no free, open-access, comprehensive online tutoring for lower division college-level mathematics was found.

Faculty at UTM recognized the need for additional tutoring in introductory mathematics courses, especially for those students located at remote sites. To this end, the CATs wiki was created.

CREATION OF THE VIRTUAL MATH LAB

In the Spring 2010, the Department of Mathematics and Statistics received university ARRA funds to create a tutoring website for college algebra. A team of seven faculty members, led by Dr. Curtis Kunkel, used a wiki to develop a pilot website with pages and tutoring modules that correspond to the topics taught in a traditional college algebra course. This tutoring website has been available to students since the Summer 2010.

This chapter will discuss the main components that went into creating the virtual laboratory, from the actual choice and implementation of the

Figure 1. Screenshot of the CATs wiki homepage

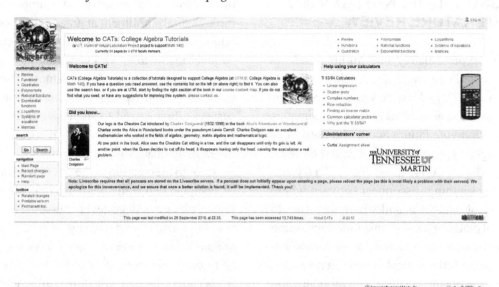

wiki format to how the team used the Livescribe SmartPens. Some thoughts and comments on other technologies that were implemented will be covered, as well as comments about various technologies that could have been used but were not.

Website and Wiki Implementation

At the start of this project, a decision had to be made as to the format in which the tutorials would be delivered. Several questions were asked, some with great trepidation from the veteran team members. The main concern was the type of website the team would be responsible for creating and maintaining. Would the information be presented using a traditional static web site focused on presenting notes and sample problems, or would the team learn new technology to produce something a little more modern and dynamic? The first realistic concern was money management. There are a lot of very reputable companies out there that would have been more than willing to construct a website for this project given the opportunity and the funding. However, on a limited budget there was a strong desire to keep outside input to a minimum and control the development and delivery of each tutorial. This meant using the

expertise of each faculty member and working within the technological limitations that tend to develop over the years. In short, the team decided that this online lab was going to be an in-house, Do It Yourself (DIY) project.

Next, the team had to decide on a medium. There was some discussion about building a traditional HTML coded website to create the environment. This idea raised some concerns from many members of our team. Several did not know how to code in HTML, and they did not feel that it would be fair to have only a few team members responsible for the bulk of the encoding. This also led to the monetary concern of purchasing HTML editing software for each person involved in this project. Time-wise, it would have involved programming lessons for some individuals before it became easy to edit the HTML code. In the end, the team decided against the traditional HTML editing software and, to save time and money, they considered more modern option.

Dr. Chris Caldwell solved the issue of finding a medium that would be user friendly and easy to access. He introduced the group to the idea of creating a wiki: in particular, a MediaWiki (www.mediawiki.org). Each page is easy to set up, and the instructions for embedding images and content were clear and concise. The moment that confirmed the use of a wiki was when everyone saw how easy it was to edit a page. It would not be necessary to send e-mails to one another to correct spelling mistakes or correct a sign change. The fear of this technology was almost non-existent compared to that inspired by the first views of HTML code. As an added bonus, MediaWiki is a free open source software option easily downloadable from their website. So, faculty were willing to try this tool and the price was just about perfect.

After seeing the results displayed and working through some of the finished tutorials, it is clear that the team made the choice that was right for them. Adding content to the wiki was very easy, including standard edits to the text along with inserting tables, pictures, downloadable files, and, most important to this discussion, embedded Livescribe *pencasts* – a video recording of SmartPen movements and drawings along with audio from the user. Adding math environments to the wiki pages was also easy, and these math environments allowed problems, equations, and notations to be displayed almost like a textbook alongside the embedded pencasts. As one might expect, some nice features were already built into the wiki environments, making the professional appearance easy to achieve: a table of contents is automatically generated on each page, usage statistics automatically track what information on the page is being accessed the most, and most importantly the wiki allowed for anyone to edit the site at anytime from anywhere.

One issue surfaced that the team did not foresee in using the wiki. While embedding the pencasts, wiki formatting does not allow links to be more than a certain number of characters, and Livescribe's preset embedding link exceeds this length. Fortunately, Dr. Caldwell came to the rescue again by creating a conversion program so that the Livescribe's preset embedding link would be

shortened considerably. This conversion program is more or less an encryption algorithm. (For more information, contact Dr. Chris Caldwell at UTM.)

Livescribe® SmartPen Pencasts

The main source of technology used in creating the dynamic tutorials for the wiki was Livescribe SmartPen Pencasts using the Livescribe's Pulse version of their SmartPen. There were several reasons for this choice. The team collaborated to build a list of technology options that they felt should be included in the tutorials. Pencasts made the list since they would serve learners who needed audio instruction as well as the visual process in real-time. The team chose Livescribe because of word of mouth recommendations and a very convincing demonstration. A conference presentation on this technology showed how easy it was to record, write, and upload basic presentations. Faculty also enjoyed seeing the paper record of the same information as their pencast where one could use the pen to touch and playback audio from any point on the page. Right away, the team knew this SmartPen was going to be the perfect tool for this project, mostly because no one was afraid of a pen, and also the price was nice. For a tool of this caliber to be around $150, it was worth a try.

The team had to find a technology that was easy to use for a variety of different people with different technology skill sets. Some professors on the team had the benefit of computer science backgrounds and technology courses, so they were not afraid of any type of technology the committee decided to use. On the other hand, there were members on the committee to consider who did have certain fears and limitations. Calculators are a daily tool, but web pages and software packages brought out great hesitation from some members. These fears went by the wayside when each team member was issued their own Livescribe Smart-Pen. One of the most common concerns shared by all members was the fact that no one wanted see their own smiling face broadcast for the whole world to see. As instructors, however, the need to be heard was essential. The team agreed that a tool of technology that they could use to record explanations while the handwritten processes could be viewed would be dynamic. This is exactly what the SmartPen could do.

Now that the team had a tool to use and a format in which the pencasts would be displayed, we were able to start creating these pencasts using the Livescribe SmartPen. The pencasts are a good choice for educators attempting to serve students who are audio-visual learners, including those who need reinforcement in a controlled environment. To this end, the pencasts and the notebooks could stand alone. In the framework of a tutorial site, these prencasts support and supplement the material covered. From a list of agreed upon college algebra topics, wiki pages were created and organized. Topics were distributed to each member of the committee and it was up to the individual to decide on the most helpful examples to use in the creation of each pencast. Professors scoured textbooks, notes, and picked each other's brains to prepare each topic as completely as possible. Then, the information reserved for the pencast was set aside. Professors took the time to practice each example, monitor voice volume and inflection, and most created a script of what should be said at which points in the presentation. The first pencasts produced were formal, stilted, and in need of more work. One hurdle that was encountered was the need to become proficient at writing and talking at the same pace. This is much easier said than done. After a couple practice runs, the team was comfortable enough with the SmartPen to relax and use it to teach instead of just presenting a problem.

The team made the decision to start each pencast with the same intro, "This pencast is intended for use by the UT Martin Virtual Math Lab …"

For the most part, these pencasts were pretty easy to create. Yes it took time and preparation to do a good job in creating each one, but that can be said about any lesson creation; online or otherwise. Each individual was pretty happy with the method chosen, until the first few were listened to in a large conference room. Unfortunately, the audio component of the technology being used had been slightly underestimated. The microphone inside of the pen is very small, but it was able to pick up chatter from the hallway through closed doors, the sound of the air conditioner turning on, and even a desktop computer's cooling fan. Some pencasts recorded distant phones ringing, the creak of a chair, and even the scratching of the pen itself. If this extra sound was too big of a distraction for the actual lesson, the only thing to do was to start that pencast over. Unfortunately there is not any post-production sound/video editing available as of yet. This also means that if a mistake is made in the middle of the pencast there is no option other than to start over. To try and combat this, the team decided to aim for each pencasts to time at or below 5 minutes in length. That way, if a mistake was made, no one lost 30 minutes of work.

There was no preset format in which material was presented in these pencasts. As such, there is a greater variety of learners that the site is able to serve. Many mathematical examples have a visual structure that is easier to follow on a dynamic example, which is what the Livescribe SmartPen allows. Most professors emphasized terminology and technique as opposed to simply working examples or discussing theoretic concepts. Some professors label pieces of the problem as they work, relating background material to the new topic. Other professors describe every step but only write out the mathematical process, never transcribing a full narrative solution. Since these pencasts were designed to be embedded into the wiki, the tools of the wiki can help a student find the voice or the style they prefer. With the wiki structure it is very easy to look at which pages a certain professor worked on or assisted with. Not every member of the team had input on every page, but the cross-collaboration should make the pages feel more cohesive.

After the pencasts were created using the notebooks and SmartPens, each pencast had to be uploaded onto a computer. The free Livescribe Desktop software that comes with the pens simplifies this process. The pen has a docking station that transfers the content from the pen into the computer. Once the information is in the computer, the content needed to be uploaded onto the Internet so that the presentations are available online. Again, Livescribe has made this an easy process. They offer multiple ways to upload and share the information. The method of choice for this team was to upload a pencast onto the Livescribe servers and to embed the files onto the wiki. This means that there is no need to pay for extra storage on another server. Livescribe gives users 500 MB storage on their servers for each registered account, regardless of how many pens are linked to that account. This amounts to approximately 50 hours of recorded material. And as an added bonus, at least at this time, they aren't strictly enforcing this maximum.

After the pencasts are uploaded to Livescribe's servers, they needed to be linked into the wiki (see Figure 2). Again, Livescribe had this option readily available for use. Note that in order to share any pencast, it must first be made available to the public, so settings were adjusted to reflect this requirement. After it is publically available, the options of what to do with the pencast include 'Email a Friend," "Download as PDF," "Get a link to this file," "Share on Facebook," "Embed this file," or "Share on our Community." Since the goal was to try and keep people actively participating in the tutorials on the wiki once they found what they were looking for, it was decided to embed these pencasts inside of our pages. Now technically they are still housed on Livescribe's servers, but

the pencasts appear as though they are an integral part of the wiki pages, and the user is not sent to a new window. This embedding process raised another hurdle for the technology savvy members of the team. The choice of using the MediaWiki brought with it some internal security to control certain pop-ups, advertising, and so on. This benefits the end user since less trash is likely to appear. However, Livescribe accomplishes this control by limiting the length of the names of the embedded files inside their wiki pages. Therefore, every one of the pencasts was reading as a blocked file since the names of the files are automatically generated as longer than allowed by MediaWiki. To get past this restriction, the team had to create a program that would take the embedding link from the *Livescribe Desktop* software and shorten it to be smaller than the blocked size. This also means we needed a program for our wiki server to internally expand this to the correct size when talking to the Livescribe servers so that the content could be accessed. Dr. Caldwell created more or less an encryption algorithm to accomplish this process and made it possible for team members to easily paste the embedding link received from *Livescribe Desktop* and then copy the converted embedding code into the wiki pages.

Now that the method was in place to go from topic or idea to pencast to embedded file on the wiki, the foundation was set for the team to fill the wiki pages with information and pencasts so that the tutorials could be used by the masses. The completion of the project was a result of the advantages in using this technology: ease of use for people with limited technology experience, little setup on the part of the user, the free server space available to each account linked to a SmartPen, the use of the *Livescribe Desktop* software to easily share the pencasts, and above all, the inexpensive costs associated with getting started.

Again, this technology is not perfect yet. There are some cons associated with using this tool: the microphone that picks up more than you want it to, no simple way to fix a mistake (it is after all,

Figure 2. Screenshot of wiki page with embedded pencasts

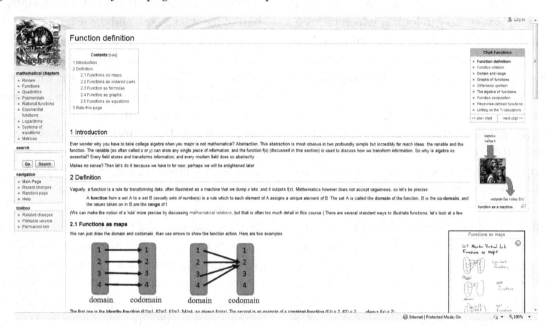

still a pen), no post-production capabilities, and being forced to use Livescribe's servers if the creations are meant to be shared. This last point was a big concern initially. The team had wanted a way to upload the tutorials completely to their servers, independent of other servers. However, there was no way around using the Livescribe servers. There has been great improvement from the first days of use; the company did not seem to be fully aware of how fast this technology would spread. There were many times that the servers were either down for maintenance or had simply crashed. This happened enough that the team was forced to insert a note about it on the main wiki page stating, "Note: Livescribe requires that all pencasts are stored on the Livescribe servers. If a pencast does not initially appear upon entering a page, please reload the page (as this is most likely a problem with their servers). We apologize for this inconvenience, and we ensure that once a better solution is found, it will be implemented. Thank you!"

One additional problem that did not occur during this process but that has plagued users since is that occasionally there are errors in uploading the pencasts from the computer onto the Livescribe servers, especially with larger files. For instance, one professor has been having a supplemental instructor use the Livescribe SmartPen in specific courses to record actual lectures this past year. Each lecture has been uploaded onto a website each week so that students have access to classroom notes if they had to miss class, needed to listen to what was said, see the example again, and so on. The larger files usually present errors in uploading. The professor may have to attempt to upload the pencasts multiple times before it actually uploads the entire pencast correctly. There does not seem to be a good, fast solution to this other than to keep trying. Yes it gets frustrating after the fifth attempt at an upload, but it will eventually get there and then all the failed uploads can be deleted.

Although the team only used the most basic of components in each pencast, faculty could have also used some of the nearly one hundred different apps currently available from the Livescribe website, some of which could translate handwriting into text or tables, could provide a dictionary at the touch of a button, or could display a scientific calculator just by tapping a few simple squares. Several of these apps could help with some accessibility issues or learning accommodations.

Other Technologies

In addition to the wiki text and the Livescribe Pencasts, the team also included demonstrations using other tools on the wiki, such as the GeoGebra program, and posted images that were captured from the Texas Instruments TI-84 Plus Silver Edition emulator software.

GeoGebra is "free mathematics software for learning and teaching" available as either a download to a personal computer or as an online applet (www.geogebra.org). This program is very similar to Geometer's Sketchpad but with the main added bonus of it being *free*! The team used this program to create most of the graphs for the tutorials on the wiki. In addition, GeoGebra was used in its interactive nature to illustrate things like how an outlier affects the line of best fit.

Texas Instruments TI-SmartView™ Emulator Software for the TI-84 Plus Family of calculators was also used. Since the University of Tennessee at Martin, like many others, has adopted the use of the TI-83 and TI-84 calculators in this level of courses, it was only natural to include some tutorials on a few of the topics students generally have difficulty on. The team used the emulator not only to capture what is seen on the screen, but also to include pointers on which buttons to press and where operations are being performed such as sketching scatter plots and finding a line of best fit using the calculator's STAT applications.

USAGE STATISTICS

Since Fall 2010, there have been approximately 22 sections of college algebra per year with around 26 students per section, giving a total of well over 1,000 students per year enrolled in the UTM college algebra course. By comparison, the main page of the CATs wiki has been accessed nearly 13,000 times over this period.

For those educators who typically teach college algebra, it will come as no surprise that the most commonly viewed pages are as follows: graphs of functions (5,962), polynomial long division (4,572), piecewise-defined functions (4,449), finding rational zeros (4,251), LinReg on the TI-83 and -84 calculators (4,210), functions (4,080), and inverse functions (4,005). This is only the list of pages that crossed the 4,000 hit mark.

Concerning other pages that have not topped the hit list, such as the factoring & foil page, the information presented on the page is complete. This page has many of the features that all content pages have including text-based definitions, examples for the students to follow along, quick feedback practice, and pencasts for the students to view. This page has been viewed 3,477 times, and the pencasts on this page have been viewed approximately 75 times. Now compare this to a more advanced topic like partial fraction decomposition. This page has been accessed only 2,585 times. However, the pencasts on this page have been accessed approximately 125 times. Clearly the need for more than just text-based presentation is required once a certain level of sophistication is met.

Since use of this site is anonymous, feedback is at the discretion of the user, and there is no way of tracking student outcomes after using this site. No grade-related statistics exist for study. Students have made it known that they think of this as a valuable resource through their responses to end-of-course evaluations and the fact that the UTM Student Success Center has purchased SmartPens that they check out to students who require accommodation to facilitate learning. Unfortunately again, due to privacy issues, success or failure cannot be discussed in any particular case.

CONCLUSION

After seeing the effects that the CATs wiki has had in the courses at UTM, the team can only hope that others institutions will consider either using this tutorial resource or create their own versions specific to their course curriculum. The hope is that, at the very least, a new awareness has been developed for the up and coming students of the 21st century who wish to have more than an office visit as a way to get help.

The Livescribe SmartPen was clearly the best choice for this faculty group based on its ease of use, price, and availability. Since the team is a group of self-proclaimed lecture capture novices, the Livescribe SmartPen can be seen as a gateway to other more ambitious lecture capture formats.

In the future, there are plans on extending this project to include topics for Trigonometry and Elementary Probability and Statistics, two other introductory courses at UTM where faculty believe this technology can be the most beneficial. There is a committee already formed that is in the process of writing an NSF proposal to extend this site to these other areas and to pull in individuals from the sciences to include more application based examples.

ACKNOWLEDGMENT

The author would like to thank the University of Tennessee at Martin for funding the project that created the CATs website. Without their funding, this project would have never made it off the ground. The author would also like to thank the West Tennessee STEM Center for Learning for hosting our CATs website on their servers.

The author wishes to recognize and thank each of the other faculty members who were involved in the project. Without their hard work and dedication to the project, the CATs wiki could not have been completed in such a timely manner. These faculty include John Bush (jbush@utm.edu), Chris Caldwell (caldwell@utm.edu), Louis Kolitsch (lkolitsc@utm.edu), Stephanie Kolitsch (styler@utm.edu), Brenda Lackey (blackey@utm.edu), and Brian Wagner (bwagner@utm.edu).

REFERENCES

Anthony, E., Sims, J., & McCullough, D. A. (2010). *Exploring placement criteria in freshman and sophomore level undergraduate mathematics courses.* Undergraduate research poster presented at the Southeastern MAA meeting, Elon, North Carolina.

Davis, E. (2010). Math tops list of most failed at UTM. *The UT Martin Pacer, 82.*

Ganter, S., & Barker, W. (Eds.). (2004). *Curriculum foundations project: Voices of the partner disciplines.* Washington, DC: Mathematical Association of America.

Katz, V. J. (2007). *Algebra: Gateway to a technological future.* Washington, DC: Mathematical Association of America.

Khan Academy. (2012). Retrieved from http://www.khanacademy.org

Lutzer, D., Rodi, S., Kirkman, E., & Maxwell, J. (2007). *Statistical abstract of undergraduate programs in the mathematical sciences in the United States: Fall 2005 CBMS survey.* Providence, RI: American Mathematical Society.

Mayes, R. (2004). Restructuring college algebra. *International Journal of Computer Algebra in Mathematics Education, 11,* 63–74.

Pollatsek, H., et al. (2004). *Undergraduate programs and courses in the mathematical sciences: CUPM curriculum guide 2004.* Washington, DC: Mathematical Association of America. Retrieved April 6, 2010, from www.maa.org/cupm

KEY TERMS AND DEFINITIONS

Embed: An embedded file is any type of multimedia file inserted into a webpage.

Emulator: A software application that can accurately imitate another device.

Math Environments: Sections of code which facilitate the view of mathematical operations and symbols.

MediaWiki: A free, web-based wiki application.

Pencast: Interactive media file that captures handwritten pages and audio recordings.

Post-Production: Final editing stage in which audio-visual changes can occur.

SmartPen: Device used to capture pencasts.

Chapter 10
Videagogy:
Using Humor and Videos to Enhance Student Learning

Peter M. Jonas
Cardinal Stritch University, USA

Darnell J. Bradley
Cardinal Stritch University, USA

ABSTRACT

Capitalist economics posits that increased competition between entrepreneurs in an economy leads to better, more consumer friendly products. As colleges compete for students, the same could be said for how modern learners have driven traditional pedagogy to new heights. In the last 30 years, education has witnessed the transformation of distance learning via the internet and home computing, the growth and inclusion of non-traditional learning methods, and most recently, the growth of a ubiquitous video culture via the usage of digital video recording, phone cameras, and web vehicles such as YouTube. This chapter attempts to connect research with the practical components of using technology in the form of humorous, short videos as a new teaching technique called videagogy: from the words video and peda-gogy, pronounced vid-e-ah-go-jee. Using humorous videos and allowing students to select video content brings self-directed learning to students in a non-threatening way that actually makes them laugh out loud.

INTRODUCTION: WHAT IS HUMOR?

In 1964 Justice Potter Stewart wrote that he could not succinctly define pornography, but that he would know it when he saw it. Humor may fall into the same category because it not only differs by individual, but because it also has many variables affecting it. There may be as many definitions of humor as there are researchers in the field. This chapter attempts to not only define humor but to provide the research behind humor and more importantly to connect humor to classroom instruction.

DOI: 10.4018/978-1-4666-3962-1.ch010

In 1970, J. Davis and A. Farina found humor to be "a whole composite of different behaviors rather than a single one, and any explanation which attempts to explain them equally would appear to be doomed to do so by explaining them marginally" (p. 175). Others have attempted to define humor by using examples, descriptors, or even through philosophy, like Sorell (1972) stating, "laughter lifts man above his animalistic state, sets him free, and gives his spirituality another dimension" (p. 11). Still others use basic characteristics of humor in their definitions, such as social, cognitive, physiological, or psychological aspects. The operational definition of humor for this discussion is defined as *a verbal or nonverbal activity eliciting a positive cognitive or affective response from listeners*. Another key element is that humor must be connected to context in order to be truly funny (Meyer, 1990). For this chapter, humor will include jokes, funny words, physical activities, exercises, stories, or even videos.

Humor is somewhat elusive partially because it changes over time with each new generation. Some things are timeless, but have you ever heard a joke on TV from a show 20 years old and it just was not funny? For example, having Ralph Cramden threatening to hit Alice by saying, "Pow, Zoom, to the moon" is not as funny today as it was years ago because of the rising concern in domestic abuse. Humor evolves as times change and new information is discovered. Each generation develops its own nuances within the culture. Today, we think it is funny to suggest that the Ethernet (a noun) is something used to catch the Ether Bunny.

There are many theories about change in history; however, Plato argues that the things people perceive to be real and permanent in life are actually not. Plato wrote that most individuals believe inanimate objects like tables, chairs, or desks are real. On the contrary, this is not true because in 100 years these items will probably not be in existence. According to Plato, the ideas or conceptualizations of a table, chair, or desk are

real because they will be the same after 100 years. The *idea* of a table is more real than the table itself because the idea can last forever. Similarly, the idea of humor is much more real than exactly what is humorous. Humor is forever and an innate response with which humans are born.

Humor is very difficult to define. The root of the English word "humor" is the Latin "*umor,*" meaning "liquid, fluid." Humor flows within us and courses through us with the ability to see what is incongruous in life—the juxtaposition of the expected and the surprising, the sublime and the ridiculous. Our sense of humor makes us notice the irregular and bizarre in human nature and human behavior. Humor is shrewd observation on the behavior of eccentrics. Through humor we understand, appreciate, and even embrace the puzzling, curious, and mismatched events and occurrences that take place in our daily lives. (Wilhelmsson, http://www.vitalchristianity.org/docs/New%20Articles/Humor-Healing2.pdf)

Humor not only involves the fluids of the body, as mentioned above, but it has to do with connections to the brain, the heart, the soul, and spirit of individuals as well as the social, spiritual, emotional, and relational aspects of people. The impact humor has on the brain partially explains the expression "growing weak with laughter." Humor as a state of mind can create balance in one's life with body, mind, and soul.

BACKGROUND: CONNECTING HUMOR TO THE BRAIN

Educators tend to believe that if they use humor in the classroom, they are not taking education seriously. Not so. Research indicates that using humor *connected to the material* not only enhances the learning environment but also increases the effectiveness of what is being learned. All of the research points in the same direction: humor has a positive effect on the learning environment when not used in a negative manner. A number of empirical studies have found that humor improves the attention, comprehension, and motivation of students (Bandes, 1988; Bryant et al., 1979; Wandersee, 1982; Gorham & Christophel, 1990). Kaplan and Pascoe (1977) found students improved their retention of material when humorous examples were used. Others like Hill (1988) and Berk (1996) found that the use of humor helped create a more positive learning environment. Many researchers like Berk (1996), Hill (1988), and Goodman (1983) found that humor builds a rapport with students which allows students to feel less intimidated and inhibited in class. When relationships improve, teaching improves (Fullen, 2001). Humor improves relationships and, therefore, teaching and learning.

Research denotes that laughter is not solely a response to jokes. Laughter is the quintessential human social signal solidifying relationships and pulling people into the fold as it connects individuals (Provine, 2000). Begley (2000) posits that "laughter seems intimately entwined with our physiology. It blocks a neural reflex that regulates muscle tone, proving that going weak with laughter is more than a metaphor" (p. 76). Humor helps teachers gain approval from students, reinforces group relationships, and builds trust within schools.

Hill (1998) and others have found that humor is not only fun but also increases retention of subject matter, especially if the humor reinforces the class material. Several empirical studies have documented similar results that teachers with a humor orientation increase student learning (Frymier and Wanzer, 1998; McGhee, 1988; Ramirez, 2002). Moreover, Jennifer (2001) and Garner (2006) found that the use of humor increased memory and meta-cognition in students. There is little question that the use of humor increases the popularity of a speaker, but there is debate over the level of effectiveness in using humor to have students learn.

MAIN FOCUS OF THE CHAPTER

Humor as a Classroom Stress Reliever

Stress causes the release of corticosteroids, which converts to cortisol and ultimately leads to an immunosuppressive effect where the body is more susceptible to disease. Laughter lowers the cortisol levels and improves the body's disease fighting capabilities, while relieving stress. When a person laughs and is joyful, the body secretes endorphins, the brain's natural painkillers, into the body. The connection between stress and high blood pressure, muscle tension, immunosuppression, and many other changes has been known for years. We now have *proof* that laughter creates the opposite effects. It appears to be the perfect antidote for stress (Berk, 2000).

Students appreciate humor, teachers like using it, and there is extant research showing its positive effect. Thompson (2000) notes that people remember information associated with jokes because they have to pay more attention to humorous items in order to *get* the joke. Remember, it is easy to be funny, but the main question is, can students take notes from the material? After all, the point of using humor is to be a more effective teacher. If students cannot take notes from your speech, then you are not appropriately connecting your humor to your actual course content.

Do not expect to be excellent the first time you attempt humor in class. Your comfort level will rise the more times you try humor. Integrating humor is like driving a car: you certainly were not great the first time you got behind the wheel, but it takes real practice, in real situations, to become proficient. Start out with contrasting incongruent ideas or making fun of concepts that do not make sense. These are prime purposes for using humor because it makes individuals feel as though they are not the only ones that do not understand a situation.

Remember:

1. Humor should never be used to embarrass, ridicule, or otherwise harm a student.
2. Humor needs to be kept appropriate to the ability level of the students.
3. Humor should be intellectually challenging.

B. L. Hurren wrote in her 2001 dissertation that when used wisely, humor facilitates attention and motivation for students, improves teacher-student rapport, and makes all subjects more fun. Creating a humor-filled environment helps students pay attention in class and renew their energy. Moreover, several linked studies provide empirical evidence on how using humor engages students, and when students are engaged they learn more (Bandes, 1988; Levine, 2006; Reynolds and Nunn, 1997).

Facts about Humor

Humor is no laughing matter. In fact, humor and laughter has been a serious research topic for more than 50 years. There have been multiple studies on what humor is, how it works, and more recently how humor increases the learning environment. *Laugh Lines for Educators* (2006) by Diane Hodges, is filled with numerous examples of jokes and stories that work well in the classroom. The examples range from elementary school aged students to high school. Other useful resources include *License to Laugh: Humor in the Classroom* by Richard Shade, and *Professors are from Mars Students are from Snickers* by Ronald Berk. Both contain excellent examples of stories and humorous quips that can be used in the classroom. Over the years, researchers have written about the Superiority Theory, Incongruity Theory, and Relief Theory of humor. Each one of these theories provides additional information on the use of humor. The facts listed below should help educators frame their use of laughter in educational environments.

1. Women laugh more than men, but males use more humor in the classroom than females.
2. "You are 30 times more likely to laugh when you're with other people than you are when you're alone" (Morreall, 1983).
3. Laughing is a social function. People will laugh at things not funny if they are in groups (Provine, 2000).
4. Funny and interesting stories related to the course content help engage students in the learning process (Bandes, 1988; Levine, 2006; Reynolds and Nunn, 1997).
5. To be perceived as effective by students, instructors should use humor that adds to the content of education and contributes to the point (Edwards and Gibbony, 1992).
6. In one study, over eighty percent of the executives claimed that lack of humor can be a sign that the company has a moral problem (Scriven and Hefferin, 1998).
7. Children laugh approximately 300 times per day while adults only laugh 17 times (Buckmann, 2010).
8. Individuals who use humor to connect material in class find students remember the information 17% longer and 37% more effectively (Jonas, 2009).

Peter Derks, a professor of psychology traced the pattern of brainwave activity in participants as related to humor. Derks along with a group of scientists at NASA-Langley in Hampton connected subjects to an electroencephalograph (EEG) to measure their brain waves when they laughed. Within four-tenths of a second of exposure to something potentially funny, an electrical wave moved through the cerebral cortex, the largest part of the brain (Marshall, July 2012, http://science.howstuffworks.com/environmental/life/inside-the-mind/laughter.htm).

When someone laughs, information is received in the brain. The amygdala, which is the emotional center of the brain, starts the process. Information flows from the amygdala to the hippocampus and then on to the thalamus. The brain gets even more complex as the information passes on to the left side of the cortex, which is the layer of cells that covers the entire surface of the forebrain, as the words and structure of the joke are analyzed. The frontal lobe then takes over to establish the proper social and emotional responses to the joke. The right hemisphere of the cortex also provides an intellectual analysis, and then information is spread to the sensory processing area of the occipital lobe, and ultimately stimulation of the motor sections evoke physical responses to the joke (Marshall, 2012, http://science.howstuffworks.com/environmental/life/inside-the-mind/laughter.htm).

Interestingly enough, laughter reduces stress hormones such as cortisol and epinephrine. The release of endorphins has also been associated with the reduction of physical pain. Laughter also boosts the number of antibody-producing cells and enhances the effectiveness of T-cells, leading to a stronger immune system. And if that were not enough, laughter is also good for your heart, according to a new University of Maryland Medical Center study (Murray, Retrieved 9/27/2012 at http://www.umm.edu/features/laughter.htm). In other words, laughter is a natural occurrence: it reduces stress, helps relieve pain, makes you live longer, and you can even lose calories the more you laugh. How cool is that?

Now all of this may seem very complex, but here is the bottom line: "Laughter is a mechanism everyone has; laughter is part of universal human vocabulary. There are thousands of languages, hundreds of thousands of dialects, but everyone speaks laughter in pretty much the same way." Babies have the ability to laugh before they ever speak (Provine, 2000). What educators need to realize is that laughter is innate to everyone and can help break down the barriers of race, language, age, and ethnicity among learners. Moreover, laughter is the shortest distance between two people.

What may surprise you even more is researchers estimate that laughing 100 times is equal to 10 minutes on the rowing machine or 15 minutes on an exercise bike. Laughing can be a total body workout! Blood pressure is lowered, and there is an increase in vascular blood flow and in oxygenation of the blood, which further assists healing. Laughter also gives your diaphragm and abdominal, respiratory, facial, leg and back muscles a workout. That's why you often feel exhausted after a long bout of laughter -- you've just had an aerobic workout (Marshall, HowStuffWorks.com).

Laughter not only helps to relieve stress but it also helps people to rid themselves of negative emotions. Research from the American Association of Therapeutic Humor (aath.org) notes that laughter is simply cathartic, which is one reason that people like comedy clubs and funny movies. We want to expel the negative emotions because they simply make us feel bad.

History of Videos in the Classroom

Some people say that bowling alleys had overhead projectors for more than 20 years before they were accepted in the classroom. We may be a little slow in education to make changes: it may even be easier to move a cemetery than change curriculum in schools. Today, bowling alleys still have better technology than most of our schools. This has to change. For more details, see *A Review of the Research Literature on Barriers to the Uptake of ICT by Teachers* (Jones, 2004) and *Enabling Teachers to Make Successful use of ICT* (Scrimshaw, 2004).

Educational Technology

Over the years, the use of instructional technology, especially involving video or film, has changed drastically. For baby-boomers, when you say the word *movie*, images of sitting in a high school class where the teacher showed a two-hour movie split over several classes come to mind. Teachers mistakenly believed that students were learning, while most of the students knew what reaction the videos produced: sleeping. The technology changed as films became videos (VHS, digital) but more importantly the control of the media changed. Bruce and Levin (1997) developed a taxonomy consisting of four levels that explain the use of technology in education, which runs the gamut from media for a) inquiry, b) communication, c) construction, and d) expression. What happened to videos over the years was that the product, the video, decreased in length as the control of the video moved from the hands of producers to teachers and ultimately to students. YouTube is a great example of how students are now developing their own videos almost instantaneously. This new sense of self-directedness needs to be reflected in the classroom. By properly using videos, teachers can reconnect and engage students. In addition, Lampert and Ball (1998) found that multimedia technology and videos in the classroom were effective tools in teacher education programs. Researchers like Stigler and Hiebert (1999); Goodman (2003); Boyatzis (1994); Zimbardo (2001); Christopher, Walter, Marek, and Koenig (2004); Aiex, (1999); and Harper & Rogers, (1999) have conducted empirical studies connecting various aspects of using videos in teaching and found positive effects on the teaching environment.

We all have heard overly ambitious and ill-supported statistics such as students remember 10% of what they hear, 30% of what they see, 50% of what they do, and 70% of what they teach, yet students do learn best when multiple modes of learning are engaged. As noted in our definition, we can represent all of these modes through *humor*, which can be the written, verbal, a picture, a gesture, or a video. Teachers can paint a picture for students through humor using words, pictures, non-verbal cues, body language and so on, using multiple modes of instruction and humor. More importantly, teachers can and should allow students to use humor.

CONCLUSION: PUTTING IT ALL TOGETHER

Videagogy is the use of technology in the form of humorous, short videos as a new teaching pedagogy (video plus pedagogy, pronounced vid-e-ah-go-jee). Videagogy is not simply showing a video in class. Teachers need to prepare and connect video to course content, helping students understand the meaning. We should be cautious using videos or any other educational technology for its own sake. Results from the research of Lawson, Bodle, and MacDonough (2007) indicate that learning associated with videos increases when teachers use guiding or structured questions. Through proper questioning, students are able to construct their own meaning to the video and course content.

Pedagogy is defined as the holistic approach to teaching: the philosophy of teachers, what we teach, how, and why. Research has identified a plethora of successful teaching styles, and now we can add the use of short videos in class to the list. As noted previously, using videos and visual effects is a great way to integrate humor, teaching, and technology. Videos engage students, they increase the level of humor, they connect humor to the content, and videos provide a way to utilize the full capacity of technology in teaching. Videos are not only fun to use for the teacher but are exciting for students who have grown up knowing and using technology.

TV commercials may be some of the best videos to use given that they are usually short and straightforward (thirty seconds to a minute long). YouTube, collegehumor.com/video, and video.google.com, provide three resources filled with excellent video content. One advantage is that these videos tend to run from 30 seconds to only a few minutes, which is long enough to get the point home but short enough not to bore the audience. For videos worth using again and again, we recommend storing a copy of the video on your hard drive, if allowed, and labeling and categorizing each so you can find the right video to match your lesson plans. Remember that the key to learning is to first connect the video to the course material and to then be sure to ask pointed questions for student discussions.

Here are a few examples to Google of videos that work really well.

- Any *South Park* clip where there the topic is PG rated
- Almost anything from TED, which are great videos with a message
- "How Not to Use PowerPoint" where Don McMillan uses funny, exaggerated examples of mistakes people make when using PowerPoint
- "Herding Stray Cats" where western cowboys talk about how to herd cats, a parody of herding cows
- "Caine's Arcade," which is a great story about a young boy who finds a multiplicity of uses for old boxes and which is full of inspiring ideas
- Abbot and Costello explaining how 13 X 7 = 28, a wonderful video for logic

These videos are just a few examples, but the latest viral video on YouTube may not be exactly what you are looking for to support your course material. If you are discussing problem solving in class, the video on *Riding the Escalator* is perfect but not easily found unless you know it is out there. Faculty can show a short, funny video and ask the students to write or discuss how it relates to the content of class. In this way, students construct their own connections to the material and store these connections more effectively in their brain because they personally built meaning and tied course content to what they already knew. Once again, the key is to find short, humorous videos that connect directly to the material being covered in class. Show the video and ask students guided questions to reflect on the material so they can connect the video in their own brain, and construct the meaning of the lesson.

Stealing a page from Dalton Kehoe, a communication-studies professor at York University, we can discuss about a particular concept in class and then ask students to take a week to research the topic and submit a short, humorous video that connects to the material discussed. After watching the videos for appropriateness, faculty can select the top videos to show in class and have students write reflections on each video, asking them to connect the content of the video to the lesson from previous weeks. And then the class may vote on the best one. The *best* video gets a prize, typically from the dollar store. In this way, students laugh and learn. They use constructivist learning theory to develop their own memory and connections to the material, which are stored longer in the brain because of the images and humor used. Moreover, students play an active role in the humor and course content as they strive to win a coveted, $1 PEZ dispenser.

REFERENCES

Aiex, N. (1999). *Mass media use in the classroom* (Bloomington, IN, ERIC Clearinghouse on Reading English and Communication, Eric Digest D-147, ED 436 016).

Bandes, B. (1988). *Humor as a motivation for effective learning in the classroom*. Doctoral dissertation, Columbia Teachers College.

Begley, S. (2000, October 9). The science of laughs. *Newsweek, 136*(15), 75-76.

Berk, R. A. (1996). Student rating of 10 strategies for using humor in college teaching. *Journal on Excellence in College Teaching, 7*(3), 71–92.

Berk, R. A. (2000, Fall). Does humor in course tests reduce anxiety and improve performance? *College Teaching, 48*(4), 151–158. doi:10.1080/87567550009595834

Berk, R. A. (2003). *Professors are from Mars, students are from snickers: How to write and deliver humor in the classroom and in professional presentations.* Dulles, VA: Stylus Publishing.

Boyatzis, C. J. (1994). Using feature films to teach social development. *Teaching of Psychology, 21*, 99–101. doi:10.1207/s15328023top2102_9

Bruce, B. C., & Levin, J. A. (1997). Educational technology: Media for inquiry, communication, construction, and expression. *Journal of Educational Computing Research, 17*, 79–102. doi:10.2190/7HPQ-4F3X-8M8Y-TVCA

Bryant, J., Comisky, P. W., & Zillmann, D. (1979). Teachers' humor in the college classroom. *Communication Education, 28*, 110–128. doi:10.1080/03634527909378339

Buckman, K. H. (2010). *Why did the professor cross the road? How and why college professors intentionally use humor in their teaching.* Dissertation Texas A & M University.

Christopher, A. N., Walter, J. L., Marek, P., & Koenig, C. S. (2004). Using a "new classic" film to teach about stereotyping and prejudice. *Teaching of Psychology, 31*, 199–202.

Davis, J. M., & Farina, A. (1970). Humor appreciation as social communication. *Journal of Personality and Social Psychology, 15*, 175–178. doi:10.1037/h0029202

Edwards, C. M., & Gibboney, E. R. (1992). *The power of humor in the college classroom.* Retrieved from ERIC Document Reproduction Service No. ED 346 535.

Frymier, A. B. & Wanzer, M. B. (Nov 1998). *"Make'em laugh and they will learn": A closer look at the relationship between perceptions of instructors' humor orientation and student learning.* Retrieved from the ERIC Document Reproduction Service No. ED 427 377.

Fullen, M. (2001). *The new meaning of educational change* (3rd ed.). New York, NY: Teachers College and University Press.

Gardner, H. (2006). *Multiple intelligences: New horizons.* New York, NY: Basic Books.

Goodman, J. (1983). How to get more smileage out of your life: Making sense of humor, then selling it. In P. E. McGhec & J. H. Goldstein (Eds.), *Handbook of humor research: Vol. 11. Applied studies* (pp. 1-21). New York, NY: Springer-Verlag.

Goodman, S. (2003). *Teaching youth media: A guide to literacy, video production, and social change.* New York, NY: Teachers College Press.

Gorham, J., & Christophel, D. M. (1990). The relationship of teachers' use of humor in the classroom to immediacy and student learning. *Communication Education, 39*, 46–62. doi:10.1080/03634529009378786

Harper, R. E., & Rogers, R. E. (1999). Using feature films to teach human development concepts. *The Journal of Humanistic Counseling, Education and Development, 38*, 89–97. doi:10.1002/j.2164-490X.1999.tb00067.x

Hill, D. J. (1988). *Humor in the classroom: A handbook for teachers (and other entertainers!).* Springfield, IL: Charles C. Thomas.

Hodges, D. (2006). *Laugh lines for educators.* Thousand Oaks, CA: SAGE Publications.

Hurren, B. L. (2001). *The effects of principals' humor on teachers' job satisfaction.* Dissertation, University of Nevada, Reno.

Jennifer, L. W. (2001). *Funny you should ask, what is the effect of humor on memory and metamemory?* Dissertation, The American University.

Jonas, P. M. (2009). *Laughing and learning: An alternative to shut up and listen.* Lanham, MD: Rowan and Littlefield.

Jones, A. (2004). *A review of the research literature on barriers to the uptake of ICT by teachers*. British Educational Communications and Technology.

Kaplan, R. M., & Pascoe, G. C. (1977). Humorous lectures and humorous examples: Some effects upon comprehension and retention. *Journal of Educational Psychology, 69*, 61–65. doi:10.1037/0022-0663.69.1.61

Lawson, T. J., Bodle, J. H., & MacDonough, T. A. (2007). Techniques for increasing student learning from educational videos: Notes versus guiding questions. *Teaching of Psychology, 34*(2), 90–93. doi:10.1080/00986280701291309

Levine, J. (Ed.). (2006). *Motivation in humor*. New Brunswick, NJ: Transaction Publishers.

Marshall, B. (April 2000). *"How laughter works" 01*. HowStuffWorks.com. Retrieved July 17, 2012, at http://science.howstuffworks.com/environmental/life/inside-the-mind/laughter.htm

McGhee, P. E. (1988). Introduction: Recent developments in humor research. *Journal of Children in Contemporary Society, 20*(1-2), 1–12. doi:10.1300/J274v20n01_01

Meyer, J. (1990). Ronald Reagan and humor: A politician's velvet weapon. *Communication Studies, 41*(1), 76–88. doi:10.1080/10510979009368289

Morreall, J. (1983). *Taking laughter seriously*. New York, NY: State University of New York Press.

Murray, M. (2012). *Laughter is the "best medicine" for your heart*. Retrieved September 27, 2012, at http://www.umm.edu/features/laughter.htm

Provine, R. (2000). *Laughter: A scientific investigation*. New York, NY: Penguin Books.

Ramirez, C. M. (2002). What is the impact of humor, message content and the leader's gender on perceptions of credibility of a leader? *Dissertation Abstracts International, 63*(05), 1864. (UMI No. 3053070).

Reynolds, K. C., & Nunn, C. E. (1997). *Engaging classrooms: Student participation and the instructional factors that shape it*. ASHE Annual meeting paper on 11/6-9/97.

Scriven, J., & Hefferin, L. (1998, February). Humor: The "witting" edge in business. *Business Education Forum*, 13–15.

Shade, R. A. (1996). *License to laugh: Humor in the classroom*. Westport, CT: Teacher Ideas Press.

Sorell, W. (1972). *The facets of comedy*. New York, NY: Grosset and Dunlap.

Stigler, J., & Hiebert, J. (1999). *The teaching gap: Best ideas from the world's teachers for improving education in the classroom*. New York, NY: Free Press.

Thompson, J. L. (2000). Funny you should ask, what is the effect of humor on memory and metamemory? (Doctoral Dissertation, American University). *Dissertation Abstracts International, 61*(8-B), 4442. (UMI 9983671)

Wandersee, J. H. (1982). Humor as a teaching strategy. *The American Biology Teacher, 44*, 212–218. doi:10.2307/4447475

Wilhelmsson, L. (n.d.). *The healing power of humor*. Retrieved September 27, 2012, from http://www.vitalchristianity.org/docs/New%20Articles/Humor-Healing2.pdf

Zimbardo, P. (2001). The power of the situation. [Video program No. 19] In *WGBH Boston (Producer), Discovery psychology: Updated edition*. South Burlington, VT: Annenberg/CPB.

KEY TERMS AND DEFINITIONS

Amygdala: The one of the four basal ganglia in each cerebral hemisphere that is part of the limbic system and consists of an almond-shaped mass of gray matter in the anterior extremity of the temporal lobe (http://www.merriam-webster.com/dictionary/amygdala?show=0&t=1349799034).

Humor: Flows within us and courses through us with the ability to see what is incongruous in life—the juxtaposition of the expected and the surprising, the sublime and the ridiculous.

Laughter: Is the quintessential human social signal. It solidifies relationships and pulls people into the fold as it helps make connections between individuals (Provine, 2000).

Stress: Is physical, chemical, or emotional concept that has an effect on the body and/or mental tension.

Videagogy: Practical components of using technology in the form of humorous, short videos as a new teaching technique, (videos + pedagogy = videagogy).

Section 4
Research-Based Best Practices

Chapter 11
Using Video and Web Conferencing Tools to Support Online Learning

Paula Jones
Eastern Kentucky University, USA

Fred Kolloff
Eastern Kentucky University, USA

MaryAnn Kolloff
Eastern Kentucky University, USA

ABSTRACT

This chapter examines effective methods for using video and web conferencing tools to support online learning. The authors discuss the concept of presence, how web conferencing can be used to support presence in online courses, and why it is important to do so. Because of the impact web conferencing can have in learning, this chapter explores a variety of teaching roles that best leverage these conferencing tools. The chapter includes information on various web conferencing software programs (paid and open source). Best practices for using web conferencing tools in online learning are also explored.

INTRODUCTION

Without physically meeting students, faculty may think it difficult, if not impossible, to provide a similar classroom experience online as in a face-to-face class, with a goal to achieve similar learning. Miller and Williamson (2008) assert that excellence in distance education courses depends in part on the instructor's subject and technical expertise but also on the instructor's willingness, both psychologically and emotionally, to acknowledge and accept differences between distance education and traditional instruction.

Faculty members can find it difficult to establish an instructional relationship with students in an online learning environment. Conrad and Donaldson (2004) state that planning for the learner's involvement and engagement is vital for success:

DOI: 10.4018/978-1-4666-3962-1.ch011

The involvement of the learner in the course, whether one calls it interaction, engagement, or building community, is critical if an online course is to be more than a lecture-oriented course in which interaction is primarily between the learner and the content or the learner and the instructor. (p. 6)

Therefore, the challenge in planning and designing online courses is in planning for interactions and *humanizing* the online learning experience. Many things change when instruction and communication are moved from a face-to-face classroom setting into an online course delivery system. Humanizing the online learning environment increases the student's comfort level and reduces the psychological distance between the instructors and students (DuCharme-Hansen & Dupin-Bryant, 2005).

Many of the challenges associated with delivering instruction via a distance can be overcome through the use of video or web conferencing. Video and web conferencing tools provide an opportunity for the instructor and students to have immediate access through synchronous communications (interaction among faculty and students occurring at the same time albeit from different locations).

Web conferencing also allows the instructor to offer immediate student support in learning content, progressing with assignments, and accessing technology. Certainly, this immediacy of information has the potential to impact the delivery of an online course. Along with immediacy behaviors (i.e., behaviors that portray a sense of closeness), web conferencing tools can help humanize the course through fostering social presence, teaching presence, and cognitive presence.

Video and web conferencing are already improving distance education by offering various degrees of support for online learning. The objective of this chapter is to identify effective methods for employing video and web conferencing tools to improve student learning in an online course.

Best practices to consider when using these tools are outlined. Various web conferencing tools are described. Recommendations for future research are provided, as well.

BACKGROUND

Online learning generally involves two types of interaction: interaction with content and interpersonal interaction among the instructor and students (Berge, 1995). Both types of interaction are related to *humanizing* the online learning environment. Humanizing the course can be accomplished using *immediacy behaviors*, which reduce the perceived distance between the teacher and the student (Anderson, 1979, Baker 2010).

Social psychologist Albert Mehrabian has been credited with defining the concept of immediacy in terms of his principle of immediacy. Mehrabian shared that people are drawn towards persons or things they like, respect or simply prefer to be involved with (1971). In an effort to support learning in an online environment, it is important to plan for interactions and methods of communication. It is also important to remove any barriers that might prevent students from engaging with the instructor. By conveying warmth and support, immediacy behavior increases the closeness or the appearance of closeness between teacher and student through behaviors such as encouraging communications and student input, the use of humor, self-disclosure, and calling students by name (Baker, 2010).

By humanizing the course and planning for immediacy, the instructor not only influences the learner's sense of belonging, but also establishes *presence*, including social, teacher, and cognitive presence. Presence creates an environment where the learner feels part of a learning community.

Humanization may include methods of communications, audio files, pictures or video clips, and instructions on where to post or "talk" with others involved in the course. The ultimate goal in humanizing a course is to create a sense of closeness between students and their instructor.

Establishing *presence* in an online course is vital in order to offer a supportive learning environment for students. Garrison, Anderson and Archer (2000) developed a conceptual model of online learning that is referred to as the "community of inquiry" model. In this model, Garrison, Anderson and Archer share three components associated with varying types of presence in order to facilitate meaningful learning. The two components that relate most closely to web conferencing are *social presence* and *teacher presence*.

Social presence creates a supportive environment where students feel comfortable and safe in expressing their ideas in a collaborative context. Online learning is often more solitary, and students report that they feel somewhat disconnected from the class (Rowntree, 2000). Even with two-way communication, "interactions between individuals at the host and remote sites are more constrained and less fluid than those taking place in the same room." (Morrison, Ross, & Kemp, 2007) The absence of social presence leads to an inability to express disagreements, share viewpoints, explore differences, and accept support and confirmation from peers and teacher.

Teaching presence is critical in online courses because this type of presence helps the learner relate to the person who serves as the subject matter expert. Establishing teacher presence in a course can help to encourage and reassure students as they call on the instructor for guidance and support throughout the learning experience. According to Anderson (2004) there are three roles involved in establishing teaching presence in an online course. First is the role in developing and designing the online course. The second role is in dialogue facilitation between students and instructor. The third role involves providing expertise through a variety of forms of direct instruction. All of these roles have the potential

of being supported through the use of video and web conferencing tools.

Educators often strive to provide an equivalent instructional experience for students whether they are meeting face-to-face or online. Smaldino, Lowther and Russell (2012) identified three core functions that an instructional telecommunication system must include in order to make online learning more comparable to face-to-face instruction. These functions include the following.

- Information presentation
- Practice with feedback
- Access to learning resources

Video or web conferencing tools improve the functionality of an instructional telecommunication system by making especially these first two functions possible. Video and web conferencing tools also influence instructor roles. Bonk, Kirkley, Hara, and Dennen (2001) describe the multiple roles of online instructors in four dimensions: (1) pedagogical, (2) social, (3) managerial, and (4) technical. The pedagogical role involves the instructor serving as the content expert and teacher for the course. The social role includes serving as a moderator and social guide. In the managerial role, the instructor serves as the overseer and manager of the course site. Finally, in the technical role, the instructor either offers technical support or resources for tech support. Because of the real time, immediate experience involved with web conferencing tools, video and web conferencing have the potential to impact each of these roles.

Establishing presence, providing communication opportunities, and planning for interactivity in an online course or through online instructional sessions are all important steps in helping the learner feel comfortable in the learning environment. Therefore, course developers need to seek ways of initiating and fostering instructional relationships. The practical challenge is to design and plan for learning activities and opportunities that provide the right balance of collaboration, communication, and feedback. Video and web conferencing are two tools that can be used to achieve this balance in an online course.

MAIN FOCUS OF THE CHAPTER

Overview of Web Conferencing and Video Conferencing

In order to teach effectively using video and web conferencing tools, faculty members would benefit from learning more about the various tools and resources currently available. In addition, more information is needed regarding the best teaching practices associated with teaching in virtual classrooms. Educators should understand the various roles they will fulfill and how the roles may change while using conferencing tools in a virtual classroom. Roles may include serving as the teacher, the moderator, a participant, as well as the tech support for students during the course.

There are distinct differences among web conferencing and video conferencing. Web conferencing allows participants to communicate in real time (Schroeder, 2009). In order to participate in in a web conference, the participants need access to the Internet and perhaps a microphone or web cam, which are optional in some cases. Web conferencing systems can accommodate synchronous and asynchronous communications since the sessions can be recorded and viewed at a later date. Web conferencing can offer a rich learning environment and simulates the face-to-face experience (Forman and Jenkins, 2005).

Video conferencing, also known as Interactive Television (ITV), requires that participants physically travel to a specific location to use the cameras and equipment setup to directly communicate with similar equipment at another location (Schroeder, 2009). Both web conferencing and video conferencing are generally planned with two-way communication in mind (i.e., participants are active in the meeting session).

Web Conferencing

Web conferencing, also known as virtual classrooms, is growing in popularity in educational settings. Web conferencing can provide benefits in most educational environments. There are several reasons why educators would want to explore using web conferencing in their online or web-supported courses. First, according to Schroeder (2009), web conferencing allows students who cannot attend face-to-face class meetings to participate in synchronous class meetings and therefore have immediate access to both class members and the instructor. Second, web conferencing can serve as a tool for supporting both *teacher presence and social presence* in an online course. Garrison and Archer (2003) describe teacher and social presence as the learner's sense of being in and part of an online or distant learning experience that is similar to a real, face-to-face experience. Finally, web conferencing allows instructors to invite professionals in the field to participate in live class meetings, allowing students to learn first-hand from experts.

Web conferencing offers many tools or resources related to methods of communicating and teaching including two-way audio, video, text-based chat, interactive whiteboards, screen sharing, presentation delivery, and feedback tools (such as surveys, polls or self-check quizzes). With these new tools and resources, faculty members and students need to be introduced to effective methods of communicating in web conference meetings and also need to be aware of web etiquette.

Web conferencing and synchronous learning have a specific place in online learning. In fact, web conferencing is recognized as a highly collaborative and social learning environment. Web conferencing can support online pedagogy in a number of ways. First, web conferencing provides tools that support communication between the student and the instructor, enabling presence to be established and maintained throughout the course. Second, web conferencing provides a didactic communication between two or more users through opportunities to interact and offer feedback on topics relevant to the course. Third, web conferencing allows students to talk through issues or questions they face in the learning process. Finally, the web conference sessions offer flexibility in supporting an anytime, anywhere learning environment that can be recorded for students to review as needed.

Video Conferencing

Video conferencing focuses on teacher presence and two-way audio and video collaboration among individuals or groups. The most familiar video conferencing situation places the user in a group with other users at an assigned location – probably a classroom or conference room outfitted with remotely controlled cameras and one or more individual student microphones. In this arrangement, the instructor is usually the central visual element. The instructor has the use of a visual presenter or document camera – a small camera focused on graphics, photos, and printed or hand-written materials. A computer is included in the system for web- or locally-generated presentation materials. Often two visual displays are available: one for students to see the presenter and one for any computer or document materials. Users in similar rooms are either located at the original site with the instructor or are able to conference with the original site using video and audio. These systems (e.g., Polycom, Tandberg) are controlled by calling into a conference bridge or multipoint control unit (MCU) and may be owned and operated by the host facility. There is the capability of extending a video conferencing room to an individual user via software (e.g., Cisco's Jabber) so that the single user can have the same features as the equipped classroom, therefore taking advantage

of the group experience without having to travel to an individual room. However, in this example, a single user absorbs the same technical resource as a full room (one port on the MCU) and therefore may not be considered cost-effective.

Web conferencing, on the other hand, has the user in their preferred location without placement being dictated. An individual's desktop or laptop computer, tablet, or smartphone allows the user access. The user is connected to other users using web-based services (e.g. WebEx, GoTo Meeting, AnyMeeting, Adobe Connect, Skype). A web cam, audio devices, as well as computer software (e.g., word processing, spreadsheet) may be integrated into the conference. Many of these conferencing programs come with whiteboard, text-based chat, user signaling devices, private messaging, polling, preview, group work spaces, and controls for the instructor or instructor-delegated students.

Example of Web Conferencing with WebEx in a Library Science Course

In one fully online library science course, the web conferencing program WebEx was used (see Figures 1 through 5). In addition to the use of Blackboard™ as the course management system, an interactive video conference was held between students and the instructor once each week during the term.

The first web conferencing session provided an opportunity for an ice-breaker session with students. Asking the students to share their computer screens with their personal photos familiarizes students with the technology of video conferencing and prepares them for student-to-student discussion and question and answer sessions.

Guest speakers were invited to share with students via various web conferencing sessions. In Figure 4, note that students were able to view the speaker and listen to the information the guest speaker shared as they displayed images for students to view. This type of delivery proved to be engaging to students and allowed students to interact directly with the guest speaker. With per-

Figure 1. Demo of Web Conference Session A. An initial web conferencing session is used to review and respond to questions students posed in the first discussion board. Using course questions that were developed and posted by students in the first session demonstrates the student-centered versus teacher-centered expectation for the course.

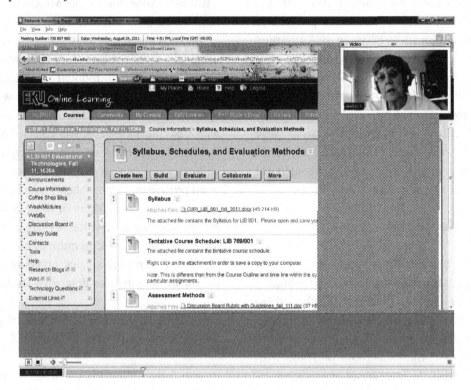

mission, the session was recorded for students to access and review, as needed after the session ended.

In addition, the course included presentation and discussion literature as well as the introduction and practice with certain computer software. With continued practice of sharing their computer screens throughout the course, the instructor was able to guide them through any specific software technical problems.

Sharing their screens with all students as well as the instructor to diagnose problems shifts the power from the teacher to the students as all participate. The final learning performance of the course is a presentation given by each student during a web conferencing session.

The student's overall learning performance was demonstrated within the presentation. Evaluation occurred through various means of self-reflection using a scoring guide. A statement of their strengths and identification of areas for continued professional growth was also included. The instructor contributed to the scoring guide and self-reflection through added observations. This allowed the student to own the learning and, most of all, allowed each to develop critical questions base on the content.

Web Conferencing Services and Resources

There are numerous web conferencing resources. However, each should be considered carefully in order to ensure the system selected meets the expectations and requirements of the teachers who plan to use them. Below is a brief list of some of the most popular free or low-cost web conferencing resources.

Figure 2. Demo of Web Conference Session B. An ice breaker is held via web conferencing as the first student-centered class experience. The screenshot shows a student sharing personal pictures of family, vacations, and so on as a means of introducing herself to other class members. This gives students experience in student-student sharing, questioning, and discussing.

Figure 3. Demo of Web Conference Session C. Guest speaker presents content and interacts with students concerning the process of reading graphic novels during this web conferencing session.

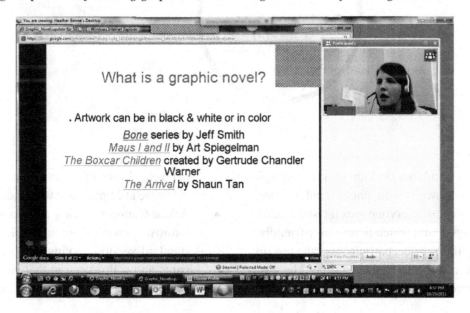

Figure 4. Demo of Web Conference Session D. Instructor interacts with one or more students based on their questions for the assigned group presentations.

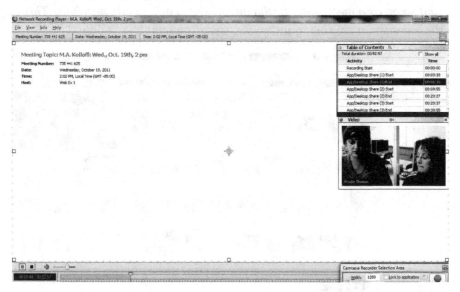

Figure 5. Demo of Web Conference Session E. A student group's course project is presented as a Prezi product and shared with other class members in a web conference.

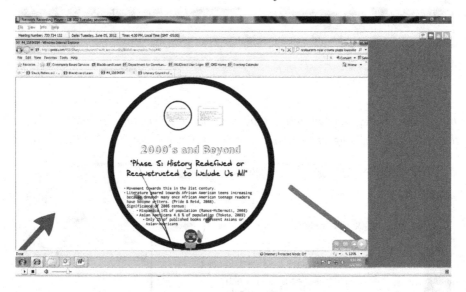

- WebEx combines desktop sharing through a web browser with phone conferencing and video, so everyone sees the same thing while you talk, which is very user-friendly. Using this service, participants can view up to seven webcam feeds at a time. The cost is approximately $500-$600 per license,

per year. More information on WebEx is available at http://www.webex.com/.

- Adobe Connect is fairly easy to use and an intuitive web conferencing tool. There is a standard version serving up to 15 participants and a Pro version that serves more. Adobe Connect and Adobe Connect Pro both include an array of useful features that support the online meeting. Sharing desktops is available. Cost is approximately $500-$600 per license, per year. More information on Adobe Connect is available at http://www.adobe.com/.

- AnyMeeting, formerly known as *Freebinar,* has expanded to offer web conferences for up to 200 participants while keeping the basic package free. The service includes screen sharing, application sharing and text conferences on the side. The services available in AnyMeeting are similar to what is available in WebEx. Though the web conferencing service is free, it is supported by advertising. Information about AnyMeeting is available at http://www.anymeeting.com/.

- Skype is a software application that allows for computer-to-computer voice or video calls over the internet. Computer-to-computer calls and screen sharing are currently free. Skype does charge for calling a cellphone or landline. Skype also has fees associated with group screen sharing. More information about Skype services is available at http://www.skype.com.

Both video and web conference meetings can be recorded for future access by the participant. Due to technological advances, web conferencing continues to grow in use. This type of technology can have a significant impact on training and learning in an online environment.

With the advent of social media, students have become accustomed to a single device such as a smart phone or tablet serving their communication needs and requirements. Therefore, it is expected that those same devices, or something similar, will serve students in their need for educational collaboration. Tablet and smart phone devices will increasingly be served as the computing cloud allows for mobility and collaboration anywhere.

There are several areas of controversy with regard to web and video conferencing because of the changes in the traditional approach of instruction. Most prominent is the claim that the instructor is not available as in a traditional class. Some critics would challenge the degree to which students are willing to contribute or interact in the open and "impersonal" online format rather than in the confines of the traditional classroom. Also, students are expected to be self-directed, a condition that they may not be prepared to meet. Technical matters of equipment, software, and necessary training are problematic.

EFFECTIVE STRATEGIES AND APPROACHES

Issues, Controversies, Problems

According to Smaldino, Lowther, and Russell (2012), student learning is the primary focus of education, whether the education is received in person or from a distance. When planning a lesson, instructional strategies must be designed and in place in order for learning to be accomplished. The instructional strategies generally fall into one of two categories: teacher-centered strategies or student-centered strategies. Often students express a preference for a mixture of student-centered and teacher-centered strategies. Students expect the teacher to add significant material not otherwise available and furnish structure to the session (Ko and Rossen, 2010). The teacher plays a vital role in designing both strategies.

Teacher-Centered Learning Environments and Web Conferencing

Teacher-centered strategies include those instructional strategies directed by the teacher. Smaldino (2012) explains that teacher-centered strategies may include instructional activities performed by the teacher, such as presentations, demonstrations, and tutorials. As the expert and authority of the content, the teacher dictates the design and structure of the teacher-centered learning environment.

In a teacher-centered learning environment, assignments are often based on memorizing basic steps or foundational information. Sometimes teacher-centered strategies allow students to practice activities that foster deeper learning of concepts and skills. Teacher-centered strategies can also engage students in higher-order thinking activities such as watching a demonstration of an experiment involving chemicals or participating in an interview of an expert (Smaldino, et al., 2012). Assessment in a teacher-centered learning environment occurs through the submission of individual assignments, quizzes, and exams.

In an online classroom, the role of a traditional classroom teacher still exists albeit in a virtual environment using a course management system such as Blackboard™. Teacher-centered strategies are quite often needed to fill this role in a web-based learning environment. In fact, this model of instruction is relatively easy to duplicate in an online learning environment. The teacher creates the instructional information, learning activities, and assignments via the course management system. Communication opportunities could be available through the use of threaded discussions. Student work can be evaluated and individual feedback posted via the online grade book available through a course management system.

Since learning occurs through the use of a course management system and possibly several other technological resources, it would be important for both the teacher and student to have solid technology skills to work within the online learning environment.

Web conferencing tools can have a positive impact on teacher-centered learning environments. With the traditional role of teacher-centered learning environments, use of web conferencing can play a vital role in directing and connecting the student to the content. Web conferencing can be used to clarify important central ideas within the structure of the course management system. For example, the teacher can arrange web conferences to demonstrate the organization and structure of course content within the course management system.

Student-Centered Web Conferencing

Within student-centered learning environments, the teacher's role is to design the learning experience in such a way that they become a *facilitator* rather than a teacher-centered lecturer. In student-centered learning environments, students are seen as capable learners, and the responsibility of learning is passed back to the student (Weimer, 2002).

Designing student-centered learning environments, either in a face-to-face setting or as a web-based course, requires a paradigm shift from traditional teaching methods by focusing on how students learn versus how teachers teach (Bilimoria & Wheeler, 1995). Weimer (2002) explains that in student-centered teaching, student learning is the focus of the class. Student-centered teaching strategies can be the best way to support student learning. Examples of student-centered strategies include discussions, discovery lessons, and problem solving activities (Smaldino, et al., 2012). One of the major challenges of the student-centered learning environment is that it defies the students' schema of the traditional teacher's role to lecture and provide resources and materials (Holden & Schmit, 2002). Weimer (2002) explains that, in order to be student-centered, instructional practice needs to change in five key areas: the balance of power, the function of content, the role of the teacher, the responsibility for learning, and the purpose and processes of evaluation.

Student-centered learning environments are described as students learning in a more active, collaborative environment with decreasing dependence on the teacher. The design of the student-centered learning environment should be built around constructive learning theories, inquiry-based learning, and the development of informed, critical and creative thinkers. In a student-centered learning environment, student dialogue focuses on the students' perception and interpretation of the assignments. Students share their interpretation of the assignment and the text or other resources while discussing various points of view. This student-centered learning environment is powered by information gathering, is driven by data, and is useful explaining how the student arrived at a particular interpretation. The learning environment allows students to express their own ideas which are based on their previous background knowledge and schema of the content as well as the gathering of new information, data, and different points of view from student-student and students-teacher interaction. The teacher's responsibility is to re-direct students away from particular misconceptions and provide additional resources.

Furthermore, within student-centered learning environments, students' questions and answers concerning the text are valued since they are based on students' current schema of the content. According to Holden and Schmidt (2002), within student-centered learning environments the students must explore multiple and even contradictory perspectives of a text resource. This corresponds with the critical thinking procedures of examining information from another perspective and the complexities of the issue or problem. When exploring various perspectives and difficulties of a problem, students are able to develop intellectually through internalizing the knowledge, skills, or abilities needed to work within a global learning and work environment.

Within the web-based learning environment, one of the most essential best practices includes preparing content ahead of time. In the student-center learning environment, the teachers' role includes preparing questions to focus students' learning on their readings and interpretations of

the text. These interpretations are posted as an initial response to the reading. Student-centered discussions are then required for the purpose of examining multiple points of view. It is assumed that, in many web-learning environments, discussion boards are an essential means of communication for the purpose of engaging student-student interaction.

It is then the teacher's responsibility to read the discussion boards and prepare for web conference sessions, which extend and elaborate on students' discussions. Based on the students' interpretations of the text, reading material, or activity, the teacher prepares questions to challenge students' misconceptions and stimulate their analytical and evaluation skills relating to various points of view, difficulty of the problem or issue, inferences relating to the problem or issue, and the central idea within the content. Engagement can take place through using the audio function of the web conferencing software or through such features as interactive whiteboard, text chat, raising hands.

Often students express a preference for a mixture of student-centered and teacher-centered strategies to be included in their learning experiences. Students expect the teacher to add significant material not otherwise available via a text book or online resource. In addition, students anticipate the teacher of the class to furnish structure to the session (Ko and Rossen, 2010).

From the information presented in this chapter, it is clear that there are several reasons to support using web conferencing sessions in online courses. There are needs that can be addressed through the use of web conferencing for both the instructor and for the learner as well. However, there are drawbacks associated with using web conferencing tools that should be considered and counterbalanced in regards to utilizing web conferencing in online courses.

Drawbacks to Web Conferencing

As noted above, offering web conferences and other types of synchronous communication sessions in an online class can be beneficial in regards to community building and the development of social and teaching presences. However, including web conference sessions in online courses has some drawbacks. Knapczyk, Chapman, Kelly, and Lu (2002) recognized that without a traditional face-to-face instructor, students in a collaborative teacher education program expressed anxiety with the video conferencing environment due to the difference in presentation format, the different roles required of the learners, and new technology skills. These and other drawbacks need to be considered and counterbalanced when supporting web conferences with students.

- There may be a learning curve in using web conferencing tools in the beginning for both the host and the participants.
- Continued tech support may be needed as students utilize the services throughout the course.
- Finding a common time for a web-based class meeting, particularly if students are spread over multiple time zones, could be challenging.
- Ensuring faculty and student hardware requirements, including webcams and headsets, are met. Some laptops have built-in cameras and microphones, but they tend to pick up a lot of extraneous noise.
- Bandwidth limitations of the presenter can cause interruptions in the conference video stream.
- Cost of equipment, software and service subscription needs to be evaluated.
- Planning for accessibility can be challenging, depending on the needs of students participating in the web conference session.
- Extensive planning may be necessary to ensure a continuous flow of information (i.e., using time well) and to keep the meeting moving along and on topic.

- As the number of participants rise, coordinating the presentation of information and methods of collaboration will become increasingly complex. Hosting a web conferencing with twelve students is a much different experience to conferencing with fifty.

Solutions and Recommendations

Preparation is important when planning one's first video or web conference. Web conferencing tools will vary, so the facilitator should plan to conduct a practice session or two in preparation to host and facilitate the session. Based on years of experience in conducting web conference sessions, the following best practices will ensure a smooth conferencing experience centered on the learners.

1. Prepare a focus for the conference.
2. Outline expectations of students by explaining their self-directed and interactive roles.
3. Prepare and upload all content items well before the conference, and arrive early to launch content. This will make the class flow more easily. Presentation slides, if used, should be planned to *guide* the information. Presenters should avoid reading slides to participants and keep slide transitions and animations to a minimum for web conferencing sessions.
4. Plan a practice session using the web conferencing tools and run through prepared content. This will help ensure the presenter has enough information planned, including opportunities for interaction and feedback. In addition, by offering a separate practice session with learners, any tech issues could be addressed before the true session actually begins.
5. If possible, have an assistant on hand to deal with issues students might have and to help facilitate the session. This lets the presenter focus on delivery, which is espe-

cially important during the first couple of web conferencing sessions.

6. Immediately before the session, complete this checklist.

   a. Plan for accessibility needs. Well before the first session, ask participants if they have assistive needs so that the session can be designed to accommodate these needs.

   b. Prepare participants and explain the most important student interaction features such as hand raising, feedback, and text chat at the beginning of the session. A whiteboard or slide should also contain a phone number for technical support, if possible. Consider asking participants to mute their microphones, if needed.

   c. Log in 15-20 minutes early. As students join, greet them; pass them the floor, and do a communications check.

   d. Have options for dealing with problems students might encounter in case these problems prevent them from participating in the live session. If possible, provide phone number to call if they are having technical difficulties.

   e. Record the session, so participants who were unable to participate in the live session can view it later. Be sure to let the participants know the session will be recorded and that they too can access the recording to review as needed.

   f. Provide audio help or guidelines to troubleshoot audio problems (i.e., test audio) before the session begins.

7. During the session, facilitators of the web conference should:

   a. Plan to engage students by requiring student feedback or interactions every few minutes (through chat, raising hands, questions and answers, participate in polls, or something similar).

   b. Be prepared to pass the microphone to students or other presenters during the session. Planning to pass the microphone over to other attendees encourages student participation and helps keep participants focused on information shared during the session.

   c. Plan for schedule breaks during the session. This is especially true if the session is scheduled to last more than 30-45 minutes. It is a good practice to schedule a 5-10 minute break about mid-way through the session, if possible.

   d. Maintain the presentation area and the screenshots shared with participants. Be sure to close content items when completed to help reduce clutter from the participant's view.

   e. Deliver *lecture* material in short segments rather than a traditional classroom format.

   f. Speak in a conversational, one-on-one tone with students. Most students are participating in the conference by themselves and not sitting with classmates.

   g. Keep students actively involved by asking students by name for participation.

   h. Utilize panels, debates, exercises, quiz formats, role playing, polls among class members, and guest experts for variety.

   i. Allow students to lead a conference session.

   j. Standardize a student question and response protocol.

   k. Summarize the discussion at the end of the conference.

FUTURE RESEARCH DIRECTIONS

There is some indication to show that students in a group receiving synchronous video conferencing with the instructor achieved at a higher grade level than a students who were not communicating via video conferencing (Han, 2011). Further research in the area of teacher presence via video conferencing and the effects on achievement and student satisfaction is needed. Questions arise as to group size, feedback, and peer critiques, as well as the effects of differing balances of teacher-centered vs. student-centered approaches in web conferencing events.

Web conferencing provides a way for individuals and group of students to bridge distances and communicate with each other in productive ways. One of the key benefits of web conferencing sessions is in the ability to record each session for future use. This opportunity for learners to be able to review recorded sessions at a later date, including faculty and student interactions, provides flexibility not generally associated with face-to-face instruction.

Another benefit includes the in-session tools permitting the instructor to engage learners and monitor learner progression. Being able to pass the microphone to students and allow them to share screens enables immediate feedback on content, in course navigation, or with technical support. Instant feedback tools such as chat windows, polls, and surveys encourage learner engagement throughout the session. These benefits need to be researched further to document impact on learning.

The use of web conferencing will most certainly continue to grow in web-based courses. Web conferencing is expected to add more resources and services customized to serve specific groups or specialized needs. Custom meeting pods that integrate specific software and services to accommodate individual classes are already available through some web conferencing resources.

Web conference providers anticipate offering more integration with learning management systems in the future. As web conferencing services and customization opportunities increase, it is anticipated that the demand for these services will increase, as well. With new web conferencing tools and features, more research will be needed.

Comparison of video conferencing tools and strategies to promote student engagement is necessary to advance progress in this area. A model of professional development for faculty members is critical and would certainly need to follow.

CONCLUSION

Teachers face challenges when moving a course from a face-to-face setting to an online environment. Providing a similar learning experience is difficult. With the demand for online courses and a goal of supporting online learners through in-depth communication and real-time instruction, video and web conferencing should continue evolving. As new or enhanced technologies become available, demands for these services are expected to grow. Conferencing has some limitations, but for many faculty the overall benefits outweigh any drawbacks. As long as the cost associated with these services remains at manageable levels, the growth pattern for video and web conferencing will continue to rise.

As Miller and Williamson (2008) suggest, excellence in distance education depends in part on the instructor's subject and technical expertise and on their willingness to accept differences between distance education and traditional instruction. Utilizing the right technology for the purpose at hand is important for both the instructor and the student. Technology should not give way to the latest flashy device or tool; instead, technology should be utilized only when it serves a specific purpose and becomes a partner in the learning process.

Advances in mobile and cloud computing have extended the reach and convenience of courses offered through distance education programs. Frequent use of social media has encouraged the use of mobile devices for instant communication with others. The *anytime, anywhere* claim of distance education has become truer than previously thought possible. Student preferences are quickly advancing toward mobile devices such as smartphones and tablets and away from ball-and-chain options such as desktop or laptop computers, neither of which are easy to locate or transport. Mobile device presents convenient access to course material during long or short free periods, and students will soon expect to see mobile web conferencing options.

With today's social networking movement and the technology to communicate, share, and learn *anywhere, anytime*, web conferencing will continue impacting how educators extend their classrooms to support student learning.

REFERENCES

Andersen, J. (1979). Teacher immediacy as a predictor of teaching effectiveness. In Nimmo, D. (Ed.), *Communication yearbook, 3* (pp. 543–559). New Brunswick, NJ: Transaction Books.

Anderson, T. (2004). Theory and practice of online learning. In T. Anderson & F. Elloumi (Eds.), *Teaching in an online learning context*. Retrieved from http://cde.athabascau.ca/online_book/

Baker, C. (2010). The impact of instructor immediacy and presence for online student affective learning, cognition, and motivation. *Journal of Educators Online, 7*(1). Retrieved from http://www.thejeo.com/Archives/Volume7Number1/BakerPaper.pdf

Berge, Z. (1995). The role of the online instructor/facilitator. *Educational Technology, 35*(1), 22–30.

Bilimoria, D., & Wheeler, J. (1995). Learning-centered education: A guide to resources and implementation. *Journal of Management Education, 29*(3), 402–428.

Bonk, C., Kirkley, J., Hara, N., & Dennen, N. (2001). Finding the instructor in post-secondary online learning: Pedagogical, social, managerial, and technological locations. In Stephenson, J. (Ed.), *Teaching and learning online: New pedagogies for new technologies* (pp. 76–97). London, UK: Kogan Page.

Conrad, R., & Donaldson, J. (2004). *Engaging the online learner, activities and resources for creative instruction*. San Francisco, CA: Jossey-Bass.

DuCharme-Hansen, R., & Dupin-Bryant, P. (2005). Course planning for online adult learners. *TechTrends, 49*(2), 31–39. doi:10.1007/BF02773969

Fenton, C., & Watkins, B. (2010). *Communication is key. Fluency in Distance Learning* (p. 240). Charlotte, NC: Information Age Publishing, Inc.

Foreman, J., & Jenkins, R. (2005). Full-featured web conferencing systems. *Innovate: Journal of Online Education, 1*(4). Retrieved from http://www.webcitation.org/ 5YbMitWTt

Garrison, D., & Archer, W. (2003). A community of inquiry framework for online learning. In Moore, M. (Ed.), *Handbook of distance education*. New York, NY: Erlbaum.

Garrison, D. R., Anderson, T., & Archer, W. (2000). Critical thinking in text-based environment: Computer conferencing in higher education. *The Internet and Higher Education, 2*(2), 87–105. doi:10.1016/S1096-7516(00)00016-6

Han, H. (2011, October). *Video-casting, social presence, interactions, and learning achievement in synchronous online learning*. Paper presented at the World Conference on E-Learning in Corporate, Government, Healthcare, and Higher Education 2011, Chesapeake, VA. Retrieved from http://www.editlib.org/p/38785

Holden, J., & Schmidt, J. S. (2002). Inquiry and the literary text: Constructing discussions in the English classroom. [Reading, English and Communication Clearinghouse.]. *Urbana (Caracas, Venezuela)*, IL.

Knapezyk, D., Chapman, C., Kelly, M., & Lu, Li-Fen (2002). *Using web-based conferencing to promote interactivity and collaboration in teacher preparation*. Society for Information Technology and Teacher Education International Conference (SITE).

Ko, S., & Rossen, S. (2010). *Teaching online: A practical guide* (3rd ed.). New York, NY: Routledge.

Mehrabian, A. (1971). *Silent messages*. Belmont, CA: Wadsworth Publishing Company.

Miller, G., & Williamson, L. (2009). *Best practices for teaching via interactive video conferencing technology: A review of the literature*. Society for Information Technology and Teacher Education International Conference (SITE).

Morrison, G., Ross, S., & Kemp, J. (2007). *Designing effective instruction* (5th ed., p. 218). Hoboken, NJ: John Wiley & Sons.

Rowntree, D. (2000). *Back to the future with distance learning: From independent learning from interdependence*. Retrieved from http://www-iet. open.ac.uk/pp/ D.G.F.Rowntree/future_dl.htm

Schroeder, B. (2009). Microsoft live meeting 2007: Web conferencing system for virtual classrooms. *Innovate: Journal of Online Education, 1*(1). Retrieved from http://innovateonline.info/pdf/vol1issue1/Rethinking Space and Time-The Role of Internet Technology in a Large Lecture Course.pdf.

Smaldino, S., Lowther, D., & Russell, J. (2012). *Connecting learners at a distance. Instructional Technology and Media for Learning* (pp. 144–172). Boston, MA: Pearson.

Weimer, M. (2002). *Learner-centered teaching: five key changes to practice*. San Francisco, CA: Jossey-Bass.

ADDITIONAL READING

Anderson, T., & Kuskis, A. (2007). Modes of interaction. In Moore, M. (Ed.), *Handbook of distance education* (pp. 295–310). Mahwah, NJ: Erlbaum.

Bacer, K. (2004). *Creating effective interactive environments for the elearner*. World Conference on E-Learning in Corporate, Government, Healthcare, and Higher Education (ELEARN), 2004.

Daniel, B., Schwier, R., & Ross, H. (2007). Synthesis of the process of learning through discourse in a formal virtual learning community. *Journal of Interactive Learning Research, 18*(4).

Galyen, K., Kumalasari, C., & Kwon, K. (2008). The digital media ZONE: A model for online digital media instruction. World Conference on E-Learning in Corporate, Government, Healthcare, and Higher Education (ELEARN), Nov 17, 2008.

Houghton, R., & Mims, N. (2003). *Does webcasting with live channel improve teaching in distance learning?* Society for Information Technology & Teacher Education International Conference (SITE), 2003.

Koumi, J. (2006). Matching media attributes to learning tasks and teaching functions. In *Designing video and multimedia for open and flexible learning* (pp. 57–91). New York, NY: Routledge.

Lee-Baldwin, J. (2005). Asynchronous discussion forums: A closer look at the structure, focus and group dynamics that facilitate reflective thinking. *Contemporary Issues in Technology & Teacher Education, 5*(1), 93–115.

Liu, M., Kalk, D., Kinney, L., Orr, G., & Reid, M. (2009). *Web 2.0 and its use in higher education: A review of literature*. World Conference on E-Learning in Corporate, Government, Healthcare, and Higher Education (ELEARN) Oct. 2009.

Liu, X., Magjuka, R., Bonk, C., & Lee, S. (2006). *Does sense of community matter? An examination of participants' perspectives in online courses*. World Conference on E-Learning in Corporate, Government, Healthcare, and Higher Education (ELEARN) Oct. 2006.

Mayes, R., Luebeck, J., Ku, H., Akarasriworn, C., and Korkmaz, O. (2011). *Themes and strategies for transformative online instruction: A review of literature*. Global Learn Asia Pacific (Global Learn), Mar 28, 2011.

Napper, V. (2008). *A literature review of models to manage participation in distance education activities for teacher education licensure programs*. World Conference on E-Learning in Corporate, Government, Healthcare, and Higher Education (ELEARN), Nov 17, 2008.

Revere, L., & Kovach, J. (2011). Online technologies for engaged learning: A meaningful synthesis for educators. *The Quarterly Review of Distance Education, 12*(2), 113–124.

Schullo, S., Siekmann, S., & Szydlo, S. (2003). *Synchronous distance education systems, choosing the right solution*. World Conference on E-Learning in Corporate, Government, Healthcare, and Higher Education (ELEARN), 2003

Yamada, M., & Akahori, K. (2005). *Raising learners' consciousness of learning objectives in communicative language learning: Videoconference system in learner-centered communication instruction*. World Conference on Educational Multimedia, Hypermedia and Telecommunications (EDMEDIA), Jun 27, 2005.

KEY TERMS AND DEFINITIONS

Humanization: Are the methods used to support communications in a web-based learning environment.

Presence: The establishment of a supportive learning environment for students. Presence involves providing opportunities for communications and socialization. Presence involves supporting students to feel comfortable in the learning environment, as if they are in and part of the virtual learning environment.

Student-Centered Strategies: A type of learning experience in which the student directs the experience and the teacher may serve more as a facilitator or guide. These strategies are used to support student learning by allowing students to be involved in more hands-on types of learning activities such as small group discussions, discovery learning, problem solving and games.

Teacher-Centered Strategies: A type of learning experience in which the teacher directs the learners in the experience. These strategies may include instructional presentations, demonstrations, or tutorials.

Video Conferencing: Synchronous video and audio communication by participants located in two or more locations especially designed and equipped for user groups.

Web Conferencing: Synchronous video and audio communication between participants located in separate locations using individual computers.

Chapter 12
Using Video to Foster Presence in an Online Course

Sharon Stoerger
Rutgers University, USA

ABSTRACT

By definition, presence makes individuals feel connected and part of a community. Yet, creating presence among the students and their instructor does not happen automatically and can be especially challenging to develop in online courses. In these learning environments, interactions are frequently text-based and asynchronous. The visual and auditory cues generally associated with face-to-face interactions are absent. However, easy-to-use, inexpensive technologies to create audio and video content are emerging, and they can foster presence in educational settings. This chapter investigates the use of rich media to promote social, cognitive, and teaching presence. Specifically, instructor-created videos were used to enhance the sense of presence in a fully online course. Responses to surveys, reflections, and unstructured follow-up interviews suggest that students prefer the richer mode of communication, indicating that they felt a greater connection to the instructor as well as their classmates.

INTRODUCTION

The availability of mobile devices, video-recording devices, and wireless Internet access is on the rise. The flexibility associated with anytime, anywhere access to information encourages learners to be more autonomous. However, online communication can be quite stark without visual and audio cues. In an email message, for example, the tone and pitch of voice as well as the speaker's body language are absent. When instruction moves online, the primary mode of communication is often asynchronous and text-based with no opportunity for face-to-face interaction among the students and the instructor.

Communication in an online environment can be a very isolating experience. Not only can purely text-based interactions result in miscommunication, but students may feel they are interacting with robots instead of real people, as well. While online

DOI: 10.4018/978-1-4666-3962-1.ch012

learning offers convenience and opportunities for reflection, this format can also hinder the development of social presence as students are physically, intellectually, and emotionally disconnected from other students and their instructors.

According to Garrison, Anderson, and Archer (2000), presence – social, teacher, and cognitive – is essential to learning and to creating a successful college experience. Social presence is built primarily through encouraging open communication and group cohesion. Cognitive presence involves the exploration, integration, and resolution of ideas and course content. A sense of teaching presence is accomplished through course design, through facilitating conversations and thought processes, and through direct, personal instruction. Together, these three presences build what Garrison, Anderson, and Archer (2000) describe as the community of inquiry framework (see Figure 1).

But how does one establish presence without face-to-face communication? By adding an audio-visual component such as video, the online instructor can enrich interaction and build a community of learners. When instructors use video to convey open, friendly, and collegial attitudes, they foster social presence. As instructors share information, inspire ideas, and connect concepts, they build cognitive presence. Teaching presence develops when video is used in course design through directing, clarifying, and authenticating conversation. Instructors may also cultivate this type of presence via direct, personal instruction such as video feedback.

New technology makes it easier for instructors to use rich media to convey information, build presence, and become visible to their online students. To augment communication in online educational spaces, Haythornthwaite et al. (2000) noted the benefits of incorporating visual cues. Barab et al. (2003) assert that simply adding pictures to profile information can help students make connections and create a stronger learning community. When instructors post a picture with their welcome

message, for example, those individuals become more than an automated bot leading the course; they become humanized.

This chapter will describe tactics to enhance presence in a fully online course. Specifically, the focus will be on the use of four types of instructor-created videos and their impact on students. The discussion will begin by examining the importance of presence in the educational process, followed by an examination in the use of technology to foster student-instructor connections and to create community in educational settings. After the video-enriched course is described, the discussion will examine the students' reaction to the videos and areas for future research.

BACKGROUND

In face-to-face courses, instructors constantly employ both audio and visual communication. According to Baker (2004), 60% of communication is non-verbal, which means that the majority of face-to-face instruction does not involve words. Students learn not just from what is said but also from their instructor's body language, visual aids, and vocal pitch and tone – all of which can be difficult to replicate online.

Figure 1. Community of inquiry framework (adopted from Garrison, Anderson, & Archer, 2000)

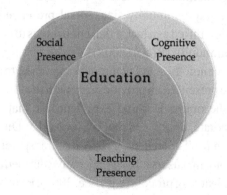

Even with a course management system (CMS), there is very little auditory, visual, and non-verbal communication (e.g., Krovitz, 2009). This lack of physical cues (e.g., Daft & Lengel, 1986) can lead to confusion and feelings of isolation. Humanizing both the instructor and students can influence online student participation (Kear, 2010). With a rich medium like video, both instructors and students are able to capitalize on physical cues necessary to create clarity and build community.

Presence and Video Technology

Creating a sense of presence is one way to build student engagement. Presence encourages students to be excited about the instructors they are learning from and the individuals they are learning with, as well as the course content. Without the instructor being physically present, creating that sense of presence is even more of a challenge and yet equally important in the online arena.

Both individual and group performance improves when there is a greater sense of presence (Fontaine, 2002; Garrison, Anderson, and Archer, 2000). Picciano (2002) agrees and asserts that there is "a definite, consistent and strong relationship among student perceptions of interaction, social presence, and learning" (p. 30). Constructivists such as Vygotsky (1978) argue that learning is a social activity. In addition to transactional distance, social equality, small group activities, group facilitation, teaching style and learning stage, and community size, social presence has been identified as a factor that contributes to sense of community (Rovai, 2002).

Technologies and techniques designed to enhance presence can provide users with the illusion that the online learning experience is "natural, immediate, direct, and real" (Lombard & Ditton, 1997, n.p.). The technology becomes transparent to the point that users no longer perceive the medium in the learning process (e.g., Lee, 2004). Rourke et al. (2001) add to this idea of the unmediated feel and argue that with an increased sense of presence, learners are able to project their personal characteristics into the community of inquiry, thereby presenting themselves as real people.

Though creating presence in a fully online course can be challenging, instructor-created videos can fill the communication gap and closely simulate the presence experienced in face-to-face classrooms. Video technology is becoming both easier to use and more affordable. Digital video recording devices such as camcorders, pocket cameras, and smartphones are typically small, versatile, and inexpensive. Most of these devices allow the user to transfer content to a personal computer and/or upload directly to social media sites such as YouTube or Facebook. Instructors can now create videos for educational purposes with minimal effort – ones that are produced and edited locally instead of by a professional team. An unpolished video bestows an authentic flair, conveying the presence of the instructor. Through these videos, students are introduced to course content as they see and hear their instructor.

Research has shown that merely adding voice enhances the instructor's online personality (e.g., Schlosser & Burmeister, 2006), contributing to teaching presence. Instructor-created videos, which convey an even greater number of communication cues, have produced favorable results, as well. Arbaugh and Hwang (2006) noted positive results with the use of video mini-lectures. Research conducted by Griffiths and Graham (2009) revealed that the use of asynchronous video in online courses, including recordings of reminders and announcements, had a positive impact on the students' learning experience and encouraged them to develop a more personal relationship with the instructor. These videos have also been found to contribute the students' sense of instructor immediacy (Jones, Kolloff, & Kolloff, 2008).

Because of the complexity of creating presence in an online course along with a growing number of technologies that enhance presence, more research is needed, particularly in online and blended courses. The following video-enriched course description will detail one instructor's use of multimedia, in particular asynchronous video content, to create a sense of presence in a fully online course.

THE VIDEO-ENRICHED COURSE

Using Garrison, Anderson, and Archer's (2000) community of inquiry framework, this course tested the ability of instructor-created, asynchronous videos to foster a sense of presence in a fully online course. This particular course was offered through an urban research institution that attracts a large and diverse group of students at both the undergraduate and graduate levels. Students can select from a variety of course options and formats: on-campus, evening, weekend, blended, and online. Like many offerings at this institution, the course under investigation was delivered through a CMS. Current CMSs operate as an educational "bank" where the primary function is to warehouse course content. While rich media content can be integrated into its framework, a reliance on text-based educational approaches remains the norm (Adams, 2006). Regardless, some instructors are taking advantage of this affordance to incorporate multimedia content into their online course curricula (e.g., Clark, Nguyen, & Sweller, 2006). In this course, instructor-created videos were used to enhance presence in an educational environment that typically relies on lean communication media.

As Kehrwald's (2008) work has highlighted, research on presence beyond solely text-based media is important. In his study, the respondents indicated that information such as personal histories, personalities, and current circumstances contributed to presence. The combination of these variables enables the instructor to become real and present in the course discussions. This idea serves to guide the design and use of video described in this chapter.

The Class: Instructional Technologies

This study examined a fully online course that lasted 16 weeks. Successful completion of a course on the use of computers for resource management was required prior to enrollment. While the course was offered through a four-year institution located in the Midwest region of the U.S., the majority of students did not live on or near campus but in neighboring communities and states. There were also a few students living in Western states, as well as in areas outside the U.S. such as Japan. A total of 23 students enrolled in the course, and they represented a diverse array of backgrounds and motivations. Their ages ranged from the mid-20s to the mid-50s; many worked full time as K-12 teachers, librarians, and information technologists. With one exception, the students in this course were at the graduate level. Like other online offerings at this institution, this course utilized the Desire2Learn (D2L) CMS.

Instructor-Created Videos

To supplement the text-based content of this course, enhance the presence of the instructor, and encourage the formation of a learning community, video content was developed. The instructor created four types of videos: 1) a personal introduction; 2) modular introductions; 3) video check-ins; and 4) modular "cool tools" introductions. While optimal video length depends on the purpose, the research indicates that students' attention begins to fade with clips lasting longer than 15 minutes (Ellis & Childs, 1999). Studies also suggest that shorter videos are more engaging for students and may lead to better learning (e.g., Gillespie, 2007). Using this research as a guide, all videos created for this course were short, and ranged from 30 seconds to less than 10 minutes. Students also appreciate locally created videos. While these videos may not appear as polished as ones developed by professional entities, students find that they are more authentic and make their instructor seem human (Symonds et al., 2010). Therefore, the videos for this course were created entirely by the instructor without assistance from a professional media outlet.

As the literature notes, images and personal information help establish connections with students and create community (e.g., Barab et al., 2003). Thus, the personal introduction was designed to set the tone for the course, help students connect with the instructor, and view her as a human being. This introduction gave students the opportunity to see and hear the instructor, as well as learn more about her academic and personal interests. Music, photographs, and images from websites are examples of information pieces that were incorporated into the video. There were seven topic modules, and each one was introduced via videos, as well. The purpose of these videos was to provide a brief overview of the readings, highlight key concepts, and present questions for the students to think about as the class moved into the online discussions. On the whole, these were the longest videos created for this course, and viewing time ranged from approximately 7 to 10 minutes.

Another type of video that was made available to students was a video check-in, where instructors give video feedback directed to the particular class they are facilitating. While the focus of these videos was less on the content of the module, they provided the instructor with an opportunity to clarify misunderstandings, address questions that surfaced during the week, and present related materials that could supplement the students' understanding. Some instructors claim that it is easy for students to "disappear" in online courses (e.g., Kaleta, Skibba, Joosten, 2007). Thus, the function of the video check-ins was to maintain the connection with students as they moved through the multi-week modules and to reinforce the idea that the instructor was there for them if needed.

One of the assignments associated with each module involved a "cool tools" presentation. For each of the module topics, students were instructed to select a cool tool to virtually present to their peers. Typically, these tools were freely available online and were ones the students found useful for educational purposes. These presentations, which investigated the positives, negatives, and pedagogical practices of the selected tools, took place in the online discussion forum. Here, the students were also given the opportunity to comment on the presentations. Videos created to introduce this portion of the course activities were shorter and more playful than the other types created for this course and emphasized creativity over content. Like the video check-ins, the purpose of the cool tools videos was to maintain a connection with students.

In the initial stages of this study, the intent was to use a digital camcorder (i.e., the Flip camera) to record the four types of videos for this course. This device was used to create videos that were made available to the students during the first weeks of the course. As the instructor became more comfortable with the video creation process and introduced a wider variety of emerging tools to the students, rich media alternatives (e.g., Jing and Animoto) were investigated. To address multiple student learning preferences and to increase the accessibility of the content, text-based versions of the videos (i.e., transcripts) were created and posted to the CMS. In addition, a YouTube Channel created for the course served as a repository for these videos and was an alternative way for students to access this content.

Evidence of Effectiveness

Because more cues can be communicated with video, students have the opportunity to see their instructor's body language and hear her tone and humor. This higher level of media richness can also add authenticity to the material. To determine whether the inclusion of this type of content had an impact on students, two open-ended surveys (midterm and end of the semester) and a reflection activity (conducted during the last module of the course) were employed. Students were strongly encouraged, but not required, to complete the surveys. In contrast, the reflection was a required activity in the course. In cases where clarification was needed to understand in greater detail the student reflection comments or survey responses, unstructured follow-up interviews were conducted.

While it is challenging for instructors to create a sense of presence in an online course, students who are given the opportunity to watch these videos see, hear, and participate in a shared experience with their instructor. At the same time, however, the comments collected from students via the midterm survey as well as their reflections indicated that more than half (n=13) of students were skeptical at first about the educational potential of videos posted to YouTube. These feelings of disbelief included the videos created by their instructor with direct links made available to them in the CMS. This sentiment about YouTube was not unexpected, and reports that share this negative tone can be found in the literature. In fact, Alex Juhasz (e.g., Jenkins, 2008) found her experience using YouTube for a college-level course to be lacking.

While Juhasz's experience was with undergraduates, this was a graduate-level course. Many of the students worked full-time as K-12 teachers or school librarians. Because content available via a number of popular social media resources was viewed as inappropriate in the K-12 setting, rules were in place prohibiting their use. Perhaps as a result of that workplace culture, students came into the course with the perception that everything they could access online is bad and creates unintended distractions. The amount of time lost when watching YouTube videos, for example, was a major concern. One student responding to the survey did not consider watching YouTube to be part of the learning process – at least not initially – and described her dislike of this form of video content in the following manner: "I have a terrible habit of getting stuck in YouTube cycles that waste hours." Others in the course made comparable statements.

The students' perceptions of the use of the instructor-created videos changed over the course

of the semester. Based on the reflection activity, students recognized the value associated with the videos. Here is what one student had to say: "I feel like this approach [the use of instructor-created videos] can be very effective, because the teacher's obligation is to surround the student with resources." Another student liked the ability to access the video content multiple times: "The videos are easily reviewable, and they ensure that students understand the concepts that they are being taught. I see videos in general as a great benefit to learning." Students found it helpful to see the ways in which the technologies we discussed in class could be put into practice: "These videos were very inspiring for me, as it showed that our recently developed capabilities are already finding their way into the learning environment."

While creating these videos took minimal effort on the part of the instructor, the collected student responses suggest that the impact on their perceptions of this course was positive. This is aligned with earlier connections among presence, community, and student satisfaction (e.g., Wise, Chang, Duffy, & de Valle, 2004; Shea, Li, & Picket, 2006). The results of this video-enriched course are not generalizable to a wider audience; however, they do show that instructor-created videos have the potential to support instruction, build understanding, and direct instruction without requiring a sizable commitment in terms of time and effort on the part of the instructor.

CHALLENGES AND RECOMMENDATIONS

Technologies come and go very quickly in today's competitive marketplace. On April 12, 2011, which was the middle of the semester described in this chapter, Cisco announced that it planned to discontinue the production of the Flip camcorder (Grobart & Rusli, 2011). Because of the ephemeral nature of devices such as the Flip, alternative video production options were investigated. The video slideshow maker, Animoto (http://animoto.

com/), and the screencasting site, Jing (http://www.techsmith.com/jing/), are examples of these sites. Animoto transformed pictures, video clips, and music into videos. With Jing Pro, full-motion videos that captured information presented on a computer screen, sound, and voice could be quickly created. Like the Flip, however, TechSmith plans to discontinue their Jing Pro product beginning February 28, 2013 and has been encouraging users to migrate to their screen capture tool, Snagit (http://www.techsmith.com/snagit.html).

While the monetary costs of creating video content for students can be low, especially when using free, online resources, there are other costs to consider. Many of these tools are easy to use, yet they still require a time investment on the part of the instructor to learn how to use them effectively. Learning a new tool, even one that is simple to use, takes time, and the life span of devices such as Flip cameras and software such as Jing Pro can be short. Fortunately, other technologically similar and inexpensive video devices are available (e.g., Sanyo Xacti, Sony Bloggie, Toshiba Camilio). A number of mobile devices such as smartphones and tablets make it possible for users to capture video content, as well. Perhaps more importantly, many of the skills needed to effectively use these technologies are transferrable.

Another aspect of creating video that can take time is editing. Not only does the instructor have to learn how to use the editing tool, but also selecting pieces of video to include or exclude is not necessarily quick. However, editing software is becoming easier to use and the options available continue to expand. Microsoft Movie Maker (Windows) and Apple iMove (Mac) are two easy-to-use video editors. Not only are these tools free or inexpensive, but some also allow users to edit on-the-go. iMovie, for example, lets users edit video directly on their iPhone or iPad.

Determining how to make the videos available to students is another point to consider. Instructors may want to create a YouTube Channel to post class-related videos. Some campuses may also have a license for a rich media platform such as Kaltura (http://corp.kaltura.com/) where instructors could post videos. In addition, this type of content could be directly uploaded to the CMS.

Addressing accessibility can be another challenge when integrating video content into the curriculum. The goal is to make course materials accessible to all and to improve the understanding of the content. Videos may pose problems for individuals who have visual or hearing impairments or who speak a foreign language, for example. In the course described in this chapter, no students had visual or hearing impairments, and all were native English speakers. Had this not been the case, extra steps would have been needed to make the content presented in the videos comprehensible to these individuals. As rich media becomes a greater part of the curriculum, the instructor may need to draft transcripts of the recording or add subtitles or closed captioning to the video. Numerous institutions have departments available to help instructors make their course content more accessible. Also, many of the technologies to add features like closed captioning or subtitles are becoming more readily available and easier to use. In fact, video sharing sites such as YouTube now offer features that enable users to add captions and subtitles to their videos (http://www.youtube.com/t/captions_about).

FUTURE RESEARCH DIRECTIONS

Presence is a complex topic with many interconnected variables that can contribute to its effectiveness. In this study, four different types of videos were used to enhance instructor presence in an online course. One avenue to be investigated in greater detail is determining the impact each type of video had on the students. Was the introduction video more effective than the cool tools introductions? Were the modular introductions more effective than the video check-ins? Deciphering the effect of each type of video would help instructors determine where to concentrate their efforts when preparing materials for class.

Expanding on this idea a bit would be to identify specific characteristics and the pedagogical purpose of these videos. Examples include examining the effectiveness of talking head shots versus demonstrating an activity. Another characteristic worth examining is video length. Studies suggest that video course content should be short to maintain the students' attention (Ellis & Childs, 1999). While students may become bored and disengage from the video when it is too long, there may be a length that is not long enough to immerse students in the material.

The literature suggests that hearing the instructor's voice alone contributes to the sense of presence (Schlosser & Burmeister, 2006). Many CMSs, including D2L, are adding the ability to provide feedback and interact with students via audio recordings. After the introduction video – one where students can see and hear the instructor – the question is whether audio and visual cues are needed. It might be equally as effective for the instructor to then rely on audio to supplement the text-based materials. Conversely, photographs and/or other forms of static visual representation may be as effective as video content.

Another area worthy of further investigation is the use of synchronous video in an online classroom. Research on synchronous communication in online courses has been favorable. Synchronous chat, for example, has been found to enhance social presence and enable active engagement in two-way communication. Im and Lee (2003/2004) found that synchronous discussions promoted social interactions and a friendly environment. Research also suggests that synchronous discussions can support active, critical reflection through peer or tutor interactions, as well as through individual reading and writing activities (Levin, He, & Robbins, 2006). Because chat tools are thought to invite more informal, interactive, and social types of conversations (Paulus, 2007), the assumption is that synchronous communication with video would create an even greater sense of presence.

CONCLUSION

Presence in online learning does not happen automatically; instead, it is something that takes work on the part of the participants (Lehman & Conceicao, 2010). While it is challenging to create a sense of presence in an online course, students watching videos such as the ones used in this course get the opportunity to see, hear, and participate in a shared experience with their instructor. The richness of the cues in these videos can add authenticity to the material. As a bonus, the combination of audio and visuals can be a powerful and effective way to convey information to students. While creating these videos took minimal effort on the part of the instructor, their impact on the students' perceptions of this course were positive in terms of managing instruction, building understanding, and directing instruction. It also gave students an opportunity to get to know the instructor as a human being – someone who was there to guide and coach them through the course – rather than a programmed robot.

The technological landscape is evolving rapidly. Within the duration of this semester-long study, the Flip video camcorder went from a "hot" device to obsolete (Grobart & Rusli, 2011). Later, an announcement was made that Jing Pro would be retired. Despite these challenges, there is evidence that students respond favorably to the addition of rich media into the curriculum. As has been noted, the research also suggests that when the sense of presence is low, students feel disconnected, especially in a fully online setting (e.g., Baker, 2010). The purpose of the videos used in this online course was to convey a feeling of "being there" for a geographically dispersed group of students, to give them a sense of community, and to create learning connections.

For the most part, asynchronous, text-based media were used to support communication among the students and the instructor. The use of video to supplement class communication enabled students to get to know the instructor, feel comfortable approaching her with questions, and view her as a real person. While the technology used to create these videos changed during the course of the semester, the intent did not. The actual technology used to construct a sense of presence remained intentionally in the background. In the end, the focus of the video creation and publication process remained on the students rather than on the technology.

REFERENCES

Adams, J. (2006). The part played by instructional media in distance education. *Studies in Media and Information Literacy Education, 6*(2), 1–12. doi:10.3138/sim.6.2.001

Arbaugh, J. B., & Hwang, A. (2006). Does "teaching presence" exist in online MBA courses? *The Internet and Higher Education, 9*(1), 9-21. Retrieved March 19, 2012, from http://www.sciencedirect.com/science/article/pii/S1096751605000783

Baker, C. (2010). The impact of instructor immediacy and presence for online student affective learning, cognition, and motivation. *The Journal of Educators Online, 7*(1).

Baker, J. D. (2004). An investigation of relationships among instructor immediacy and affective and cognitive learning in the online classroom. *The Internet and Higher Education, 7*, 1–13. doi:10.1016/j.iheduc.2003.11.006

Barab, S. A. MaKinster, J. G. & Scheckler, R. (2003) Designing system dualities: Characterizing a web-supported professional development community. *The Information Society, 19*, 237-256.

Clark, R., Nguyen, F., & Sweller, J. (2006). *Efficiency in learning: Evidence-based guidelines to manage cognitive load.* San Francisco, CA: John Wiley & Sons. doi:10.1002/pfi.4930450920

Daft, R. L., & Lengel, R. H. (1986). Organizational information requirements, media richness and structural design. *Management Science, 32*, 554–571. doi:10.1287/mnsc.32.5.554

Ellis, R., & Childs, M. (1999). The effectiveness of video as a learning tool in on-line multimedia modules. *Journal of Educational Media, 24*(3), 217–223. doi:10.1080/1358165990240305

Fontaine, G. (2002). Presence in teleland. In Rudestam, K. E., & Schoenhotz-Read, J. (Eds.), *Handbook of online learning: Innovations in higher education and corporate training* (pp. 21–52). Thousand Oaks, CA: Sage.

Garrison, D. R., Anderson, T., & Archer, W. (2000). Critical thinking in text-based environment: Computer conferencing in higher education. *The Internet and Higher Education, 2*(2), 87–105. doi:10.1016/S1096-7516(00)00016-6

Gillespie, D. (2007). On-demand video system enhances visual learning. *District Administration, 43*(9), 25–26.

Griffiths, M., & Graham, C. (2009). Using asynchronous video in online classes: Results from a pilot study. *Instructional Technology and Distance Learning, 6*(3), 65-75. Retrieved March 22, 2012, from http://www.itdl.org/journal/mar_09/article06.htm

Grobart, S., & Rusli, E. M. (2011). For Flip video camera, four years from hot start-up to obsolete. *New York Times.* Retrieved April 12, 2011, from http://www.nytimes.com/2011/04/13/technology/13flip.html

Haythornthwaite, C., Kazmer, M. M., Robins, J., & Shoemaker, S. (2000) Community development among distance learners: Temporal and technological dimensions. *Journal of Computer Mediated Communication, 6*(1). Retrieved May 1, 2012, from http://jcmc.indiana.edu/vol6/issue1/haythornthwaite.html

Im, Y., & Lee, O. (2003-2004). Pedagogical implications of online discussion for preservice teacher training. *Journal of Research on Technology in Education, 36*(2), 155–170.

Jenkins, H. (2008). Learning from YouTube: An interview with Alex Juhasz. *Confessions of an Aca-Fan*. Retrieved July 13, 2012, from http://henryjenkins.org/2008/02/learning_from_youtube_an_inter.html

Jones, P., Kolloff, M., & Kolloff, F. (2008). Students' perspectives on humanizing and establishing teacher presence in an online course. In K. McFerrin et al. (Eds.), *Proceedings of Society for Information Technology & Teacher International Conference 2008* (pp. 460-465). Chesapeake, VA: AACE.

Kaleta, R., Skibba, K., & Joosten, T. (2007). Discovering, designing, and delivering hybrid courses. In Picciano, A. G., & Dziuban, C. D. (Eds.), *Blended learning: Research perspectives* (pp. 111–143).

Kear, K. (2010). Social presence in online learning communities. *Proceedings of the 7th International Conference on Networked Learning*. Retrieved April 23, 2011, from http://www.lancs.ac.uk/fss/organisations/netlc/past/nlc2010/abstracts/PDFs/Kear.pdf

Kehrwald, B. (2008). Understanding social presence in text-based online learning environments. *Distance Education, 29*(1), 89–106. doi:10.1080/01587910802004860

Krovitz, G. (2009). Increasing instructor presence in an online course. *Educator's Voice, 10*(4), 1-7. Retrieved March 19, 2012, from http://www.pearsonecollege.com/Newsletter/EducatorsVoice/EducatorsVoice-Vol10Iss4.learn

Lee, K. M. (2004). Presence, explicated. *Communication Theory, 14*, 27–50. http://www.fineminddesign.com/site/media/Readings/Week%2010/Lee(2004)_Presence%20Explicated_CT.pdf doi:10.1111/j.1468-2885.2004.tb00302.x

Lehman, R. M., & Conceicao, S. C. O. (2010). *Creating a sense of presence in online teaching: How to "be there" for distance learners*. San Francisco, CA: Jossey-Bass.

Levin, B., He, Y., & Robbins, H. (2004). Comparative study of synchronous and asynchronous online case discussions. In C. Crawford et al. (Eds.), *Proceedings of Society for Information Technology and Teacher Education International Conference 2004* (pp. 551-558). Chesapeake, VA: AACE.

Lombard, M., & Ditton, T. (1997). At the heart of it all: The concept of presence. *Journal of Computer-Mediated Communication, 3*(2). Retrieved April 19, 2011, from http://jcmc.indiana.edu/vol3/issue2/lombard.html

Paulus, T. (2007). CMC modes for learning tasks at a distance. *Journal of computer-Mediated Communication, 12*(4). Retrieved, January 7, 2012, from http://jcmc.indiana.edu/vol12/issue4/paulus.html

Picciano, A. G. (2002). Beyond student perceptions: Issues of interaction, presence, and performance in an online course. *Journal of Asynchronous Learning Networks, 6*(1), 21–40.

Rourke, L., Anderson, T., Garrison, D. R., & Archer, W. (2001). Assessing social presence in asynchronous, text-based computer conferencing. *Journal of Distance Education, 14*(3), 51–70.

Rovai, A. P. (2002). Sense of community, perceived cognitive learning, and persistence in asynchronous learning networks. *The Internet and Higher Education, 5*(4), 319–332. doi:10.1016/S1096-7516(02)00130-6

Schlosser, C. A., & Burmeister, M. (2006). Audio in online courses: Beyond podcasting. *Proceedings of E-Learn 2006 World Conference on E-Learning in Corporate, Government, Healthcare, and Higher Education,* Honolulu, HI. Retrieved March 22, 2012, from http://www.scribd.com/doc/27071823/Audio-in-Online-Courses-Beyond-Podcasting-Schlosser-Burmeister

Shea, P., Li, C. S., & Pickett, A. (2006). A study of teaching presence and student sense of learning community in fully online and web-enhanced college courses. *The Internet and Higher Education*, 9(3), 175–190. doi:10.1016/j.iheduc.2006.06.005

Symonds, S., Jamieson, A., Bell, A., Wood, B., Ryan, A., & Patterson, L. (2010). Taking sociology online: Boosting teacher presence and student engagement through rich media. In C. H. Steel, M. J. Keppell, P. Gerbic, & S. Housego (Eds.), *Curriculum, Technology & Transformation for an Unknown Future: Proceedings ASCILITE Sydney 2010* (pp. 948-950).

Vygotsky, L. S. (1978). *Mind in society: The development of higher psychological processes*. Cambridge, MA: Harvard University Press.

Wise, A., Chang, J., Duffy, T., & del Valle, R. (2004). The effects of teacher social presence on student satisfaction, engagement, and learning. *Journal of Educational Computing Research*, 31(3), 247–271. doi:10.2190/V0LB-1M37-RNR8-Y2U1

KEY TERMS AND DEFINITIONS

Community of Inquiry Framework: A model developed by Garrison, Anderson, and Archer (2000) that is comprised of three types of presence – social, cognitive, and teaching. These three interconnected elements are essential to learning and to creating successful educational experiences.

Digital Camcorder: A small, portable electronic device that captures audio and video components.

Engagement: A psychological investment of a student in the learning process. In other words, the student willingly and positively participates in educational activities.

Lean Media: Modes of communication that convey the least amount of information. Lean media contain few cues. In some situations, however, they may be more efficient than richer communication modes.

Media Richness: The degree to which media carry data and symbolic information. Ranking criteria may be based on the types of cues (e.g., immediate feedback, alteration of a message, transmission of emotions) that are conveyed via a medium.

Online Education: Teaching and learning that is supported electronically. Courses that are conducted fully online do not include a face-to-face component.

Presence: A feeling of being connected to and forming a community with other individuals.

Rich Media: This is a broad term for multimedia content that can lead to interactivity. Increasingly, rich media are being incorporated into online courses and tools.

Chapter 13
Media and the Moving Image:
Creating Screen Media Literacy

Paul Chilsen
Carthage College, Rosebud Institute, USA

ABSTRACT

We are immersed in a culture of spoken media, written media, and – like it or not – screen media. Just as writing and speaking skills are keys to functioning in society, we must consider that the future increasingly demands proficiency in "mediating" as well. Doing anything less leaves this powerful medium in the hands of a relative few. By offering instruction in what screen media is, how it is created, how it relates to other literacies, how the internet is changing it, and how this all informs everyday teaching and learning, the Rosebud Institute seeks to make screen media literacy more broadly understood and accessible. This chapter follows a program developed by the Rosebud Institute and looks at how – using simple, accessible technology – people can become more screen media literate by creating digital films and ePortfolios themselves. Developed along with Rosebud's program manager, Christine Wells, the creation process enables deeper, more authentic learning, allowing us all to communicate more effectively, to self assess more reflectively, and to thrive in a screen-based world.

SCREEN MEDIA: AN INTRODUCTION

Have you looked at a screen today? You may of course be reading this text on paper, but chances are growing ever stronger that you may well be looking at a screen right now as you read this chapter. In many cases, it seems not that big of a deal. After all, it is simply words on a page and the medium of delivery may not be all that crucial.

Inverting the classic phrase of communication scholar Marshall McLuhan for a moment, the medium does not really seem to alter or affect the message all that much in this particular case. Or does it?

With the tectonic media shift in which we find ourselves, the lines we think we know, and think we can count on, seem to be blurring. The myriad machinations and goings on in our convergent

DOI: 10.4018/978-1-4666-3962-1.ch013

media world, while a fascinating and rich topic, understandably extend beyond the scope of this chapter. Rather the focus here is to look more at what we can do now. Now that the explosive growth and pervasive penetration of new media is upon us, what can we do to get a firmer grip on the reins? How can we go beyond handing out expensive devices designed to simply access the conversation, and instead convey real skills that allow more people to effectively join in, to make clear meaning, and to affect the change they seek?

One way is to take a step back – get back to basics a bit and begin to give people some simple tools that they can use to more effectively be a part of the burgeoning world of what is happening on screens around the world. As mentioned, you may be looking at a screen right now but if not, you have probably looked at one if not several already today and most certainly – unless you make a concerted effort to the contrary – you will be bombarded with screen images all day, telling you what to do, what to think, what to like – even what to say.

And the trend is only growing. As Eva and John Waterworth state in their discussions on mediated presence "Our everyday lives are more and more pervasively experienced through media… There are very few places where one is out of reach of [these] devices…" (Waterworth & Waterworth, 2010)

This ever-expanding world of screen-based electronic media encompasses such an understandably and incredibly broad array of media types, paradigms, and histories that even finding a name or term to refer to it all can prove difficult. For our purposes here, we prefer the term *screen media*. It is a term we are becoming more and more comfortable with to specifically describe media produced, created for, and unfolding on the screen yet it is general enough to encompass a broad array of different media, both moving (film, video, television, and gaming) as well as those which are generally more static (websites, social media, blogs). As mentioned, this chapter has a necessarily refined scope. We will look at a very practical and doable approach to giving people a baseline way to become more active and informed members of a screen media world. Interestingly, it is in this more simple approach that the potential becomes highly expansive, giving people the tools to literally go wherever they want, much like the effect of teaching a person to write or to read.

But what *people* or *persons* are we talking about? Who is this for? To say everyone may well elicit a raised eyebrow or two but literally, screen media literacy is so crucial that virtually everyone will need some baseline understanding of what it is and how it works. This is not a new concept of course. The term media literacy has been around since the 1970's and in 1988, one of the most relevant and enduring quotes comes from a former president of the Carnegie Foundation for the Advancement of Teaching, Ernest Boyer: "It is no longer enough to simply read and write. Students must also become literate in the understanding of visual images" (Boyer, 1988). What is new however, is how far-reaching and therefore undeniable the screen has become. If screen media is virtually everywhere, then its literacy is in demand virtually everywhere if we are to have an informed and literate public. "The ability to both read and write visual information; the ability to learn visually; to think and solve problems in the visual domain—will, as the information revolution evolves, become a requirement for success in business and in life." (Gray, 2008) That said, keeping our sites on achievable goals and not biting off more than is manageable, the immediate audience addressed mostly herein are students and educators – both in a K-12 environment and in post-secondary education as well.

Without delving too deeply into program specifics, we will outline a broadly prescriptive approach – a program that takes achievable steps towards reducing and addressing what has been referred to as our rampant media *illiteracy* (Baker, 2012). While the method is simple enough, there are of course roadblocks, speed bumps and various difficulties along the way but the promise of a more informed, empowered, and literate digital citizenry seems a worthy enough cause to overcome the surmountable obstacles.

Toward the end of the chapter, we will look at program efficacy thus far and explore ideas for growth, refinement, and expansion, giving attention to where we can go from here and furthering the mission of creating screen media literacy for all.

THE PRESENT AND FUTURE EFFECT

It has been said that those who control the media, control the future. Setting aside a more manipulative connotation of "control," and focusing rather on an interpretation more aligned with understanding and effective use, it seems a natural, logical extension that in order to more positively affect our future we must increase the number of, and more fundamentally educate future media makers (Chilsen & Wells, 2012).

If you accept this "proliferating mediation of our everyday lives" (Waterworth & Waterworth, 2010) as an unstoppable fact and embrace the intrinsic notion that we are therefore irreversibly immersed in a screen media culture, then one could argue that just as we are taught and know how to write and speak in a text-based society, now, in order to function competently in a screen-based society, we all would do well to start becoming more proficient at "mediating" as well.

Given the massive realignment that continues to unfold in the broad world of digital media, it seems both right and pressing that we realign the thinking and approach taken towards defining what screen media is, who ought to know how it works

and how we can democratize the understanding and use of these powerful and exploding media.

Unlike fashionable pedagogical trends, the need for screen media literacy and ability is here to stay. Embracing and expanding what Elizabeth Daley, of USC's School of Cinema-Television once called "the greatest digital divide," the approach outlined herein seeks to close the chasm between those who can read and write in screen media, and those who cannot (Van Ness, 2005). Put simply, because so many now have access to and can therefore create media for the screen, everyone ought to be learning the basics of how to read and write in the language of the screen. To do anything less leaves this awesome and expanding power in the hands of a relative few.

It is from this wellspring of possibilities that the Rosebud Institute was formed. Given the somewhat prescriptive nature of this chapter, it seems prudent to at least briefly discuss this umbrella organization, in the interest of giving a point of reference for the approach taken. To that end, it is important to point out the Rosebud Institute is at least partly inspired in name and independent spirit by the enigmatic and prodigious filmmaker Orson Welles, (*Citizen Kane, The Magnificent Ambersons, Touch of Evil*). The institute seeks to embody both Welles' revolutionary approach to motion pictures as well as a sort of can-do, hands-on approach to addressing a growing need – a need to better equip future media makers in a world virtually drowning in images on the screen.

PREPRODUCTION: THE ROSEBUD INSTITUTE

At Carthage College in Kenosha, Wisconsin, the Rosebud Institute has found an appropriate and constructive association. A private, liberal arts institution, nestled between the twin metro areas of Chicago and Milwaukee, the newest department at Carthage is Communication and Digital Media (CDM). Tangentially affiliated with CDM, the Rosebud Institute finds obvious alignment with a substantial portion of the department's stated mission in that CDM is devoted to the advancement and development of a student's knowledge and ability in screen media. Grounded in the liberal arts, and taking a modest, non-film-school approach – just far enough away from the trappings of the entertainment industry – the Rosebud Institute seeks an appropriate combination of exploring where and how education may change in the area of screen media literacy. It is neither an easy nor insular task, and challenges, encouragement, input and even inspiration are sought from every corner. Even the very name Rosebud Institute – derived partly, as mentioned, from a Wellesian sensibility – has a geographic alignment; Orson Welles was born in Kenosha and lived there for the first formative years of his life.

Irrespective of any ethereal inspiration Welles may provide, it is the broader notion that all students need at least a basic, core knowledge of making media, wherein exists a powerful motivator – for Carthage, for the Communication and Digital Media department, and for the Rosebud Institute. This motivation lead to action and the Rosebud Institute was formed. Since then, its Founder/Director and its Program Manager have put together the beginnings of a program that is seeking and finding better ways to teach screen media literacy. Building on this, and collaborating with a large and robust Education department as well as a growing Adult Education division, the Rosebud Institute's larger, more universal mission – defining and exploring screen media literacy for all in order to better equip individuals to communicate and thrive – seems connected at Carthage College, both in ideal and setting.

SHOULD WE OR SHOULDN'T WE: *A MEDIAFESTO*

When one currently teaches writing or speaking, it is not necessarily to create great novelists or orators. That may happen, but the main driver is literacy and all that comes with it – especially cultural, social and political literacy and along with that cultural, social and political efficacy. As Carl Casinghino (2011) asserts in the preface of his text *Moving Images*, we do not teach math to young students in order to prepare them all to become professional mathematicians. Similarly, we are not teaching motion picture studies to crank out a new generation of Spielbergs. Instead we are "helping learners to develop cooperative skills, to enhance their problem-solving abilities, and to participate in cultural and social processes as capable, engaged interpreters" (Casinghino, 2011). Rosebud is interested in pushing the idea of skills development further, insisting that both reading and *writing* in screen media are important, and intrinsically interconnected.

In short, we need both. It seems increasingly a given that education needs to improve student understanding of how screen media work, how they make meaning, and how they construct (or reconstruct) reality. But more and more are coming to understand that true screen media literacy must also provide students with the ability to *create* media products. (Baker, 2012). With the written word, we know that people are better readers if they have at least a working understanding of how to write, and the same seems to hold true for media.

The notion of cultural context pushes the importance further still. David Buckingham (2007) in his piece on Digital Media Literacies, extracts this notion from the discourse on "multiliteracies": that literacy education cannot simply be confined to the acquisition of skills but rather must include a framing by cultural and social contexts. In screen media, there is always a maker and there is always an audience. Without an understanding of who made what, for whom, and for what reason, there will always exist a danger of painting media with too broad a brush. It seems everyone has an opinion and the conversation can quickly get confusing, even political. When discussing media, interesting yet often tangential arguments surface on all sides of this discussion, a good portion of which come under the "media is too..." lead in: media is too violent, it's too much about entertainment, it's too difficult, it's too expensive, it's too liberal, it's too sexy and perhaps the biggest one in education circles: it's just too much more for teachers to teach. However, one could easily make the argument that media is simply too important – too important now to just let it go.

If you take a moment to look around and notice, you may quickly come to the conclusion that the average teenager seems to do precious little thinking outside of the four walls of the screen. Given the chance, they will let the addictions of Facebook, YouTube and any number of current online trends usurp their time, (e.g., Pintrest, Twitter, StumbleUpon) But we currently give them no formal training to navigate these byways even in the most basic of ways, to say nothing of inculcating them with any sense of how best to spend their time there. We somehow expect them to develop some kind of sensibility on their own and basically give them the keys to drive without requiring they obtain any kind of license. By comparison, if we took an average child, but one who had been given no formal training in any of the disciplines of reading, writing and speaking, and set them down anywhere in a modern culture, leaving them to their own devices, expecting them to develop culturally recognized proficiency solely from the multiple channels of stimuli around them, would they be able to function in society? Some of them certainly would, eventually, but intrinsically, we recognize that many of them would not function all that well, and that overall their proficiencies would remain at the lower end of that functionality. Just as a rising tide lifts all boats, in this case, the opposite is also true. Our reasons for teaching any basic literacy may seem to be a given to many, but in this case it requires a retrospective, even deconstructed look. We teach these basic literacies for many reasons, not the least of which is to elevate our society and level the playing field, as it were. The more who know the language of the land, the more who are able to come to, and participate at, the tables of

meaningful discourse. If we accept the fact that screen media is here to stay, in perpetuity, and recognize that its literacy is important and unique, then it stands to reason that we must take a more formal approach to its pedagogy (Chilsen & Wells, 2012). Screen media has become, in effect, how we communicate…now.

And yet, in at least the broadest sense, we are generally taking the opposite approach. "Most uses of computers in schools signally fail to engage with the complex technological and media-saturated environment in which children are now growing up. For the most part, they are narrowly defined, mechanical and unimaginative" (Buckingham, 2007). If that is the case, then what we are apparently doing is leaving it up to the surrounding stimuli to teach our children how to read and write in this pervasive, growing medium. In that way, students – and the general public – are developing a skewed and undiscerning way of relating to screen media in general. A University of Wisconsin and Northwestern University colleague, Laura Kipnis, has referred to this phenomenon as a "marginally-trained sensibility" – one based almost entirely on the unregulated consumption of commercial television, film and internet programming in a comparatively indiscriminate fashion. If the educational system produces students with little or no formal training in screen media literacy, we are passing on that legacy and sending them out into the world as comparative babes in the wood, rather ill-equipped to function at the level the rapidly-converging world demands. Filmmaker, George Lucas has been quoted as saying "If people aren't taught the language of sounds and image, shouldn't they be considered as illiterate as if they left college without being able to read and write?" (Lucas, 2004). This may seem a strong and biased opinion but it raises a valid point. If we can begin to address the often-vast differences in a student's understanding of how screen media is made, how its language works, and how it affects change in ourselves and the culture around us, we will start students on a path of developing and refining the tools they need to function as capable, engaged individuals in a digitally mediated world.

As the downward trend in cost and the concurrent upward trend in quality in consumer electronics continue to expand both the reach and cultural power of screen media technology, the core knowledge of making media is even further democratized. And as accessibility spreads, so do the expectations of a modern culture. The whole idea of "media making" becomes a lingua franca of the future. In order to keep up, people – students and their teachers – need a basic tool kit of these specific skills as they venture out into the real and professional world, regardless of their eventual vocation. It is a new literacy – a language that continues to be accessible and used by greater numbers of people. It is a natural step then to guide, educate, and form the possible ways students can use this language across virtually all professions, in a more engaged, enlightened and effective manner (Chilsen & Wells, 2012).

CREATING THOSE WHO CAN

The challenge for the Rosebud Institute was to begin to translate its mission and ideals into action and come up with an approach that can address a need in current and future pedagogy. To this end, the Rosebud Institute launched a pilot program, the first version of which took place near the end of June 2010.

Originally offered under Rosebud's program header *Summer Series for Teachers*, the pilot program was designed as an intensive course for teachers and graduate students in education, titled *Media & The Moving Image*. Using current resources at Carthage College, this summer offering targeted elementary, middle and high school teachers who, while accumulating important summer enrichment or graduate credits, were interested in learning to better understand screen media themselves, perhaps begin to teach it in their classrooms, and encourage the attendant screen media literacy that would follow – both for themselves and their students.

The intensive, five-day seat time portion of the course was flanked by considerable asynchronous, pre and post work but the core instruction took place in the highly regulated and rigorous classroom component. The concentrated graduate-level course was designed to address new approaches for teaching media literacy by exploring the basics of reading and writing in the language of screen media.

Following a dynamic yet simple hands-on approach, participants learned a two-pronged approach to screen media. They each created two somewhat modest media pieces designed to help them begin to find their own voice in the often-cacophonous world of screen media. Participants conceived of a simple, relevant motion picture project, which they wrote, shot and edited, trying their own hand at using basic cinematic language to tell a simple, visual story. Alongside the film project, they each built an ePortfolio website of their own design, creating a timely, accessible and expandable way to display, manage, and share their projects, their ideas and even themselves. The film was not simply a slideshow movie and the ePortfolio was not simply another website repository, but rather both projects carried the weight of audience and were a true expression of what one could call the maker's *digital self*. While the projects may have seemed modest in scope, they were rife with importance and significance. The gratification of getting a solid grip on using technology more effectively, coupled with the thrill of truly creating something from nothing, lent a palpable air of accomplishment to the work. All of the projects were done in a guided, supportive learning environment where collective work, feedback, interaction, and sharing were all fostered and encouraged.

Creating a short first film of this nature seems to give most people a heightened sense of ownership along with the empowering feeling of "I can do this." They get to see how it is done, and – contrary to their assertions at the beginning of the course – they learn to become *better* watchers of film and television, not "ruined" as they often fear. An additional benefit of both projects is a deeper, richer and more authentic learning experience. We have found this to be even more significant in younger students but literally, one cannot help but learn something more deeply by going through the process of having to create a piece of screen media about it. The very creation process itself, seems to imbue the creator with knowledge and insight that reportedly surpasses any number of pedagogical activities. As inverted classrooms and project-centered learning continue to grow in importance and efficacy, this is one of the areas we are most excited about exploring further.

As mentioned, both projects have a strong sense of audience – the idea of *who is watching*. In an attempt to address this issue even further, we give some focus to ePortfolios as a form of self-distribution. Again, these are not simply a way to show work, but rather ePortfolios can also give the maker a sense of the potential power and reach of their creations. This is not art or expression created in a vacuum. This is work that potentially the world can see, and that is a lot of power and responsibility to consider.

With the pervasive spread of social networking, and its ever-younger-skewing clientele, a concurrent and integrated approach to creating, managing and distributing digital assets seems a viable, connected and crucial initiative to pursue. The additional benefit is to stimulate teachers to think about instructing their students on some of the how and why – and need – of managing their digital personae…their digital selves. As stories continue to hit the news about school-age sexting and other inappropriate interactions on the web, and as employers, schools and organizations increasingly support their personnel decisions by what they find on someone's Facebook site (Hechinger, 2008), the time seems ripe for educating students in the art of representing themselves appropriately in virtual reality, at a young enough age to begin building essential and culturally suitable lifelong skills. It is hoped that eventually there will come a day where most everyone is able to instantly capture, identifiably own, intelligently store, and instinctively know what to do with their digital assets (Chilsen & Wells, 2012), but until that time, we need to guide, to prod, even to insist.

Exploring the Media and the Moving Image program further, lectures, seminars, hands-on instruction, and classroom discussions all build toward the notion of how best to *communicate* in screen media. The motion media component, while relying on basic precepts of moviemaking, is decidedly removed from a Hollywood mode and instead approaches film grammar as new language of expression and making meaning. To lay the groundwork for effective communication, the coursework introduces a process encompassing fundamental aspects of *Preproduction*, (i.e., treatments, scripting, storyboarding and planning), *Production* (i.e., basic camera use, angles and filming), and *Postproduction* (i.e., importing and editing clips, exporting, and delivery), as well as addressing issues of aesthetics, ethics and cultural impact. The ePortfolio component extends communication beyond creation and into the arenas of audience and distribution via internet presentation. Participants build a base of knowledge with which to create their own purposeful, comprehensive collection of work and information. Through the process of building their own site throughout the course, they learn about the collaborative potential of online portfolios as well as the means by which they are able to create, upload and share their own original media in the form of video and audio podcasts.

Instruction emphasizes the demystification of the technical interface involved in these undertakings, in favor of a more basic exploration of reading, writing and presenting in the language of the screen. With beginning film projects, it is important to help participants become comfortable with adopting the grammar of motion media language by emphasizing connections with things they already know. Perhaps more than any other medium, cinema is a great re-appropriator, borrowing heavily from almost everywhere in its earnest need to communicate and create meaning. The challenge is to show participants that much of what they already know – the patterns, influences and structures of most if not all other intellectual pursuits – share a commonality with the basics of motion media language. This phenomenon crosses many disciplines but a prevailing example is how film productions often turn to art history for inspiration. Christopher Bowen, in his text, *Grammar of the Shot* (2009), points out that certain aspects of lighting, especially in painting, (chiaroscuro, angle, quality), become an important touchstone for the crew and actors working together on a film.

Additionally the Rosebud Institute focuses on the initial use of narrative to tell a simple screen story, giving first-time filmmakers a solid handle that they and their audiences understand – the ability to tell and read a story. It creates an important commonality at a crucial juncture where they are taking their first tentative steps in new language.

In a tangential fashion, the veritable explosion of social networking, self-promotion, and digital media distribution via the internet creates another opportunity for learning. As mentioned above, the sheer accessibility of virtually anything, anywhere at anytime necessitates that students learn to build, discern, shape, maintain, organize, and share their own *original* selves through the creation and management of their online presence. Especially for young people, it is important to "think twice about the online personae they are presenting to the world" (Coutu, 2007). What they post today will be available for years, and they may not understand this until they are sitting in a job interview years from now, and the potential employer opens a file that includes their résumé as well as their latest online rantings and party photos (Coutu, 2007). In short, students must manage and contextualize their digital selves, and if they do not, someone will begin to do it for them.

As the discussion of mediating continues to unfold, a natural progression continues to build towards presentation; the dovetailing of ePortfolios or other Web 2.0 interfaces with motion media is a natural occurrence and a means of distributing originally created digital media via the use of a well-designed, well-placed, and well-managed websites. As designed, anyone can simply take the course for their degree, their enrichment or their professional development, but teachers taking the class have the additional option of coming away with interrelated curriculum modules which they may want to use in their own classrooms.

Since the initial offering in June 2010 the Rosebud Institute has offered additional, follow-up courses under the Summer Series. *Media & The Moving Image*, (MMI 1) was repeated in summer 2011 along with a new course, *Media & The Moving Image 2* (MMI 2), providing a next step where participants now learned how sound worked with the moving image as well as building their knowledge and integration of Web 2.0 tools as they further developed and designed their digital presence.

MMI 1 has also been offered to Adult Ed students at Carthage in a 7-week format to see if it could adapt to a more regular schedule. The courses have worked well in that format, so much so that the current idea is to take the offerings more in that direction, partly owing to the challenges that the intensive summer courses prompted, with issues like conflicting work schedules, level of focused intensity for some, and not aligning with other summer school program schedules. Additionally, the courses are finding a connection with a much broader array of constituencies beyond education, such as professional development and undergraduate distribution coursework.

A third and more specific program is also underway with the Rosebud Institute. Launched as a pilot with a local high school in spring 2011, the Intensive Onsite Training Approach (IOTA) program gives individuals working within their organizations the chance to work closely with Rosebud Institute instructors to implement their own version of teaching the MMI series directly in their schools. Four highly successful IOTA programs have been completed to date including an Illinois College professional development program working under a 2011 Mellon grant.

Another exciting measure of the program's success has been the development and piloting of a new program by a recent IOTA teacher, Cindy Renaud. Ms. Renaud will be running her own version of the Rosebud screen media approach at her high school, launching this new coursework in the fall of 2012 at Harborside Academy, an Experiential Learning (EL) school in Wisconsin. Ms. Renaud may not exactly be the rule, in that she is a very driven teacher who is drawn specifically to more intentional use of technology in the classroom, but as a highly effective classroom teacher, her words are convincing and cut to the core of a broader necessity for more integrated screen media instruction:

Today's students will live their lives in a competitive, technology-driven global society. The ability to create relevant, content-specific, professional quality products using screen media will give students a foundation for being proficient digital citizens.... The aim of today's educator, then, is to engage the media-centric population of youth and prepare them for the competiveness of a global society and economy. (Renaud, 2012)

Before Renaud's successful IOTA program in the 2011-2012 school year, the Rosebud Institute had decided to take a cart-before-the-horse view of its programming by launching a pilot summer camp for students ages 13-17 in summer 2011. Called *Screen Media Boot Camp*, this weeklong overnight camp essentially takes the same type of program

offered to the adults, tweaks the coursework and activities for a younger audience, and takes kids through the steps to make their own movies and ePortfolios with intentionality and purpose.

All of these steps – the programming, the outreach, the camp – are highly intentional and are attempting to address what is seen by more and more as a core necessity. As screen time increases for students, up to one quarter of their day and rising (Herring & Notar, 2011), the need to educate to, through and with screen media is becoming crucial. With this in mind, the current Rosebud approach, albeit developing, offers recurring rotation of courses, enabling participants to expand both their own skills in making media, as well as guide and assess the work of their peers, graduates and students. When applicable, course credit has been configured for the necessary flexibility in today's transfer-laden and professional development landscape. Credit can be applied toward a Master of Education degree. Additionally, other types of credit options offer more choices for virtually anyone seeking general professional development, giving individuals and teachers more – and more media-savvy – options that can apply toward advancement, and licensure renewal, extending their abilities, their strengths and their screen media literacy.

With the IOTA onsite exceptions mentioned above, most classes currently meet on the campus of Carthage College. But as the IOTA program demonstrates, the courses are a movable feast of sorts, able to go virtually anywhere and effectively instruct at almost any level. Altered as appropriate for various constituencies, programs attempt to offer realistic and useful options for participants, giving them differing viewpoints and ideas through a number of atypical sessions including film screenings, story circles, panel discussions, emerging technology lectures, and relevant supplemental coursework. What has been witnessed in programs thus far is that the close-knit structure of the course and the necessity to collaborate offers ample opportunity for participants to work and learn together while networking and sharing with their peers.

By offering instruction in this manner, focusing on what screen media is, how its language is constructed, what it looks like, how to make it, how it impacts the culture around us, and how it informs everyday teaching, learning, discourse and commerce, the Rosebud Institute seeks to make screen media literacy more broadly accessible, allowing us all to communicate and thrive in an increasingly media-saturated world (Chilsen & Wells, 2012).

CUT TO: FASTFORWARD...

Where to go from here is almost as challenging and exciting as arriving at this point in the first place. Recognizing the interconnected nature of this kind of literacy exploration – a pioneering attempt to define, codify and teach a basic screen language and the subsequent screen media literacy it will hopefully engender – is most certainly not an isolated undertaking, nor should it be. Instead, it demands input, guidance and molding not only from the ongoing development of learning technologies and teaching, but from the many other pursuits – academic, social, and professional – which will continue to shape its content as well as its analysis.

Therefore a look forward involves not only assessing the results of the ongoing and expanding programs of the Rosebud Institute – their overall acceptance, efficacy and usefulness according to the participants – but also seeking and considering a veritable multitude of other viewpoints and approaches. As mentioned earlier, just as screen media is not created in a vacuum, so too, the analysis, definition and program development toward broader screen media literacy – even the most basic grammar, syntax and structure of the language as well as how best to teach this

literacy – is an ongoing and multi-dimensional subject which, like most areas of study across the academy, will thrive best as it becomes part of the rich discourse on how we now communicate, interact and get along.

Would that it were a sitting target. It is not, and complicating this discourse is the fact that it's all changing, often before we can grasp what happened yesterday. Kathryn Montgomery, noted theorist and pundit on children and youth interactions with media, pointed out over a decade ago that "the explosion of the new digital media culture is occurring so rapidly that its growth is surpassing the ability of scholars...and educators to grasp fully its nature, its direction and its impact..." (Montgomery, 2000). And it's only gotten worse.

All the more reason it seems, to work to get a better understanding of it now. In the interest of not chasing the elusive dragon of expanding media portals and their pervasive, seemingly unruly effects on our culture, the Rosebud Institute takes a more stripped-down, basic approach. How can educators arm themselves in what many see as a battle for attention in an ever-dizzying cacophony?

One way is by realizing that there is a *me* in media. As the personal increasingly becomes public, it will be the clearer voices that rise above the din. As with any form of communication, if you want to be heard you must strive to be the more effective communicator. More and more, what the world seems to want and even demand are unique and personal views. Witness how the phenomenon of "mommy blogging" has become an important resource for those in search of the best consumer goods. As with the voyeuristic attraction of cinema, the more personal someone is on the screen, the more drawn in the viewers seem to become. Why else would the seeming mundanity of Twitter be so engaging for so many? The Rosebud coursework outlined herein is designed to give individuals the tools they need to find their voice and become more effective "mediators." The approach is simple. The equipment is accessible. The results are measurable (Chilsen & Wells, 2012).

Initial, pre-course feedback from Rosebud Institute program participants thus far reveals that a general and pervasive fear of technology poses a significant initial hurdle, especially among established professionals who are looking for fewer challenges in their busy days, not more. *Digital Natives* – kids who grew up with technology, and "spent their entire lives surrounded by and using computers…phones, and all the other toys and tools of the digital age" (Prensky, 2001) – seem to have a great deal less of this anxiety. In many cases they are naturals, but it still does come up. In view of this fear, it is important to assess the effectiveness of the coursework's attempt to demystify and deemphasize the technical interface, in favor of a more basic exploration of reading and writing in the language of the screen. Does the program ultimately encourage participants to first embrace and then look beyond the technical, towards a future that will eventually equate camera and screen technology with pencil-to-paper technology? Can cloud computing, where digital assets and computing resources are delivered over the web, be accepted by educators as a natural extension of teaching, learning and self-assessment? Will we be willing to start down the road of affirming that "writing" with a camera in a basic cinematic language or communicating with images on a website, are no more or less "natural" than depositing ink on the page or even painting on the walls of a cave?

Early analysis of post-coursework comments and survey results indicate that many aspects of the initial offerings of the program have been successful. Comments such as the following are representative:

- "I'm getting a lot of ideas that I can take back to the classroom."
- "The ePortfolio portion of the course was also inspiring."

- "I learned more technology in this one week than I've learned in my whole life. It's been an amazing class."
- "I think it's interesting that every single person in this class is going to do something different with what they've learned once they leave."
- "I was afraid of this stuff at first. But when my work heard I took this course, they asked me to make a film for our company website; I did, and they loved it!"

These comments seem to indicate that the general structure of the program is headed in the right direction and is garnering the kind of ownership, engagement and buy-in initially hoped for.

Further assessment, refinement and development of the coursework and its results will also include investigation of participants' responses to and incorporation of the two aforementioned curriculum modules. The Movie Module is designed to weave basic cinematic language and screen media literacy into current curricula, and the ePortfolio Module is designed to instruct students on the how and why of managing their digital presence and the distribution of created assets through the related use of ePortfolios. How the participating teachers accept and ultimately deploy the modules is of particular interest, because it will be a direct indicator of their capacity and their willingness to inject screen media literacy into the ebb and flow of day-to-day teaching and learning.

Assessment, development, and refinement of the professional development angle also needs to be addressed, especially along the lines of creating streamlined yet organizationally specific approaches that can be remapped onto different circumstances according to need. Potential school in-service visits to directly introduce, assess, and promote further program application and efficacy are also being explored. The hope is that such follow-up activities will nurture a more complete, ongoing acceptance and integration of the foundational principles that the Rosebud Institute espouses and embodies.

Continuing the look forward, program outcomes will be extrapolated across a vision for further coursework modification, integration and expansion in order to continue to effectively meet the needs of professionals, both within education and outside of it, as well as the mediated learning abilities of their constituencies.

TEACHING CONVERGENCE

A few final thoughts revolve around the much-touted notion of convergence – that we indeed find ourselves nearing what feels to many like an apex in mediating, a veritable explosion of old ways and a tumultuous, aggressive and often calamitous scramble for finding a new modus operandi. While access to technology remains an issue, it seems to be turning more into a matter of effectively accessing one's own voice. "When people talk to me about the digital divide, I think of it not being so much about who has access to what technology as who knows how to create and express themselves in this new language of the screen" (Lucas, 2004). Even more so today, with phones becoming cameras and cameras becoming mobile devices and iPods becoming iPads and tablets and movie screens and televisions, and everyone scrambling to reach the almighty consumer where they live, eat, breath and sleep, the time does indeed seem to be now. While not everyone agrees how this will unfold, most are clear that as the crescendo ensues, the best way to use this new power and reach cannot be left to its own devices:

Learning depends crucially on the exact character of the activities that learners engage in with a program, the kinds of tasks they try to accomplish, and the kinds of intellectual and social activity they become involved in...technology may provide *interesting and powerful learning opportunities, but these are not taken automatically; teachers and learners need to learn how to take advantage of them. (Salomon & Perkins, 1996)*

Since simply having technology in the classroom "does not automatically inspire teachers to rethink their teaching or students to adopt new modes of learning" (Hiltzik, 2012), handing out $2000 pencils is not enough. Technology is here to stay and digitally native students relate to it differently. We therefore need a different approach (Chilsen & Wells, 2012). We can't simply add screen media literacy "to the curriculum menu, hiving off 'information and communication technology' into a separate subject" (Buckingham, 2007). Rather, in a world that is increasingly dominated by screen media, we need to reconceptualize our definition of *literacy*. We have both the ability and the duty to educate young and old alike in the language of the screen; to do anything less would be to leave them unprepared in an often hostile world – a world where the immediacy, manipulation and message of today's media have the potential to dramatically alter the classic modes of teaching, learning and communicating.

REFERENCES

Baker, F. W. (2012). *Media literacy in the K-12 classroom*. International Society for Technology in Education - ISTE

Boyer, E. (1988). *Media literacy: Sayings*. Retrieved from http://www.medialiteracy.com/sayings.htm

Buckingham, D. (2007). Digital media literacies: Rethinking media education in the age of the Internet. *Research in Comparative and International Education*, 2(1), 43–55. doi:10.2304/rcie.2007.2.1.43

Casinghino, C. (2011). *Moving images: Making movies, understanding media*. United States: Delmar Cengage Learning.

Chilsen, P. J., & Wells, C. R. (2012, June). *Media and the moving image: Creating those who thrive in a screen media world*. Paper presented at Ed-Media World Conference On Educational Media & Technology, Denver, CO.

Coutu, D. (2007, June). We Googled you. *Harvard Business Review*, *85*(6), 37–47.

Gray, D. (2008, May 22). *Web log message*. Retrieved from http://www.davegrayinfo.com/2008/05/22/why-powerpoint-rules-the-business-world/

Hechinger, J. (2008, September 18). College applicants, beware: Your Facebook page is showing. *Wall Street Journal*, p. D1.

Herring, D. F., & Notar, C. F. (2011). Show what you know: ePortfolios for 21st century learners. *College Student Journal*, *45*(4), 786.

Hiltzik, M. (2012, February 4). Who really benefits from putting high-tech gadgets in classrooms? *Los Angeles Times*, p. B1.

Lucas, G. (2004, September 14). *Interview by J. Daly [Personal Interview]. Life on the screen: Visual literacy in education. Edutopia*. Retrieved from http://www.edutopia.org/life-screen

McLuhan, M. (1964). *Understanding media: The extensions of man*. New York, NY: McGraw-Hill.

Montgomery, K. (2000). Youth and digital media: A policy research agenda. *Journal of Adolescent Youth*, *27S*, 61–68. doi:10.1016/S1054-139X(00)00130-0

Prensky, M. (2001). Digital natives, digital immigrants. *On The Horizon, 9*(5). Retrieved July 16, 2012 from http://www.marcprensky.com/writing/

Renaud, C. (2012). *Creating a digital media curriculum for the high school*. Unpublished Master's thesis. Carthage College, Wisconsin.

Salomon, G., & Perkins, D. N. (1996). Learning in wonderland: What computers really offer education. In S. Kerr (Ed.), *Technology and the future of education* (pp. 111-130). NSSE Yearbook. Chicago, IL: University of Chicago Press.

Thompson, R., & Bowen, C. J. (2009). *Grammar of the shot* (2nd ed.). Amsterdam, The Netherlands: Focal Press.

Van Ness, E. (2005, March 6). Is a cinema studies degree the new M.B.A.? *New York Times*, p. M1.

Waterworth, E., & Waterworth, J. (2010). Mediated presence in the future. In Bracken, C. C., & Skalaski, P. D. (Eds.), *Immersed in media: Telepresence in everyday life* (pp. 183–196). New York, NY: Routledge.

KEY TERMS AND DEFINITIONS

Digital Asset: An originally created piece of work that has been imported or converted into digital format and therefore can be deployed in any number of digital media. Digital assets can include but are not limited to: photos, videos, music, blog entries, podcasts, files, résumés, and/or any other work created in an academic setting.

Digital Immigrant: A person born before the existence or current pervasive nature of digital technologies who is not naturally familiar or instinctively comfortable and therefore must adapt to using digital technology, interfaces, and software.

Digital Media Literacy: The acquired ability to understand, access, evaluate, and analyze types and avenues of information created online or with available software and hardware to communicate and participate in civic life as competent media consumer, contributor, and creator of media in the online community.

Digital Native: A person who is indigenous to the digital world, has grown up with and uses a wide variety of available and continually evolving technology with an inborn, instinctive sense of how to communicate, record, understand and share in society.

ePortfolio: A website created for or by an individual, that manages their digital assets and online presence, communicating learning or professional progress, which continues to change as long as its creator continues to develop and refine the content to reflect current experience, skill, and/or career focus.

Media Convergence: The natural, continual, accelerating evolution of technology resulting in a more integrated, inescapable coming together of multiple avenues of information, entertainment and online communication.

Mediate: To create original work for and effectively communicate through the technology, tools, and language of the screen.

Screen Media: Any media that is produced for or distributed via the screen, including the entire spectrum of what constitutes *the screen*: the cinematic screen, the television screen, the computer screen, and the small screens accessed on a smartphones and other handheld devices.

Section 5
Student-Centered Learning and Student-Created Videos

Chapter 14
Digital Story-Making in Support of Student Meaning-Making

Gail Matthews-DeNatale
Northeastern University, USA

ABSTRACT

Learning design is critical to success when using visual media to enhance learning. This process involves beginning with the end goals in mind and working backwards to craft a thoughtful learning sequence. Through a pair of case studies, this chapter demonstrates the role student-generated digital stories can play in helping students make meaning of firsthand learning experiences. Digital story-making engages students in a multi-modal, multi-sensory experience that deepens engagement and improves the memorability of learning. Educators are under increasing pressure to provide evidence of the impact that coursework has on student learning, and student-generated digital stories provide valuable artifacts of learning.

INTRODUCTION

Stories are the large and small instruments of meaning, of explanation, that we store in our memories. – Roger Schank

Technology speaks with a loud voice. Whether the topic is digital storytelling, ePortfolios, or online learning, one of the first questions asked is "What software do you use?" We've got it all wrong, and student learning suffers as a result. The first questions should be "What do the students need to learn?" "What strengths do they bring to the class?" and "What have been their greatest challenges in learning?" This is a critical distinction, because in a book dedicated to enhancing instruction with visual media, it might be tempting to focus on visual media at the expense of considering what we mean by "enhancing instruction."

Educators often begin with an idea for an activity, select the tool, use it, and assess the results as a last step. Wouldn't it make more sense to begin with the end in mind and focus first on our hopes and dreams for student learning? With an eye

DOI: 10.4018/978-1-4666-3962-1.ch014

toward the destination, necessary steps fall into place – including the selection and use of technology – and the journey is much more meaningful for all participants (Wiggins & McTighe, 2005). This approach to learning design makes outcomes easier to assess and share with decision-makers who want to see evidence of learning (Brown and Diaz, 2011).

Through a pair of case studies, this chapter focuses on the role of student-generated digital stories in helping students make meaning of firsthand learning experiences. The story-making process helps students increase their capacity to reflect, assess, and shape their own learning. Digital story-making engages students in a multi-modal, multi-sensory experience that deepens engagement and improves the memorability of learning. Because digital story-making combines physical and mental intensity, attention to detail and reflection, it is in itself a meaning-making endeavor.

WHAT IS DIGITAL STORYTELLING?

Bryan Alexander observes "we've been telling stories with digital tools since the first computer networks linked nodes" (Alexander, 2011). Even in the early days of ARPANET in the 1960s, informal narratives were transmitted as asides to formal communication. The origin of the term is unclear, but it is usually attributed to Joe Lambert, Executive Director of the *Center for Digital Storytelling*, whose stories combine words, images, and audio in short, three- to five-minute-long narrative videos.

Any story that can be told verbally or in writing can also be told digitally, and the technical tools required to do so have become increasingly ubiquitous and easy to use. In the web site *50+ Ways to Tell a Story*, Alan Levine writes:

It was not long ago that producing multimedia digital content required expensive equipment and deep levels of technical expertise. We are at the point now where anyone can create and publish very compelling content with nothing more complex than a web browser (Levine, 2012).

In 2010 Jim Groom, Director of Teaching and Learning Technologies at the University of Mary Washington, founded *ds106*, a Massive Open Online Course (MOOC) on Digital Storytelling. The site has since grown to include a repository of assignments contributed by faculty from a range of institutions of higher education (DS106, n.d.).

A review of current resources on Digital Storytelling confirms that the major emphasis is usually placed on the *way* that a story is produced from a technical perspective, rather than on the pedagogical process of infusing student-generated digital storytelling into the learning experience. One notable exception is Georgetown University's Center for New Designs in Learning and Scholarship, whose Digital Storytelling Multimedia Archive poses three research questions:

1. **Multimedia Distinctive:** What about student learning in digital storytelling is distinctive to the media?
2. **Social Pedagogy:** How does the explicitly social aspect of this process change student learning?
3. **Affective Learning:** How does the emotional aspect of this process work to improve learning? (CNDS, n.d.)

According to Joe Lambert, humans are "overwhelmed by stories that we can't process. Our minds construct a sense of memory immediately after being part of an experience, and unless we … recite the story of the experience, it slowly diminishes in our memory" (Lambert, 2010, p.1). Ellen Goodman, a Simmons College professor who participated in Lambert's Digital Storytelling workshop, made the following observations about her story-making experience:

There was something about working so intensely and in a concentrated fashion with the dialogue and matching photographs or a visual image to it. As a producer, you're so present with the material and the message that you're trying to convey. You have to think much more deeply and complexly about what it is that you want to say.

And I think through that process of analyzing it, you can come up with different versions, you think "Geez, I've thought about it so much, I actually feel a little bit different about it – now I want to say something different than I thought I was going to say when I started." And I think that's the feedback loop. You're really introspective and you're reflective ... the telling of the story transforms you and transforms the story. (Matthews-DeNatale, What's the Educational Value of Digital Storytelling? 2008, 00:39)

The story-making process, during which students translate firsthand experience into reflective narratives, enhances both the motivation of the learner while creating the story and the memorability of the learning itself. According to educational researcher Raymond Wlodkowski, "motivation binds emotion to action" because:

From a neuroscientific viewpoint, at the micro level, learning is long-lasting change in existing neuronal networks ... As we experience our world, events that are accompanied by feelings receive preferential processing in the brain ... We are much more likely to remember things that engage us emotionally. It appears that the more powerful the feeling that accompanies an experience, the more lasting the memory (Wlodkowski, 2008, pp. 2-21).

This means that, from a physiological standpoint, learning is literally a process of changing your mind. Digital story-making creates a space for this cognitive change to develop. The process of digital story-making provides a framework for

students to see the proverbial forest for the trees, to extract a take-home story from the complexity of experiential learning. The physicality of manipulating and methodically arranging digital images, audio, and text "makes students slow down and think about their work in new ways" (CNDS, n.d.), resulting in reflective meaning-making.

This chapter provides two case study examples of course assignments that used digital story-making to enhance students' capacity for reflective meaning-making, distilling firsthand experience into narratives that could be shared with peers, professors, family, and future learners.

STORYTELLING IN THE AGE OF THE INTERNET: TWO CASE STUDIES

NOTE: The following learning experiences were designed for use in an undergraduate-level course taught by the author at Simmons College, Boston, in 2006. In addition to gathering written reflections at the end of the course, select students were interviewed several months after completing the course to gain insight into their long-term perceptions of the experience. To access detailed lesson plans, rubrics, and other collateral materials see Matthews-DeNatale (2008), *Digital Storytelling: Tips and Resources.*

Storytelling in the Age of the Internet is a Multidisciplinary Core Course, a "required course for all First-Year students ... that involves engaging students in critical thinking and writing and addressing the challenges and opportunities of living in a multiracial and multicultural society" (Simmons College, n.d.). Of the 18 students enrolled in this course, all were female, approximately two thirds came to the college from suburban and rural communities, one third were either international students or New Americans whose parents immigrated to the United States, and one was from Boston proper. The new urban environment disoriented many of these students: some were afraid for their safety because they had no prior experience navigating a city, and almost all were extremely homesick within three to four weeks after the start of the course.

The pedagogical challenge was to help students move out of their intellectual comfort zone when they were already feeling the discomfort of first-year college life. Digital storytelling was used at the beginning of the course as a strategy for helping students become acclimated to the experience of urban living, and again at the end of the course as a vehicle for critical analysis of their assumptions and perspectives about race and culture.

Boston Story Map

The course began with a Story Map assignment designed to help students literally find a legitimate place to stand within the new, urban environment in which they lived. It was an introductory exercise that helped students make connections between day-to-day life experiences, issues associated with cultural diversity, and their academic work.

Students were instructed to select a setting in the Boston area to visit and write about. They were provided with a list of suggested places, but they were also free to select a site of their own choosing. The list included safe places, such as a nearby art museum, but it also included public spaces in communities that differed from many of the students' cultures of origin (e.g., a grocery store in Chinatown or a local community action organization dedicated to preserving affordable community housing in a historically Puerto Rican neighborhood undergoing gentrification).

The assignment was to observe, journal, and document their place in a thoughtful and respectful manner. "Criteria for Excellence" helped focus and guide student attention, as they were charged with authoring a firsthand account of the observation experience that conveyed:

- A Sense of Place (rich description of sights, sounds, and smells)

- People or Culture (heritage, values, beliefs, and perspectives)
- Insight, Questioning, Reflection (what ideas, issues, and concerns the experience raised)
- Intellectual Connection (meaningful reference to a course reading, discussion, etc.)
- Broadened Horizons (interacting with an unfamiliar place or culture)

After several weeks of journaling, story sharing, feedback, and revision, each student turned her observations into a web-based story. In constructing the online version of their story, students were asked to consider whether or not it would be appropriate or culturally sensitive to include audio, video, and images. Visual media were used intentionally, not automatically. In this regard, the decision to *not* incorporate a visual element was part of a larger conversation about the culture of self-disclosure and the consequences of over sharing, a concern that pre-dates Facebook but is largely a consequence of user-friendly online publishing tools. The stories were linked to a Google Map, creating a map-based compilation of the students' work (see Figure 1). Viewers could click pushpin-type buttons on the map to read the story that was written about that place.

On a practical level, the process of pooling and mapping these narrative experiences created a visual representation of their new environment. They developed an annotated visual guide that they could use in navigating the new space in which they lived. On a conceptual level, digital storytelling provided a structure for a larger conversation about place, identity, belonging, and self-and-other. In both regards, the result was larger than the sum of its parts.

Digital Stories of Service Learning

The culminating experience in *Storytelling in the Age of the Internet* was a digital storytelling project that grew out of students' experiences with

Figure 1. Screenshot of the Boston story map (© 2008, Matthews-DeNatale presentation)

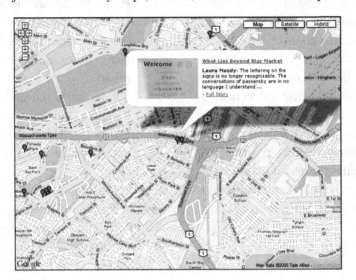

service learning. The assignment was designed to help students make intellectual connections, translating the particulars of a firsthand experience into a larger meaning that could be "stored in memory" (Schank, 1992).

About five weeks into the 13-week semester, students selected a service-learning placement. Options included a home for the elderly, an after school mentoring program for middle school children, and a tutoring program for English-as-second-language learners. At least two students were assigned to each site.

Students were expected to work at their placement for a minimum of twenty hours. Each student had a private journaling space in the course's learning management system and was expected to post at least one message per week to document the experience in writing. In addition to writing, students were encouraged to document their placement experiences with digital pictures, video, and drawings as appropriate. Some used their smartphones to record video and images, others used digital cameras, and a few used disposable cameras.

In the final third of the semester, students participated in sessions that prepared them for story planning and production. These sessions were based on the digital storytelling workshop developed by Joe Lambert at the Center for Digital Storytelling (CDS).

From elementary school through high school, students are taught how to write a five-paragraph essay. This structure introduces a topic, identifies at least three points, expands upon each point within a series of paragraphs, and summarizes points made. The focus is on fleshing out thoughts; the structure is linear. In contrast, the CDS advocates engaging story-makers in a cyclical and recursive process that distills narratives into an essence. The process is as much about meaning-making as it is about story-authoring.

In class, each student was paired with another student who had worked at the same placement. Each dyad discussed what they learned from the service experience after comparing the points of agreement and divergence in their journals. They discovered that two people could have radically different experiences and perspectives within the same work setting. For example, in one pairing a student whose first language was English compared notes with a student whose first language was Hindi. They had both worked at a drop-in center for adult English Language Learners. The Hindi-speaking student assumed that her work would be a piece of cake, because she grew up translating for her parents. To her surprise, the experience was quite challenging, because the process of interpreting is very different from the process of teaching a person to speak a language. In contrast, the native English speaker discovered a passion for helping others communicate and find their voice in a new language. This counterintuitive finding was the kernel of their digital story. See Figure 2 for a visual representation of the digital story in production.

Students used a modified form of the CDS rubric as a guide for providing feedback and improving their story plans:

- Point (of View)
- Dramatic Question
- Emotional Content
- Script and Voice
- Sense of Audience
- Images (visuals support and add new dimension to what is being said)
- Balance of Economy and Detail
- Pacing

- Grammar and Writing

Over the course of three weeks they shared plans with the class, critiqued peers' plans, revised plans, created preliminary storyboards, wrote scripts, selected images, correlated images with script, recorded audio, revised storyboards, produced a video, and celebrated with an in-class screening. On the face of it, this part of the experience was procedural, but it also constituted thought-in-action.

Evidence of Learning

As mentioned at the beginning of this chapter, academic technologists are under increasing pressure to demonstrate that the resources they provide are having a positive impact on student learning, and that the expense is fiscally responsible. According to Malcolm Brown and Veronica Diaz:

The calls for more accountability in higher education, the shrinking budgets that often force larger class sizes, and the pressures to increase

Figure 2. A digital story in production (© 2008, Matthews-DeNatale presentation)

degree-completion rates are all raising the stakes for colleges and universities today, especially with respect to the instructional enterprise. As resources shrink, teaching and learning is becoming the key point of accountability ...

Apart from the fiscal and accountability pressures, the pace of technology change continues unabated. Facing so many options but constrained budgets, faculty and administrators must make careful decisions about support for teaching and learning: what practices to adopt and where to invest their time, effort, and fiscal resources. On an almost daily basis, faculty and their support staff must decide whether or not to use a technology or adopt a new teaching practice. This again argues for evidence-based practice that includes evaluations to inform future decisions (Brown and Diaz, 2011).

When combined with student-authored reflections, student-generated digital stories are valuable artifacts of learning. This type of evidence has been described as "visible knowledge" or "making thinking visible" (Center for New Designs in Scholarship, n.d.; Collins et. al., 1991). The stories provide an external representation of student thinking: rich data that yield insight into the interior world of the learner.

This evidence of learning is not without its limitations. The online medium is inherently volatile. The student websites and blogs in which the stories are usually embedded come and go, often disappearing upon graduation, which complicates longitudinal study and makes it difficult to assess the long-term educational impact of story-making. The stories are also self-reported and anecdotal, more useful in assessing students' new media literacy than traditional academic conceptual learning (Jenkins et al, 2006).

But all mediums have their disadvantages. For example, this book illustrates the limitations of printed text. Screenshots cannot do justice to the

interactive power of hypertext and the multimodal engagement of digital stories. It is incumbent upon the reader to imagine the combination of sounds, images, transitions, pacing, and linkages of the Service Learning Digital Stories and Boston Story Map described in this chapter.

How can we know if digital story-making is achieving the desired pedagogical result? At this point the outcomes are anecdotal. Learning through digital story-making is a complex process that includes many variables: course and assignment goals, the life experiences that students draw upon in creating their stories, the quality and ease of use in the story-making tools, the support provided by technologists, and feedback provided by faculty and peers during the story-development process. Educators are connecting the dots in recent research on the neuroscience of learning, student observations and interviews, and their own intuition as teachers. Skeptics will want to see scientifically valid, statistically significant research on the effectiveness of digital storytelling for achieving content-related and conceptual learning. Proponents would also welcome verification of the learning that they believe is taking place, but this type of research is both expensive and labor intensive. How ironic that the research critical to justifying funding for student-generated digital storytelling is currently cost prohibitive!

With these caveats in mind, *Storytelling in the Age of the Internet* did endeavor to document both short-term and long-term pedagogical impact. At the end of the course, students were asked to write a final reflection on the experience. Six months, and again one year after the course, four of the students were interviewed to assess the immediate and long-term impact of the experience. Six years after completing the course, a final round of follow-up communication took place with several of the same students via LinkedIn. Student Rachel Franchi consented to share her final course reflection, an excerpt from the follow-up interview, and the LinkedIn correspondence as evidence of her long-term learning:

Final Reflection (Submitted on the Last Day)
It is not the importance of stories that I learned, nor is it that they can be as diverse as we are as a human race. What it is about stories that I learned and is now embedded into my own definition of stories, is how we all can relate to them, on some level, even if that level is mere compassion, or interest, or lack thereof of being able to relate. Common threads people share through stories isn't always the literal common thread, but the fact that both the storyteller and the person listening care about forming a common thread that doesn't yet exist.

The digital stories many people in the class did about the International Learning Center at the YMCA were not experiences I could relate to. I only speak English, I have never tutored anyone in a language, nor spent a great deal amount of time with any struggling immigrants. However, I still became connected to their stories—the ones of the immigrants, and the stories the MCCer's told through iMovie. Why? Because I was an active listener to their stories, I was interested, I took it all in, and now have it in me forever. …Thank God for Storytelling in the Age of the Internet or I would have been missing out… only appreciating the things I was already familiar with, and not those that are most important to be exposed to… the stories and things that are new and different! (R. Franchi, personal communication, May, 2006)

Follow-Up Interview (Conducted Approximately Six Months after the Course)
When I think back to when I've done term papers, you do have to be very, very structured. Even though it's a first draft, it needs to have a topic sentence, and a thesis statement and things like that. So I think your thinking is very constricted in a way. Whereas with storytelling, digitally, I think that you can start with your raw thoughts –

whatever they may be – and then you can fine-tune them to decide what you want your story to be. … You have all these thoughts in your head about what you want it to be, and you have all these experiences, and you have your journaling. For you to get across your message and what you're trying to say in a way that's visual, audio, and with text, I think is really using different parts of your brain.…you're using all the senses versus just reading it. (Matthews-DeNatale, What's the Difference Between Writing and Digital Storytelling? 2008, 00:50)

LinkedIn Communication (Six Years after Completion of the Course)
I remember the course being very unique and unlike any other course offerings at Simmons, which is why it piqued my interest. It was one of the most creative, non-structured academic environments I had ever been in. What I will always remember is that you had us all sit at a big conference table instead of in a lecture hall or at desks. The physical environment of the classroom alone was extremely engaging. … While I haven't had to use iMovie for any other projects I still got a lot out of the multidimensional project experience- interviewing, recording, reflecting, taking photos, incorporating them into a meaningful storyline and then using technology to deliver that story.

Being a biochemistry major at Simmons and now being a fourth year medical student, it's safe to say I have never taken another course like this in the many years of school I've had, but that is what has made it so memorable. …This course allowed me to wear a completely different hat, be creative in ways I never had before, and have a lot of fun. (Franchi, personal communication, May 26, 2012)

In these three passages, Rachel speaks to both the practical and conceptual enhancement of learning that takes place when students generate their own visual media. On a pragmatic level, creating visual media allows students to think outside the box. In this instance, the *box* could be defined as the structure of a five-paragraph essay, lecture hall learning, or course assignments that do not allow students to problem-solve for themselves. Digital story-making creates an opportunity for students to collaborate with one another, draw from a rich and diverse set of data (interviews, photos, journal entries), and use "different parts of the brain" to transform "raw thoughts" into a coherent message. On a conceptual level, visual story-making allows students to find the essence of an idea, and then aggregate individual stories to gain a larger perspective; the stories are in them forever.

Aggregated Learning

In *Composing a Life*, Mary Catherine Bateson likens the process of turning life challenges into meaning to stringing beads into a "necklace of elegance and beauty" (Bateson, 1990, p. 240). If digital stories are the beads, how do they become a necklace? When we take a story-making approach to learning design, involving students in the construction of narratives about their learning, the next logical step is for students to reflect upon the relationship between individual stories and their larger learning journeys.

In the same way that digital story-making helps learners see the trees of the forest in discrete courses, ePortfolio-making helps learners see the forest as a whole by aggregating stories into meaning over an extended period of time. From a technical standpoint, ePortfolios are designed to accommodate many forms of media, from text files to still images and videos. Traditional and progressive work can coexist, with digital stories housed alongside term papers. More important, ePortfolios are designed to support a process in which learners examine the interrelationship between stories and other artifacts of learning, *reflecting on* experience in order to *learn from* experience (Matthews-DeNatale, n.d.).

Following her work with digital-story-making at Simmons College, the author expanded her use of technology to include ePortfolios when she joined the faculty of Education at Northeastern University in 2011. In January of 2012, the Masters Program decided to require all students to keep ePortfolios of their learning. See Figure 3 for a sample page from an ePortfolio.

While this initiative is still young, preliminary evidence suggests that the initiative is having the

Figure 3. Sample page from an ePortfolio. (©2012, Alisha Cardwell, Used with permission)

desired result, based on the following responses to a recent questionnaire:

Student A: My ePortfolio has helped me realize encompassing lessons, themes and interests I have accumulated throughout my time at Northeastern. In my undergraduate program, I had a "set it and forget it" attitude about my courses—I hyperfoucsed on the material at hand but then quickly moved on once the course was over. At the graduate level, everything I learn I try to apply to my current position or utilize when looking for new career opportunities. Maintaining an ePortfolio can be a lot of work, but now I feel like a have a map of my whole graduate career that I can personally reference or share with employers. As a visual learner, I especially liked saving videos or images since sometimes the emotional reactions or thought-processes produced from media is hard to save in words.

Student B: An ePortfolio enables one to keep material in its raw form. A traditional, paper portfolio limits the type of material one can place in it. For example, multimedia presentations do not translate effectively into a paper portfolio as the essence and complexity of the work is lost. Whereas traditional reflections and portfolios may stifle creativity and creativity, the ePortfolio and its digital format enable the user to spread their wings and flex their creativity. It is empowering rather than limiting. In keeping completed assignments or other multimedia sources in their raw form, students can maintain a true representation of their learning experiences, knowledge, and skills.

The benefits of compiling and reflecting upon my work in an ePortfolio are extensive. Course content and concepts, assessments, and discussion can easily be forgotten or lost if one is not challenged to reflect. The ePortfolio empowered me to synthesize material from each course I took while also giving me the opportunity to store my work for future reference. What separates the ePortfo-

lio from other reflection tools is that I can easily access information from previous courses and make meaningful connections across courses and content areas. If concepts, knowledge, and skills remain isolated throughout my learning experience, then the potential benefits of my academic program are incomplete and unfulfilled. The goal of the ePortfolio is to reduce this isolation so that students get the most out of their program.

Student C: Through the digital format I am able to share my learning in a colorful, creative way … This format allows me to bring words to life, it allows my reader to see inside my journey and not just words on a paper. Some images and videos I choose to include convey meanings that are otherwise hard to capture. The use of video allows me to speak my ideas to my audience, through my voice you are able to hear my passion and purpose for my work.

CONCLUSION

The tools used for creating and aggregating digital stories are much less important than the process and goals for learning. Tools are transitory; each new generation lowers the barrier to entry through increased ease of use. From an instructional design perspective, the effectiveness of student-generated media depends on the clarity of learning goals. Digital storytelling is not an inherently superior teaching strategy, and the tools are not a panacea; educators need to keep an eye on the prize of substantive, reflective, course- and program-appropriate learning.

The value of digital story-making is that it provides students with a rich and multi-faceted experience, creating a differentiated learning environment that engages all of the learners' senses. The stories themselves are rich artifacts, providing evidence of learning to students, their teachers, and those who need to verify that technology investment has pedagogical value. When combined with written reflection, for example in an ePortfolio, these stories help make learning memorable at both a pragmatic and conceptual level, and they also help make knowledge visible. The stories may be transitory but, through the act of their creation, the memories will stay with the makers for the rest of their lives.

ACKNOWLEDGMENT

The author wishes to thank Jamie Traynor and Lesley Weiman of Simmons College for the support they provided in orienting students to digital storytelling tools, Jamie Traynor for support in developing the *Digital Storytelling: Tips and Resources* booklet, and Doug DeNatale for his feedback on earlier drafts of the chapter. Thanks also to Rachel Franchi, Ellen Goodman, and Vaughn Rogers for participating in interviews and follow-up communication about the learner's perspective of digital story-making. Thanks also to Mary Church, Stefani Harvey, Travis DiJoseph, and Claire Weiss Lewis for providing written responses to interview questions about learning ePortfolios.

REFERENCES

Alexander, B. (2011). *The new digital storytelling: Creating narratives with new media*. Westport, CT: Prager.

Bateson, M. C. (1990). *Composing a life*. New York, NY: Plume.

Brown, M., & Diaz, V. (2011). Seeking evidence of impact: Opportunities and needs. *Educause Review, 46*(5). Retrieved May 18, 2012, from http://net.educause.edu/ir/library/pdf/ERM1152.pdf

Center for New Designs in Scholarship (CNDS). Georgetown University. (n.d.). *Digital story multimedia archive*. Retrieved May 19, 2012, from https://pilot.cndls.georgetown.edu/digitalstories

Center for New Designs in Scholarship (CNDS). Georgetown University. (n.d.). *Visible knowledge project*. Retrieved May 19, 2012, from https://cndls.georgetown.edu/about/grants/vkp

Collins, A., Seely Brown, J., & Holum, A. (1991). Cognitive apprenticeship: Making thinking visible. *American Educator, 15*(3), 6–46.

ds106. (n.d.). Retrieved August 10, 2012 from http://ds106.us

Jenkins, H., Purushotma, R., Clinton, C., Weigel, M., & Robison, A. (2006). *Confronting the challenges of participatory culture: Media education for the 21st century*. Project New Media Literacies. Retrieved May 18, 2012 from http://www.newmedialiteracies.org/files/working/NMLWhitePaper.pdf

Lambert, J. (2010). *Digital storytelling cookbook*. Retrieved May 18, 2012, from http://www.storycenter.org/storage/publications/cookbook.pdf

Levine, A. (2012). *50+ web 2.0 ways to tell a story*. Retrieved May 18, 2012, from http://50ways.wikispaces.com http://50ways.wikispaces.com

Matthews-DeNatale, G. (n.d.). *Reflecting for learning*. Retrieved August 10, 2012, from https://northeastern.digication.com/master_of_education_eportfolio_resources/Reflecting_for_Learning

Matthews-DeNatale, G. (2008). Digital Story-Making: Understanding the Learner's Perspective. Session presented at The *Educause Learning Initiative Annual Conference, San Antonio, TX*. Retrieved May 19, 2012 from http://www.educause.edu/Resources/DigitalStoryMakingUnderstandin/162538

Schank, R. (1992). *Tell me a story: Narrative and intelligence.* Evanston, IL: Northwestern University Press.

Simmons College. (n.d.). *Multidisciplinary core course.* Retrieved May 18, 2012, from http://www.simmons.edu/enews/orientation_061809/core.html

Wiggins, G., & McTighe, J. (2005). *Understanding by design.* Upper Saddle River, NJ: Prentice Hall.

Wlodkowski, R. (2008). *Enhancing adult motivation to learn.* San Francisco, CA: Jossey Bass.

ADDITIONAL READING

Center for Digital Storytelling. (n.d.). *Storycenter. org.* Retrieved May 18, 2012, from http://www.storycenter.org

Division of Information Technology, University of Maryland, Baltimore. (n.d.). *Digital stories.* Retrieved May 18, 2012, from http://www.umbc.edu/oit/newmedia/studio/digitalstories

Matthews-DeNatale, G. (2007). *Digital storytelling: What and how are students learning?* Session presented at "Digital Natives, Digital Immigrants" Colleges of the Fenway Conference, Boston, MA. Retrieved May 19, 2012, from http://www.slideshare.net/gmdenatale/digital-storytelling-what-and-how-are-students-learningcof2007

Matthews-DeNatale, G., & Alexander, B. (2007). *Web 2.0 and digital storytelling: Educause learning initiative "ELI in Conversation" podcast series.* Retrieved May 19, 2012, from http://connect.educause.edu/blog/gbayne/eliinconversationweb20and/46133

Matthews-DeNatale, G., Maxfield, S., Perna, M., & Makofske, F. (2007). *Digital storytelling.* Retrieved May 19, 2012, from http://www.slideshare.net/gmdenatale/digital-storytelling-hbs-braingain-0807

Narrations, C. (n.d.). *Storiesforchange.net.* Retrieved May 18, 2012, from http://storiesforchange.net

Ohler, J. (2008). *Digital storytelling in the classroom: New media pathways to literacy, learning, and creativity.* Thousand Oaks, CA: Corwin/Sage.

Robin, B. R. (2005). *Educational uses of digital storytelling.* Retrieved May 18, 2012, from http://www.coe.uh.edu/digital-storytelling

Chapter 15
Video Projects:
Integrating Project-Based Learning, Universal Design for Learning, and Bloom's Taxonomy

Marianne Castano Bishop
Indiana University South Bend, USA

Jim Yocom
Indiana University South Bend, USA

ABSTRACT

Video projects offer valuable opportunities for students to engage in the academic enterprise and demonstrate what they are learning. This chapter explores what will be referred to as the Helix-Flow: an amalgam synthesizing and strengthening three theoretical frameworks of instruction, including Project-based Learning, Universal Design for Learning, and Bloom's Taxonomy of Cognitive Domain. The Helix-Flow captures the essence of these three theories and serves as a backdrop for understanding and appreciating video projects as a learning artifact. As a helix, the spirals wrap around the cylinder or cone. Each spiral represents one of the theories and the cylinder or cone represents student engagement with video projects. The spirals or theories support the cone or student engagement with video projects. Each theory or spiral has its own inherent and prescribed set of principles and guidelines. Each theory integrates with the others while keeping its own strengths, providing a comprehensive approach to instruction and student engagement. Each theory scaffolds differentiated instruction. This chapter will also examine the five Rs as guidelines for multimedia projects – Rationale, Roles, Resources, Rubric, and Readiness as well as the design of video assignments, assistance, production phases, and assessment.

DOI: 10.4018/978-1-4666-3962-1.ch015

INTRODUCTION

Schwartz and Hartmann (2007) argued the paucity of empirical evaluations on the use of video for learning. They reviewed abstracts from ten issues of five different peer-reviewed journals published before October 2005 on learning interventions at all ages and from diverse topics, comparing the number of research articles that focused on video-aided learning (VAL) with computer-aided learning (CAL). Relevant findings include the following: of the 48 journal abstracts on *learning and instruction*, they found that only 6.3% were on VAL and 16.6% were on CAL; the 31 journal abstracts on *cognition and instruction* also yielded low results for VAL at 3.2% but a higher result of 25.8% for CAL. Because of an apparent need for more data that highlights the affordances of video as a tool for learning, this article seeks to add to the scholarship of teaching and learning: (1) by reviewing how video projects have been used by faculty and students from various disciplines to enhance instruction and increase student engagement; (2) by highlighting three theoretical frameworks that scaffold teaching and learning in the context of video projects; and (3) by discussing faculty and student preparedness in producing videos.

We start with a discussion of video projects and how they impact teaching and learning. To provide a theoretical framework for video projects, we underscore the principles and guidelines of Project-based Learning (PBL), Universal Design for Learning (UDL), and Bloom's Taxonomy of Cognitive Domain. We propose a model for applying these three theories – the Helix-Flow. We also discuss the five Rs for developing and assessing multimedia, particularly video projects. We provide issues and considerations to keep in mind before we conclude.

Almost every day, we hear about new multimedia resources like smart devices that could be used to take video- and audio-clips. Multimedia can include any combination of media formats such as text, graphical images, audio, and video for the purpose of providing information and/or instruction (Yocom & Bishop, 2010). For this chapter we will focus on video projects. With a buffet of multimedia-rich resources available, the use of video for teaching and learning is increasingly becoming the technology du jour. Students nowadays are asking their instructors to have the option of submitting video projects as part of coursework. Faculty are increasingly using videos for teaching. (Bishop & Yocom, 2011; Yocom & Bishop, 2010)

Video projects highlight the many dimensions of teaching and learning. Not only does video accommodate different learning styles – auditory, visual, kinesthetic – video projects also foster teamwork, time management, self-efficacy, and technology skills. Don Knezek of the International Society of Technology in Education noted, "Now and in the future, effective teachers of digital-age learners will be challenged to move away from models of teaching and learning as isolated endeavors. As they model work and learning that reflects inventive thinking and creativity, teachers must become comfortable as co-learners with their students and with colleagues around the world" (ISTE, 2008, p. i).

Some examples of video projects for teaching and learning are exemplary in their own right. These video projects address the paucity of video-aided learning resources found by Schwartz's and Hartmann's literature review on journal abstracts on or before 2005 and demonstrate increasingly more resources are being made available to educators and students.

Video Projects Online

Multimedia Educational Resource for Learning and Online Teaching (MERLOT) ELIXR is an initiative that hosts a digital repository from more than 70 discipline-specific multimedia case stories. These digital stories are currently being used for faculty development and include real-life experiences that spotlight exemplary teaching strategies as well as the process of implementing them (MERLOT, n.d.). MERLOT also features student-created videos as part of coursework. Videos on MERLOT are licensed by Creative Commons to be shareable – meaning others can copy, distribute and transmit these case studies but the videos cannot be altered, cannot be transformed or built upon, and cannot be used without making attributions to the original authors or creators unless permission is first granted from the original authors or creators (Creative Commons, n.d.).

One of the digital case stories is from Regina Austin, professor at the University of Pennsylvania Law School, who developed a visual legal advocacy course. She taught visual legal advocacy with the goal of training law students "to become producers and directors of visual legal advocacy which is…advocacy made on behalf of clients and causes that are directed at achieving social justice." "The videos are wonderful device for getting students to get out into the world with their cameras as a cover perhaps and to have contact with people who have real problems and people who need the law to help them with their problems. If the problem can be visualized, other people will come to understand those problems and might be given more of an incentive to help to solve them" (http://elixr.merlot.org/case-stories/teaching-strategies/nurturing-student-creativity-with-video-projects/student-video-projects-in-law-school2, 2010). Lawyers who have used video documentaries and testimonials inspired her.

Jacqui Sadashige and others whose works are featured in MERLOT ELIXR share Austin's sentiment. In Sadashige's case, as faculty at the University of Pennsylvania's Center for Programs in Critical Writing, she is not teaching her students how to make film; rather, her students create mashups (i.e., video clips from several sources that provide a digital collage of their message) as a teaching tool after her students decide on their topics as a group. Sadashige came up with this idea when her students asked her if they could do video projects as a way to demonstrate writing abilities.

Examples of topics her students have worked on are racism at Disney, changes in workplace etiquette, and self-portrayal in hip-hop videos. Students post their videos in Facebook and other social networks and are usually eager for their friends to see what they have accomplished. The roles in video production that students take on help them "gain greater appreciation of what this medium is about." (http://elixr.merlot.org/case-stories/teaching-strategies/nurturing-student-creativity-with-video-projects/nurturing-student-creativity-with-video-projects4/, 2010).

Under the auspices of the Oakland Unified School District, the Urban Dreams Video Project emerged as part of the Urban Dreams Technology Innovation Challenge Grant and Youth Media Project. The Urban Dreams Video Project used a team of filmmakers who worked with the Oakland public high school teachers and students to produce videos on human rights and social justice. Student filmmakers described the projects they were interested in and developed concepts for their video projects. Together with the Urban Dreams Video Project team, several videos were produced. They included topics that focus on issues that were meaningful to Oakland youth. One of these videos was entitled "Education – What does it mean? What is it worth?" In this video, student filmmakers discuss Frederick Douglass' life as a former slave in the 1800s who became a leader of the abolitionist movement, a social reformer, orator, writer, and statesman. Students also interviewed other students and asked them questions such as, "what does getting an education mean to you," "do you and your friends take getting an education seriously," and "what do you think the future would be like without an education," with reflections at the end. Another video, "Young Sisters on the Street," had students researching youth issues in the US and developing countries where Oakland had *sister city* relationships. The group focused on child prostitution in Brazil and its impact on AIDS, health care, child labor, and educational opportunities. The video also included a narrative on a friend's life of prostitution in the US. "Gay Marriage: A Right? Or Wrong?" featured the student group's investigation of the historical context of gay rights and gay marriage and how these issues affect the nation. An excerpt from the students' concept paper noted that "by presenting interview subjects, a brief history, and an in-depth look at all sides, we feel we can better inform the public." Toward the end of their video, they posed the questions of "who decides," "who cares," "who wins," and "who loses" (Oakland Unified School District Urban Dreams Video Project, n.d.).

At Duke University, Kevin Caves had his students work in teams during their capstone course "to design, build and deliver customized assistive devices for people with disabilities in the community" (Center for Instructional Technology, n.d.). Using flip video cameras, students recorded their interviews with clients with disabilities. The video featured clients explaining what they could do on their own and what they could do with the assistive prototypes developed by students. As students designed the devices, they referred to the preliminary video as a memory aid. For those instructors who couldn't attend the meeting with clients, the video was also a resource for review. The final presentation was the final cut of the video with interviews and demonstration of the devices they designed (Center for Instructional Technology, n.d.).

At Georgetown University, Digital Storytelling as a social pedagogy combined video, sound, images, and the creator's voice. Students worked individually or collaboratively to investigate issues that have relevance in and outside their classrooms and, more importantly, are meaningful to them. Students "work on authentic assignments, develop their personal and academic voice, represent knowledge to a community of learners and receive situated feedback from their peers. Due to their affective involvement with this process and the novelty effect of the medium, students are more engaged than in traditional assignments.

These factors can create a spiral of engagement, drawing students into deeper and deeper engagement with their topics." (Duke University Digital Storytelling, n.d.)

The Helix-Flow and Theoretical Frameworks

These educational video projects support at least three theoretical frameworks that we refer to as the Helix-Flow. Most of the examples above relate to Project-based Learning, Bloom's Taxonomy of Cognitive Domain, and Universal Design for Learning. The focus on these three theoretical frameworks was purposely designed since they work from and with each other in scaffolding best teaching practices and student engagement. The common thread that weaves through these theories or spirals is that they focus on projects that are both authentic and meaningful to the learner, support differentiated instruction, and move the learner to acquire skills they may not have thought possible had they not actively engaged in producing an artifact or end-product as part of coursework. The Helix-Flow supports student-centered pedagogy and practice. The artifact, as far as this article is concerned, is a video project that the student has developed.

A helix is a three-dimensional spiral curve that turns on an axis and surrounds the surface of a cylinder or cone at an upward constant angle from the base. The cylinder or cone represents student engagement through video projects and each of the three spirals represents each of the theories previously mentioned. Each spiral or theory wraps around the cylinder or cone, supporting student engagement. Each spiral or theory integrates with the other two while keeping its own strengths, providing a comprehensive approach to instruction and student engagement. Each theory has its own inherent and prescribed set of principles and guidelines (See Figure 1).

We start with a discussion of Project-based Learning (PBL) since it underscores the creation

Figure 1. The helix-flow of project-based learning, universal design for learning, and Bloom's taxonomy of the cognitive domain

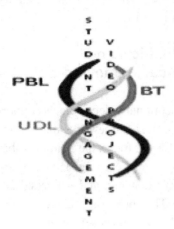

of meaningful projects in response to an authentic problem. In many of the scenarios mentioned above from the video projects online, PBL seems to be the foundation from which video projects were created as learning artifacts. Universal Design for Learning and Bloom's Taxonomy of Cognitive Domain support this foundation to enhance student engagement.

Student Engagement

EDUCAUSE refers to student engagement as the "rendezvous between learning and the digital tools and techniques that excite students" (EDUCAUSE, n.d.). With the easy availability of resources for producing video projects – cameras on smart phones and mobile devices, web-based storage areas, and affordable video cameras, software programs and apps – faculty should not be surprised if the use of video projects as part of coursework increases through the years.

Psychologist David Myers (2006, 2009, 2011) defined learning as a relatively permanent change in one's behavior due to experience. When students are able to work on projects that excite them, using video production tools and techniques, and end up with a relatively permanent change in how they

see the world and themselves through their newly acquired knowledge, skills, and understanding, one could say that the students have learned what they needed to learn.

The National Survey on Student Engagement website (NSSE, n.d.) states that student engagement represents two critical features of collegiate quality: student-focus and institution-focus. The amount of time and effort students apply to their studies and related educationally purposeful activities is the first feature. The second feature relates to resource deployment, curriculum organization and other learning opportunities offered by the institution to motivate students to participate in activities that have been linked to student learning from decades of research studies.

From the video projects online discussed above, it appears that students put a significant amount of time and effort into their projects, and the faculty and educational institutions provide them with resources both on-campus and online to create their video projects. Resources available to faculty and students as discussed above have facilitated effective and efficient use of these resources in video projects.

Project-Based Learning (PBL)

Bender (2012) defined Project-based Learning (PBL) as "an instructional model based on having students confront real-world issues and problems that they find meaningful, determine how to address them, and then act in a collaborative fashion to create problem solutions" (p. 1). PBL uses authentic, real-world projects, each involving a highly motivating and engaging question, task, or problem, so that students learn academic content within the context of cooperative and collaborative problem-solving situations (Bender, 2012, p. 8). PBL supports differentiated instruction (Bender, 2012, p. 2) which starts where students are and builds on their strengths.

Differentiated instruction is a theory of teaching based on the premise that educators need to vary their instructional approaches and adapt them to meet individual and diverse learners in the same class (Tomlinson, 2001). The shift in perspective for educators is such that curriculum and presentation of information to learners are adjusted for the learners' benefit rather than expecting learners to modify themselves to fit the curriculum. Differentiating instruction meets each student where he or she is and assists in the learning process.

With PBL, learners work on artifacts, which are items created to represent possible solutions to problems or aspects of a solution to the problem (Bender, 2012, p. 9). Videos or video projects are examples of artifacts that represent what students have learned. They also demonstrate that students took on responsibilities based on their individual skills or talents.

Two essential components of projects (Houghton Mifflin, n.d.) include a) a driving question or problem, necessarily anchored in the real world, and b) a culminating product or multiple representations such as a series of artifacts or tasks, which meaningfully address the driving question. Students pursue solutions to these nontrivial problems by:

1. Asking and refining questions,
2. Debating ideas,
3. Making predictions,
4. Designing plans and experiments,
5. Collecting and analyzing data,
6. Drawing conclusions,
7. Communicating their ideas and findings to others,
8. Asking new questions, and
9. Creating artifacts (Houghton Mifflin, n.d.).

Students creating video tend to go through most, if not all, of these nine solution-finding endeavors. They tend to learn about real life issues, policies, trends, and so on. Their video end-product is testament to their understanding of the driving question and to finding ways to demonstrate their understanding.

Video projects mentioned earlier from MERLOT ELIXR had students collaborating together to solve a particular problem that is interesting and meaningful to them, such as racism, education, assistive technology application, civil rights, and social justice. They were actively engaged in the solution-finding endeavor and were proud to present their video projects to classmates, faculty and whoever might be interested, including Facebook subscribers and clients.

PBL and Universal Design for Learning share the same instructional goal: to determine ways to apply differentiated instruction.

Universal Design for Learning (UDL)

Universal Design for Learning (UDL) highlights differentiated instruction as well as inclusive learning or equitable learning, where every learner receives the opportunity to learn by maximizing talents, skills, and strategies. For educators, UDL provides a "blueprint for creating instructional goals, methods, materials, and assessments that work for everyone--not a single, one-size-fits-all solution but rather flexible approaches that can be customized and adjusted for individual needs" (CAST, n.d.). With its curriculum-designed approach, UDL seeks to "increase flexibility in teaching and decrease the barriers that frequently limit student access to materials and learning in classrooms" (Hall, Strangman and Meyer, 2009).

UDL supports the three primary brain networks: recognition, strategic, and active. The recognition network focuses on multiple means of representation, where information and content are presented in different ways. The strategic network refers to the multiple means of action and expression, where students can express themselves and what they know in different ways. The active network highlights multiple means of engagement, where interest and motivation for learning are stimulated. *Multiple-ness* is key to UDL.

UDL enables faculty to be more acutely aware of their instructional strategies and curricular designs. While developing learning objectives and outcomes, faculty build on students' skills and strengths to move students toward their full potential. Though not easy, providing students with multiple chances to succeed results in student and faculty success – a mutually beneficial endeavor.

When students create video projects, they typically choose their own roles in the production process, appropriate to their comfort level. Students express themselves – their talents, strengths, skills, work ethic, time management ability, and self-efficacy – in ways that lead to learning. Learning may manifest in the acquisition of new skills and attitudes about the educational process, leading to a relatively permanent change in knowledge, skills, view of the discipline, or view of the world.

Supporting diversity in talents, skills, and strategies as well as respecting students' natural beginnings, video projects enhance student learning. Students self-identify where in the video production flow their talents and skills are best applied. In the beginning, students may struggle in finding the role best suiting their talents. Even so, students experience the subject matter, production work, and collaboration as they grow and learn about themselves. This support for the natural progression in realizing a student's potential makes UDL truly effective for self-actualization. When faculty are able to provide multiple resources through multiple means of representation, action and expression, and engagement, students have less road blocks to achieving their developmental potential throughout their academic and professional careers.

Through UDL guidelines, video projects foster learning through the three primary brain networks – recognition, strategic, and active –

which are often associated with the type of learner. Resourceful and knowledgeable learners usually have a stronger recognition network. Faculty can appeal to the recognition network by showcasing multiple means of representation. Learners who tend to be strategic and goal-directed are seen as having a better strategic network. Faculty can appeal to the strategic network by demonstrating and encouraging multiple means of action and expression including physical action, expression and communication, and executive functions. Purposeful, motivated learners typically have a stronger active network and benefit from multiple means of engagement.

Video projects can scaffold differentiated learning, equitable and inclusive learning by starting where students are and finding ways to optimize their strengths. These projects also promote UDL guidelines and approaches.

UDL also accommodates Multiple Intelligences (MI). Howard Gardner (2003) posits that each individual has a combination of nine types of Multiple Intelligences, ranging from linguistic, mathematical and logical, musical, spatial, bodily-kinesthetic, interpersonal, intrapersonal, naturalistic, and existential. Individuals may have some intelligences more pronounced than other intelligences. In a video project, a group member with a more acute linguistic intelligence could serve as the scriptwriter, for example, and someone else with stronger musical intelligence could be the audio and music coordinator. If several members have high interpersonal intelligences, group work will be more efficient and effective.

UDL emphasizes inclusive or equitable learning where educators find ways of supporting and expressing the strengths of *all* learners so that students may find meaning and enhance learning. Group projects, particularly video production projects, provide the opportunity for learners to build on each other's strengths; to gain confidence as they contribute successfully to the project;

and to acquire skills in time management, group dynamics, and collaboration.

UDL and Multiple Intelligences are related to Bloom's Taxonomy of Cognitive Domain. Building on the students' strengths, differentiated instruction could scaffold individual learning and move the learner from one level of cognition or mastery to the next. The hope is that the learner will eventually reach the highest level of cognition or learning through the application of instructional strategies geared toward optimizing the learner's potential.

Bloom's Taxonomy of Cognitive Domain (BT)

Since 1956, educators and learners have regarded Benjamin Bloom's Taxonomy of Cognitive Domain as the universal go-to pedagogical and instructional resource. In collaboration with other educational psychologists, Bloom developed a system for classifying levels of behavior for how we learn.

Different levels correspond to degrees of difficulty so that the earlier level must sometimes be mastered before reaching the next level. In this way Bloom's Taxonomy of Cognitive Domain provides a framework for instructional scaffolding where lower level objectives should be mastered before climbing to the higher dimensions of the taxonomy.

The six major levels are as follows.

1. **Knowledge:** Recalling data or information, often described as simple regurgitation of information
2. **Comprehension:** Understanding meaning, translating and interpreting instructions and problems, and stating a problem in one's own words
3. **Application:** Using a concept in a new situation and applying what was learned in the classroom to new situations outside the classroom
4. **Analysis:** Separating material or concepts into component parts so that its organizational structure may be understood and distinguishing between facts and inferences
5. **Synthesis:** Building structure or pattern from diverse elements, forming a whole by putting parts together, and emphasizing the creation of new meaning or structure
6. **Evaluation:** Making judgments about the value of ideas or materials and justifying a stand or decision (Performance Juxtaposition, 1999; Overbaugh and Schultz, n.d.)

In the 1990s, Lorin Anderson, a former student of Bloom's, and other cognitive psychologists updated the taxonomy to address 21st century instructional considerations. Anderson's updated categories featured verbs instead of nouns, and the fifth and six categories were reversed. Anderson's version of Bloom's Taxonomy of Cognitive Domain includes:

1. Remembering,
2. Understanding,
3. Applying,
4. Analyzing,
5. Evaluating, and
6. Creating.

Both the original and updated versions provide a list of verbs to guide activities. For instance, with *remembering*, can the student list, repeat, state, or match? For *understanding*, can the student describe, paraphrase, discuss, or explain? For *evaluating*, can the student argue, defend, or support?

Video projects can support different learning styles, theoretical foundations, and instructional processes. These projects promote gradual learning, from one level to another. Because video projects are multi-sensory, these multiple stimuli enhance the learning experience. Ultimately, learners engage in video projects to create a new product or point of view, the highest category in Anderson's updated taxonomy.

The Helix-Flow of the three theoretical foundations – Project-Based Learning (PBL), Universal Design for Learning (UDL), and Bloom's Taxonomy – supports instruction and student engagement through video projects. Before embarking on a video project, though, both faculty and students have several considerations to address.

FIVE R'S OF MULTIMEDIA PROJECTS

We advocate 5 R's of multimedia projects to serve as guidelines for faculty and students: rationale, roles, resources, rubrics, and readiness (Yocom and Bishop, 2010; Bishop and Yocom, 2011).

- A clear *rationale* should be developed to explain how a video project fulfills course requirements.
- Faculty and students need to agree on what *roles* will be assumed for the project. Faculty may act as coach in content development while students divide other roles among themselves.
- Faculty must consider the availability of *resources* such as technology support, content support, and equipment. Students need to acquire resources, whether borrowed or owned, such as cameras, musical scores and lights as well as people for interviewing.
- *Rubrics* may be generated by both faculty and students or by faculty alone. Enabling students to contribute to the discussion of the final rubric can motivate students to perform better as students feel invested in the project and validated (Bishop and Yocom, 2009; Yocom and Bishop, 2010).
- *Faculty readiness* could be achieved through faculty development workshops or one-on-one consultations with multi-

media experts. *Student readiness* may be assessed beforehand through surveys on prior experience and skills relevant to video production. Faculty can support student readiness through discussions of group project requirements and expectations and even through hands-on workshops on how to use video equipment and peripherals. Faculty may conduct these workshops or have an on-campus expert from the media department or teaching center work with students.

Issues and Considerations

Before implementing student-created video projects, we should at least consider the design of video assignments, assistance, production phases, and assessment.

Design of Video Assignments

While students in general grow more sophisticated in their ability to produce and share video online, production skill levels vary widely. A well-designed survey of student production skills will inform decisions on the complexity of the assignment, what technology tools will be recommended, and how much assistance should be given. Assessing project management and group interaction skills may be useful when grouping students. Complex projects will benefit from including at least one technologically-adept student and one organizationally-skilled student.

While grouping, extra care must be taken to ensure a clear understanding of roles, expectations, and the assessment process. Small groups of two to four students usually work well for video. Consideration should be given as to whether to assess the group project as a whole, to assess the efforts of individual students, or to do some combination of both. Project tasks may be divided into subtasks – such as writing or planning, video recording and editing – and assigned to individuals.

Assistance

Because online video projects typically use emerging multimedia technology, faculty must be careful to develop realistic projects based on available campus and online resources. At most universities, students have access to video production assistance through the library or media center, though students may not be aware of such assistance and where to find it. Instructors should include specific, up-to-date instructions on what types of assistance are available and where.

Students should be given a list of carefully vetted web resources that fit the assignment and are appropriate for the skill level of the students. By providing this list, students use a common point of reference in approaching the project, which makes troubleshooting simpler. Testing a project in advance will expose any problems with resources, links, or departmental services.

If students need help locating media sources, librarians will likely be helpful. If faculty feel unable to answer difficult technical questions, resource contacts could be given to students for technical support around campus such as the media center or online. Video lends itself well to student-centered learning, so faculty may want to assess students in part on their ability to resolve technical issues.

To prepare library and technical staff, faculty can provide copies of the syllabus or assignment instructions. In this way, problems may be anticipated, and solutions made readily available while departments prepare for increased equipment usage or staff during peak times.

Students are increasingly self-reliant in finding solutions to technical problems either with the help of their peers or through the plethora of help available on the web. So while instructors may answer some video production questions, students naturally find their own answers through online or campus resources.

For students to work collaboratively and for professors to evaluate video projects, some means of sharing must be in place. Course management systems such as Blackboard, Moodle, Canvas, or Oncourse CL from Sakai serve as portals to access both video project work and web resources. Social software such as YouTube, Google Apps, and Flickr can be used to share and submit coursework, but care must be taken to ensure that sensitive or copyrighted material is password-protected. Data storage sites such as Box and Dropbox offer yet another way to share files and collaborate.

Video assignments add complexity to the course and can pose challenges to faculty. Faculty development and support staff can assist faculty with issues related to technology and pedagogy, ranging from best practices in the design and assessment of video project work to providing assistance in locating appropriate online and campus resources for students with technical issues. Web-based programs that allow for real-time videoconferencing, such as Adobe Connect, can be used for virtual office hours. Faculty could also create audio or video recordings modeling some of the required features of video projects. By actively participating in video production workshops faculty are better prepared to assist students.

Production Phases

Traditionally, the task of creating video has been divided into three phases: pre-production, production, and post-production. We add a fourth phase for distribution. These four phases may be useful in splitting assignments into subtasks, dividing students into groups, and developing an assessment rubric.

Pre-production involves planning, scriptwriting, storyboarding, and developing production timelines. Conceptual, language, and organizational skills are required in the design and refinement of the message. Students may be required to consider the intended audience. Production timelines can provide useful milestones for project monitoring and assessment.

Production includes recording video and audio content. Students will either be required to have access to and some understanding of a video camera or be required to find and incorporate existing sounds and images. In either case, students who are able to apply principles of visual composition are apt to acquire more pleasing images.

Post-production is the editing phase. Students may need to transfer media to a computer, convert media from one format to another, and use editing software. General computing skills are helpful in this phase.

Distribution involves storing and sharing the final video. Videos must inevitably be shared with the instructor, and video projects are oftentimes shared with and critiqued by other students, as well. Offline delivery, such as a DVD or portable memory device, is simpler and more private. Online sharing, whether through a learning management system or other web-based solutions, provides easier access for peer review and critique and can be highly motivational, especially if videos are shared publicly. The public nature of online delivery, particularly on social media sites, provides an opportunity to explore copyright issues. Students' familiarity with the tools of online video delivery can streamline the production process.

Assessment

Assessment of student readiness may help faculty adjust coursework parameters to suit the range of skills and experience of students in each class. Faculty could poll at the start of the semester to determine students' level of expertise in project management, group interaction, computing, and media production. Based on student responses, faculty will be able to gauge the video expertise of their students and group students to balance these skills, where each group has at least one member experienced with project management, research, video recording, sound editing, and video editing.

Video coursework can be difficult to assess through traditional metrics. Faculty should develop meaningful assignment and assessment protocols for student engagement and optimal

learning. Video is inherently subjective in its design, so a well thought-out video projects *rubric* should include clear, specific, and measurable objectives for the assignment. Rubrics may include *criteria* for assessing content development, message design, production values, application of copyright guidelines, and teamwork principles. Rubrics can help avoid assessing projects on video quality alone.

Faculty should be clear and succinct in conveying project expectations to students. When students understand how they will be graded, there is no confusion about expectations during the project or when the end-product is presented. Evaluation guidelines and rubrics can be posted at the start of the semester along with audio or video instructions. Ideally, students will use these rubrics while reviewing each other's work. A web-based rubric creation program such as Rubistar can be used by both instructor and students.

Group projects require additional consideration to ensure each student is graded fairly. Faculty may elect to grade their students based on both individual and collaborative work. Students may evaluate other individuals in the group based on a common rubric. Evaluation criteria can include the ability to work with groups, submit tasks on time, provide quality work, and perform technical tasks. The group could also provide an overall grade for themselves with an explanation as to why they thought they deserve that grade. These assessments, including a critical look at student evaluations of each other, are often combined for the final grade.

CONCLUSION

Weighing the practicality of student-created video against the value it adds to the learning experience needs to be explored in more detail. More research is also needed in how best to adapt for teaching and learning the proliferation of Web 2.0 tools in social media, screen capture, and community-building.

Video production tends to be the technology du jour due, in part, to the smorgasbord of topics available through the web, including MERLOT ELIXR, YouTube, and other online services that make it easy to post and share videos. However, issues surrounding Copyright, Fair Use and the TEACH Act need to be discussed. The notion that anything on the web is acceptable to reuse is a mistake, and students must understand that using someone else's work requires attribution and, in many cases, permission.

Video projects support student abilities to engage with material in which they are already interested while scaffolding the learning process and encouraging skills such as team work, creative project design, personal time management, group management, and critical thinking. These video projects have become more practical due to the proliferation of inexpensive multimedia production tools, an increase in broadband internet penetration, and ready availability of technology tutorial resources.

Benefits include an opportunity to accommodate multiple intelligences; multiple means of representation, action and expression, and engagement from Universal Design for Learning; and an opportunity to provide multiple resources to optimize their academic performance via Bloom's Taxonomy of Cognitive Domain. Students choose to work on projects they feel passionate about, culminating in authentic and meaningful artifacts from Project-based Learning.

These three theoretical frameworks – Project-based Learning, Universal Design for Learning, and Bloom's Taxonomy of Cognitive Domain – work together in what we call the Helix-Flow: a model wherein each theoretical framework provides pedagogical adventures and *aha* moments through fluid experiences. The common dynamic in this helix is the knowledge, skills, and experience acquired by students through authentic engagement, teamwork, and creative video projects, supporting differentiated instruction and student-centered teaching and learning.

While instructors need not be experts in video production, faculty must ensure that students have access to resources including online tutorials and instructions on submitting and sharing project work. Successful design and assessment of video assignments depends on several factors like assessing student readiness; setting specific, measurable objectives; and developing a meaningful rubric (Bishop and Yocom, 2009; Yocom and Bishop, 2010, 2011). Student-created video assignments provide students with creative opportunities to apply themselves in myriad ways that they do not sometimes anticipate but end up successfully delivering. Video projects as part of coursework could evolve from being technology *du jour* to technology *universal*.

REFERENCES

Bender, W. N. (2012). Project-based learning: Differentiating instruction for the 21st century. Thousand Oaks, CA: Corwin, a Sage Company.

Bishop, M. C., & Yocom, J. (2009, August). *Designing and evaluating multimedia projects in an online environment.* Board of Regents of the University of Wisconsin System for the 25th Annual Conference on Distance Teaching and Learning, Madison, WI

Bishop, M. C., & Yocom, J. (2011, August). *Education, multimedia and social media: Are we ready for showtime?* Board of Regents of the University of Wisconsin System for the 27th Annual Conference on Distance Teaching and Learning, Madison, WI.

CAST (Center for Applied Special Technology). (2008). *Universal design for learning (UDL) guidelines – Version 1.0.* Retrieved from http://www.cast.org/publications/UDLguidelines/version1.html

Center for Instructional Technology. (n.d.). *Student video fellowship: Biomedical engineering capstone video project*. Retrieved from http://cit. duke.edu/blog/2010/03/student-video-fellowship-biomedical-engineering-capstone-video-project/

Creative Commons. (n.d.). *Attribution-NoDerivs 3.0 United States* (CC BY-ND 3.0) Retrieved from http://creativecommons.org/licenses/by-nd/3.0/us/

Duke University Digital Storytelling. (n.d.). *Social pedagogy*. Retrieved from https://pilot.cndls. georgetown.edu/digitalstories/social-pedagogy/

EDUCAUSE. (n.d.). *Student engagement*. Retrieved from http://www.educause.edu/ EDUCAUSE+Quarterly/EQVolume322009/ EDUCAUSEQuarterlyMagazineVolum/192952

Gardner, H. (2003). *Multiple intelligences after twenty years*. Retrieved from http://www. pz.harvard.edu/PIs/HG_MI_after_20_years.pdf

Hall, Strangman & Meyer (2009). *Differentiated instruction and implications for UDL implementation*. Retrieved from http://aim.cast.org/learn/ historyarchive/backgroundpapers/differentiated_instruction_udl

Houghton Mifflin. (n.d.). *Project-based learning space: The basics*. Retrieved from http://college. cengage.com/education/pbl/background.html

ISTE. (2008). *National educational technology standards for teachers – NETS-T* (2nd ed.). International Society for Technology in Education.

MERLOT ELIXR. (n.d.). *Welcome to MERLOT ELIXR*. Retrieved from http://elixr.merlot.org/ merlot_elixr?noCache=730:1349067763

MERLOT ELIXR. (n.d.). *Visual legal advocacy course with Regina Austin*. Retrieved from http:// elixr.merlot.org/case-stories/teaching-strategies/ nurturing-student-creativity-with-video-projects/ student-video-projects-in-law-school2

MERLOT ELIXR. (n.d.). *Nurturing student creativity – Critical writing*. Retrieved from http:// elixr.merlot.org/case-stories/teaching-strategies/ nurturing-student-creativity-with-video-projects/ nurturing-student-creativity-with-video-projects4/

Myers, D. (2006, 2009, 2011). *Psychology*. New York, NY: Worth Publishers.

National Survey of Student Engagement (NSSE). (n.d.). *Student engagement*. Retrieved from http:// nsse.iub.edu/html/about.cfm

Oakland Unified School District Urban Dreams Video Project. (n.d.). *Urban dreams video project video library*. Retrieved from http://urbandreams. ousd.k12.ca.us/video/index.html

Overbaugh, R. C., & Schultz, L. (n.d.). *Bloom's taxonomy*. Old Dominion University. Retrieved from http://ww2.odu.edu/educ/roverbau/Bloom/ blooms_taxonomy.htm

Performance Juxtaposition. (1999). *Bloom's taxonomy of learning domains*. Retrieved from http:// www.nwlink.com/~donclark/hrd/bloom.html

Schwartz, D. L., & Hartman, K. (2007). It's not video anymore: Designing digital video for learning and assessment. In Goldman, R., Pea, R., Barron, B., & Derry, S. J. (Eds.), *Video research in the learning sciences* (pp. 335–348). New York, NY: Erlbaum.

Tomlinson, C. A. (2nd. Ed., 2001). How to differentiate instruction in mixed-ability classrooms (2nd ed.) Alexandria, VA: ASCD.

Yocom, J., & Bishop, M. C. (2010). *4 Rs in multimedia projects: Rationale, resources, roles, and rubrics*. Board of Regents of the University of Wisconsin System for the 26th Annual Conference on Distance Teaching and Learning, Madison, WI.

ADDITIONAL READING

Center for Social Media. (2008, Nov.). *The code of best practices in fair use for media literacy education.* American University School of Communication's Center for Social Media. Retrieved from http://www.centerforsocialmedia.org/resources/publications/code_for_media_literacy_education/

Dartmouth University. (2007). *Student video projects at Dartmouth: Preparing the assignment.* Retrieved from http://www.dartmouth.edu/~videoprojects/prepare.html

Dartmouth University. (2007). *Student video projects at Dartmouth: Suggestions for evaluating student video projects.* Retrieved from http://www.dartmouth.edu/~videoprojects/evaluate.html

Dartmouth University. (2007). *Student video projects at Dartmouth: Online multimedia assignment form.* Retrieved from http://www.dartmouth.edu/~videoprojects/form.html

David, B. Wiegle Information Commons. (n.d.). *ELIXR MERLOT faculty development initiative nurturing student creativity with video projects.* Retrieved from http://wic.library.upenn.edu/elixr.html

Duke University Library. (2007). *Integrating library resources into your course.* Retrieved from http://library.duke.edu/services/instruction/faculty/

Educational Technology Resources. (2002). *Assessment: Teacher process for digital video.* Retrieved from the http://edtech.guhsd.net/video/Assess.htm

Gardner, H. (1999). *Intelligence reframed: Multiple intelligences for the 21st century.* New York, NY: Basic Books

Georgetown University, Center for New Designs in Learning and Scholarship. (n.d.). *Digital storytelling multimedia archive: Grid.* Retrieved from https://pilot.cndls.georgetown.edu/digitalstories/grid/

Gnovis (n.d.). *Multimedia.* Georgetown University Journal of Communication, Culture and Technology (CCT). Retrieved from http://gnovisjournal.org/multimedia/

Green, T. D., & Brown, A. (2002). *Multimedia projects in the classroom: A guide to development and evaluation.* CA: Corwin Press.

Heinich, R., Molenda, M., Russell, J., & Smaldino, S. (1999). *Instructional media and technologies for learning* (6th ed.). Merrill/Prentice Hall.

ISTE. (2008). *National Educational Technology Standards for Teachers* (NETS-T), 2nd ed. International Society for Technology in Education (ISTE).

ISTE HyperSIG. (2011). *Multimedia mania 2004 – Judges' rubric.* Revisions by North Carolina State University. Retrieved from http://www.ncsu.edu/mmania/mm_docs/mm_judge_rubric2.html

Kaplan, A. M., & Haenlein, M. M. (2010). Users of the world, unite! The challenges and opportunities of social media. *Business Horizons*, *53*(1), 59–68. Retrieved from http://www.sciencedirect.com/science/article/B6W45-4XFF2S0-1/2/600db1bd6e0c9903c744aaf34b0b12e1 doi:10.1016/j.bushor.2009.09.003

McCullen, C. (2011). Multimedia project rubric. *MidLink Magazine.* Retrieved from http://www.ncsu.edu/midlink/rub.mmproj.htm

MERLOT ELIXR. (n.d.). *Engage students through productions.* Retrieved from http://elixr.merlot.org/case-stories/teaching-strategies/teaching-strategies-for-engaging-learners/engage-students-through-productions

MERLOT (Multimedia Educational Resources for Learning and Online Teaching). (n.d.). Retrieved from http://www.merlot.org

Penn State University. (2007). *Creating and assessing video assignments*. Retrieved from http://digitalcommons.psu.edu/node/416

Penn State University. (2011). *Penn State learning design community hub*. Retrieved from http://ets.tlt.psu.edu/learningdesign/webdesign/media/video

Prensky, M. (2001). Digital natives, digital immigrants. *Horizon, 9*(5). Retrieved from http://www.marcprensky.com/writing/Prensky%20-%20Digital%20Natives,%20Digital%20Immigrants%20-%20Part1.pdf doi:10.1108/10748120110424816

Schrock, K. (2011). *Kathy Schrock's guide for educators*. Retrieved from http://school.discoveryeducation.com/schrockguide/assess.html

University of Texas-Austin. (2007). *Assessing media projects*. University of Texas at Austin's Division of Instructional Innovation and Assessment. Retrieved from http://www.utexas.edu/academic/diia/dms/faculty/assessment/index.php

University of Wisconsin-Stout. (2008). *Video project rubric*. Retrieved from http://www.uwstout.edu/soe/profdev/videorubric.html

University of Wisconsin-Stout. (2011). *Video and multimedia project rubrics*. Retrieved from http://www.uwstout.edu/soe/profdev/rubrics.cfm#video

Utah Education Network. (2011). *Multimedia presentation rubric*. Retrieved from http://www.uen.org/Rubric/rubric.cgi?rubric_id=16

KEY TERMS AND DEFINITIONS

5 R's of Multimedia Projects: Rationale, Roles, Resources, Rubrics, and Readiness – guidelines for faculty and students engaged in creating multimedia projects (e.g., video) as part of coursework.

Artifact: End-product resulting from a multimedia coursework such as video project.

Bloom's Taxonomy of Cognitive Domain: A universal go-to pedagogical and instructional resource that highlights a system for classifying six levels of behavior for how we learn; provides a framework for instructional scaffolding where lower level objectives (e.g., knowledge, comprehension, application) should be mastered before reaching the higher dimensions of the taxonomy (e.g., analysis, synthesis and evaluation).

Differentiated Instruction: A theory of teaching based on the premise, that to be effective, educators should vary their instructional approaches and adapt them in ways that meet individual and diverse needs of learners in the class.

Helix-Flow: An amalgam synthesizing and strengthening three theoretical frameworks of instruction, including Project-based Learning, Universal Design for Learning, and Bloom's Taxonomy of Cognitive Domain.

Learning: A relatively permanent change in one's behavior due to experience.

Multimedia: Any combination of media formats such as text, graphical images, audio, and video for the purpose of providing information and/or instruction.

Production Phases for Video Creation: Framework for creating video projects that include four elements - Pre-production, Production, Post-production, and Distribution; provides useful guidelines for splitting assignments into subtasks, dividing students into groups, and developing an assessment rubric.

Project-Based Learning: A model of instruction wherein students engage in confronting issues surrounding a driving question or problem anchored in the real world that are meaningful to them, and creating a product or artifact (e.g., video) that address the driving question.

Student Engagement: The "rendezvous between learning and the digital tools and techniques that excite students" (EDUCAUSE, n.d.); represents two critical features of collegiate quality – a) the amount of time and effort students apply to their studies and related educationally purposeful activities, and b) the resource deployment, curriculum organization and other learning opportunities offered by the institution to motivate students to participate in activities that have been linked to student learning from decades of research studies. (NSSE, n.d.)

Universal Design for Learning: A blueprint for the creation of instructional goals, methods, materials, and assessments that include flexible approaches that are customizable and adjustable for individual needs.

APPENDIX: ADDITIONAL RESOURCES

Assessment/Evaluation of Course Requirements

- **Teacher Process for Digital Video:** http://edtech.guhsd.net/video/Assess.htm
- **Crafting an Assignment Containing a Video Component:** http://digitalcommons.psu.edu/node/418
- **Creating and Assessing Video Assignments:** http://digitalcommons.psu.edu/node/416
- **Multimedia Project Rubric:** http://www.ncsu.edu/midlink/rub.mmproj.htm
- **Video Project Rubric:** http://www.uwstout.edu/soe/profdev/videorubric.html

Library Resources

- **Role of libraries in assisting students to do multimedia research and projects:** http://www.emeraldinsight.com/Insight/ViewContentServlet?Filename=/published/emeraldfulltextarticle/pdf/0721091105.pdf

Presentations and Production

- **Add images to PowerPoint:** http://presentationsoft.about.com/od/nextstepsinpowerpoint/ss/add_pics.htm
- **Buy and use a flip camera:** http://www.ehow.com/how_4546191_use-flip-camera.html and http://www.youtube.com/watch?v=mh6s9gNoFro video with good tips on dos and don'ts when shooting
- **Conduct an audio interview:** http://www.feedforall.com/how-to-conduct-podcast-interview.htm
- **Create a blog:** http://www.youtube.com/watch?v=BnploFsS_tY
- **Download and use Audacity:** http://www.how-to-podcast-tutorial.com/17-audacity-tutorial.htm
- **Fifteen videos on intermediate to advanced aspects of video interview technique:** http://www.ehow.com/videos-on_7691_film-conduct-video-interview.html
- **Free software program for screen capture with audio. Includes a site for posting screen:** http://jingproject.com/
- **Record an oral history (covers process rather than equipment):** http://dohistory.org/on_your_own/toolkit/oralHistory.html
- **Use a webcam:** http://www.microsoft.com/canada/home/communications-and-mobility/articles/webcam-basics-how-do-they-work.aspx and http://www.mahalo.com/how-to-use-a-webcam

Distribution

- **How to post to Facebook:** http://www.wikihow.com/Post-a-YouTube-Video-on-Facebook and http://www.mahalo.com/how-to-post-on-facebook
- **How to post to Picasa:** http://www.wonderhowto.com/how-to/video/how-to-create-web-albums-for-your-pictures-in-picasa-171035/
- **How to post to YouTube:** http://www.youtube.com/watch?v=9w-gQAwS2uc&feature=fvw

Chapter 16
Putting *Me* in Media:
Communicating and Creating Screen Media with a Purpose

Christine Wells
Carthage College, Rosebud Institute, USA

ABSTRACT

Like learning to read or write, or acquiring the fundamentals of mathematics, screen media literacy is rapidly becoming an essential life skill. This dominant and expansive interface for contact, culture, and commerce has become the way we communicate now. Given the power and reach of the screen, it seems essential that as with any other fundamental skill, we must begin to understand and create within this medium in a more foundational, intentional way. But the language of the screen is complicated, rapidly becoming almost as multidimensional and multifaceted as the number of users it encompasses. Additionally, given its reliance on technology, it is an ever-changing landscape fraught with the challenges of chasing the elusive cutting edge. This chapter looks at a more back to basics approach to screen media literacy by offering instruction in what screen media really is and how to create it in a more foundational and transferable fashion. Using simple, accessible technology, people become more screen literate and the creation process enables deeper, more authentic learning, with the credence and accountability of a potentially world wide audience. Focusing on an integral part of a process developed by the Rosebud Institute – an organization committed to making screen media literacy more broadly understood and accessible – this step-by-step, integrated method delivers a new understanding of media literacy. Using simple, accessible technology, participants create dynamic, original ePortfolio websites themselves and distribute their work to an ever-expanding audience. Developed along with Rosebud's founder and director, Paul Chilsen, the process encourages individuals to find their own voice and embrace the me in media, moving us towards a future where people will instantly capture, identifiably own, intelligently store, and instinctively know what to do with their digital assets, allowing us all to communicate more effectively and thrive in a media-saturated world.

DOI: 10.4018/978-1-4666-3962-1.ch016

INTRODUCTION

What do you look like to the online world? Did you know anyone was watching?

Media Convergence – the coming together and overlapping of film, television, websites, social media, news, and advertising – is changing the way we communicate and interact at an alarming rate. Every day we are engulfed in video, images, and text, and most of it is coming to us on a screen. Screen media is everywhere and the "noise" it is delivering at an increasingly feverish pace is more and more becoming a desensitizing hum. How do we begin to deal with this? We could continue to let it wash over us, becoming more and more detached, allowing what Mike Wesch references as a "whatever" feeling towards screen media to take over, a general sense that we are "increasingly disconnected, disempowered, tuned out, and alienated" (Wesch, 2012). But a more progressive answer seems fundamentally rooted in *understanding*. If we are to understand how screen media works, and more importantly, if we are to have a personal voice that rises above the desensitizing hum of the screen, we need a more back to basics approach that strips away the "sexiness," and the bells and whistles that we see in commercial screen media. Like learning to read or write, acquiring the fundamentals of mathematics, or even learning to play a musical instrument, the screen is another medium of communication, and we need to learn to understand and create using a more foundational, building blocks approach. This chapter discusses an intentional, focused, adaptable exploration of screen media in a more deliberate, screen-savvy, engaged fashion, and presents part of a programmatic method to increase screen media literacy through the design, development and publishing of a unique online presence through the creation of an ePortfolio.

Technology continues to evolve and change at lightning speed, warping our definition of "educational technology" and what defines effective technology education, both in K-12 institutions and higher education. Is it simply learning to organize files, navigate software, word process documents, or press buttons on the latest gadgets we bought yesterday that are now virtually obsolete today? Is it learning an interface? Learning to type? Technology will always change, will continue to advance and evolve, and there will always be some new tool or app or something expensive that will claim to solve all of our technology needs. But at its core, what does technology help us to accomplish? What does it do? What are the advantages to having screen-based, constant, overwhelming access to information that may or may not be accurate? What do we do with the ability to over-inform people we are barely connected to, with endless status updates? If we pare all that away and walk behind the "curtain" comprised of gadgets, functionality, and "new"ness, technology can become a more effective way for us to communicate and connect with each other.

So what do we do? How do we change course and choose not to simply consume and be manipulated by commercial screen media? Rather than assuming the role of uninformed media consumers, we need to be brave enough to harness the control, the opportunity, and the basic skills in creating an intentional digital presence. We must learn to "manage" our digital selves, the information we choose to share, and the original work and opinions we *do* create, so that what we share online is unique, appropriate, and *real*. We must recognize the importance of teaching the younger generations that come behind us, evermore besieged by pervasive access and opportunity to the screen not to be swallowed by screen media, but to share carefully, to write appropriately, and to learn to express a clear voice that rises above the din. And most importantly, we must come to understand and accept that in the online world, the personal has become public, and *now*, with the world as the audience, it matters so much more that we manage our individual online presence.

It seems clear to many observers that the world does not need another $3,000 pencil.

There is a better path, not simply a "means to an end" view that reduces technology to an expensive word processing tool, but a back to basics look at screen media as a medium unto itself – a way to effectively communicate, express original ideas, and rise above the technology din.

The relatively prescriptive focus of this chapter is to present such an approach – one that is systematic and intentional towards creating, maintaining, and sharing a unique digital presence in the form of an ePortfolio. We will discuss the program, the benefits, and the issues at hand in creating an individualized, competent, and empowering course of action to put the *me* in media.

BACKGROUND: THE ROSEBUD INSTITUTE AND THE EVOLUTION OF THE EPORTFOLIO

As human beings, creating and maintaining connections to other people are paramount to our quality of life. From our human connections, we derive feelings of self-esteem and self-worth, informing the weight of our impact on the world around us. Screen media gives us incredible opportunity, platform, and endless options to establish and maintain meaningful connections with others, but we struggle to find a balance as the screen continues to overtake personal, human connections. Are the connections we create in the virtual world real? Do they have as much weight and value as the connections we maintain in person on a daily basis? Most of us see screen media and the possibilities of screen media education as either the opportunity to re-appropriate and quote someone else, use someone else's images, "tag" an article or a post we like, avoid stating opinions by "liking" what someone else shares online, waste time watching a funny video that someone else created, pontificate on what we ate for breakfast that morning or share baby photos with virtual friends and acquaintances. There is a veritable

cacophony of information, over-sharing, and commercial media that desensitizes and manipulates our ability to disseminate truth, find meaning, or make our own opinions regarding what we see and hear on the screen. The landscape of technology and technology education continues to change and we must transform our thinking and our approach.

While most of our classrooms were built under the assumption that information is scarce and hard to find, nearly the entire body of human knowledge now flows through and around these rooms in one form or another, ready to be accessed by laptops, cell phones, and iPods. (Wesch, 2008)

The time that students spend in front of a screen, from watching television, to surfing the Internet, to using a smartphone, has drastically increased. "Today's kids are media savvy. They are spending as much as one-fourth of the day using media and for two of those hours, they are using more than one type of media at the same time" (Herring & Notar, 2011). Marc Prensky suggests that as a result, the way we learn and assimilate information has also changed. "Digital Natives are used to receiving information really fast. They like to parallel process and multi-task. They prefer their graphics before their text rather than the opposite" (Prensky, 2001). If this is true, it seems to follow that we need to take a harder look at the way we consume media and by extension way we teach media education.

We must think about technology differently, and we must view and teach technology and technology skills through the lens of communication, with intentionality, focus, and attention to the notion of a potentially worldwide audience. Instead of allowing screen media to wash over us, participating only as simple media consumers, let us teach the basic tools and thought processes behind understanding and creating more intentional screen media. By doing so, we will learn to understand the importance and relevance of maintaining our digital presence. We can look at media more carefully and understand this medium with more depth and meaning. Instead of haphazardly posting our life for anyone and everyone to view, let us be intentional and appropriate about creating, managing, and sharing a unique, focused digital presence that deliberately and intelligently shows the outside world what we *want* them to see.

As mentioned, the method laid out in this chapter is tied directly to a two-pronged approach developed under an umbrella organization, the Rosebud Institute. An educational organization tangentially affiliated with a small liberal arts college in the Midwest, the Rosebud Institute is dedicated to the advancement and development of a student's knowledge and ability to create screen media (Chilsen & Wells, 2012). While either prong of Rosebud's program can be restructured to stand on its own – and curriculum restructuring continues successfully in various situations with diverse constituencies – the basic Rosebud idea is a more holistic approach to screen media literacy. Therefore, in order to outline and talk about the effective, proven ePortfolio approach developed under the Rosebud Institute, as well as the background theory and need for addressing this medium appropriately in the current climate of technology, we need first to discuss the evolution and continued direction of the institute itself.

Founded in 2009 on the campus of Carthage College in Kenosha, Wisconsin, the Rosebud Institute set out to address the current "noise" in technology and media education, teaching participants the value, meaning, and clarity that can be found in creating original screen media. Combining public K-12 education perspectives with the integrated philosophy and opportunity of a small liberal arts college, Rosebud has an aligned focus towards creating students and teachers that are better able to understand and create meaningful screen media projects. The process nurtures their ability to establish, develop, and maintain meaningful connections to communicate effectively, thus setting them apart from the cacophony on the screen. Those who go through the program better understand how screen media really works *and* how to communicate original, personal ideas. The Rosebud Institute continues to evolve its philosophy and approach in the direction of current needs in education, issues of access, Internet propriety and etiquette, and of course the proliferation of original ideas and work; but effective communication, discovering possibilities, and building connections remain at its core.

Originally designed as a graduate-level course for teachers to address new approaches to teaching screen media literacy, Rosebud's back to basics method addresses screen media as its own literacy, and teaches participants the foundational building blocks of reading and writing for the screen. The two-pronged approach to finding a personal screen media voice, involving the sequential process of creating two relevant pieces of screen media, dovetail and integrate with each other for a final presentation of work. In one part of the program, students conceive of a simple, original, visual story to tell as a short, motion picture piece, through which they learn the basics of the language of motion media and the skills to tell their story in an original short film. In the other part of this approach, each participant builds an original ePortfolio website, partially for the distribution of their original film, but also as an intentional, creative, evolving résumé of their work, achievements, and goals.

Though the process continues to evolve with the changing needs of teachers and students, the differing access to technology, and the often-inconsistent school environments where it has been implemented, this step-by-step, integrated method has met with great success to date. It provides participants with an understanding of motion media as well as a dynamic, effective, original ePortfolio website that they can be proud of sharing with an ever-expanding audience.

The focus in this chapter is the ePortfolio piece of this approach, but it has been both possible and highly effective to teach this two-pronged method of screen media literacy in a parallel, aligned way that intertwines most effectively in a presentation of original work and progress. What begins as an overload of overwhelming and new information – presented in such a different, hands-on, get-dirty approach than most students are accustomed to – becomes an enlightening, empowering, collaborative exploration and expression of self. This all takes place in a guided, supportive learning environment where collective work, feedback, interaction, and sharing are all fostered and encouraged. An adaptation of this program, which will be subsequently outlined in greater detail, has proven successful with a pilot group of fifth grade music students, experienced K-12 teachers, a high school honors sociology class, eighth grade language arts students, and a freshman crew in an expeditionary learning school, with more ideas and avenues for creating programs in the near future. We will explore the proven method and keys to the program's success and adaptability.

Creating a basis and understanding for the background history and evolution of ePortfolios will help set the stage for taking this idea yet another step forward. We manage our time, we manage the details in our actual lives, but usually the only driving force behind managing our "digital selves" is common sense (or lack thereof) coupled with the fear of the wrong personal information entering the wrong hands. Instead, the opportunity and access to manage this digital area of our lives, which we often access more frequently than making eye contact with another human being, is now within reach, and there is no better time than now. "Today's average college grads have spent less than 5,000 hours of their lives reading, but over 10,000 hours playing video games (not to mention 20,000 hours watching TV)" (Prensky, 2001). Opportunity, access, and now an urgency

brought on by cautionary tales in the news media are virtually forcing our hand.

Focusing on an effective, proven pedagogy and approach to creating ePortfolios requires that we first take a look at the origins, value, and evolution of its predecessor: the in-hand portfolio. The in-hand portfolio has long been a common and valuable tool for freshly graduated college students to display and share artifacts and work completed in college courses over their years of study, showing career potential and acquired skills.

Portfolio is a concept taken from the world of architecture and the fine arts, where portfolio constitutes an extensive curriculum vitae with which the artist or architect presents his or her work... the idea of a portfolio first and foremost as a collection or inventory. (Meestus, Questier, & Derks, 2006)

For working professionals in fields from education and visual arts to business and finance, maintaining an organized, detailed portfolio that shows work experience in a more visually interesting, media-rich, detailed manner is a valuable tool for acquiring a desired position. More than a collection of artifacts, an in-hand portfolio might have included images, writing samples, videos, recordings – anything that illustrates with more depth and detail what a résumé can not possibly tell on a page, and more than an interview candidate can articulate during the course of a brief job interview. For college students, a portfolio mimics work experience they cannot possibly yet have, offsetting the challenge of entering the professional workforce armed with only their college courses, internships, and a desire for financial success. For working professionals, a portfolio works to "prove" work experience and flesh out specific skills and previous job-specific experience – again, in a more visually dynamic way.

Shift forward to the advent of the Internet, website creation, and the explosion of access to information, and in the early 1990's, the ePortfolio is born. This began a transformation, allowing companies and individuals to create their own web presence either in the form of a webfolio that acts as a repository of online-accessible, static documents and hyperlinks to other related sites, or to a more dynamic, changing, moldable ePortfolio site that shows learning or professional progress and continues to change as long as its creator continues to develop and refine the content to reflect current experience, skill, and career focus. An ePortfolio refers to "database-driven, dynamic web sites, not static, HTML-driven sites" (Batson, 2002). In a day and age where even the older generations, often referred to as "Digital Immigrants" live quite comfortably in the world of email, web research, and social networking, the younger generation, or "Digital Natives," are almost constantly connected online and disconnected from in-hand anything, unless it involves a screen. Digital natives "have spent their entire lives surrounded by and using computers, videogames, digital music players, video cams, cell phones, and all the other toys and tools of the digital age" (Prensky, 2001). It only makes sense, then, that as access and opportunity have driven the ability to create original websites for any purpose, without the need for extensive HTML or web design experience, the digital native generation already has, and should further embrace the opportunity and ability to create an ePortfolio: a living, breathing, online-accessible record of experience and skills, showing unique personality and potential. "EPortfolio systems are not new—they have been promoted and studied for nearly two decades" (Okoro, Washington, & Cardon, 2011). Though this is decidedly the case, and the use of ePortfolios continues to grow in all levels of education, the nebulous, indefinable, technology-reactive nature of the how, the why, and the reality of implementing ePortfolio use on a large scale is under much research and debate. A fully integrated shift has yet to occur,

and a realistic focus on effective approaches to creating original, effective, visually dynamic ePortfolios has yet to surface – until now.

ME MEDIA: CREATING OR RECREATING OUR DIGITAL SELVES

Although further research, varied approaches, and educational pedagogy behind ePortfolios continues to develop, we must continue to focus on and use the ePortfolio as a way to communicate personality, professionalism, experience, and competency with a potentially much wider audience. Those that learn to articulate themselves in this fashion and format – and work to do it well – will be ahead of the curve, as the shift from in-hand portfolios to a focused, highly articulate presentation of oneself online continues to change with technology, educational pedagogy, and shifting expectations of a screen-based world. "EPortfolios are helping students become critical thinkers and aiding in the development of their writing and multimedia communication skills" (Lorenzo & Ittelson, 2005). The critical thinking, writing for the screen, and multimedia communication proficiencies that students must develop in order to present themselves competently in an ePortfolio are now fundamental life skills to develop in the current technology environment – they are infinitely usable, enduring, and highly transferable to other disciplines.

One could argue that while many students use the Internet for research and finding information, connecting with other people on a daily basis, gaming, keeping up with news in the world around them, etc. that often the constant inundation of information readily available can disallow and dis-motivate students from creating and sharing their own original thoughts. "21st Century learners should not be just consumers of knowledge, but producers of knowledge" (Herring & Notar, 2011). In our experience with students at the Rosebud

Institute, it is their personal and private challenge to write, design, organize and share *original* thoughts and work without leaning on a high level of reappropriation. The idea of ePortfolios is a good one, and makes sense in the current climate of technology, level of online connectivity, as well as the connection between employment and technology: "ePortfolio provides students a safe environment to research, read, write, collaborate, and publish to their space on the web" (Herring & Notar, 2011). However, we need to take great care and approach the idea not simply as another test to grade, a paper to hand in at the end of a class, or a means to an end of articulating learning outcomes at the end of a semester, but rather as a way for students to learn to express themselves and their own original ideas. Otherwise, we are just loading teachers and their students with more things to do. "Such problems are especially prevalent in education, where the Internet (which must be the most remarkable creativity and collaboration machine in the history of the world) often enters our classrooms as a distraction device" (Wesch, 2012).

In short, we must be careful not to add to the noise.

The goal is effective communication through creating an ePortfolio that will change, grow, and show progress over time. Establishing an ePortfolio is just the beginning of creating an intentional, intelligent online "self" – the learning and the progress in managing that entity will occur over a much longer period. And the growth of the individual is potentially limitless.

To a degree, the transformational shift has begun to occur in the classroom format: arguments and research abound towards a change from teacher-centered instruction and lecture format to the "flipped" classroom – lecture and teacher-centered instruction may take place in recorded format or in an asynchronous setting outside of the classroom, freeing the in-class time for skill application and more student-centered learning. The ePortfolio process as described in this chapter

is highly aligned with a student-centered learning approach. The disconnect that occurs between digital immigrants and digital natives is one of pedagogical approach – teaching and learning the same way it has always been done – even though it is becoming increasingly clear that through evolving technology, highly connected, multi-tasking students most certainly learn, assimilate and apply information differently (Prensky, 2001). The concept of choice, ownership, and responsibility in creating and maintaining an ePortfolio reflects the changing nature of technology, and the way education must change to more actively engage students. In challenging students to become responsible for their own knowledge, and proving that they are able to gain that knowledge and skill set via the design, writing, and distribution of their original work online, we recognize that "the world is now the audience and students take on the responsibility for becoming the expert on the content" (Herring & Notar, 2011). In a research study conducted with Masters degree candidates in an education program, Wickersham and Chambers (2006) acknowledge this responsibility and value as well: "Through the use of electronic portfolios, the responsibility of learning is transferred to the students. It allows them to be involved and engaged in the learning process and therefore keeps the focus on the learner-centered environment" (p.744). The strengthening connection between student as creator and a real world audience lends real authenticity and heightened pressure to "perform" better, and to be responsible for the content and demonstration of knowledge via an online portfolio. When we are made aware that someone is watching, we care more.

The researched and common sense benefits of creating an ePortfolio continue to proliferate: ePortfolios "enhanced technological skills and provided a mechanism for ease of storage and accessibility" (Chambers & Wickersham, 2007); that focused use "provide(d) students with a means of demonstrating their skill set, education, and relevant experiences" (Chatham-Carpenter, Seawel, & Raschig, 2010); and "they give students the opportunity to create a digitized showcase of their work and skills that can be presented to prospective employers" (Lorenzo & Ittelson, 2005). These are just a few of many recognizable examples that concentrate on the learner-centered approach to education, where students become responsible for their learning now and in the future. It is already happening – "Students are reading and writing to their online space outside the classroom" (Herring & Notar, 2011). One can argue even further, however, that with the evolution of technology and the ability to manage one's online presence, the résumé is no longer enough in the widening circles of our global economy. The tables have now turned, and the well-planned and designed résumé that passes on and off the desks of potential employers, along with the in-hand paper portfolio that may sit on a shelf, go the way of the Oldsmobile and the cassette. A strong web presence, an online résumé and an ePortfolio that shows depth, thought, and originality, is becoming the valuable communication and "selling" tool to get hired now and in the future (Mannix, 1994). And again, since a complete shift towards an exclusively online job search and hiring system has yet to occur, those that present themselves well in this way are ahead of the curve.

We need to harness the potential to engage students in this way, *before* they are even close to entering the workforce. By transferring the ownership of learning and knowledge to the individual, and giving audience and weight to their shared work, in a multiple presentation format, we allow students at a critical time in their cognitive development to form the understanding that there *is always* an audience, and that they must be careful and intentional about how they present themselves anywhere on the screen – through quality writing, appropriateness, relevant images, and original thoughts and ideas. With the right direction and clear educational and pedagogical research behind this approach, students will learn that "an electronic portfolio is really a living

history of lifelong learning" (Barrett, 2001). We don't just hand students the $3,000 pencil and the vague idea of creating an effective web presence; we begin with an intentional, focused approach to learning the language of the screen.

THE ROSEBUD INSTITUTE APPROACH

There are too many labels and approaches to count in documenting the evolution of the ePortfolio. To name a few: Formative or summative ePortfolios (Barrett, 2001); ePortfolios that end at the end of a semester or college career and focus mostly on college learning outcomes (Chatham-Carpenter, Seawel, & Raschig, 2010); and showcase, assessment, or development ePortfolios (van Tartsijk & Driessen, 2004). The truth is, there is no one method or set of rules that will necessarily fit an educational institution or an individual. However, there is a process to identify direction, content, and audience in a way that renders each approach to creating an ePortfolio a unique, focused approach. The Rosebud Institute has created a program that includes developing a clear sense of purpose, site creation and development, continual revision, collaboration and feedback, and a presentation of progress and learning process. This course of action has thus far proven successful in a variety of situations: Adult Education, graduate Education students, high school students, and even middle school students have gone through the process and continue to update, maintain, and share their ePortfolio with a variety of audiences and peers. Two important notes on the Rosebud Institute Approach: 1) each learning environment and group of students is different. Learning outcomes, goals, and the process must be flexible to accommodate different environments, access to technology, and the abilities of students and teachers. 2) The point is not to create technology-savvy web developers that will go on to successful careers in graphic or web design. Rather, the goal of implementing a successful ePortfolio program lies in helping students to create, manage, and share an articulate, well-written, well-organized online portfolio that showcases their best original work and unique ideas (Chilsen & Wells, 2012).

The most closely aligned pedagogy with the Rosebud Institute ePortfolio approach states that there are "three types of online portfolios: informal, organizational, [and the] personal digital portfolio" (Waters, 2009). An informal electronic portfolio is designed mostly as a repository for work, some limited collaboration with other students, with a brief timetable such as a semester or a year for creation and development, and the ability to share with classmates in a course and/ or a professor. An organizational portfolio gives more attention to the design, navigation, and purpose of sharing a collection of work over a longer period of time, with more depth, and perhaps with a wider audience. The Rosebud Institute encourages and teaches what Waters calls the "holy grail" of ePortfolios: the personal digital portfolio.

As you will see in the steps outlined below, this process is a highly adaptable, extremely reflective and collaborative process, as well as a continually personal and rewarding learning experience. Remember that while the process outlined below has successfully been used on its own, the ePortfolio piece of the program is normally used in conjunction with the two-pronged approach mentioned earlier in this chapter. This method is a blended approach that includes differing measures of asynchronous pre-work, initial and continued onsite training, continual electronic feedback, reflection, and expected revisions, along with a final presentation component in front of a live audience.

1. Choosing a Focus, Purpose, and Audience

Students begin by researching other example ePortfolios, thoughtfully considering the pos-

sibilities of what information about themselves they would like to share. After gathering their thoughts, ideas, and research, students write a purpose statement to establish a direction and focus, and create an outline of their site in terms of its intended navigation, content and development. It is highly important that students write a clear, concise purpose statement that begins to give form and focus to the unique personal "voice" they will use in writing and designing for the screen. Students use the vehicle of the purpose statement to describe personal and professional goals, intended audience, and outlines a plan for creation, development, and distribution. This part of the process is articulated to a group; informal feedback is given to help students further refine and focus the direction of each ePortfolio site towards the intended audience and aligning with their desired outcomes for the site. It is important to note, however, that the purpose statement is intended not as copy that should be reappropriated and recycled directly or necessarily anywhere on the ePortfolio site itself, but as a narrative tool and transferrable medium to focus ideas and direction towards a singular purpose. The purpose statement and outline, both of which require continual revision throughout the scope of the project, establish a framework and workable scope and sequence for site creation and development.

2. Get Organized

An ePortfolio is the organized, navigable, visual output of quality work that has already been completed. In order to design such a site, participants must organize what they want to show. This means collecting *digital assets* such as personal and professional images, previous work examples, an updated résumé, external links, and other digital media that may include documents, recordings, and videos. As students develop their individual sites and complete further work examples to showcase, the created ePortfolio will require further revision and re-organization to show the individual's learning process, development and progress over time (Chilsen & Wells, 2012).

The Rosebud Institute approach carries with it the weight and responsibility of creative licensure – students are encouraged to use their *own* images, their *own* work, and not to rely on the vast and abundant (and easily copied) digital media out on the web. And when it is appropriate or necessary to quote or reference other organizations, individuals, or media, those sources must be duly credited, correctly cited, and permission obtained.

This organization piece is a challenging step in the process, more of a process within itself really, and it requires that students learn to better organize, maintain, and review their digital assets both for the scope of developing an effective ePortfolio site, but also for their future. Currently, students who walk through this process must dig back into their previous work, revise some of that work as needed, and also plan for a future of better organizing and more intentional creation of work for their ePortfolio sites. We realize that this will not always be the case. As hopefully ePortfolios become de rigueur in education, students will *begin* their education with the idea that they must create work for sharing in an ePortfolio, and they must set up a system for organizing and storing their work in a way that makes managing individual digital assets much less tediously time consuming, and much more straightforward.

3. Creating and Managing Our Digital Selves

EPortfolio creators need to choose a repository that works for them. With that in mind, the RBI continues to focus on accessible, user-friendly technology interfaces for ePortfolios. A multitude of web-based, free or nearly free web site creation software options are now much improved, have become readily available, and do not require knowledge of html code or complex software programs to navigate successfully. It is important to de-emphasize the technology interface component of this step in the process and choose a repository and web design tool that retains a good balance between ease of use and dynamic visual representation.

Part of establishing and developing a professional, intentional online presence is to organize and add meaningful content. Images, documents, hyperlinks, narrative page introductions, contextualization of work that connects media elements with the focus and purpose of the site are just some of the examples of this ongoing step in the ePortfolio process. As mentioned above, students must also discuss proprietary measures, copyright guidelines, as well as appropriate online discussion and writing etiquette and some basic design guidelines for site development.

4. Reflection, Revision, and Collaboration

Students continually reflect, articulate, and hear feedback on their progress from others, giving credence and accountability to their work before it appears in a presentation forum for a wider audience. Based on peer and instructor feedback, both electronically and in person, students make changes and improvements. Timeliness in improving and adding content makes for quicker feedback, which in turn begets more opportunities to reflect, revise, and thereby improve the visual identity, content, and organization. Most students would likely report that the continual revision process is where they learned the most, but is also the most challenging and difficult step in creating an ePortfolio. Here's why: "Authors of paper portfolios often consider their portfolio to be "done" while electronic portfolio authors are more likely to consider their portfolios "a work in progress" (Fiedler & Pick, 2004). Though we provide an "ending" of sorts with the opportunity to present and share work with a live audience, the understanding is there that this is only the beginning, the ePortfolio is not officially finished; a digital presence created must continue to be managed, continue to grow and change to showcase the best work and appropriate personal voice possible (Chilsen & Wells, 2012).

In the implementation of an ePortfolio project, oftentimes the assumption is that the experience will be a solitary one, collecting artifacts and staring at a screen for hours, designing and formatting a website. The Rosebud Institute seeks a more collaborative, community approach where the gathering of elements, some writing, and some design take place outside the classroom environment, but the rest of the pieces: initial design, integration, formatting and layout, selecting *meaningful* and *relevant* digital content, and overall site development often happen inside the classroom (Chilsen & Wells, 2012). Students learn to articulate their opinions regarding their own work, and the more they understand the basic building blocks for how to create this type of screen media, the more they share openly and honestly with each other.

Widening the Communication Lens: The World as Audience

Recognizing and giving a wider, online audience to work completed in a college classroom is not necessarily new, but also does not necessarily happen. Turning in a final paper, even one that is peer-reviewed, is finished, turned in to a professor to read, graded, and often shelved or filed, perhaps even forgotten. Where is the authenticity and real-world connection with learning within that framework? We need to shift that thinking to make learning a more real, authentic experience that matters, both to the student and the audience of the world around them. "Unlike print portfolios, the ePortfolios are easily shown to classmates and other students. ePortfolios can have a more public and conversational function" (Kryder, 2011). An essential tenet of the Rosebud Institute approach does exactly this, in the showcase, distribution,

and articulation of work in a public forum where conversation and feedback are encouraged.

Because the audience might often *be* the potential employers or decision makers, the ePortfolio carries with it the weight of reality and the idea of permanence – a strong sense that this *matters*. The ePortfolio is published, online, and always accessible to the public. This idea of audience certainly lends a higher level of engagement and certainly authenticity to their learning: the pressure is on, and participants create ePortfolio sites with better, more creative, more concise writing, clearly developed content, appropriate images, and hopefully the beginning of the best representation of their best online self for others to see, not just one instructor, for one class, in one finite timeframe. Our students think intentionally about how they will distribute their information, and this is where good writing, an eye for simple design, and good organizational skills become highly obvious and very important to communicating in this medium. "ePortfolios are excellent reflection tools. Students become acutely aware of their strengths and weaknesses, more so than by developing résumés" (Okoro, Washington, & Cardon, 2011). The self-awareness that students develop by virtue of creating an ePortfolio and presenting to a real audience is an empowering tool for future development of self and more effective communication.

THE ISSUES AT HAND

Understandably, the Rosebud Institute approach to creating ePortfolios and other screen media is not without its particular challenges, and is not claimed to be able to be successful in all arenas and educational situations. In this intentional, pedagogical, sequential approach to teaching communication via a continually evolving technological interface, we want to recognize the observable issues, arguments and problems thus far.

Information Overload

With either the ePortfolio approach or the two-pronged screen media method that also includes producing a short silent film, there is some necessary front-loading and pre-work that students need to do to think about screen media with a different perspective than they are typically accustomed to as media consumers. The change in perspective, along with film views, discussion involving some simple deconstruction of screen media, and research into portfolio examples, can sometimes be overwhelming. The Rosebud Institute approach addresses this issue by approaching the foreign concept of creating original screen media through narrative writing and other means of communication students are already familiar with and capable of communicating with others. By breaking down the steps and focusing on some primary and basic tenets of screen media, we address and stem the potential for information overload.

Technology Access

Though the screen is ubiquitous, and technology and personal access to a screen is more assumed now than ever before, the Rosebud Institute is careful to focus only on the available technology and access for a given group. Making no assumptions about round-the-clock access to a personal computer or the internet, we are aware that technology access for some continues to be difficult, both in and out of school. Care is taken to supplement technology where appropriate, and to use interfaces and software that are readily available to the students at hand.

Privacy and Copyright

Recognizing that the broad umbrella of educational "fair use" doctrine has many gray areas, students are encouraged to write their own original ideas, create and share original work, and not to rely on the re-appropriation of the readily accessible work of others. This of course is much more challenging and a very personal journey. "Portfolios are often considered a very personal reflection of self, and this constraint can be a source of dissatisfaction" (Fiedler & Pick, 2004). Students are encouraged to research examples to help them gather ideas and formulate a clear direction and focus for an ePortfolio site, but when it comes down to creating a site, copyright rules must be respected and students must learn to think and articulate for themselves.

Ownership

Educational Institutions that are beginning to implement larger scale ePortfolio programs struggle with the issue of site ownership, as well as establishing parameters of digital etiquette. Does the school own the domain and hand that entity over to the student at graduation? Does the site get deleted after graduation? On an individual scale "students manage their own portfolios: they decide on the objective, content and format of their portfolio" (Meestus, Questier, & Derks, 2006). Students create their own ePortfolios, and thereby should be the owners, developers, and distributors responsible for the quality and appropriateness in their own work.

Development

Though the communicative platform of the ePortfolio allows many opportunities for "enhanced technological skills and provide(s) a mechanism for ease of storage and accessibility" (Chambers & Wickersham, 2007), students often run into problems when developing their site. Overwhelming design options for non-design students, lack of organization and ability to locate artifacts, and some floundering when deciding how to organize pages and content is quite common. The Rosebud Institute approaches this particular issue with continual peer and instructor feedback, as well as with common touch-point conversations with students, asking them to verbally articulate the ideas that they want to communicate visually.

Assessment and Evaluation

Like the informal and organizational ePortfolios we have previously discussed (Waters, 2009), oftentimes an ePortfolio approach has too narrow a time period for "completion," and too narrow a focus in regards to assessment and evaluation. Evaluation rubrics can be helpful, and implementing an ePortfolio project as a part of a class begets the need to perhaps regulate or require certain content. The challenge lies in recognizing and avoiding the potential to over-assess, over-evaluate, and lose sight of the potential engagement, audience, and creativity components of a project such as this one. In that instance, an ePortfolio can be relegated to online repository of work, to be downloaded, printed, graded, and, as we said before, forgotten. Avoiding a didactic approach, where "students basically collected their work, selected examples to showcase, and reflected on what they learned" (Lorenzo & Ittelson, 2005), the more challenging and more rewarding focus lies in the online personal digital portfolio, where students create and communicate original ideas in a way that reflects personality and interests. There must necessarily be assessment components, and those evaluation measures must align with the curriculum at hand, but there is a challenge to keep focus on the possibilities of maintaining and showing growth in an ePortfolio beyond the confines of a semester.

Technology Training: Learning the Interface

The Rosebud Institute approach to learning screen media focuses on the notion that technology will continually evolve and change. Therefore, if we focus on the communicative aspects of creating meaning in the original screen media projects students create, students learn a skill set that is transferrable to different interfaces and platforms. With digital natives, often the only issue here is access in public schools to viable software and hardware. Creating a multi-faceted, multimedia-rich ePortfolio even within the framework of a free online interface using available Web 2.0 technologies takes considerable technology resources. Reliable technology is one issue here, and the other is that there is always a learning curve and different aptitude levels towards learning a new technology interface.

Once students become more familiar with the concept of ePortfolios and comfortable with the technology itself that the technology will no longer be seen as a barrier and students will be able to relate more to the concepts of self knowledge and knowledge transfer. (Wickersham & Chambers, 2006)

Unlike other educational processes, we expect students to get up to speed quickly and stay there. However, for the most part, this doesn't seem to be an issue for digital natives, especially if they are introduced to the process at an early age.

Maintenance and Follow-Up

Because this particular approach to screen media and ePortfolios forces us to rewire our thinking from a single deadline or projected completion date to a more nebulous, continually self-paced track of maintenance and growth, it is difficult and sometimes frustrating to think that an ePortfolio, if it is to be a truly effective representation of one's digital personae, must continually be updated and maintained. "One of the greatest challenges they faced is 'for students to engage with their ePortfolios initially and then maintain their participation in the light of student study pressures and priorities'" (Chatham-Carpenter, Seawel, & Raschig, 2010). This evidence is compounded by the fact that the highest level of support and accountability lies within the confines of the project or course, and the only one that drives the bus to continue to show ePortfolio growth is the individual that created it. The Rosebud Institute continues to maintain connections with past program participants, and encourages continued communication and support, but as the program grows, this becomes more and more difficult to sustain. We continue to make every effort to find other audience, feedback, and networking opportunities beyond the scope of a single project to continually support the efforts of sustained growth and using the skills students have learned.

"It's Just More Work."

From experienced, stressed public school teachers who do not want one more challenging educational technology project to learn, to college students struggling to finish courses successfully and establish a career path, the ePortfolio might seem like it is "just more work." It *is* more work, and it takes time, thought, and careful planning to create an ePortfolio that effectively communicates an articulate personal voice. Some students maintain that "developing their portfolio electronically "forced" them to become more organized with more space to store information and allowed for a professional looking documentation of the ePortfolio" (Wickersham & Chambers, 2006). Though it is more work to set up an ePortfolio, and those that have a lot of work to locate, effectively contextualize, and display in an organized way might find the task somewhat daunting, there is a high level of value and real-world importance in maintaining a well-organized ePortfolio, and this must balance against the "extra work." Tipping the scales is the current environment of a much more competitive workplace. As stated before, the résumé is no longer enough, and competent job applicants will want to set themselves apart, showing their career potential and acquired experience in a more visually dynamic way. The world is already turning in this direction; "it's just more work" turns into "do this, or be left behind."

LOOKING FORWARD

After three years of program development and success in many arenas, the Rosebud Institute continues to look for feedback and ideas to further develop and adapt a communication-based method to learning screen media literacy – for different constituencies and populations, across different subject areas and disciplines, and varied age groups that include both digital natives and digital immigrants. Like the overall Rosebud Institute approach, as this program continues to grow and evolve, it is something that needs input, guidance and acceptance from a broad array of educators, academics and end users to be successful, meeting both the needs and expectations of the elusive, ever-changing medium of the screen. In our experience, we do recognize that there are sustainable truths and persevering ideas that will continue to inform and shape the direction of our approach and our ability to change with the times. We do not claim to have all the answers. But even though ePortfolios are not a new idea, this stripped down, back to basics, collaborative approach implemented in a more intentional, informed and interconnected manner is a unique direction the Rosebud Institute believes will continue to be the most broadly beneficial.

Recognizably, while the ever-changing trajectory of technology can seem vexing as we try to nail down a solid method – or even one clear method that always works – the Rosebud Institute program, with its emphasis on flexibility and tailoring the program to meet the needs and expectations of specific groups of students, can help us attain a more fundamental understanding of the use and intertwining of ePortfolios into the fabric of education and our professional lives.

We can start here: thinking about technology and technology education in a more application and communication-based way that challenges those who walk through the door to form and express their *own* ideas – to create something from nothing. In doing so, the whole approach becomes a more integral part of education – and consequently, people will experience less organizational whiplash. Then, the "where's all my stuff and how do I organize it" feeling will become the exception, not the rule. Almost like they automatically do now with pictures on Facebook or Picasa or wherever, eventually we will come to the day where people will instantly capture, identifiably own, intelligently store, and instinctively know what to do with their digital assets.

As stated earlier, maintenance, follow-up, sustainability and accountability are cause for concern in any current model for implementing ePortfolios. We must continue to search for a better mechanism for keeping people engaged in continuing to update and further develop their ePortfolios. The continued maintenance and careful monitoring of an established online presence can be a cause of consternation for some, tedious for others, and simply may get sloppy over time without a professor or established, consistent audience looking over the shoulder of the creator. Is there a way to sprinkle some Facebook dust on the process for kids so they really *want* to keep it moving forward? Are there perhaps better ways to add accountability *without* ruining the creative and life-long learning aspects of owning and proliferating an ePortfolio? And what of digital immigrants, who may find the task of organizing, uploading, managing, and organizing already created more daunting than valuable? We believe that starting from the perspective of creative communication, as well as creating goals that are manageable and attainable, are paramount to prevailing over these obstacles, but continued research, observation, and direct participant feedback continue to be valuable in finding more definable solutions.

While technology has become more complex and advanced, equipment and software have actually become much more affordable for individuals and educational institutions alike.

However, universal access to technology cannot and should not be assumed (Page, 2002). Recognizing that there is a disparity among different populations of students, we must continue to actively and creatively explore ways to level the technology playing field, increasing and equalizing access for disadvantaged constituencies. The inconsistencies of access coupled with the way technology is taught, both in and out the classroom, further complicates the issue for economically disadvantaged students. "Performativity, workability, and complexity (continue to shape) schools' efforts to deploy new technologies for academic preparation" and adaptation of these systems continues to vex administrators and teachers alike (Warschauer, Knobel, and Stobel, 2004). The Rosebud Institute is built on the premise that the technology we use should be affordable and accessible, but improving access to basic technology required for this approach, especially to those in higher need areas, remains an issue. Writing grants for educational technology funding, pursuing and supporting government incentive programs, and an expansion of Rosebud's IOTA program – Immersive Onsite Training Approach (Chilsen & Wells, 2012) are all on the table, but need further exploration.

Also mentioned above, assessment is a very important aspect of technology education, and we continue to define and refine what effective assessment means in the realm of ePortfolios. Assessment may offer a key, both in the efficacy of an ePortfolio program but also (carefully) using ePortfolios themselves as an assessment tool. On the latter, it may be that ePortfolio assessment can possibly drive the desire for students to want to continually or at least regularly update and maintain their sites. However, those that are intrinsically motivated to present themselves in a professional, original way online may not require this, and will likely surpass the expectations of assessment.

The advantages... include providing a comprehensive picture of learners' achievement and growth, enlarging the view of learning outcomes, involving students in the assessment process, motivating independent learning, communicating learning outcomes to faculty and parents, and creating an intersection for instruction and assessment. (Okoro, Washington, & Cardon, 2011)

For most, though, it may come down to the notion of "if they have to they will." But eventually, hopefully, we will be able to encourage and further develop both the intrinsic motivation to prove themselves in this way, but also impress upon Digital Natives and Immigrants alike, the real-world weight and importance of maintaining a competent representation of self for the online world. And like many things in education – math skills, writing skills, speaking skills – "mediating" skills too will eventually become part of how people conduct their everyday lives once they venture forth in the real, now very screen-based world. Much as a life skill learned in school that can be respected for its real-world application, like counting change or measuring square footage, the skill set one builds in creating an ePortfolio is highly valuable, transferable, and usable – and perhaps the one that matters most. The ideas behind creating an ePortfolio are infinitely more complex, highly personal, and carry the weight and reality of a real-world audience. Therefore, as we further research our pedagogy, adaptations of the program, and ways to effectively assess, we must continue to keep the importance of those ideals in mind.

CONCLUSION

As commercial and social media convergence advances at a rapid pace, and the unstoppable evolution of screen media continues, the time for change is indeed now. Gone are the days of saying "that's something we're going to have to deal with" because the issue of media convergence is being "dealt with" without our input. It seems generally and genuinely understood that students learn differently now. They engage in different ways – This is not necessarily a new phenomenon, and eventually these students will be adults. "Several hours a day, five days a week, sharply focused attention—does that remind you of anything? Oh, yes—video games! That is exactly what kids have been doing ever since Pong arrived in 1974" (Prensky, 2001b). Digital immigrants are becoming the new digital natives, so a day will come when we'll all be marching to a similar tune.

If we agree that establishing and maintaining a competent individual online presence is both timely and necessary, then interweaving ePortfolios into technology education seems to be a natural fit to meet this need. A back to basics approach, rooted in learning the fundamentals of how screen media really works, giving screen media the credence it deserves as its own medium of communication, sets the stage for better understanding and effective use of technology and communication skills. The Rosebud Institute approach to creating ePortfolios is one such method that works well – it is intentional, foundational, and basic – and it works. Using ePortfolios in this intentional, focused, adaptable fashion allows the needed flexibility at a time where we as a society, we as educators and educational policy creators, and we as individuals try to embrace the transformational shift and siren call of the screen without being consumed by it.

An important tenet of this transformative approach is the notion of creating something from nothing, empowering students and people to believe and know that they are creating original, meaningful, expressive, important work that carries the weight of self-reflection.

What is needed more than ever is to inspire our students to wonder, to nurture their appetite for curiosity, exploration, and contemplation, to help them attain an insatiable appetite to ask and pursue big, authentic, and relevant questions, so that they can harness and leverage the bounty of possibility all around us… (Wesch, 2012)

This process can and does inspire, nurturing in students the drive to do better, to communicate more effectively, and to take responsibility for their own learning. The more we can impress upon them the importance of audience, the more students are driven to be articulate, engaged, and appropriate members of a screen-based society. It ups the ante of performance and accountability; when people are watching, we do better. The ePortfolio platform offers advantages to the digital generation of students by "giving them creative opportunities for meaningful reflection through interactive displays of performance and engagement" (Okoro, Washington, & Cardon, 2011)

Screen media doesn't have to be a $3,000 pencil. Fully embraced in a more intentional fashion, it can be a challenging, multi-faceted, exciting way to find a personal voice and express, connect, and communicate effectively in the most pervasive, permanent, evolving medium of the day.

The challenge then, is how to interweave screen media into the fabric of life. The screen is everywhere, and pervades almost every aspect of what we do and the way we live. The evolution and saturation of screen media is already happening on its own, and it will continue to happen whether we take action or not – we need to make it happen now, and we need to make it happen better. This back to basics approach to screen media offers one way to cultivate a better direction, creating confident, screen-savvy media consumers who can authentically create and purposefully thrive in a screen-based world.

REFERENCES

Baines, L. (2012, June 20). *Web log message*. Retrieved from http://lifeboat.com/blog/2012/06/a-future-of-fewer-words

Barrett, H. C. (2001). *Expert showcase: Dr. Helen Barrett on electronic portfolio development*. Retrieved from http://ali.apple.com/ali_sites/ali/exhibits/1000156/

Batson, T. (2002). *The electronic portfolio boom: What's it all about?* Retrieved October 9, 2003, from http://www.syllabus.com/article.asp?id=6984

Borzo, J. (2011, January 21). Employers tread a minefield: Firings for alleged social-media infractions sometimes backfire on companies. *Wall Street Journal*. Retrieved from http://online.wsj.com/article/SB10001424052748703954004576089850685724570.html

Brandes, G., & Boskic, N. (2008). EPortfolios: From description to analysis. *International Review of Research in Open and Distance Learning*, *9*(2), 1–17.

Chambers, S. M., & Wickersham, L. E. (2007). The electronic portfolio journey: A year later. *Education*, *127*(3), 351–360.

Chatham-Carpenter, A., Seawel, L., & Raschig, J. (2010). Avoiding the pitfalls: Current practices and recommendations for eportfolios in higher education. *Journal of Educational Technology Systems*, *38*(4), 437–456. doi:10.2190/ET.38.4.e

Chilsen, P. J., & Wells, C. R. (2012, June). *Media and the moving image: Creating those who thrive in a screen media world*. Paper presented at Ed-Media World Conference On Educational Media & Technology, Denver, CO.

Fiedler, R. L., & Pick, D. (2004). *Adopting an electronic portfolio system: Key considerations for decision makers*. Association for Educational Communications and Technology, 27th Conference.

Herring, D. F., & Notar, C. F. (2011). Show what you know: ePortfolios for 21st century learners. *College Student Journal, 45*(4), 786.

Kryder, L. G. (2011). EPortfolios: Proving competency and building a network. *Business Communication Quarterly, 74*(3), 333–341. doi:10.1177/1080569911414556

Lorenzo, G., & Ittelson, J. (2005). *An overview of e-portfolios*. Educause Learning Initiative. Retrieved from http://net.educause.edu/ir/library/pdf/ELI3001.pdf

Mannix, M. (1994). Your credentials plus a song and dance. *U.S. News & World Report, 117*(17), 102.

Montgomery, K. (2000). Youth and digital media: A policy research agenda. *Journal of Adolescent Youth, 27S*, 61–68. doi:10.1016/S1054-139X(00)00130-0

Montgomery, K., Gottliev-Robles, B., & Larson, G. O. (2004). *Youth as e-citizens: Engaging the digital generation*. Center for Social Media.

Mossberger, K., Tolbert, C. J., & McNeal, R. S. (2008). *Digital citizenship: The internet, society, and participation*. (1 ed., Vol. 1). Hong Kong: Massachusetts Institute of Technology.

Okoro, E. A., Washington, M. C., & Cardon, P. W. (2011). E-portfolios in business communication courses as tools for employment. *Business Communication Quarterly, 74*(3), 347–351. doi:10.1177/1080569911414554

Page, M. S. (2002). Technology-enriched classrooms: Effects on students of low socioeconomic status. *Journal of Research on Technology in Education, 34*(4), 389–409.

Prensky, M. (2001a). Digital natives, digital immigrants — A new way to look at ourselves and our kids. *On the Horizon, 9*(5), 1-6. Retrieved from http://www.marcprensky.com/writing/prensky - digital natives, digital immigrants - part1.pdf

Prensky, M. (2001b). Digital natives, digital immigrants part ii: Do they really think differently? — Neuroscience says yes. *On the Horizon, 9*(6), 1-8. Retrieved from http://www.marcprensky.com/writing/prensky - digital natives, digital immigrants – part2.pdf

Richert, R. A., Robb, M. B., & Smith, E. I. (2011). Social partners: The social nature of young children's learning from screen media. *Child Development, 82*(1), 82–95. doi:10.1111/j.1467-8624.2010.01542.x

Ring, G., Weaver, B., & Jones, J. H. (2008). Electronic portfolios: Engaged students create multimedia-rich artifacts. *Journal of the Research Center for Educational Technology, 4*(2), 103–114.

Salomon, G., & Perkins, D. N. (1996). Learning in wonderland: What computers really offer education. In S. Kerr (Ed.), *Technology and the future of education*. (p. 111-130). NSSE yearbook. Chicago, IL: University of Chicago Press.

Van Tartwijk, J., & Driessen, E. (2006, April 26). E-portfolio scenarios. *Insight: Observatory for new technologies and education*. Retrieved from http://insight.eun.org/ww/en/pub/insight/school_innovation/eportfolio_scenarios/portfolios_types.htm

Warschauer, M., Knober, M., & Stone, L. (2004). Technology and equity in schooling: Deconstructing the digital divide. *Educational Policy, 18*(4), 562–588. doi:10.1177/0895904804266469

Waters, J. K. (2009). E-portfolios come of age. *T.H.E. Journal, 36*(10), 24–29.

Waterworth, E., & Waterworth, J. (2010). Mediated presence in the future . In Bracken, C. C., & Skalaski, P. D. (Eds.), *Immersed in media: Telepresence in everyday life* (pp. 183–196). New York, NY: Routledge.

Wesch, M. (2008, Oct 21). *Web log message.* Retrieved from http://www.britannica.com/blogs/2008/10/a-vision-of-students-today-what-teachers-must-do/

Wesch, M. (2012, June). *The end of wonder in the age of whatever.* Keynote speech presented at EdMedia: World Conference on Educational Media & Technology, Denver, CO.

Wickersham, L. E., & Chambers, S. M. (2006). E-portfolios: Using technology to enhance and assess student learning. *Education, 126*(4), 738–746.

Zhang, S., Olfman, L., & Ractham, P. (2007). Designing ePortfolio 2.0: Integrating and coordinating web 2.0 services with eportfolio systems for enhancing users' learning. *Journal of Information Systems Education, 18*(2), 203–214.

ADDITIONAL READING

Campbell, R., Martin, C. R., & Fabos, B. (2006). *Media & culture.* Boston, MA: Bedford/St. Martin's.

Fitch, D., Peet, M., Reed, B., & Tolman, R. (2008). The use of eportfolios in evaluating the curriculum and student learning. *Journal of Social Work Education, 44*(3), 37–54. doi:10.5175/JSWE.2008.200700010

Grant, A. E., & Wilkinson, J. S. (2009). *Understanding media convergence: The state of the field.* New York, NY: Oxford University Press.

Graves, N., & Epstein, M. (2011). E-portfolio: A tool for constructing a narrative professional identity. *Business Communication Quarterly, 74*(3), 342–346. doi:10.1177/1080569911414555

Prensky, M. (2001). Digital natives, digital immigrants. *On The Horizon, 9*(5). Retrieved July 16, 2012 from http://www.marcprensky.com/writing/.

Wilber, R. (2011). *Future media.* San Francisco, CA: Tachyon Publications.

Williams, R. (2008). *The non-designer's design book* (3rd ed.). Berkeley, CA: Peachpit Press.

KEY TERMS AND DEFINITIONS

Digital Asset: An originally created piece of work that has been imported or converted into digital format and therefore can be deployed in any number of digital media. Digital assets can include but are not limited to: photos, videos, music, blog entries, podcasts, files, résumés, and/or any other work created in an academic setting.

Digital Immigrant: A person born before the existence or current pervasive nature of digital technologies who is not naturally familiar or instinctively comfortable and therefore must adapt to using digital technology, interfaces, and software.

Digital Media Literacy: The acquired ability to understand, access, evaluate, and analyze types and avenues of information created online or with available software and hardware to communicate and participate in civic life as competent media consumer, contributor, and creator of media in the online community.

Digital Native: A person who is indigenous to the digital world, has grown up with and uses a wide variety of available and continually evolving technology with an inborn, instinctive sense of how to communicate, record, understand and share in society.

ePortfolio: A website created for or by an individual, that manages their digital assets and online presence, communicating learning or professional progress, which continues to change as long as its creator continues to develop and refine the content to reflect current experience, skill, and/or career focus.

Media Convergence: The natural, continual, accelerating evolution of technology resulting in a more integrated, inescapable coming together of multiple avenues of information, entertainment and online communication.

Mediate: To create original work for and effectively communicate through the technology, tools, and language of the screen.

Screen Media: Any media that is produced for or distributed via the screen, including the entire spectrum of what constitutes "the screen": the cinematic screen, to the television screen, the computer screen, and including the small screens we connect to on a smartphone.

Webfolio: A precursor to the current ePortfolio. A site created for or by an individual to act as a repository of online-accessible, static documents and hyperlinks to other related sites.

Chapter 17
Flipped or Inverted Learning:
Strategies for Course Design

Christine Davis
Walden University, USA

ABSTRACT

A number of researchers have explored the use of multimedia to support instruction in inverted classrooms providing a functional approach for university face-to-face and hybrid courses. Students in inverted learning work online before class listening to prerecorded lectures and completing related activities reserving class time for problem solving, projects, authentic applications, and reflection. The purpose of this chapter is to explore the value of cognitive and metacognitive elements in flipped – also known as inverted – learning that promote active learning. Practical strategies for course design and technical considerations related to how multimedia tools can be used to deliver and support instruction are also addressed.

INTRODUCTION

Inverted learning is a unique learner-centered approach to teaching and learning. This instructional model adjusts the design and delivery of instruction so students take the lead and responsibility for learning before class so the instructor can spend class time working on applied learning activities. The model relies on the active involvement of the learner and results in increased teacher-student interaction (Kahn, 2011). This chapter will review the theoretical background for inverted learning as well as the instructional design and technical considerations involved in planning and implementing the model. Objectives related to this chapter focus on flipped/inverted learning and strategies for course design:

1. Explore the concerns for meeting the needs of the learner;
2. Understand the constructivist design features of inverted learning;

DOI: 10.4018/978-1-4666-3962-1.ch017

3. Analyze the cognitive and metacognitive features of multimedia used to promote learner engagement online;

4. Understand the structure, components, and process used in developing an inverted course;

5. Consider important guidelines and technical considerations for course design; and

6. Summarize the special features and future research areas related to inverted learning in higher education.

BACKGROUND

Inverted learning is an emerging instructional approach that can be used to support or change the pedagogy of teaching in education. The system customizes the student's learning experiences promoting student discovery and management of learning. Concerns about traditional learning models in higher education coupled with an increasing desire to meet the learning needs of the adult student have resulted in the recent interest and experimentation with inverted learning. Inverted learning is rooted in the constructivist model and the fields of active, social, situated, learner-centered, and virtual or e-Learning (see *Key Terms and Definitions*).

Most universities still deliver instruction based on a *philosophy of a teacher-controlled learning model that promotes passive learners.* It is a formal, impersonal learning environment created by direct instruction with an emphasis on gaining information, note taking, and following procedures (Cole, 1990) with less focus on the learner and how learning occurs. This lecture-based format fails to engage students (Trees & Jackson, 2007) developing passive, non-thinking learners (McKeachie, 2002). Meyers and Jones (1993) reported students exposed to a lecture format were inattentive 40% of the time affecting both learning and retention (p.78). Gleason (1986) observed that passive learners also appeared dis-

connected from the instructor, classmates, as well as the course content. Arum and Roska (2011) questioned the effectiveness of traditional learning in higher education and used the *Collegiate Learning Assessment* (CLA) to assess content retention in college students. They reported most students demonstrated limited growth in learning and retention. Bok (2006) determined students in lecture courses only remembered 42% of material taught and found retention a week later deteriorated to 20% (p. 123). Crouch and Mazur (2001) also found students in lecture classes were unable to relate or retain content knowledge. It appears direct instruction often results in inefficient or ineffective learning.

Another consequence of the lecture model is the *amount of teacher-instructor contact time.* Khan (2011) found instructors in a traditional class spent less than 5% of instructional time interacting and working with students (n. p.) affecting the scope and depth of exposure to course content and limiting the time available for problem-solving, critical thinking, as well as the application and transfer of learning needed to move skills from theory to practice. Some instructors may ask questions or conduct an activity but most courses can be described as lecture heavy. In contrast to straight lecture, Marton and Saljo (1976) recommended a learner-centered approach that results in developing *deep* and reflective learning. In learner-centered classrooms, effective learners frequently pause and reflect for understanding, adjusting learning strategies as needed. Brockbank and McGill (2007) described this process of reflection as *third order learning* (p. 49) important for the growth and efficiency in learning. It appears "what we know about good learning is almost wholly contrary to the structure and conditions of lecture courses" (Foreman, 2003, p. 14). Traditional instructional methods typically used in higher education also seem inconsistent with the core learning theories found in psychology and education.

ISSUES AND PROBLEMS: MEETING LEARNER NEEDS

There are a number of researchers concerned about *accommodating the learning styles and needs of the millennial student*. These students use technology in a seamless way to socialize, communicate, and access information. Technology tools are embedded in their lifestyle and learning style. Universities need to adjust instructional methods to accommodate a generation of tech-savvy students entering higher education with new learning preferences and needs. Frand (2000) studied the millennial student and identified their learning approaches and beliefs. The millennial student considers computers and the Internet ubiquitous and find technology is engaging and more accessible for entertainment and learning. They spend most of their time online and fewer hours watching television. They feel what is viewed is subjective and can be altered by technology creating suspicion for what is authentic or real. They consider *doing* far more important than *knowing*. This principle is inherent in how the millennial student lives and learns. Learning preferences favor the trial-and-error approach used in electronic gaming rather than linear thinking and logic. These students stay connected through technology and find it essential for socializing, working, and living and express little patience for delays in a culture that expects access to people and information 24/7 (p. 15-24).

Higher education also recognizes the *value of critical thinking* (Halpern, 1998) and considers it an essential skill for college graduates (Arum & Roska, 2011). The skills involved in critical thinking are complex, sensitive to context, and require reflection and correction for forming judgment, (Lipman, 1988, p.39) problem solving, and decision-making. Since many instructors rely on lecture, they fail to provide students with opportunities to analyze, evaluate, and make inferences, considered important pre-requisites for developing critical thinking (Facione, 1990). The Association of American Colleges and Universities (2005) reported only 6% of college seniors were proficient in critical thinking (p. 10). Bok (2006) believed higher education demonstrated little effort to help students develop critical thinking and problem solving skills and found few students could apply skills in authentic ways or even transfer skills from one course to another (p. 83). Clearly there is a need for a more effective learning model in higher education. See Table 1 for a comparison between traditional and active/inverted learning.

INVERTED LEARNING

Inverted learning is a functional model that changes how faculty and students view and approach learning. The model constructs interaction between instructor and student in new ways both virtually and face-to-face. In contrast to the traditional passive learning model, inverted learning promotes student engagement before (pre-tests, lectures, discussion, activities) and after class (extended reading, application, and assessment) through multimedia materials, freeing classroom time for hands-on application of skills. Inverted learning focuses on the student, his/her active engagement and control of the learning process enabling more effective use of classroom time.

Active learning is a major focus in inverted learning. Active learning in inverted courses requires student engagement in thinking and doing so that the learner forms a relationship with content and constructs meaning. Gibbs (1992) compared the characteristics of a course designed for *surface learning* (high workload and contact hours, lack of student involvement and depth of thinking) with a course designed for *deep learning* (structured knowledge base, active learning, and interaction with others) (p.10-11). Courses designed for *deep learning* were found to be effective in promoting active learning and higher-level thinking. Based upon the need for active learning in lecture-based

Table 1. Comparison between traditional and active/inverted learning

	Traditional	Impact on Student	Active/Inverted Learning	Impact on Student
Instructional Design	Instructor centered, creates scripted materials and assessments	Passive	Student centered, activities designed to promote constructivist learning, assessments applied content and learning process	Active learner, accountable for learning, increased social learning; Students retain and apply information
Course Delivery	Course delivered face-to-face, regular schedule	Passive, receiver of information, attends weekly class	Delivery before, during, and after class in online and face-to-face sessions; Majority of class involves direct interaction with students.	Engages in online work before and after class; Exposed to a variety of learning styles and interactive and shared learning activities, teaches others
Lecture Format	Provides facts and information; Targets middle of the class; Uses singular approach	Passive, may take notes on facts, may feel disconnected from content, instructor, peers	Student interacts with online lecture, student controls access, reviewing as needed for understanding; Multiple learning approaches and activities	Develops responsibility for learning, controls learning pace, develops background knowledge, exposure to different learning styles; Increases interest, motivation, focus, and time on task; Achieves better retention and recall
Learning Activities	May be included when or if time permits	May engage in discussion or an activity with peers	Individual and collaborative activities offered before, during, and after class for higher-level thinking and authentic application to solve real-world problems	Engages in variety of collaborative, authentic activities; Engages in authentic applications; problem solving
Type of Materials	Notes, handouts, PowerPoint Presentation, video	Reviews distributed materials	Interacts with media clips, podcasts, learning modules, discussion forums, webinars, prerecorded lectures	Multimedia materials activities constructivist learning, increases interest, focus, and time on task, achieves better retention and recall
Discussion Format	Inserted in lecture or at the end of the class	Passive unless he/she volunteers or are called upon	Designed to promote active involvement before, during, and after class to develop critical thinking and reflection	Demonstrates critical thinking, applied, and authentic problem solving, reflection and evaluation of conclusions and decisions
Assessments	Essay, multiple choice, traditionally administered at the end of the course	Rote learning to recall or explain key facts	Integrates multiple types of assessments and feedback before, during, and after the learning process; Applied and authentic assessments, presentations, portfolio work	Applies higher-level thinking, deeper understanding, and reflection on content, applications, and the learning processes used

classrooms Foreman (2003) identified five design considerations for promoting learner involvement: (a) *Customize* learning environments providing learners with a variety of content and hands-on activities designed to meet different learning styles and needs; (b) *Provide immediate feedback* to expand on knowledge, provide clarification, or extend concepts; (c) *Construct* learning through an authentic, active learning environment, featuring multisensory activities so learners can explore, discover, and develop learning strategies as well as core content skills; (d) *Motivate* through modeling, observing, and interacting with others to spark learner interest and extend time engaged in practice with skills; and (e) *Include enduring*

reinforcement and application for long-term recall and generalization (p.14).

Another key design element of an inverted classroom (Lage & Platt, 2000) is the *integrated technology* used to deliver and support instruction since a great deal of time is spent out of class working online either preparing for class or reflecting on skills learned after class. Inverted learning capitalizes on the features of online or 'just in time learning" with access to the course content 24/7. The learning environment employs a cognitive learning model using multimedia tools to deliver essential background information, related web-based learning activities, and discussion forums to promote learner interaction.

Multimedia is considered is a viable system for supporting online learning in inverted classrooms. It involves a combination of hardware and software applications that integrates print, audio, graphics, video, and animation materials (Fenrich, 1997) for individualized learning. Other software programs offer sound and image editing that produce realistic 3-D models, designs, and complex animations to create realistic simulations and digitally-created learning environments. Animations are a powerful element in media that supports the development of imagery and the mental models needed to understand concepts (DeLeng, Dolmans, & van de Wiel, 2007) using unique properties that attract, engage, and focus learners (Stone, 1999) resulting in increased levels of learner participation. Repetition with media materials permits the learner to review and interact with skills as often as necessary for understanding without fear of embarrassment or consternation. Bruner and Olson (1986) refer to the benefit of 'learning by seeing' experiences provided by media (p. 226). Video clips also have the power to deliver information in a vicarious manner (Reddi & Mishra, 2003) providing authentic snap shots of procedures and best practices found in the real world. Herrington and Oliver (2000) describe how media creates *situated* learning experiences when an expert models skills and breaks down tasks, preparing the learner for practice. Media can also effectively support the cognitive learning processes by delivering context while satisfying the interactive and social nature of learning (Gee, 2000).

In inverted classrooms, many aspects of lecture (fact gathering and background knowledge) are accomplished through online work, whereas complex relationships and extended concepts are explored during class time. This structure promotes the development of *convergent* learners who prefer to problem-solve and experiment with new ideas (Kolb, 1984) in the online segment; and *assimilating* learners who listen, analyze, and transform information and ideas in the classroom segment (Kolb, 1984; Buerck, Malmstrom, & Peppers,

2003). Such higher-level activities are by nature *active* involving shared learning among students and between the instructor and students (Gannod, Burge, & Helmick, 2007). The system also tends to personalize learning by appealing to different learning styles (Lage, Platt, & Treglia, 2000) through a wide-range of instructional activities also designed to activate higher-level thinking. This concept of self-discovery of knowledge through active learning (Mathie, et al., 1993) replicates the type of cognitive work expected in the real world. See Figures 1 and 2 for active/inverted learning models.

A Case Study

Davis and Froriep (2009) experimented with two different sections of a literacy course with 32 pre-service teachers. The goal was to incorporate more meaningful learning experiences designed to better prepare the pre-service teachers for clinical experiences working with children in elementary schools. They studied the value of using online multimedia clips of teachers modeling effective teaching and assessment strategies in reading. The key investigative question for the study asked if teacher candidates found value in viewing video clips online and if it helped them better understand best practice techniques for teaching and assessing reading skills.

Throughout the semester, video clips were incorporated into the online instructional content, using *BlackBoard Academic Suite* eEducation Platform (2002). The multimedia clips, were linked to credible professional websites (reading and department of education) depicting master teachers providing instruction to elementary school students (K-6) in the essential skills of reading including phonemic awareness, phonics, fluency, comprehension, and vocabulary. The media clips detailed both the required content and the correct techniques used to focus, cue, teach, reinforce, and assess each reading skill. Students viewed and reviewed the multimedia clips online as often

Figure 1. Multimedia model for active/inverted learning

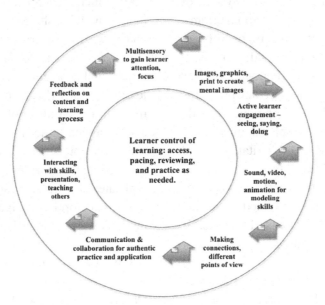

as necessary for understanding. The instructors then used class time to extend and apply skills providing students with opportunities to model, practice, and critique as classmates demonstrated instructional and assessment techniques.

The instructors collected anonymous responses to a four-point Likert-scale (Strongly Agree to Strongly Disagree) questionnaire at the end of the semester to determine student opinions about their learning experiences. The teacher candidates in this study reported value in viewing the online video clips and indicated that the process helped them better understand best practice techniques for teaching and assessing reading skills. All students (100%) agreed that the viewing of the online video clips helped them better understand the instructional techniques involved in teaching each skill. Most students (84%) felt that viewing the video clips helped them better understand techniques for assessing each of the essential reading skills; and 72% of students indicated their experiences reviewing the online multimedia materials enhanced their understanding and ability to model the essential reading skills (p.2). Prior exposure to expert teachers modeling skills

enhanced student readiness and confidence in performing these skills in a classroom and clinical setting. This study has positive implications for inverted learning as students entered class with a greater understanding of the process and techniques involved in teaching reading skills permitting the students to practice and apply the skills in class under the coaching and supervision of the instructor. The additional work before class resulted in increased time available in class for teacher-student interaction and student practice with skills with perceived benefits expressed by the students.

Benefits of Inverted Learning

There are a number *benefits for students engaged in inverted learning*. Researchers (Lage, Platt, & Treglia, 2000; Papadopoulos, Santiago-Román, & Portela, 2010) concluded students preferred inverted learning to traditional lecture-based classes. Inverted learning is user-friendly and student-centered. It accommodates different learning styles while exposing students to the working styles of others. Students benefit from first

Figure 2. Inverted student-centered learning model

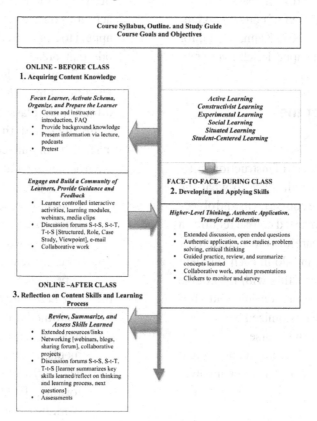

exposure and the ability to control when and how often they access and review concepts (Foertsch, Moses, Strikwerda, & Litzkow, 2002). The diverse activities assigned before, during, and after class keep students actively engaged increasing student time on task. The multimedia materials used in inverted learning presents an enjoyable and interactive format for learning (Bransford, Brophy, & Williams, 2000; Lage, Platt, & Treglia, 2000), providing visual images that promote cognitive effort, increasing student motivation and focus (Juwah et al. (2004). The learning structure encourages *deep thinking* through discussions and shared decision-making. Students are given ample opportunities to ask questions, make predictions, evaluate and refine ideas, transferring and applying learning. Students are aware of expectations

and performance criteria minimizing questions and reducing frustrations.

There are also *benefits expressed by instructors*. The model promotes student ownership of learning while it accommodates and meets the needs of a variety of learning styles (Lage, Platt, & Treglia, 2000). It personalizes learning at a distance, creating virtual learning communities promoting social connections, instructor-student interaction and rapport (Lage, Platt, & Treglia), resulting in more efficient use of class time. Instructors also reported increased opportunities to monitor student progress, provide guidance and feedback, and identify skills in need of remediation (Chickering & Gamson, 1987; Juwah et al. 2004; Solvie & Kloek, 2007). Finally, the key benefit expressed by instructors involved the increase in student contact time in class enabling the extension and application of concepts (Gannod, Burge, & Helmick, 2007; Kahn, 2011), for applied problem solving (Zappe, Leicht, Messner, Litzinger, & Lee, 2009).

The Components of the Inverted Course

In inverted learning, the focus of instruction shifts from what the instructor will *teach* to what the students will *do* to achieve course goals and objectives. The design of an inverted course requires a unique framework and careful consideration for what students will read and do in each segment of the learning process, starting with the course introduction as well as before, during, and after class. Many elements are customized based upon the content and nature of the course.

This emphasis requires careful planning and preparation for every aspect of learner involvement.

1. **Preparing the Course - Online:** Course preparation is customized according to subject area and planned learning outcomes. Preparation may involve the recording of a course introduction, recording lectures for each online session, selecting online and print resources, readings, learning modules, as well as the development of assignments, discussion forums, pretests, quizzes, and exams. Each segment should be designed to prepare the learner for class work while supporting and developing skills. The online course template should permit easy navigation between different sections of the course management system so students may review specific content, catch up on material missed, or prepare for quizzes and course assessments. Lage and Platt (2000) and Lage, Platt, and Treglia (2000) suggest

offering a multimedia "menu" of learning activities online that can accommodate and appeal to a preferred learning style or methods that presents information in different ways. They consider this approach as user-friendly, of high interest, and unmatched in a traditional classroom (p. 32). Lage, and Platt suggested the course management system be organized into distinct learning environments including:

a. *The Philosophical Foundation of the Course* (presenting the course syllabus, course and instructor introductions, related vocabulary terms, and student learning and performance expectations);

b. *The Learning Desk* (recorded lectures, multimedia materials, learning modules, podcasts, webinars, and assessments organized by week or session);

c. *The Coffee House* (discussion and chat forums, FAQ forum, collaborative working groups, student communication boards, blogs, and surveys); and

d. *The Library* (offering course resources, Internet links, search engines, references, bibliographies, and links to library databases) (p.10).

2. **Preparing the Learner for the Course – Online:** Students should feel confident and knowledgeable about the course format, content, expectations, and planned learning outcomes through the course outline and study guide. At this stage students should be introduced to the concept of inverting learning, how the course will be structured, what the instructor will do, and what students are expected to do before, during, and after class by week or session. Each student must clearly understand his/her responsibility to be active throughout the course. Course preparation can include a recorded course

introduction, pre course readings, and an opportunity to assess self-management skills and a personal readiness for learning online. A *Question and Answer Forum* can answer questions about the course or related assignments while reassuring students reducing their concerns.

3. **Preparing the Learner for Class – Online:** Students must enter class prepared for active learner involvement. Student engagement before class increases cognitive levels so students enter class with the schema and background knowledge necessary for higher-level thinking, reasoning, and application. Effective student preparation can be accomplished through a number of interactive activities designed so that the student can formulate and self-discover key concepts. Students should explore Internet links that provide theoretical, historical, and current information about the session topic. Next students should listen to and view *pre-recorded lecture*(s) on the session topic(s) *and view related media or video clips* of experts modeling skills that can be reviewed as needed. Finally students engage in *learning modules*, simulation, and interactive activities to develop a working knowledge base. Additional preparation for class can involve surveying student opinions or completing a self-assessment of entry-level skills.

4. **During Class – Face-to-Face:** During class, the role of the instructor changes from providing information to one of applying information and monitoring student participation through observing, questioning, and guiding work. A variety of learning experiences are recommended during class to sustain active student engagement and learning. The instructor can plan simulations, role-playing, student presentations, projects, experiments, or demonstrations (Baker, 2000). Open-ended and critical thinking questions can stretch the application of skills to solve authentic problems found in the real world and collaborative work can engage the learner in social and shared learning experiences so students benefit from the exchange of ideas and from teaching others. Finally, the instructor can use technology tools such as clickers (Johnson, 2007; Rice & Bunz, 2006; Stowell & Nelson, 2007) to aid in engaging students and assessing their progress with learning.

5. **After Class – Online:** After class work often involves online activities designed to extend and apply concepts including: follow-up discussion forums, additional collaborative work on special projects, and/or to provide opportunities for students to reflect on or summarize learning experiences. Online surveys, quizzes, and exams can measure learning outcomes; and course evaluations can assess the achievement of course goals and objectives as well as the effectiveness of the course design and instructional activities.

Instructional Design for Inverted Learning

The theoretical framework for developing an inverted learning environment involves a pedagogical shift from developing didactic instruction based upon behavioral learning theories to developing constructivist learning using multimedia tools to promote cognitive interaction and authentic practice with skills. The most efficient method for *inverted course design* is the backward design process as described by Wiggins and McTighe (2005). This involves working from planned student learning outcomes.

Step 1: Develop the course outline, identifying the significant learning goals and outcomes students are expected to achieve. Explain the inverted learning structure and student expectations for each learning segment.

Step 2: Develop a *course content outline and session map* best suited for direct instruction, lectures, or activities (face-to-face and online) that will help students acquire foundation skills, course content, learning goals and objectives. Package and sequence course content by topics. Make decisions about the delivery of content and when students will engage in direct instruction, interactive activities, reflection, and assessment experiences (before, during, or after class) (online and face-to-face) for each topic by session.

Step 3: *Create online lecture materials* designed with text, graphics, and narration using a variety of software applications including *Articulate* (Studio, 2009), *Camtasia* (Tech-Smith, 2010), *Jing* (TechSmith, 2010), *Captivate* (Adobe, 2010), *PowerPoint* (Microsoft, 2010), *VoiceThread* (Educause, 2009) or *Keynote* (Apple, 2009). Final products can be exported as a *Flash* file (Adobe, 2012) or a *QuickTime* (Apple, 2012) movie for student retrieval as a streaming video for immediate viewing or downloaded for future viewing. Each lecture should be carefully designed to explain introductory as well as more complex information the learner cannot formulate from readings or from other types of learning experiences. Locate and evaluate media clips, Internet links, and online resources for quality and value.

Step 4: Design and create *classroom projects and applied learning activities* (see Figure 3).

Step 5: Create *online social experiences* to foster collaborative relationships among students. Such experiences can consist of small as well as large group sessions delivered through web-conferencing systems that engage and support virtual learners such as *Wimba* (Blackboard, 2011), *Elluminate* (Blackboard, 2010), *and Blackboard Collaborate*

(Blackboard, 2012). Additional n*etworking tools* such as webinars, blogs, and podcasts can be included to encourage social learning with peers and experts in the field.

Step 6: Develop *discussion forums* designed to exchange ideas, probe and explore student thinking. Discussion forums offer a platform for accommodating both the social and active learning elements necessary in inverted learning. Moore (1989) described three types of interaction for distance-learning environments: learner-content interaction to promote a cognitive and intellectual relationship with the content; the learner-instructor relationship molded by the instructional design of the system; and learner-learner interaction through discussion and knowledge sharing (p. 2-4). The instructor can personally guide discussion(s) or defer to a student leader. Specific questions can act as an introduction for face-to-face work.

Step 7: *Design student reflection and assessment activities* (online and face-to-face).

Step 8: *Develop strategies to scaffold teaching* and learning activities.

Step 9: *Organize and load online content,* lectures, media files, Internet resource links, and multimedia materials into the course management system by session. *Include resource materials, references, and* supplemental readings that can stretch student discovery and thinking.

Step 10: *Evaluate the design of each activity* for academic value, constructivist approach, and alignment with learning outcomes. Determine the degree to which: (a) There is a comprehensive presentation of content through manageable units with authentic applications; (b) Course content and learning activities meet course goals and objectives; (c) The online materials (audio and visual) and navigation aids are current, accessible; (d) The multimedia materials (audio and visual) are of high quality, promote critical and higher-level thinking, and lead to student achievement of course content; (e) The multimedia materials accommodate different learning styles and rates, are flexible, user-friendly, and easy to manage and control; (f) The multimedia materials attract, focus, engage, and help the learner construct learning, promoting interaction between students and the instructor. Evaluate the course for levels of student achievement, interaction, and student satisfaction.

Instructors should consider the instructional design skills and time required to develop a quality course. Consider the learning needs of the adult student and balance the content and workload planned for each learning segment (before, during,

Figure 3. Designing the inverted learning course

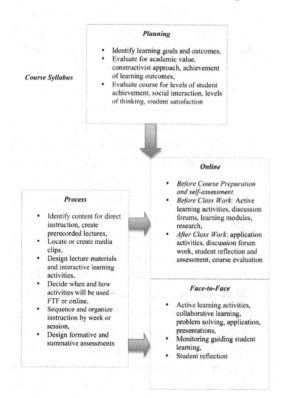

and after class). The format of the course must be framed to maximize student involvement (see Table 2 for a course planning guide). The learner should reflect on the essential skills needed for inverted learning including information and technology literacy skills, study skills, as well as the ability to manage time, self-assess, and self-correct to complete assigned work and achieve course outcomes. When students recognize instructor expectations for inverted learning, he/she will understand responsibilities and expectations for being prepared before class and active during class in order to succeed in the course. The success of the learner may well depend on his/her understanding and acceptance of the principles of active and inverted learning.

Researchers in the Field of Inverted Learning

A number of university professors have investigated the field of inverted learning based on two major topics for inquiry: a.) Does inverted learning support student *learning styles and needs* increasing the levels of student engagement and thinking?; and b.) What is the *value of multimedia materials* for content delivery, modeling, cognitive development, and skill acquisition?

1. **Learning Styles and Needs:** Some researchers have focused on how inverted instruction addresses different learner needs and learning styles. Lage, Platt, and Treglia (2000) flipped 5 of 35 sections of an introductory course in microeconomics. Participating students viewed prerecorded lectures, engaged in discussion forums, completed worksheets, and online quizzes spending class time on active student engagement through hands-on activities and group work (p. 33-34). Researchers attributed higher student motivation and ownership in learning to increased levels of interaction and active learning experiences (p. 37).

Table 2. Inverted learning course planning guide

Course:
Learning Goals:

Objective	Wk	Directed Learning Activities	B	D	A	Student Learning Activities [Active or Multimedia]	B	D	A	Student Reflection & Assessment Activities	B	D	A	Resources [Print or Internet]

B - Before Class
D - During Class
A - After Class

Baker (2000) flipped a graphic design course using web-based lecture notes, discussion forums, and online quizzes to free class time for higher-level thinking and application with skills. Students reported experiencing more control over learning, more opportunities for collaboration, and receiving more personal attention than in other courses. Broad, Mathews, and McDonald (2004) also studied how technology in inverted accounting classes provided a richer learning environment that supported learner needs and styles. They found students explored and discussed concepts more in depth then those in traditional college courses. Solvie and Kloek (2007) investigated if inverted learning could create a constructivist-learning environment, able to meet learner needs and styles in a pre-service teacher course. Bates and Galloway (2012) surveyed student reactions in an inverted physics course and found evidence of high quality student learning. They concluded, "we are convinced that, due to student efforts outside of class, we covered as much content but uncovered a great more understanding" (p. 8). Other researchers found students in graduate statistics courses became more aware of the learning process when taught in an inverted class (Frederickson, Reed, & Clifford, 2005).

2. **The Value of Multimedia:** Other researchers used multimedia materials to deliver lectures, model skills, and support learners. Herrington and Oliver (2000) investigated the value of multimedia in creating authentic and situated learning experiences for pre-service teachers. They found multimedia materials provided an effective framework for the development, reflection, and assessment of complex skills. Zappe, Leicht, Messner, Litzinger, and Lee (2009) explored the value of prerecorded videos of lectures in an inverted architectural engineering course. The majority of students (75%) reported that the videos and the additional time spent problem solving in class improved their understanding of complex methods and concepts (p.8). Others created podcasts to deliver lectures online to engineering students using class time to model, support, observe and guide student decision-making and progress with engineering projects (Gannod, Burge, & Helmick, 2007). Liao (2012) also found video clips focused learners, increasing interest and stimulating critical thinking (p.

53). Khan (2011) developed media tutorials on a range of math skills to better prepare students for classroom work and found inverted learning promoted active student engagement and increased teacher-student interaction (n.p.).

Solutions and Recommendations

While researchers have explored the benefits of active participation for students, it is understood that some learners may still choose to participate less often or do so in a more passive manner. Pedagogical strategies that promote learner involvement are critical for involving the learner in an inverted course. As a result, learning activities must take into account how learners make sense of information, acquire skills, and internalize concepts (Bransford, Brown, & Cocking, 2000) while incorporating essential constructivist principles of learning. Instructional design for inverted learning requires careful and creative planning for how and when instruction and learning activities will be delivered (Reddi & Mishra, 2003) based on an analysis of learner needs.

Course designers must consider the knowledge required for the achievement of course goals, the kinds of thinking required for the application of skills (critical, creative, and practical thinking), and the essential connections that must be made within the course, with other courses in the program, and with authentic applications found in the real world (Fink, 2003). Good instructional design is important for achieving learner outcomes in inverted learning environments. The design of course activities will determine the degree of involvement and ultimate achievement of the learner as well as the success of the inverted learning program. Instructors must take the time to create well-designed learner-centered activities that foster self-discovery and a responsibility for learning. Recommendations:

1. **Implement Well-Designed Activities:** Constructivist learning occurs when the learner builds on prior knowledge and personal experiences, making connections, constructing and demonstrating new knowledge (Newby, Stepich, Lehman, & Russell, 1996; Walker & Lambert, 1995). Instructors should incorporate an authentic purpose for assignments and provide criteria to guide student work and measure student performance. Learning approaches should prepare and support the learner to handle more complex content and promote the cognitive effort required for understanding and higher-level thinking.

2. **Use a Learner-Centered Approach:** In a learner-centered environment, the focus is on the student and the process of learning, what the student is learning, how he/she is learning, and how he/she can use and apply what is learned (Weimer, 2002). Grunert (2000) outlined the key elements found in a learner-centered course indicating the syllabus should convey the philosophy and purpose of learner-centered instruction, the logistics and conceptual framework of the course, the student's role and responsibilities and suggested learning activities that can activate and sustain learning (p. 2). Learner-centered activities and structured discussion forums should be formulated to promote student interaction, collaborative/social learning, critical thinking, and opportunities for evaluation and self-reflection of skills learned. The work of Weimer (2002) served as the basis for the development of specific ways to involve students before, during, and after class.

   a. **Preparation for the Course - Online:** Survey students and edit the course syllabus to include personal goals related to course outcomes. Encourage shared decision-making about the details of assignments and criteria for scoring rubrics. Have students assess personal levels of readiness for active and inverted learning by rating a list of essential skills. Collaborate with students to create assessment checklists so students can evaluate work before submission. Ask students to complete a quiz on the syllabus.

b. **Before the Class - Online:** Discuss the purpose of activities and assignments and question students to clarify their understanding of course expectations. Introduce lectures with thought-provoking questions to promote connections between previous skills learned and new material presented. Create or use media clips in which skills are modeled and explained. Assign tasks before, during, and after viewing media clips. Encourage students to practice and evaluate skills. Use summary discussion forums so students can reflect what they have learned.

c. **During Class:** Prepare students to take an active role in developing the learning climate in an inverted course. Students can contribute a list of conditions and acceptable procedures as well as expectations for active learning in the class. Use matrices and concept maps to organize, sequence, and break tasks into steps. Make students aware of the strategies and approaches used in thinking, learning, and problem solving. Students should also defend or explain personal reasoning, approaches, or solutions used when completing tasks. Allow time for students to debrief and share what they have learned. Ask students to self-assess progress with assignments and projects.

d. **After Class –Online:** Some instructors include post class online work for closure and assessment. Assessment of student performance is usually guided by rubrics and grading scales and should include a variety of ways the learner worked within the course including being prepared and actively involved by initiating, responding, collaborating, questioning, answering, reacting, summarizing, and assessing his/her work as well as the work of others.

3. **Incorporate Opportunities for Evaluation and Feedback:** Researchers (Juwah, et al., 2004) developed principles for providing effective feedback for e-Learners: (a) Facilitate dialogue, self-reflection, and self-assessment of learning throughout the course; (b) Help clarify and define expectations for good performance (standards, criteria, rubrics, checklists); (c) Provide opportunities to close the gap between current and desired performance; (d) Deliver high quality information about learning (provide timely feedback and relate corrective feedback to criteria); and (e) Use information obtained to inform instructional planning (identify problems, concerns, understandings) (p.2).

4. **Construct Adequate Learner Supports:** Reddi and Mishra (2003) recommend an *e-Learner support system* that is sensitive and responsive to student needs (p. 25). There are significant considerations involved in designing a student support system in inverted learning so students can construct, organize, and evaluate levels of learning. (a) First instructors need to create a climate for active learning by helping students understand the need, purpose, and framework for active learning; (b) Second, instructors need to foster in students a responsibility for learning and develop the skills and strategies for processing and retaining information; (c) Third, instructors need to design opportunities for students to communicate, collaborate, and learn with others; (d) Finally, students

need to think about and assess what they have learned as well as the effectiveness of the selected learning approaches used.

Technical Considerations and Guidelines for the Use of Multimedia

Those involved in inverted courses need to consider the technical aspects of the technology tools used to organize, deliver, and support the online aspects of the course.

1. **Use Quality Technology Tools:** Inverted learning relies on the delivery of multimedia materials often affected by memory, bandwidth speed, and the quality of computer possessing and course management systems. Poor technical elements can reduce the speed of downloading files affecting the listening and viewing experience of the student. Some management systems restrict the size of media files and process them at slower speeds significantly increasing the time it takes to load the file into the course management system. Some media files load in 30-seconds while others take 30-60 minutes or more. Instructors also need access to computer equipment and software applications required for the development of quality multimedia materials (Reddi & Mishra, 2003). The purchase and use of hardware and software can be expensive and often requires additional professional development. Instructional designers should understand that the creation and loading of media materials into the course template is labor intensive and time consuming.

2. **Use Quality Media Clips:** The creation of media clips requires some knowledge of the process of working with both audio and visual files. Selected media should be evaluated for value of the content as well as for technical aspects of appearance and other design features that attract and engage the viewer. The presenter should be evaluated for his/her expertise in the field and knowledge of current trends and best practices. The video should have clarity on both the video and audio tracks and be of moderate duration (approximately 20-30 minutes (Zappe, Leicht, Messner, Litzinger, & Lee, 2009, p.11). The video should provide enough time to model and share sufficient practice and/ or authentic ways to convey the scope and sequence of the skill(s). Videos that are too long or are of poor quality can cause fatigue and a loss of interest. For more complex concepts, guided practice and anticipation guides can support media clips by reinforcing key principles, special techniques, or sequential steps important to the skill. Designers should select only those of high quality and whenever possible compress files or reduce the size of each media clip.

    Quality media clips can also be found on websites sponsored by research and professional organizations. Media clips on these sites are often commercially developed and are a cost effective alternative to creating media materials in the home or on campus. Some require memberships or fees, while research sites usually offer access to media clips free of charge. There could be limited availability of media clips in certain subject areas and it may be time consuming to research, locate, and link files to course management systems. Media clips on private sites are available at the pleasure of the hosting organization and can be moved or removed at any time. Whether linking or uploading files, each media clip should be field tested for ease of access and use. Links must be tested on a regular basis to make sure they are still accessible and must be used in compliance with copyright regulations.

3. **Design Interactive Discussion Forums:** Discussion forums provide the social aspects critical to the learning process. Researchers

have reported students enjoy and want such interactions (Grooms, 2000) and found they contributed to a more satisfying learning experience (Anderson, 2002). Discussion forums are considered an effective constructivist tool for e-settings (Bannan-Ritland, Dabbagh, & Murphy, 2000; Hung, 2001; Hung & Nichani, 2001) and require careful development to promote the construction of learning with others. The work of Sorensen and Baylen (2009) and Davis (2010) can served as a basis for the development of a number of discussion board formats that can be used to create a constructivist and active learning environment promoting student participation, interaction, and higher-level thinking in inverted coursework. (a) In a *Structured Discussion Forum*, a student leader poses a key question, provides background knowledge, posts related resources and summarizes and synthesizes the key points of the discussion at the end of the session (Sorensen & Baylen, 2009, p. 77); (b) *In a Case Analysis Forum*, learning teams are assigned to an authentic case study for shared research, discussion, and analysis. After a presentation [online or in class] each team reviews and critiques the findings of another team (p. 78); (c) *In a Discussion Role Forum*, each student assumes a different role for postings including: initiating, supporting, challenging, monitoring, and summarizing (p. 79); (d) *In the Viewpoint Forum*, students are assigned different perspectives or points of view for research, gathering evidence, and for the development and presentation [online or in class] of solutions (Davis, 2010, p.2); and e.) *In a Summary Forum,* students evaluate and reflect on key concepts learned during the session (p.2).

Scoring discussion forum work can be based upon an analysis of the levels of student thinking, participation, and his/her ability to engage in self-directed learning. This can

be achieved by using the work of several cognitive processing systems. Bloom (1994) recognized six cognitive processing levels including: knowledge, comprehension, application, analysis, synthesis, and evaluation) (p. 1-8) and Henri (1992) developed an analytical model for the scoring critical thinking using five dimensions related to the degree of participative, social, interactive, cognitive, and meta-cognitive work (p.125). Garrison, Anderson, and Archer (2000) assessed the degree of community learning using three criteria: cognitive, teaching, and social presence measuring the degree to which participants constructed meaning through sustained communication among students and between students and the instructor (p.88). Some instructors also consider the frequency or the length of postings.

4. **Provide Ongoing Support:** Those involved in inverted learning should develop a philosophy and commitment to a paradigm shift in teaching and learning. A plan for implementation should include professional development and ongoing support for participating faculty. Professional development should deal with both the theoretical basis of inverted learning as well as a discussion of the pedagogical learner-centered approaches that have been found effective in promoting student responsibility and active involvement in the learning process. Finally, the university needs to provide an efficient and user-friendly course management system and knowledgeable personnel to assist with course design and development as well as the ongoing technical support necessary for implementation.

Students will also need both training and support. Learning modules can prepare students for working online and help them understand expected roles and responsibilities in an inverted course. Students must be informed of technology requirements, have access to good technology tools, and ongoing technical and academic support systems considered essential for inverted learning so students can focus on learning content, not on troubleshooting technology.

FUTURE RESEARCH DIRECTIONS

With a good body of research on the merits of and efficacy of learning online, future work could determine how best to frame and deliver inverted learning to improve student learning and enhance virtual learning delivery options. Inverted learning has been used in a variety of university programs including economics, mathematics, education, engineering, marketing, and computer science. The approach takes advantage of technology tools to promote and support active learning at a distance. While some researchers have concentrated on promoting active learning, others have focused on meeting student learning styles. Both research approaches have used different media materials to deliver online activities with a focus on the cognitive benefits of multimedia to support and promote learning.

Faculty in higher education will continue to research the value of inverted learning as well as the design and delivery of strategies that motivate learners, connecting them to essential concepts in authentic ways while promoting his/her active, ownership in the learning process. This field will require further work into best practices related to the delivery of specific subject areas, the quality and delivery of technology tools, effective course design, and the professional development and support of faculty involved in inverted learning. Emerging trends may well address how inverted learning meets the needs of the millennial and e-Learning student. Future research will likely be conducted from the perspective of both the student and the instructor related to the characteristics of effective instructional design and the value of multimedia technology tools. Several

possible areas for future study will likely focus on the *pedagogy of the inverted learning model, design features of inverted learning and the effectiveness of technology tools in inverted learning.* Inverted learning is a promising field in the area of technology-enhanced learning environments. The key to the success of inverted learning relies on the ability of the instructor to construct a learning environment that helps students engage in the intellectual work of learning. Studies to date have had promising results with implications for designing effective hybrid or blended courses.

CONCLUSION

Inverted learning capitalizes on the combination of a number of effective learning theories. Inverted learning promotes *active learning,* both online and in the classroom. More important, inverted learning results in increased teacher and student interaction (Gannod, Burge, & Helmick, 2007; Kahn, 2011), with significant benefits related to thinking and learning (Bates & Galloway, 2012). It establishes *cognitive expectations* for the learner including being prepared, taking responsibility for controlling the learning process (Lage, Platt, & Treglia, 2000), and applying skills to solve problems in related or new situations (Zappe, Leicht, Messner, Litzinger, & Lee, 2009). The system is based on *constructivist learning,* when the learner makes connections and constructs knowledge through individual and collaborative concrete, abstract, and authentic learning activities. Inverted learning promotes the *development of meta-cognitive skills* in the learner through self-evaluation and reflection on content, as well as the thinking and learning processes used.

Multimedia in inverted learning provides the necessary tools to attract, develop interest, focus, and engage learners through technology tools embedded in online course management systems. First, students listen and observe lecture material on demand, considered a personalized approach appealing to different learning styles (Lage, Platt, & Treglia, 2000). Second, students engage in online learning activities designed to activate schema and promote the development of necessary background knowledge to better prepare students for class. Third, inverted learning uses online discussion forums and shared or collaborative learning activities (online or face-to-face) to create the social aspects essential to the learning process. Well-designed discussion, regardless of location, promotes reflection and higher-level thinking, a goal in higher education. This is the heart of active learning in the classroom and a contrast to the passive learning style found in traditional lecture-based classrooms.

It is clear this approach requires unique instructional design considerations and skills. An efficient and effective program will depend on how the instructor organizes and uses the course management system. Educational institutions must prepare both the instructor and the student for new roles in teaching and learning. Students must understand expectations for coursework and possess the entry-level skills for learning online including the self-management and organizational skills required to function as an independent learner. The challenge is to determine how instruction and technology can best support inverted learning and the unique needs of the learners enrolled.

REFERENCES

(2009). *Keynote*. Cupertino, CA: Apple, Inc. [Computer software]

(2009). *VoiceThread*. Boca Raton, FL: Educause Inc. [Computer software]

(2010). *Camtasia: Mac, Version 1.1*. Okemos, MI: TechSmith. [Computer software]

(2010). *Captivate*. San Jose, CA: Adobe. [Computer software]

(2010). *Elluminate*. Washington, DC: Blackboard Inc. [Computer software]

(2010). *Jing*. Okemos, MI: TechSmith. [Computer software]

(2010). *PowerPoint (12.0)*. Redmond, VA: Microsoft Corp. [Computer software]

(2011). *Wimba*. New York, NY: Blackboard, Inc. [Computer software]

(2012). *Flash*. San Jose, CA: Adobe. [Computer software]

(2012). *Quicktime*. Cupertino, CA: Apple, Inc. [Computer software]

Alessi, S. M., & Trollip, S. R. (2001). *Multimedia for learning* (3rd ed.). Boston, MA: Allyn & Bacon.

Amer, A. (2006). Reflections on Bloom's revised taxonomy. *Electronic Journal of Research in Educational Psychology*, *4*(1), 213–230.

Anderson, T. (2002, May). *An updated and theoretical rationale for interaction*. ITFORUM. Retrieved from http://it.coe.uga.edu/itforum/paper63/paper63.htm

Articulate Rapid E-Learning. (2009). *Computer software*. San Francisco, CA: Studio Pro.

Arum, R., & Roska, J. (2011). *Academically adrift: Limited learning on college campuses*. Chicago, IL: University of Chicago Press.

Association of American Colleges Universities. (2005). *Liberal education outcomes: A preliminary report on student achievement in college*. Washington, DC. Retrieved from www.aacu.org/advocacy/pdfs/leap_report_final.pdf.

Baker, J. W. (2000). The "classroom flip": Using Web course management tools to become the guide on the side. In J. A. Chambers (Ed.). *Selected Papers from the 11th International Conference on College Teaching and Learning* (pp. 9-17). Jacksonville, FL: Florida Community College at Jacksonville.

Bandura, A. (1977). *Social learning theory*. New York, NY: General Learning Press.

Bannan-Ritland, B., Dabbagh, N., & Murphy, K. (2000). Learning object systems as constructivist learning environments: Related assumptions, theories, and applications. In D. A. Wiley (Ed.). *The instructional use of learning objects*. Retrieved from http://reusability.org/read/chapters/bannab-ritland.doc

Bates, S., & Galloway, R. (2012). *The inverted classroom in a large enrollment introductory physics course: A case study*. University of Edinburgh, Higher Education Academy. Retrieved from http://www.heacademy.ac.uk/assets/documents/stem-conference/Physical%20Sciences/Simon_Bates_Ross_Galloway.pdf

Blackboard Collaborate. (2012). *Computer software*. Washington, DC: Blackboard Inc.

Bloom, B. S. (1994). Reflections on the development and use of the taxonomy. In Anderson, L. W., & Sosniak, L. A. (Eds.), *Bloom's taxonomy: A forty year retrospective* (pp. 1–8). Chicago, IL: Chicago University Press.

Bok, D. (2006). *Our underachieving colleges: A candid look on how much students' learn and why they should be learning more*. Princeton, NJ: Princeton University Press.

Bonwell, C. C., & Eison, J. A. (1991). *Active learning: Creating excitement in the classroom*. ASHE- ERIC Higher Education Report Washington, DC: School of Education and Human Development, George Washington University.

Bransford, J., Brophy, S., & Williams, S. (2000). When computer technologies meet the learning sciences: Issues and opportunities. *Journal of Applied Developmental Psychology, 21*(1), 59–84. doi:10.1016/S0193-3973(99)00051-9

Bransford, J. D., Brown, A. L., & Cocking, R. R. (Eds.). (2000). *How people learn: Brain, mind, experience, and school*. Washington, DC: National Academy Press.

Broad, M., Mathews, M., & McDonald, A. (2004). Accounting education through an online-supported virtual learning environment. *Active Learning in Higher Education, 5*(2), 135–151. doi:10.1177/1469787404043810

Brockbank, A., & McGill, I. (2007). *Facilitating reflective learning in higher education* (2nd ed.). McGraw Hill.

Brown, R. (2001). The process of community building in distance learning classes. *Journal of Asynchronous Learning Networks, 5*(2), 18–35.

Bruner, J., & Olson, D. (1986). Learning through experience and learning through media. In Gerbner, G., Gross, L. P., & Melody, W. (Eds.), *Communications technology and social policy: Understanding the new "cultural revolution"*. New York, NY: Wiley.

Buerck, L. A., Malmstrom, T., & Peppers, E. (2003). Learning environments and learning styles: Non-traditional student enrollment and success in an Internet-based versus a lecture-based computer science course. *Learning Environments Research, 6*(2), 137–155. doi:10.1023/A:1024939002433

Chickering, A. W., & Ehrmann, S. C. (1996). Implementing the seven principles: Technology as lever. American Association of Higher Education. *AAHE Bulletin, 49*(2), 3–6.

Chickering, A. W., & Gamson, Z. (1987). Seven principles for good practice in undergraduate education. *AAHE Bulletin, 40*(7), 3–7.

Cole, N. (1990). Conceptions of educational achievement. *Educational Researcher, 19*(3), 2–7.

Crouch, C., & Mazur, E. (2001). Peer instruction: Ten years of experience and results. *American Journal of Physics, 69*(9), 970–977. doi:10.1119/1.1374249

Davis, C. (2010). Using student-centered discussion forums to enhance student participation in online courses. In *Proceedings: 26th Annual Distance Teaching and Learning Conference*, (pp. 1-5). Madison, WI.

Davis, C., & Froriep, K. (2009). Using multimedia for modeling reading instruction in teacher education. In *Proceedings: 25th Annual Distance Teaching and Learning Conference*, (pp. 485-488). Madison: WI.

DeLeng, B., Dolmans, D., & van de Wiel, M. (2007). How video cases should be used as authentic stimuli in problem-based medical education. *Medical Education*, *41*(2), 181–188. doi:10.1111/j.1365-2929.2006.02671.x

Dewey, J. (1990). *The school and society and the child and the curriculum*. Chicago, IL: The University of Chicago Press.

Facione, P. A. (1990). *Critical thinking: A statement of expert consensus for purposes of educational assessment and instruction*. Millbrae, CA: The California Academic Press.

Felder, R. M., & Brent, R. (1996). Navigating the bumpy road to student-centered instruction. *College Teaching*, *44*(2), 43–47. doi:10.1080/87567555.1996.9933425

Fenrich, P. (1997). *Practical guidelines for creating instructional multimedia applications*. Fort Worth, TX: Harcourt Brace.

Fink, L. D. (2003). *A self-directed guide to designing courses for significant learning*. San Francisco, CA: Jossey-Bass.

Foertsch, J., Moses, G., Strikwerda, J., & Litzkow, M. (2002). Reversing the lecture/homework paradigm using e-teach web-based streaming video software. *Journal of Engineering Education*, *91*(3), 267–274. doi:10.1002/j.2168-9830.2002.tb00703.x

Foreman, J. (2003, September/October). Next-generation educational technology versus the lecture. *EDUCAUSE Review*, *35*(5), 12–22.

Frand, J. K. (2000, September-October). The information-age mindset: Changes in students and implications for higher education. *EDUCAUSE Review*, *35*(5), 15–24.

Frederickson, N., Reed, P., & Clifford, V. (2005). Evaluating web-supported learning versus lecture-based teaching: Quantitative and qualitative perspectives. *Higher Education*, *50*, 645–664. doi:10.1007/s10734-004-6370-0

Gannod, G. C., Burge, J. E., & Helmick, M. T. (2007). Using the inverted classroom to teach software engineering. In *Proceedings of the 30th International Conference on Software Engineering* (Leipzig, Germany, 2008) ICSE '08, (pp. 777-786). New York, NY: ACM.

Garrison, D. R., Anderson, T., & Archer, W. (2000). Critical thinking in a text-based environment. Computer conferencing in higher education. *The Internet and Higher Education*, *2*(2), 87–105. doi:10.1016/S1096-7516(00)00016-6

Gee, J. P. (2000). The new literacy studies: from: "socially situated" to the work of the social. In Barton, D., & Ivanic, R. (Eds.), *Writing in community*. London, UK: Sage.

Gibbs, G. (1992). *Improving the quality of student learning*. Bristol, UK: TES.

Gleason, M. (1986). Better communication in large courses. *College Teaching*, *34*, 20–24. doi:10.1080/87567555.1986.10532325

Graziadei, W. D., Gallagher, S., Brown, R. N., & Sasiadek, J. (1997). *Building asynchronous and synchronous teaching-learning environments: Exploring a course/classroom management system solution*. Retrieved from http://horizon.unc.edu/projects/monograph/CD/Technological_Tools/Graziadei.asp

Griffin, M. M. (1995). You can't get there from here: Situated learning, transfer and map skills. *Contemporary Educational Psychology, 20,* 65–87. doi:10.1006/ceps.1995.1004

Grooms, L. (2000). *Interaction in the computer-mediated adult distance-learning environment: Leadership development through on-line distance education.* Unpublished doctoral dissertation, Regent University, Virginia Beach.

Grunert, J. (2000). *The course syllabus: A learning-centered approach.* Bolton, MA: Anchor Publishing.

Halpern, D. F. (1998). Teaching critical thinking for transfer across domains: Dispositions, skills, structure training, and meta-cognitive monitoring. *The American Psychologist, 53*(4), 449–455. doi:10.1037/0003-066X.53.4.449

Henri, F. (1992). Computer conferencing and content analysis. In Kaye, A. R. (Ed.), *Collaborative learning through computer conferencing: The Najaden papers* (pp. 116–136). Berlin, UK: Springer-Verlag. doi:10.1007/978-3-642-77684-7_8

Herrington, J., & Oliver, R. (2000). An instructional design framework for authentic learning environments. *Educational Technology Research and Development, 48*(3), 23–48. doi:10.1007/BF02319856

Herrington, J., & Standon, P. (2000). Moving from an instructivist to a constructivist multimedia learning environment. *Journal of Educational Multimedia and Hypermedia, 9*(3), 195–205.

Hung, D. (2001). Design principles for web-based learning: Implications for Vygotskian thought. *Educational Technology, 41*(3), 33–41.

Hung, D., & Nichani, M. (2001). Constructivism and e-learning: Balancing between the individual and social levels of cognition. *Educational Technology, 41*(2), 40–44.

Johnson, C. (2007, January). Clickers in your classroom. *Wakonse-Arizona E-Newsletter, 3*(1), 71–77.

Jonassen, D. H. (1999). *Constructing learning environments on the web: Engaging students in meaningful learning. EdTech 99: Educational Technology Conference and Exhibition 1999: Thinking Schools.* Learning Nation.

Juwah, C., Macfarlane-Dick, D., Mathew, B., Nicol, D., Ross, D., & Smith, B. (2004). *Enhancing student learning through effective formative feedback.* York, UK: Higher Education Academy.

Khan, S. (2011, March). *Salman Khan: Let's use video to reinvent education.* TED 2011. Retrieved from http://blog.ted.com/2011/03/09/lets-use-video-to-reinvent-education-salman- khan-on-ted-com/

Kolb, D. A. (1984). *Experiential learning: Experience as the source of learning and development.* Englewood Cliffs, NJ: Prentice-Hall, Inc.

Lage, M. J., & Platt, G. J. (2000). The Internet and the inverted classroom. *The Journal of Economic Education, 31*(11). Retrieved from http://www.jstor.org/stable/1183338

Lage, M. J., Platt, G. J., & Treglia, M. (2000). Inverting the classroom: A gateway to creating an inclusive learning environment. *The Journal of Economic Education, 31,* 30–43.

Lave, J., & Wenger, E. (1991). *Situated learning: Legitimate peripheral participation.* Cambridge, UK: University of Cambridge Press. doi:10.1017/CBO9780511815355

Liao, W. C. (2012, February). Using short videos in teaching a social science subject: Values and challenges. *Journal of the NUS Teaching Academy, 2*(1), 42–55.

Lipman, M. (1988). Critical thinking: What can it be? *Educational Leadership, 46*(1), 38–43.

Manninen, T. (2000). Interaction in networked virtual environments as communicative action – Social theory and multiplayer games. In *Proceedings of CRIWG2000 Workshop*, Madera, Portugal, (pp. 154-157). IEEE Computer Society Press.

Marton, F., & Saljo, R. (1976). On qualitative differences in learning: Outcome and process. *The British Journal of Educational Psychology*, *46*(1), 4–11. doi:10.1111/j.2044-8279.1976.tb02980.x

Mathie, V. A., Beins, B., Benjamin, L. T., Ewing, M. M., Hall, C. C., & Henderson, B. . . . Smith, R. A. (1993). Promoting active learning in psychology courses. In T. V. McGovern (Ed.), *Handbook for enhancing undergraduate education in psychology*, (pp. 183–214). Washington, DC: American Psychological Association.

Matlin, M. W. (2002). Cognitive psychology and college-level pedagogy: Two siblings that rarely communicate. In Halpern, D. F., & Hakel, M. D. (Eds.), *Applying the science of learning to university teaching and beyond* (pp. 87–103). San Francisco, CA: Jossey-Bass. doi:10.1002/tl.49

McKeachie, W. J. (2002). *McKeachie's teaching tips: Strategies, research, and theory for college and university teachers* (11th ed.). Boston, MA: Houghton-Mifflin.

Meyer, C., & Jones, T. B. (1993). *Promoting active learning: Strategies for the college classroom*. San Francisco, CA: Jossey-Bass.

Moore, M. G. (1989). Editorial: Three types of interaction. *American Journal of Distance Education*, *3*(2), 1–6. doi:10.1080/08923648909526659

Newby, T. J., Stepich, D. A., Lehman, J. D., & Russell, J. D. (1996). *Introduction to instructional technology. Instructional Technology for Teaching and Learning*. Englewood Cliffs, New Jersey: Educational Technology Publications.

Newman, F., & Scurry, J. (2001). Online technology pushes pedagogy to the forefront. *The Chronicle of Higher Education*, *47*(44), B7.

Newmann, F. (1996). *Authentic achievement: Restructuring schools for intellectual quality*. San Francisco, CA: Jossey-Bass.

Papadopoulos, C., Santiago-Roman, A., & Portela, G. (2010, October). *Developing and implementing an inverted classroom for engineering statics*. Paper presented at the annual meeting of the 40th ASEE/IEEE Frontiers in Education Conference, Washington, DC. Retrieved from http://fie-conference.org/fie2010/papers/1741/pdf

Phillips, D. (2000). *Constructivism in education*. Chicago, IL: University of Chicago Press.

Piaget, J. (1971). *Genetic epistemology*. New York, NY: W. W. Norton & Company, Inc.

Ponti, M., & Ryberg, T. (2004). Rethinking virtual space as a place for sociability: Theory and design implications. In *Proceedings of Networked Learning Conference 2004*, Sheffield University.

Reddi, U. V., & Mishra, S. (Eds.). (2003). *Educational multimedia: A handbook for teacher-developers*. New Delhi, India: The Commonwealth Educational Media Centre for Asia.

Resnick, L. B. (1987). Learning in school and out: 1987 presidential address. *Educational Researcher*, *16*(9), 13-20+54. Retrieved from http://links.jstor.org/sici?sici=0013-189X%281 98712%2916%3A9%3C13%3AT1PALI%3E2.0 .CO%3B2-X

Rice, R. E., & Bunz, U. (2006). Evaluating a wireless course feedback system: The role of demographics, expertise, fluency, competency, and usage. *Studies in Media & Information Literacy Education*, *6*, 1–10. doi:10.3138/sim.6.3.002

Roblyer, M. D. (2006). *Integrating educational technology into teaching* (4th ed.). Upper Saddle River, NJ: Pearson Prentice Hall.

Slavin, R. E. (1990). *Cooperative learning theory, research and practice*. Needham Heights, MA: Allyn & Bacon.

Solvie, P., & Kloek, M. (2007). Using technology tools to engage students with multiple learning styles in a constructivist learning environment. *Contemporary Issues in Technology & Teacher Education, 7*(2), 7–27.

Sorensen, C. K., & Baylen, D. M. (2009). Learning online. In Orellana, A., Hudgins, T., & Simonson, M. (Eds.), *The perfect online course: Best practices for designing and teaching* (pp. 69–86). Charlotte, NC: Information Age Publishing.

Sparrow, L., Sparrow, H., & Swan, P. (2000). Student-centered learning: Is it possible? In A. Hermann & M. M. Kulski (Eds.), *Flexible Futures in Tertiary Teaching: Proceedings of the 9th Annual Teaching Learning Forum*. Perth, Australia: Curtin University of Technology. Retrieved from http://lsn.curtin.edu.au/tlf/tlf2000/sparrow.html

Sternberg, R. J., & Grigorenko, E. L. (2002). The theory of successful intelligence as a basis for instruction and assessment in higher education. In Halpern, D. F., & Hakel, M. D. (Eds.), *Applying the science of learning to university teaching and beyond* (pp. 45–54). San Francisco: Jossey-Bass. doi:10.1002/tl.46

Stone, L. L. (1999, Summer). Multimedia instruction methods. *The Journal of Economic Education*, 253–258.

Stowell, J. R., & Nelson, J. M. (2007). Benefits of electronic audience response systems on student participation, learning, and emotion. *Teaching of Psychology, 34*, 253–258. doi:10.1080/00986280701700391

Trees, A., & Jackson, M. (2007). The learning environment in clicker classrooms: Student processes of learning and involvement in large university-level courses using student response systems. *Learning, Media and Technology, 32*, 21–40. doi:10.1080/17439880601141179

Walker, D., & Lambert, L. (1995). Learning and leading theory: A century in the making. In Lambert, L., Walker, D., Zimmerman, D., Cooper, J., Lambert, M., Gardner, M., & Slack, P. (Eds.), *The constructivist leader* (pp. 1–27). New York, NY: Teachers College Press.

Weimer, M. (2002). *Learner-centered teaching: Five key changes to practice*. San Francisco, CA: Jossey-Bass.

Wiggins, G., & McTighe, J. (2005). *Understanding by design* (2nd ed.). Alexandria, VA: ASCD.

Zappe, S., Leicht, R., Messner, J., Litzinger, T., & Woo Lee, H. (2009). *Flipping the classroom to explore active learning in a large undergraduate course*. American Society of Engineering. Retrieved from soa.asee.org/paper/conference/paper-view.cfm?id=10046

KEY TERMS AND DEFINITIONS

Active Learning: Active learning involves the cognitive processes used when the learner is actively involved in the learning process. Active learning builds on the learner's knowledge and guides how he/she strategically approaches new tasks and problems. Learning effectiveness is based on how and when the learner uses these strategies for thinking and learning. This metacognitive work is the foundation for active and learner-centered learning. Active learners tend to learn more content (Bonwell & Eisen 1991; Slavin, 1990) understand, (Meyers & Jones 1993), communicate, (Fink, 2003) and retain concepts longer (Newman & Scurry, 2001). Chickering and Gamson (1987) identified active learning as one of the seven principles of good practice in higher education.

Constructivist Learning: The theory of constructivism deals with the *cognitive* processes involved in forming understanding. Constructivism engages the learner in inquiry, experience, and discovery in both the *construct* (Brunner, 1960; Piaget, 1971; Phillips, 2000) and *control* (Bransford, Brown, & Cocking, 2000) of learning. Constructivist approaches to learning are therefore derived from active learning theories in which learners benefit from observing, interacting, and interpreting personal (Alessi & Trollip, 2001) and shared learning experiences. *Metacognition* deals with the learner and his/her conscious awareness of the learning conditions around them. Metacognitive skills help the learner understand, manipulate, and control cognitive efforts. These skills are more effective when internalized to the point when they become automatic and useful to aid in activating and monitoring the learning process. The implications of metacognition are significant for constructivism as the learner can be more productive when aware of personal metacognitive strengths and weaknesses, are actively engaged in learning, and are able to control, self-monitor, and adjust strategies to facilitate learning (Amer, 2006). The role of an instructor in a constructivist classroom is to design and shape learner involvement as they progress through the course engaged in cognitive and higher-level thinking. The instructor develops the content and shapes the learning experiences so the learner constructs, understands, and applies knowledge in authentic ways.

Inverted Learning: Inverted learning implies that traditional lectures and readings usually delivered during classroom time are completed in a constructivist way by the learner outside the classroom (Lage, Platt, & Treglia, 2000). This concept of *classroom flipping* (Baker, 2000) permits time for conducting active learning activities in the classroom so content can be extended and applied through guided discussion, critical thinking, and collaborative problem solving.

Learner-Centered Learning: Roblyer (2006) advocates *learner-centered* rather than *instructor-centered* classrooms where learners are engaged in a variety of hands-on activities and performance-based assessments. In a learner-centered course the role of the instructor shifts from disseminating

information to one who facilitates and supports the learner (Jonassen, 1999). In this constructivist environment, the responsibility for managing learning experiences shifts to the student as a self-directed learner (Felder & Brent, 1996; Sparrow, Sparrow, & Swan, 2000) making them active producers and evaluators of learning (Ponti & Ryberg, 2004). Many universities advocate the use of active and learner-centered approaches for face-to-face as well as online courses based upon the conclusion that students learn and retain more skills in a learner-centered model (Matlin, 2002; Sternberg & Grigorenko, 2002). Weimer (2002) identified five effective components of a learner-centered teaching model that can be used as a road map for developing active learning: (a) First is the shift in the role and responsibility of the instructor from a teacher-centered didactic approach to a learner-centered constructivist approach to teaching. (b) Second is the function of how content is delivered through a variety of interactive activities designed to promote the development of core knowledge for further learning and application of skills. (c) Third is the philosophical belief and approach to instruction that encourages efficient learning and learner responsibility for coursework completion. (d) Fourth involves formative and summative assessments for the continual improvement (through self-monitoring, reflection, and peer assessment). (e) Finally, Weimer advocates shared decision-making between instructor and students when developing course policies and procedures (p. 8-17).

Situated Learning: In situated learning (Griffin, 1995; Lave & Wenger, 1991) the learner forms a relationship with a specific contextual content. Situated learning experiences are meaningful since they link the learner with the real world to co-construct learning and problem solve with others. These are useful and important skills for lifelong learning. In the classroom situated activities immerse learners in authentic settings through observing, role-playing, or simulating. Students seem to benefit when engaged in such rich and stimulating learning environments; discovering and developing skills; and applying them to create realistic and useful products (Newmann, 1996).

Social Learning: Social learning theory is based upon the premise that people learn best with and from each other. It is the foundation for learning and work in the real world. Concerned about the state of learning in U.S. schools, Resnick (1987) advocated increased opportunities for *shared cognition* and learning as found in the world-of-work as opposed to *individual cognition* and learning typically found in traditional classrooms (p.13). Social learning involves the sensory and social involvement of the learner through observing, modeling, experiencing, and reflecting with others (Dewey, 1990). Bandura (1977) described three variations of observational learning typically found in social learning experiences: a.) A live demonstration or modeling of the target behavior; b.) Verbal instructions, descriptions, or narrations of the target behavior; and c.) A symbolic model or representation using multimedia tools (p. 24-28). Many believe the future of virtual learning is rooted in the field of social learning. There has been a technological convergence in e-Learning to support social and collaborative learning.

Virtual, E-Learning: Virtual, online, distance, and e-Learning settings are electronic-based learning systems delivered in *synchronous* or *asynchronous* formats using course management programs to provide the resources and communication tools necessary to support learning (Graziadei, Gallagher, Brown, & Sasiadek, 1997). These flexible 24/7 virtual learning environments replicate both classroom and real world contexts through a variety of technology tools. Learners explore, interact, solve problems, (Manninen, 2000) and experience authentic learning through a variety of multimedia materials (graphics, text, audio, animation, and video) (Fenrich, 1997; Vaughan, 2003). In e-Learning, students benefit from timely feedback and opportunities to reflect on and self-assess progress with learning (Chickering & Gamson, 1987; Chickering & Ehrmann, 1996). Ideally, these components promote student-teacher and between student interaction with the instructor guiding and challenging the learners. A number of researchers (Brown, 2001; Herrington & Standon, 2000) considered the design of student-centered, online learning communities as active and/or constructivist-based.

Chapter 18
Making Learning Reel:
Student–Made Videos on Mobile Devices

Rochelle Rodrigo
Old Dominion University, USA

Kristopher Purzycki
Old Dominion University, USA

ABSTRACT

As more students bring powerful pocket-sized computers to class in the form of their smartphones and tablets, faculty need to take advantage by devising curriculum that incorporates mobile video production as a means of contributing to the discourse of the university and the world at large. Projects where students use mobile devices to make videos create active learning environments where they are more likely to build and connect their classroom learning with what they already know. These types of projects also develop student digital composing skills while navigating several issues pertinent to a 21st century participatory culture. These assignments engage students with themes and issues that not only promote success in higher education but throughout their careers.

INTRODUCTION

While watching Father Guido Sarducci's comedic skit "Five Minute University," many college faculty laugh uneasily because we recognize the "truth" in the skit. Not only is it difficult to teach so that the material is retained beyond the final exam, instructors must also impart to students the confidence to apply their learning to situations outside of the classroom. Since Tagg and Barr's 1995 article in *Change*, which flipped scholarly focus on pedagogy from *faculty teaching* to *stu-dent learning*, most "new" pedagogical strategies have focused on ways to better facilitate students learning and knowledge transfer; in short, student learning requires active engagement with both the content being taught as well as with other individuals.

No longer regarded as only a source for entertainment, communication, and engagement, the mobile phone and smartphone have also developed into tools that facilitate community involvement and social collaboration. No longer limited to only telephonic capabilities, these sophisticated

DOI: 10.4018/978-1-4666-3962-1.ch018

devices allow users to not only capture but also edit and then distribute images and video. Assignments designed to take advantage of all the capabilities many mobile devices offer provide instructors and students alike with the tools to immerse themselves within teaching and learning. Specifically, instructors can develop mobile video assignments that ask students to make connections between their learning and context by recognizing the meaning-making opportunities that exist within their community, recording a significant concept or event, and then sharing their interpretation with a wider audience.

In this chapter, we will outline strategies and assignments that prompt students to produce their own videos using mobile devices through a curriculum that aids learning and the transfer of knowledge. Furthermore, we will discern many of the considerations instructors must weigh before incorporating these lessons into their syllabi.

BACKGROUND

With increasing calls for accountability, many faculty in higher education are paying more attention to which teaching strategies better promote student learning – with most realizing that they are uninterested in students simply echoing facts as evidence of knowledge retention. Instead, instructors want their classes to demonstrate the complex levels of learning that usually rank higher on Bloom's Taxonomy of the Cognitive Learning Domain (Bloom, Engelhart, Furst, Hill, & Krathwohl, 1956); faculty are explicitly interested in learning that demonstrates analysis, synthesis, and evaluation.

More recent scholarship about teaching and learning has expanded both concepts of knowing and learning. Kalantzis and Cope (2008) outline a shift in "ways of knowing" from confidence in concrete truths based upon a single way of creating knowledge to an epistemological relativism and a more skeptical approach to both the process and product of knowing, (p. 189). The authors then

outline "knowledge repertoires," a more contemporary and diverse understanding of knowledge that accounts for legitimized methods of knowing with respect for difference (p. 189). There has also been an explosion of scholarship that discusses the neurological aspects of knowing and learning. Zull (2002) reminds us that learning must occur within specific sections of the brain and knowing physically changes the brain.

The more contemporary neurological research on learning has reminded many faculty that Bloom's Taxonomy did not only include the cognitive domain. The affective domain (Krathwohl, Bloom, & Masia, 1964) and the psychomotor domain (Simpson, 1972) greatly impact student learning. Since Sutton-Smith's landmark articulation of the relationship between play and learning in *The Ambiguity of Play* (1997), many in higher education have sought a curriculum that unites these once conceptually polarized concepts. Lack of stress (Medina, 2008), coupled with positive, even fun (Zull, 2002), learning activities that engage all of the senses (Medina, 2008; & Zull, 2002) are more likely to facilitate learning.

Seeing this shift towards a more robust understanding of knowing and learning helps make sense of Fink's (2003) Taxonomy of Significant Learning. The first three categories resemble Bloom's Cognitive Taxonomy: Foundational Knowledge, Application, and Integration (Fink, 2003). The next two expand learning to include a "Human Dimension" that facilitates learning about oneself and others as well as a "Caring" which facilitates "developing new feelings, interests, and values" (p. 30). The final category is more metacognitive with a focus on "Learning How to Learn" (p. 30). Kalantzis and Cope (2008) also characterize students' "new" learning as a process of "social cognition and collaborative learning" that is fueled by "distributed knowledge, with more people as active knowledge makers" (p. 189).

Once faculty acknowledge this expansive shift in how we understand knowing and learning, they also realize their teaching, their actual classroom practice, has to change accordingly. Weimer (2002) and Blumberg (2009) discuss five changes that many faculty need to make in their teaching:

- Change the focus on memorizing content to (socially) constructing knowledge and meaning;
- Shift the teacher's role from disciplinary expert and content deliverer to learning experience facilitator;
- Motivate and teach students how to take more responsibility for the learning, shifting from passive to active learners;
- Change from an exclusive use of summative assessment to more frequent formative, peer, and self-assessments, providing frequent feedback and space for revision/learning; and
- Shift the balance of power in the classroom, giving students more control over determining what and how they learn, as well as how they are assessed. (Weimer, 2002, p. 8-17)

In other words, faculty who care about student learning have a plethora of theory and research-based strategies to rely upon, most of them suggesting students need to be more actively engaged in the learning process.

While many faculty members are trying to make the shift to active, learning-centered teaching, they are also being told students need to develop various 21st century skills and digital literacies. Several educational organizations have endorsed or published a variety of lists and guidelines that include things like using technology to gather, analyze, and synthesize information (ASCD, 2008; Association of Colleges and Research Libraries, 2000; Council of Writing Program Administrators [CWPA], 2008; National Council of Teachers of English [NCTE], 2008; & Partnership for 21st Century Skills, 2011) as well as describe, explain, and persuade with technology (Conference on College Composition and Communication, 2004; CWPA, 2008; Intel, n.d.; NCTE, 2005; NCTE 2008; & Partnership for 21st

Century Skills, 2011). In short, many of these 21st century skills can be summed up within Jenkins (2006) types of participatory culture:

- **Affiliations:** Memberships, formal and informal, in online communities centered around various forms of media;
- **Expressions:** Producing new creative forms;
- **Collaborative Problem-Solving:** Working together in teams, formal and informal, to complete tasks and develop new knowledge; and
- **Circulations:** Shaping the flow of media. (p. 3)

The skills that Jenkins (2006) lists that students will need to successfully participate in our 21st century digital participatory culture closely resemble a mix of the desired learning objectives by many faculty in higher education, the higher order thinking goals outlined in Bloom's Taxonomy of Cognitive Learning Domain, as well as the characteristics of active learning and knowledge making: play, performance, simulation, appropriation, multitasking, distributed cognition, collective intelligence, judgment, transmedia navigation, networking, and negotiation (p. 4). With this long list of skills, it isn't surprising that students say "they are not fully confident that they have the technology skills to meet their needs" (Dahlstrom, de Boor, Grunwald, & Vockley, 2011, p. 20). That same edition of EDUCAUSE's annual student technology usage survey claims students say that "technology can make learning a more immersive, engaging, and relevant experience" (p. 10).

Students are often asked to engage technology on the terms of the institution—using specific hardware and software most relevant to their discipline's curriculum. For examples of this, consider the differences between labs housed within the schools of engineering and, say, visual arts. However, instead of providing an arsenal of creative tools for use in the classroom, these tools are often reduced to ones of rote production. Compounding the situation, the school often requires students to accommodate it's own proprietary technology – such as browser-based education software like Blackboard and distance learning platforms – that often presents more barriers for students (and faculty alike) because they can be difficult to use and privilege specific ways of teaching and learning. EDUCAUSE's annual student technology usage survey (Dahlstrom, et. al., 2011) reminds us that "students tend to most highly value the technologies that they see their instructors using" (p. 19).

The immobility of desktop and (to a lesser but still considerable degree) laptop computers prevents students from learning through creation within a diversity of places and spaces. Unlike these more cumbersome devices, whose tacit complexity often intimidates the novice user, the smartphone has enjoyed widespread adoption despite possessing a level of technological intricacy that parallels many basic desktops. As of February 2012, 46% of American adults own smartphones (Smith, 2012, p. 1) with more "average" college aged adult ownership in even higher: 18-24 years = 67%, 25-34 years = 71%, and 35-44 years = 54% (p. 4). And "most students come to campus with multiple technology devices – a majority of students own about a dozen" (Dahlstrom, et. al, 2011, p. 4): 87% arrive with laptops, 62% with iPods, 55% with smartphones, 11% with netbooks, 8% with an iPad or other tablet (p. 7). And although "e-reader and iPad ownership is more prevalent among more affluent students" (p. 7), Pew reports both Black (49%), and Hispanic (49%) smartphone ownership is higher than White (45%) (Smith, 2012, p. 4).

Smartphone and tablet technology has emerged as one of the most widespread communications and information dissemination methods. The Pew Internet and American Life project reports that 86% of smartphone owners use their phone for "just-in-time" information (Rainie & Fox, 2012, p. 2). Similarly, 18-24 year olds who do not attend college are "a bit less likely to go online wirelessly than either undergraduate or graduate students,

but notably more likely than the overall adult population" (Smith, Rainie, & Zickuhr, 2011, para. 5). The EDUCAUSE survey reports that 45% of students used their devices "to look up information on the Internet *in class*" (Dahlstrom, et. al., 2011, p. 14). In short, students need to be more actively engaged as learners and are in growing numbers bringing their own devices upon which they want to learn how to use more effectively; why not take advantage of this?

While handheld devices have undoubtedly increased general access to the entertainment and information found on the Internet, they are often considered grossly inadequate as utilities for word processing and spreadsheet creation and thus poor platforms for learning the skills crucial to succeeding in school and beyond. This limitation in productivity has distracted instructors from recognizing the mobile device's potential as an instructional tool. Therefore most discussion of "learning" with mobile devices is focused on "teaching": how to deliver content via traditional written texts, image, and video to the mobile device (Rodrigo, 2011). We are proposing that instructors reimagine the learning activities that prompt students to produce texts using their mobile devices so that the assignments reflect the relationship between the user and technology.

Although there are considerable limitations to these portable devices (imagine composing long-form text using only one's thumbs!), there are several creative methods of incorporating these devices into higher education curricula that take advantage of some of their educational potentials. With the unprecedented ability to record and share information, instantaneous user dissemination is the hallmark of the mobile device. For the college student, this promises new approaches to learning, knowledge construction, and communication. In a study about incorporating wireless laptops in a writing classroom, instructors described how the technology "allowed for a flexible arrangement and rearrangement of the classroom space" and that "laptops are less intrusive, particularly in the space between students" (Hochman & Palmquist,

2009, p. 122). In that same study, faculty felt themselves shifting toward a "less directive style of teaching" and that students were taking "more responsibility for their own learning" (p. 122). One faculty member mentioned that the students' shifts to hands-on activities helped them "abandon the attitude of mere listener and notetaker" (p. 125).

Working with handheld devices not only helps engage the student, the personal connection he or she has with the device might help the student make a similarly intimate connection to the course content. Furthermore, they may then network the course content out among personal relationships managed through the mobile device:

Students work differently with m-learning devices than they do with tethered desktop computers. Public-lab computers are precisely that....Even personally owned desktops retain an external, semipublic face, their screens readable by passersby or, worse yet, roommates. But mobile machines become personally intimate; they are held close to the body—in a purse, on the lap, in a pocket, on the floor next to the user. Their screens are easily hidden from prying eyes. Emotional investments increase, even with shared devices. (Alexander, 2004, para. 6)

Through what Alexander refers to as "m-learning," students may personally connect with their subject matter using their mobile devices – engaging cognitive, affective, and psychomotor domains while composing dynamic texts that incorporate images, videos, and sound into their words and their worlds.

IDEAS FOR MOBILE VIDEO ASSIGNMENTS

Many of the assignment ideas listed below require the students to actively participate in their academic, social, and cultural environments. Instead of being sent to the musty corners of the library, students will explore the world around

them and respond to their experiences while engaging course content. By incorporating mobile devices into more traditional assignments and the course overall, student learning is contextualized, authenticating the experience for the user (Jeng et al., 2010). Furthermore, allowing emergent, critical thinkers to tailor the assignment so that it challenges them to straddle disciplines, aids in the creation of what Diane Penrod (2007) refers to as "assignments and learning environments that not only build upon students' dominant multiple intelligences but also strengthen their weaker competencies" (p. 120).

We have divided the types of assignments into three categories: projects that develop the ability to synthesize and present information, contextually immersive "on the town" or "in the world" tasks, and those where students use their devices for collecting research data. While categorizing these activities, we'll also discuss how and why they will better facilitate content learning, knowledge transfer, and/or learning assessment.

Synthesizing and Presenting Assignments

This category of assignments asks students to synthesize a concept or process they have learned and create a video that presents the material in a new or different manner. The core assignment is to have a student, or a group of students, compose a video that illustrates a concept that is central to the course but has given them trouble. For example, someone might talk through how someone who is cutting up a pizza or cake is using the mathematical concept of fractions. As a project that asks students to focus on and reflect upon the subject, higher order thinking as well as knowledge making is being enlisted to reinterpret the project in a subjectively impactful way.

Similarly, instructional videos are popular methods of online learning. These easily accessible tutorials are often referred to for quick insight into any given subject; why not have students make their own how-to video? Undergraduate students, perhaps uncertain in their own standing in the university, may not consider themselves steeped in their chosen fields enough to aid their peers. To bolster their knowledge and confidence within their own academic discipline, students create a conceptual or instructional video that provides direction on a specific topic or process. Interviewing the faculty, exploring the facilities where the bulk of their courses will be carried out, and surveying student colleagues, mobile videographers carry out a brief introduction into their arena. For example, nursing students might make a video about proper hand washing procedures that includes interviews with practicing nurses. These projects are excellent ways for students to not only participate in the disciplinary discussion but, through media, also contribute to a library of video instruction.

In a course where students are learning different disciplinary processes, students can be asked to document procedures specific to their field. In classes where students have labs, like various science courses, students can record one another working, noting specific steps as they progress. Subsequent assignments could include reflective essays to review the video, or compare numerous videos, to analyze their own practices. As a collaborative effort, this particular project might be especially valuable as a means of documenting individual processes and comparing each within a peer group. These reflective activities challenge students to take increasing responsibility for their own learning and meta-awareness of themselves as learners.

"On the Town" or "In the World" Assignments

This category of assignments asks students to capture examples of impressions, procedures, or events that they have learned out in "the real world." The core assignment asks students to shoot video of a concept, talking through the video about how and why the example does or does not work in demonstrating the course premise. Furthermore, these activities ask students to apply what they've learned and circulate their understandings with their classmates to socially construct meaning. For example, artistic design or engineering courses might ask students to shoot video or make a video montage of compiled images, representing specific precepts. By having the students do this assignment the course quickly builds a repository of good, bad, and ugly examples of any given notion.

One method of aiding student retention beyond the school is to tie the curricula to their anticipated career or personal interests. By using these devices to aid in their understanding of their chosen fields, students' skills with portable technology transcend beyond those utilized for entertainment and connecting with their classmates and future colleagues. Instructors can ask students to make mini-documentary videos about specific careers or how specific processes, skills, or theories are applied on the job. Students can compile audio, image, and video recordings to make videos that demonstrate what it means to be a social worker or anthropologist. A theater student might tour the backstage area, exploring the nooks and crannies while describing how actors behave behind the scenes. Like the instructional videos mentioned above, documentary videos provide students the opportunity to demonstrate what they've learned in a manner that benefits other members of the class and field at large.

Collecting Research Data Assignments

Using video to conduct and report out upon research provides the ultimate opportunity for active learning where students are making knowledge. This category of assignments asks students to use the mobile devices to capture "real world" data that they then can analyze later for a research project. Spinuzzi (2009) reminds us that the "genie's out of the bottle" in terms of citizen journalism; therefore, why aren't we capturing research data the same way? The core assignment is for students to collect notes, audio, images, and video while in the field that they might analyze, and possibly compile into a video, later.

Rather than using their mobile devices to answer "big picture" questions, students might focus on the minutiae of the moment. This assignment requires students to narrow their perspective as an exercise in mindfully addressing the dramatic changes that occur in deceptively mundane spaces. Students can compile a time-lapse video over a more expansive period of time and/or space, honing in on the devil in the details. Discerning a subject matter will likely be the most challenging aspect of this assignment. For example, a biology student might film the growth of a small plant; marketing instructors might consider a series of the same storefront taken from the same location at the same time (much like Harvey Keitel does in the movie *Smoke*) to analyze advertising efforts. Given the time constraints of this project, it should be assigned early in the semester to serve, perhaps, as a capstone assignment.

Another assignment might require students to incorporate an active research project from another course and capture the environment that contextualizes the task they're performing. Considering the spaces where scholarship is conducted, students of any discipline can explore the laboratory, interviewing room, or even the library. For example, our biology student might create a movie describing the lab and discuss how the physical space influences her motivations for studying biology or show how a specific setup might influence the results of an experiment. Students of the humanities, as another example, might create a video describing the variety of study environments within a library or tour science, engineering, or medial labs.

LOGISTICS AND LEGALITIES

Several issues surface when incorporating mobile video assignments into a course, and instructors should discern the various logistics of these assignments, including: access to hardware and software, technological support, and assessment. There are also a variety of legal issues that might impact these types of assignments, including copyright, accessibility, and privacy.

Hardware and Software

When considering these assignments, it mustn't be assumed that all students have access to mobile devices and video editing software. Prior to developing the project outlines, it is advisable to determine what resources are available at the institution, or local libraries, or media centers. The Pew research reminds us there is a rapidly growing number of smartphone and tablet owners and:

groups that have traditionally been on the other side of the digital divide in basic internet access are using wireless connections to go online. Among smartphone owners, young adults, minorities, those with no college experience, and those with lower household income levels are more likely than other groups to say that their phone is their main source of internet access. (Zickuhr & Smith, 2012, p. 2).

There are also variations in demographic uses of mobile technologies that should be taken into consideration. For example, Hispanics a very likely to use their smartphone for photography while blacks and Hispanics alike are more likely to use their smartphone as an audio-video recording device (Zickuhr & Smith, 2012, p. 21). With this in mind, it is important for faculty not to assume who does and does not have access and to assess each class of students for their access to hardware and software.

Since there is not, as of this writing, a robust mobile platform for video production, editing may be conducted on a suitable computer with editing software. Projects composed of still images, such as a slideshow videos, offer some reprieve for the technological difficulties students might face producing a video. Compiling a group of still images avoids the complexities of video production altogether. Presented as an animated GIF file, this project may be compiled in *Adobe Photoshop* or even on several free browser-based slideshow applications available online like *Animoto* and *Photopeach*.

Access not only involves possession but also knowing what to do and how to do it. The complexities of video editing can easily intimidate instructors and students unfamiliar with the time-devouring process of timeline structures, cutting and splicing video clips, and coordinating audio tracks. Instructors should assess individual comfort levels as much as possible and allow for students to interpret their own adequacies and aptitudes.

One of the easiest ways to improve access is to have students work in groups, where students follow more structured group roles typically outlined within robust collaborative learning assignments (Millis & Cottell, 1998). For example, students who better understand how to edit and compile the video might do those jobs while other students write scripts and shoot. Having students work in groups also facilitates socialized knowledge construction promoted by Jenkins (2006) and Kalantzis and Cope (2008).

While text-based documents may be composed collaboratively across mobile devices using applications such as *Google Drive*, at the time of this writing there is a dearth of options that allow multiple users to work together on a common video project. Collaborative video editing applications such as *WeVideo* are still in developmental stages and seem hindered by logistical issues. Mobile applications for collaborative video composition and editing will most certainly grow over the coming years given the rapid expansion of high-speed networking and dropping smartphone costs. One possible solution is to create an online depository such as a blog space, video channel, or shared *Dropbox* where students can collect and thematically contextualize the group's videos and reflections. Instructors at schools that employ educational software packages, such as *Blackboard*, should also be able to take advantage of virtual meeting spaces and discussion boards.

Technological Support

Perhaps the most daunting barrier to overcome when incorporating mobile video production into the syllabus is the spectrum of technological experience levels. It is vital that instructors assess the gamut of skill among the students. In an average sized classroom, how many varieties of expertise with mobile devices are represented? Applications available for one device may not be on another. Some students may not have access to a mobile device with adequate video capabilities. On the other hand, what problems will arise from device incompatibility and stubborn cross-platform disagreements?

Student expertise should not be discounted. Considering that each is an expert user of their respective devices, these assignments also provide a wonderful opportunity to "level" the classroom. Instructors should not shy away from learning themselves – one person could not possibly keep up with every application and innovation in mobile technology. As part of an initial skill assessment, ask students to share their preferred methods of creative production.

Having students work in groups will facilitate technology support as students help one another figure out how to use the hardware and software. At the same time, instructors should slowly build a stockpile of resources (e.g., websites, *YouTube* videos, and direct mobile numbers to friendly folks in IT). As many college writing centers expand to accommodate multiliteracy (Sheridan & Inman, 2010) by providing digital publishing assistance, faculty should survey student academic support resources, as well. As the Bring Your Own Device (BYOD) movement grows, Chief Information Officers (CIOs) in higher education plan for an increasing number of student devices. Faculty should befriend campus instructional designers, technologists, and IT support staff, most of whom will be excited by these projects and will want students to succeed.

Assessment

Some projects might fall into low-stakes, write-to-learn style assignments (Bean, 2011) where students not only explore the content and concepts but also familiarize themselves with the capabilities of their devices. These assignments shouldn't require more from the students than "point and shoot" and perhaps a little reflection to demonstrate their knowledge.

Many multimedia composition scholars suggest students do a variety of meta-reflective work to help assess assignments and to produce more polished video projects while demonstrating that they have learned, even mastered, the content (Borton & Huot, 2007; Alexander, 2007; Kuhn, 2010). Instructors and students should agree to a very distinct purpose and audience for their video project (Borton & Huot, 2007; Alexander, 2007): with a focused task, it is easier to comment on why a project did or did not complete the task. Students should reflect and discuss how and why they composed the video (Borton & Huot, 2007; Alexander, 2007; Kuhn, 2010). Finally, students should keep a detailed journal or log of the production and editing process where they discuss both what they did and why they did it (Borton & Huot, 2007; Alexander, 2007). All of these meta-reflective materials will help instructors assess the video projects.

Copyright

Just as students struggle to adequately provide attribution of outside resources in traditional, written papers, students will struggle to understand the importance of citing other work (especially music). When everyone is capable of producing and sharing media, our participatory culture is faced with a bit of a quandary. If students publish their videos publically to the web, copyright issues need to be explained; however, students should not be deterred from producing multimedia work that they can share with their friends and family. Instead of forcing students to only publish their work in "safe" environments, like the institutional learning management system, students should be encouraged to incorporate work that is in the public domain or licensed for reuse (like *Creative Commons* licensing). Using these assignments as a platform, students develop an understanding of copyright issues through discerning which license to apply to their own publicly distributed works as members in a digital participatory culture. Introducing students to websites like *Jamendo* and *ccMixter* will help them keep them from using copyrighted music. Of course, you still need to teach them or have them research appropriate attribution practices.

Accessibility

As with issues related to copyright, discussing accessibility with students as they produce their videos will help make the finished products more comprehensive and user-friendly. At a minimum, if students produce higher quality videos that might be published to the web or used in future courses, they should provide transcripts of the audio content; ideally, students would produce a captioned version of the video. Students may be asked to fully develop and share their process using storyboards and transcripts, which help make the final product more accessible. As previously mentioned, the assignment itself can be made more accessible by using group project strategies to allocate students with different levels of technological access, knowledge, and production ability to balanced groups and by growing a library of support materials accessible to all groups of learners.

Privacy

Having students produce and publish videos will bring up a host of privacy concerns to consider.

First, actually publishing the student work might violate the student's own privacy under FERPA (Family Educational Rights and Privacy Act). You can easily avoid this by having students sign a release to publish the project, publish under a pseudonym, or by keeping the final project private. In our experience, students are excited to share this work; therefore, we suggest you work out language with your department and legal office for a release form.

Students recording other individuals may be potentially harmful to those individuals' rights to privacy. For example, if nursing students are working in a school lab with a dummy, recording the dummy is not an issue. If those same students were to record real patients they worked with while on internship, that could potentially be violating HIPAA (Health Insurance Portability and Accountability Act). Similarly, if students collect videos of individuals as primary data for a research project, the project would first need to be approved by an Institutional Review Board to protect the rights of the human research subjects.

CONCLUSION

The Pew studies have noticed the mobile difference:

once someone has a wireless device, she becomes much more active in how she uses the internet-not just with wireless connectivity, but also with wired devices. The same holds true for the impact of wireless connections and people's interest in using the internet to connect with others. (Zickuhr & Smith, 2012, p. 14)

As media that inherently combines so many of the skills we want to impart on our students, mobile video embraces the dynamic and burgeoning intrasocial learning economy.

Given the potential issues involved in these assignments, it might seem like incorporating robust mobile video assignments is not worth

the time or energy. However, the opportunity to promote student authority over their own modes of learning should not be overlooked. Designing and delivering these learning activities is complex, and therefore faculty need plan plenty of preparation time but the increase in learning and the ability to foreground student expertise makes these efforts worthwhile. In studies about how faculty incorporate new technologies into their teaching, scholars find that it takes a lot of time (Giest, 2010) and faculty are usually most concerned and need the most help with pedagogical issues (Hochman & Palmquist, 2009; Rodrigo, 2009).

Video production, like writing, entails personal openness but to a greater degree in that the audience is potentially much larger than a single instructor or a few hesitant peer reviewers. While the composer may regard this vulnerability as a negative, this contextual exposure of mobile video assignments is what creates an impactful learning experience. As the pedagogical vision shifts to accommodate "m-learning," it is vital that the higher education embraces this pocket technology. As contemporary workspaces shift from cubicle to living room and telecommuting grows in prominence, these skills will only serve students' career goals that much more.

Acknowledging the benefit towards professional development is merely the penultimate goal, though. Composing mobile video urges students to invest themselves in their task through the use of an instrument with which they are intimately adept. What's more, through a more intuitive process of production and presentation, the learning curve of most mobile video applications is forgiving, allowing students to explore the medium, take risks, and bask in the serendipitous moment of creativity.

If institutions of higher education truthfully mean to provide a stage for personal growth, our syllabi should reflect the student's chosen communication device, their cognitive development as a multi-disciplinary learner, and their identities as creative individuals who learn from social interaction and reflection.

REFERENCES

Alexander, B. (2004). Going nomadic: Mobile learning in higher education. *EDUCAUSE Review*, *39*(5), 28–35. Retrieved from http://educause.edu

Alexander, K. P. (2007). More about reading, responding, and revising: The three Rs of peer review and revision. In Selfe, C. L. (Ed.), *Multimodal composition: Resources for teachers* (pp. 113–131). Cresskill, NJ: Hampton Press.

ASCD. (2008). *21st century skills*. Retrieved from http://www.ascd.org/research-a-topic/21st-century-skills-resources.aspx

Association of Colleges and Research Libraries. (2000). *Information literacy competency standards for higher education*. Retrieved from http://www.ala.org/acrl/standards/informationliteracycompetency

Barr, R. B., & Tagg, J. (1995). From teaching to learning-A new paradigm for undergraduate education. *Change*, *27*(6), 13–25. doi:10.1080/00091383.1995.10544672

Bean, J. (2011). *Engaging ideas: The professor's guide to integrating writing, critical thinking, and active learning in the classroom* (2nd ed.). San Francisco, CA: Jossey-Bass.

Bloom, B. S., Engelhart, M. D., Furst, E. J., Hill, W. H., & Krathwohl, D. R. (1956). *Taxonomy of educational objectives: The classification of educational goals; Handbook I: Cognitive domain*. New York, NY: Longmans, Green.

Blumberg, P. (2009). *Developing learner-centered teaching: A practical guide for faculty*. San Francisco, CA: Jossey-Bass.

Borton, S. C., & Huot, B. (2007). Responding and assessing. In Selfe, C. L. (Ed.), *Multimodal composition: Resources for teachers* (pp. 99–111). Cresskill, NJ: Hampton Press.

Conference on College Composition and Communication. (2004). *CCCC position statement on teaching, learning, and assessing writing in digital environments*. Retrieved from http://www.ncte.org/cccc/resources/positions/digitalenvironments

Coogan, D. (2006). Service learning and social change: the case for materialist rhetoric. *College Composition and Communication*, *57*(4), 667–693.

Council of Writing Program Administrators. (2008). *WPA outcomes statement for first-year composition*. Retrieved from http://wpacouncil.org/positions/outcomes.html

Dahlstrom, E., de Boor, T., Grunwald, P., & Vockley, M. (2011). *The ECAR national study of undergraduate students and information technology, 2011 (Research report)*. Retrieved from http://educause.edu/

Fink, L. D. (2003). *Creating significant learning experiences: An integrated approach to designing college courses*. San Francisco, CA: Jossey-Bass.

Giest, H. (2010). Reinventing education: New technology does not guarantee a new learning culture. *E–Learning and Digital Media*, *7*(4), 366–376. doi:10.2304/elea.2010.7.4.366

Hockman, W., & Palmquist, M. (2009). From desktop to laptop: Making transitions to wireless learning in writing classrooms. In Kimme Hea, A. C. (Ed.), *Going wireless: A critical exploration of wireless and mobile technologies for composition teachers and researchers* (pp. 109–131). Cresskill, NJ: Hampton Press.

Intel. (n.d.). *Technology literacy*. Retrieved from http://www.intel.com/education/technologyliteracy/index.htm

Jenkins, H., Clinton, K., Purushotma, R., & Robison, J. A. J., & Weigel, M. (2006). *Confronting the challenges of participatory culture: Media education for the 21st century*. Retrieved from http://digitallearning.macfound.org/

Kalantzis, M., & Cope, B. (2008). *New learning: Elements of a science of education.* Port Melbourne, Australia: Cambridge University Press. doi:10.1017/CBO9780511811951

Krathwohl, D. R., Bloom, B. S., & Masia, B. B. (1964). *Taxonomy of educational objectives; The classification of educational goals. Handbook II: The affective domain.* New York, NY: Longman, Green.

Kuhn, V. (2010). Speaking with students: Profiles in digital pedagogy. *Kairos: A Journal of Rhetoric, Technology, and Pedagogy, 14*(2). Retrieved from http://kairos.technorhetoric.net/14.2/interviews/kuhn/index.html

Medina, J. (2008). *Brain rules: 12 principles for surviving and thriving at work, home, and school.* Seattle, WA: Pear Press.

Millis, B. J., & Cottell, P. G. (1998). *Cooperative learning for higher education faculty.* Phoenix, AZ: American Council on Education & Oryx Press.

National Council of Teachers of English. (2005). *NCTE position statement on multimodal literacies.* Retrieved from http://www.ncte.org/positions/statements/multimodalliteracies

National Council of Teachers of English. (2008). *NCTE definition of 21st century literacies.* Retrieved from http://www.ncte.org/positions/statements/21stcentdefinition

Partnership for 21st Century Skills. (2011). *Framework for 21st century learning.* Retrieved from http://www.p21.org/overview/skills-framework

Penrod, D. (2007). *Using blogs to enhance literacy: The next powerful step in 21st-century learning.* Lanham, MD: Rowman & Littlefield Education.

Rainie, L., & Fox, S. (2012). *Just-in-time information through mobile connections.* Retrieved from http://pewinternet.org

Rodrigo, R. (2009). *Motivation and play: How faculty continue to learn new technologies* (Doctoral dissertation). Retrieved from ProQuest. (1790315301)

Rodrigo, R. (2011). Mobile teaching versus mobile learning. *EDUCAUSE Quarterly, 34*(11). Retrieved from http://educause.edu/

Sheridan, D. M., & Inman, J. (2010). *Writing center work, new media, and multimodal rhetoric.* Cresskill, NJ: Hampton Press, Inc.

Simpson, E. J. (1972). *The classification of educational objectives in the psychomotor domain.* Washington, DC: Gryphon House.

Smith, A. (2012, March). *46% of American adults are smartphone owners.* Retrieved from http://pewinternet.org/

Smith, A., Rainie, L., & Zickuhr, K. (2011). *College students and technology.* Retrieved from http://pewinternet.org/

Spinuzzi, C. (2009). The genie's out of the bottle: Leveraging mobile and wireless technologies in qualitative research. In Kimme Hea, A. C. (Ed.), *Going wireless: A critical exploration of wireless and mobile technologies for composition teachers and researchers* (pp. 255–273). Cresskill, NJ: Hampton Press.

Sutton-Smith, B. (1997). *The ambiguity of play.* Cambridge, MA: Harvard University Press.

Weimer, M. (2002). *Learner-centered teaching: Five key changes to practice.* San Francisco, CA: Jossey-Bass.

Yu-Lin, J., Ting-Ting, W., Yueh-Min, H., Qing, T., & Yang, S. J. H. (2010). The add-on impact of mobile applications in learning strategies: A review study. *Journal of Educational Technology & Society, 13*(3), 3–11. Retrieved from http://www.ifets.info/

Zickuhr, K., & Smith, A. (2012). *Digital differences.* Retrieved from http://pewinternet.org/

Zull, J. E. (2002). *The art of changing the brain: Enriching the practice of teaching by exploring the biology of learning*. Sterling, VA: Stylus.

KEY TERMS AND DEFINITIONS

Access: When working with technologies in educational environments, access is a complex issue. Not only do instructors need to worry about basic availability of hardware and software, they also need for students to understand how to use the technologies. When asking students to produce multimedia works, access also becomes an issue associated with the finished project. Instructors need to think about a variety of individuals with different abilities both producing and consuming the assigned videos.

Active Learning: Active learning incorporates teaching philosophies, pedagogies, and learning activities that require students to *do* things as a part of their learning process. Different active learning philosophies, pedagogies, and activities ask students to engage with the course content, course processes, as well as one another, usually while producing new texts and knowledge.

Application: With regard to mobile devices, the term application refers to the individual software programs that perform any number of functions. Nearly all devices have a standard core set of applications that allows users to access email, play games, as well as record and edit pictures and videos. Additionally, these may also be downloaded from a vast number of online resources, the most popular being Apple's *iTunes* and *App Store* and Google's *Google Play*. The quality of these applications ranges from amateur products of limited capability to ones of a nearly professional scope.

Attribution: To prevent copyright infringement, individuals should provide some form of citation, or attribution, that lists what resource was used in the new text as well as where the original resource may be accessed. Attribution is complex in video texts for two reasons: first, it is difficult to identify the exact text being quoted (you can not just put in quotation marks around specific clips, images, or sounds within a video); and second, what format and location the citations take (especially in the age of *YouTube* where videos can be embedded separately from their original supporting websites and documentation).

Handheld Device: When discussing handheld devices, individuals are usually referring only to smartphones and tablet computers. Handheld devices are very small, usually highly personalized, and connect to the internet through WiFi or cellular phone technologies. The extreme portability of these devices makes it easier for users to take them just about anywhere.

Mobile Device: A discussion of mobile devices usually includes laptops, tablets, netbooks, eReaders, and cell or smart phones. Connected to the Internet via one of the many iterations of wireless local area networking (cellular, WiFi, 3G, and 4G are currently available), most devices are able to download software applications from any number of sources. When discussing video production, the most relevant of these applications would include software that allows the device to serve as portable image, audio, and video recording equipment.

Multiliteracy: As Internet users often encounter modes of composition that entail more than text, the notion of multiliteracy implies a mode of "reading" that negotiates text with images, film, and other dynamic elements. Multiliteracy also includes discourse that traverses national, ethnic and cultural delineations.

Slideshow Video: A video made up of static images that have been compiled with transitions and usually audio. Different slideshow video applications allow for various levels of editing in terms of image focus, zooming, and panning; transitional methods, and audio synchronization.

Smartphone: Smartphones are generally handheld computers that have telephonic capabilities and primarily connect to the internet through cellular technology. Smartphones have a base operating system (ie., iOS, Android, Windows) and run a variety of software applications colloquially referred to as "apps."

Student Learning: Student learning is the focus of active learning philosophies, pedagogies, and classroom activities. The idea is to focus on whether or not students are actually learning the course content, as opposed to focusing on what and how teachers are teaching, or delivering, the course content.

Teaching: Teaching refers to the course design and content delivery facilitated by the course instructor. Teaching, however, is only part of the equation. Contemporary active learning philosophies, pedagogies, and activities focus attention on whether or not the students are actually learning the course content. In other words, to be a learning focused classroom, instructors need to articulate what, how, and why their teaching practices better facilitate student learning.

Transmedia: A unified composition, often digital in nature, which is created utilizing several methods of production. Comprised of movies, static and animated images, as well as text, the transmedia project incorporates several mediums – sometimes both digital and physical in nature – to produce a cohesive narrative.

Video Editing: Basic video editing applications will allow users to clip shot sequences, incorporate shot transitions, and synchronous one, or more, audio tracks to the video. Students producing video will also need the ability to compile and publish, or export, the video in a format best suited for the intended audience or publishing venue.

Compilation of References

(2009). *Keynote*. Cupertino, CA: Apple, Inc.[Computer software]

(2009). *VoiceThread*. Boca Raton, FL: Educause Inc. [Computer software]

(2010). *Camtasia: Mac, Version 1.1*. Okemos, MI: TechSmith. [Computer software]

(2010). *Captivate*. San Jose, CA: Adobe. [Computer software]

(2010). *Elluminate*. Washington, DC: Blackboard Inc. [Computer software]

(2010). *Jing*. Okemos, MI: TechSmith. [Computer software]

(2010). *PowerPoint (12.0)*. Redmond, VA: Microsoft Corp.[Computer software]

(2011). *Wimba*. New York, NY: Blackboard, Inc.[Computer software]

(2012). *Flash*. San Jose, CA: Adobe. [Computer software]

(2012). *Quicktime*. Cupertino, CA: Apple, Inc.[Computer software]

17 USC § 512 - *Limitations on liability relating to material online*. (2009). Cornell University Law School, Legal Information Institute. Retrieved from http://www.law.cornell.edu/uscode/text/17/512

About HowStuffWorks. (2012). *HowStuffWorks*. Retrieved May 17, 2012, from http://www.howstuffworks.com/about-hsw.htm

Adams, J. (2006). The part played by instructional media in distance education. *Studies in Media and Information Literacy Education, 6*(2), 1–12. doi:10.3138/sim.6.2.001

Aiex, N. (1999). *Mass media use in the classroom* (Bloomington, IN, ERIC Clearinghouse on Reading English and Communication, Eric Digest D-147, ED 436 016).

Alessi, S. M., & Trollip, S. R. (2001). *Multimedia for learning* (3rd ed.). Boston, MA: Allyn & Bacon.

Alexander, B. (2004). Going nomadic: Mobile learning in higher education. *EDUCAUSE Review, 39*(5), 28–35. Retrieved from http://educause.edu

Alexander, B. (2011). *The new digital storytelling: Creating narratives with new media*. Westport, CT: Prager.

Alexander, K. P. (2007). More about reading, responding, and revising: The three Rs of peer review and revision. In Selfe, C. L. (Ed.), *Multimodal composition: Resources for teachers* (pp. 113–131). Cresskill, NJ: Hampton Press.

Allen, I. E., & Seaman, J. Babson Survey Research Group. (2011). *Going the distance: Online education in the United States, 2011*. Babson Park, MA: Babson Survey Research Group.

Allen, M., Witt, P. L., & Wheeless, L. P. (2006). The role of teacher immediacy as a motivational factor in student learning: Using meta-analysis to test a causal model. *Communication Education, 55*(1), 21–31. doi:10.1080/03634520500343368

Amer, A. (2006). Reflections on Bloom's revised taxonomy. *Electronic Journal of Research in Educational Psychology, 4*(1), 213–230.

American Counseling Association. (n.d.). *Resources*. Retrieved April 1, 2012, from http://www.counseling.org/resources/

Andersen, J. (1979). Teacher immediacy as a predictor of teaching effectiveness. In Nimmo, D. (Ed.), *Communication yearbook, 3* (pp. 543–559). New Brunswick, NJ: Transaction Books.

Anderson, T. (2002, May). *An updated and theoretical rationale for interaction*. ITFORUM. Retrieved from http://it.coe.uga.edu/itforum/paper63/paper63.htm

Anderson, T. (2004). Theory and practice of online learning. In T. Anderson & F. Elloumi (Eds.), *Teaching in an online learning context*. Retrieved from http://cde.athabascau.ca/online_book/

Anderson, T. D., & Garrison, D. R. (1998). Learning in a networked world: New roles and responsibilities. In Gibson, C. C. (Ed.), *Distance learners in higher education: Institutional responses for quality outcomes* (pp. 97–112). Madison, WI: Atwood Publishing.

Anthony, E., Sims, J., & McCullough, D. A. (2010). *Exploring placement criteria in freshman and sophomore level undergraduate mathematics courses*. Undergraduate research poster presented at the Southeastern MAA meeting, Elon, North Carolina.

Anthony, L. (2004). AntConc: A learner and classroom friendly, multi-platform corpus analysis toolkit. *IWLeL 2004: An Interactive Workshop on Language e-Learning*, (pp. 7-13).

Anthony, L. (2012). AntConc (3.3.1w) [Computer Software]. Tokyo, Japan: Waseda University. Available from http://www.antlab.sci.waseda.ac.jp/

Apple. (2012). Retrieved May 29, 2012, from http://www.apple.com/

Arbaugh, J. B., & Hwang, A. (2006). Does "teaching presence" exist in online MBA courses? *The Internet and Higher Education, 9*(1), 9-21. Retrieved March 19, 2012, from http://www.sciencedirect.com/science/article/pii/S1096751605000783

Archive, I. (2010). *Wayback machine beta FAQs*. Retrieved April 30, 2012, from http://faq.web.archive.org/what-is-the-wayback-machine/

ArtBabble. (n.d.). *Home*. Retrieved May 17, 2012, from http://www.artbabble.org/

Articulate Network. (2012). Screenr | Instant screencasts: Just click record. *Screenr*. Retrieved May 14, 2012, from http://www.screenr.com/

Articulate Rapid E-Learning. (2009). *Computer software*. San Francisco, CA: Studio Pro.

Arum, R., & Roska, J. (2011). *Academically adrift: Limited learning on college campuses*. Chicago, IL: University of Chicago Press.

Arvidson, P. S., & Huston, T. A. (2008). Transparent teaching. *Currents in Teaching and Learning, 1*(1), 4–16.

ASCD. (2008). *21st century skills*. Retrieved from http://www.ascd.org/research-a-topic/21st-century-skills-resources.aspx

Association of American Colleges Universities. (2005). *Liberal education outcomes: A preliminary report on student achievement in college*. Washington, DC. Retrieved from www.aacu.org/advocacy/pdfs/leap_report_final.pdf.

Association of Colleges and Research Libraries. (2000). *Information literacy competency standards for higher education*. Retrieved from http://www.ala.org/acrl/standards/informationliteracycompetency

Baines, L. (2012, June 20). *Web log message*. Retrieved from http://lifeboat.com/blog/2012/06/a-future-of-fewer-words

Bain, K. (2004). *What the best college teachers do*. Cambridge, MA: Harvard University Press.

Baker, F. W. (2012). *Media literacy in the K-12 classroom*. International Society for Technology in Education - ISTE

Baker, J. W. (2000). The "classroom flip": Using Web course management tools to become the guide on the side. In J. A. Chambers (Ed.). *Selected Papers from the 11th International Conference on College Teaching and Learning* (pp. 9-17). Jacksonville, FL: Florida Community College at Jacksonville.

Baker, C. (2010). The impact of instructor immediacy and presence for online student affective learning, cognition, and motivation. *The Journal of Educators Online, 7*(1).

Baker, J. D. (2004). An investigation of relationships among instructor immediacy and affective and cognitive learning in the online classroom. *The Internet and Higher Education, 7*, 1–13. doi:10.1016/j.iheduc.2003.11.006

Bandes, B. (1988). *Humor as a motivation for effective learning in the classroom.* Doctoral dissertation, Columbia Teachers College.

Bandura, A. (1977). *Social learning theory.* New York, NY: General Learning Press.

Bannan-Ritland, B., Dabbagh, N., & Murphy, K. (2000). Learning object systems as constructivist learning environments: Related assumptions, theories, and applications. In D. A. Wiley (Ed.). *The instructional use of learning objects.* Retrieved from http://reusability.org/read/chapters/bannab-ritland.doc

Barab, S. A. MaKinster, J. G. & Scheckler, R. (2003) Designing system dualities: Characterizing a web-supported professional development community. *The Information Society, 19*, 237-256.

Bardine, B., Bardine, M., & Deegan, E. (2000). Beyond the red pen: Clarifying our role in the response process. *English Journal, 90*(1), 94–101. doi:10.2307/821738

Bargeron, D., Grudin, A., Gupta, E., Sanocki, F., & Leetiernan, S. (2002). Asynchronous collaboration around multimedia applied to on-demand education. *Journal of Management Information Systems, 18*(4), 117–145.

Barrett, H. C. (2001). *Expert showcase: Dr. Helen Barrett on electronic portfolio development.* Retrieved from http://ali.apple.com/ali_sites/ali/exhibits/1000156/

Barr, R. B., & Tagg, J. (1995). From teaching to learning-A new paradigm for undergraduate education. *Change, 27*(6), 13–25. doi:10.1080/00091383.1995.10544672

Barthes, R. (1974). *S/Z* (Miller, R., Trans.). New York, NY: Hill and Wang.

Basili, J. N. (2008). Media richness and social norms in the choice to attend lectures or to watch them online. *Journal of Educational Multimedia and Hypermedia, 17*(4), 453–475.

Bates, S., & Galloway, R. (2012). *The inverted classroom in a large enrollment introductory physics course: A case study.* University of Edinburgh, Higher Education Academy. Retrieved from http://www.heacademy.ac.uk/assets/documents/stem-conference/Physical%20Sciences/Simon_Bates_Ross_Galloway.pdf

Bates, T. (2006). *Technology, e-learning and distance education.* New York, NY: Abingdon.

Bateson, M. C. (1990). *Composing a life.* New York, NY: Plume.

Batson, T. (2002). *The electronic portfolio boom: What's it all about?* Retrieved October 9, 2003, from http://www.syllabus.com/article.asp?id=6984

Batson, T., & Bass, R. (1996). Primacy of process: Teaching and learning in the computer age. *Change, 28*(2), 42–47. doi:10.1080/00091383.1996.9937750

Beach, R. (1989). Showing students how to assess: Demonstrating techniques for response in writing conferences. In Anson, C. (Ed.), *Writing and response: Theory, practice, and research* (pp. 127–148). Urbana, IL: National Council of Teachers of English.

Beach, R., & Friedrich, T. (2006). Response to writing. In MacArthur, C., Graham, S., & Fitzgerald, J. (Eds.), *Handbook of writing research* (pp. 222–234). New York, NY: Guilford.

Bean, J. (2011). *Engaging ideas: The professor's guide to integrating writing, critical thinking, and active learning in the classroom* (2nd ed.). San Francisco, CA: Jossey-Bass.

Begley, S. (2000, October 9). The science of laughs. *Newsweek, 136*(15), 75-76.

Bell, T., Cockburn, A., McKenzie, B., & Vargo, J. (2001). Flexible delivery damaging to learning? Lessons from the Canterbury Digital Lectures project. In the *13th Proceedings of the ED-MEDIA 2001 World Conference on Education Multimedia & Telecoummunications,* Tampere, Finland.

Bender, W. N. (2012). Project-based learning: Differentiating instruction for the 21st century. Thousand Oaks, CA: Corwin, a Sage Company.

Berge, Z. (1995). The role of the online instructor/facilitator. *Educational Technology, 35*(1), 22–30.

Berk, R. A. (1996). Student rating of 10 strategies for using humor in college teaching. *Journal on Excellence in College Teaching, 7*(3), 71–92.

Berk, R. A. (2000, Fall). Does humor in course tests reduce anxiety and improve performance? *College Teaching, 48*(4), 151–158. doi:10.1080/87567550009595834

Berk, R. A. (2003). *Professors are from Mars, students are from snickers: How to write and deliver humor in the classroom and in professional presentations*. Dulles, VA: Stylus Publishing.

Bilimoria, D., & Wheeler, J. (1995). Learning-centered education: A guide to resources and implementation. *Journal of Management Education, 29*(3), 402–428.

Bishop, M. C., & Yocom, J. (2009, August). *Designing and evaluating multimedia projects in an online environment*. Board of Regents of the University of Wisconsin System for the 25th Annual Conference on Distance Teaching and Learning, Madison, WI

Bishop, M. C., & Yocom, J. (2011, August). *Education, multimedia and social media: Are we ready for showtime?* Board of Regents of the University of Wisconsin System for the 27th Annual Conference on Distance Teaching and Learning, Madison, WI.

Blackboard Collaborate | Online Collaboration Software for Engaging, Collaborative Learning. (2012). *Blackboard Collaborate*. Retrieved May 29, 2012, from http://www.blackboard.com/platforms/collaborate/overview.aspx

Blackboard Collaborate. (2012). *Computer software*. Washington, DC: Blackboard Inc.

Bligh, D. A. (2000). *What's the use of lectures?* San Francisco, CA: Jossey-Bass.

Bloom, B. S. (1994). Reflections on the development and use of the taxonomy. In Anderson, L. W., & Sosniak, L. A. (Eds.), *Bloom's taxonomy: A forty year retrospective* (pp. 1–8). Chicago, IL: Chicago University Press.

Bloom, B. S., Engelhart, M. D., Furst, E. J., Hill, W. H., & Krathwohl, D. R. (1956). *Taxonomy of educational objectives: The classification of educational goals; Handbook I: Cognitive domain*. New York, NY: Longmans, Green.

Blumberg, P. (2009). *Developing learner-centered teaching: A practical guide for faculty*. San Francisco, CA: Jossey-Bass.

Bok, D. (2006). *Our underachieving colleges: A candid look on how much students' learn and why they should be learning more*. Princeton, NJ: Princeton University Press.

Bolter, J., & Grusin, R. (2000). *Remediation: Understanding new media*. Cambridge, MA: MIT press.

Bonk, C., Kirkley, J., Hara, N., & Dennen, N. (2001). Finding the instructor in post-secondary online learning: Pedagogical, social, managerial, and technological locations. In Stephenson, J. (Ed.), *Teaching and learning online: New pedagogies for new technologies* (pp. 76–97). London, UK: Kogan Page.

Bonwell, C. C., & Eison, J. A. (1991). *Active learning: Creating excitement in the classroom*. ASHE- ERIC Higher Education Report Washington, DC: School of Education and Human Development, George Washington University.

Borton, S. C., & Huot, B. (2007). Responding and assessing. In Selfe, C. L. (Ed.), *Multimodal composition: Resources for teachers* (pp. 99–111). Cresskill, NJ: Hampton Press.

Borzo, J. (2011, January 21). Employers tread a minefield: Firings for alleged social-media infractions sometimes backfire on companies. *Wall Street Journal*. Retrieved from http://online.wsj.com/article/SB10001424052748703954004576089850685724570.html

Boyatzis, C. J. (1994). Using feature films to teach social development. *Teaching of Psychology, 21*, 99–101. doi:10.1207/s15328023top2102_9

Boyer, E. (1988). *Media literacy: Sayings*. Retrieved from http://www.medialiteracy.com/sayings.htm

Brandes, G., & Boskic, N. (2008). EPortfolios: From description to analysis. *International Review of Research in Open and Distance Learning, 9*(2), 1–17.

Bransford, J. D., Brown, A. L., & Cocking, R. R. (Eds.). (2000). *How people learn: Brain, mind, experience, and school*. Washington, DC: National Academy Press.

Bransford, J., Brophy, S., & Williams, S. (2000). When computer technologies meet the learning sciences: Issues and opportunities. *Journal of Applied Developmental Psychology, 21*(1), 59–84. doi:10.1016/S0193-3973(99)00051-9

Brecht, H. D., & Ogilby, S. M. (2008). Enabling a comprehensive teaching strategy: Video lecture. *Journal of Information Technology Education, 7*, 71–86.

Brent, R., & Felder, R. M. (1996). Navigating the bumpy road to student-centered instruction. *College Teaching, 44*(2), 43–47. doi:10.1080/87567555.1996.9933425

British Universities Film & Video Council. (2006). *The Newsfilm online digitization project.* Retrieved May 17, 2012, from http://newsfilm.bufvc.ac.uk/

Broad, M., Mathews, M., & McDonald, A. (2004). Accounting education through an online-supported virtual learning environment. *Active Learning in Higher Education, 5*(2), 135–151. doi:10.1177/1469787404043810

Brockbank, A., & McGill, I. (2007). *Facilitating reflective learning in higher education* (2nd ed.). McGraw Hill.

Brookfield, S. D. (2006). *Skillful teacher: On techniques, trust, and responsiveness in the classroom.* San Francisco, CA: Wiley, John & Sons.

Brotherton, J. A., & Abowd, G. D. (2004). Lessons learned from eClass: Assessing automated capture and access in the classroom. *ACM Transactions on Computer-Human Interaction, 11*(2), 121–155. doi:10.1145/1005361.1005362

Brown, M., & Diaz, V. (2011). Seeking evidence of impact: Opportunities and needs. *Educause Review, 46*(5). Retrieved May 18, 2012, from http://net.educause.edu/ir/library/pdf/ERM1152.pdf

Brown, J. S. (2006). New learning environments for the 21st century: Exploring the edge. *Change, 38*(5), 18–24. doi:10.3200/CHNG.38.5.18-24

Brown, R. (2001). The process of community building in distance learning classes. *Journal of Asynchronous Learning Networks, 5*(2), 18–35.

Bruce, B. C., & Levin, J. A. (1997). Educational technology: Media for inquiry, communication, construction, and expression. *Journal of Educational Computing Research, 17*, 79–102. doi:10.2190/7HPQ-4F3X-8M8Y-TVCA

Bruner, J., & Olson, D. (1986). Learning through experience and learning through media. In Gerbner, G., Gross, L. P., & Melody, W. (Eds.), *Communications technology and social policy: Understanding the new "cultural revolution".* New York, NY: Wiley.

Bryant, J., Comisky, P. W., & Zillmann, D. (1979). Teachers' humor in the college classroom. *Communication Education, 28*, 110–128. doi:10.1080/03634527909378339

Buckingham, D. (2007). Digital media literacies: Rethinking media education in the age of the Internet. *Research in Comparative and International Education, 2*(1), 43–55. doi:10.2304/rcie.2007.2.1.43

Buckman, K. H. (2010). *Why did the professor cross the road? How and why college professors intentionally use humor in their teaching.* Dissertation Texas A & M University.

Buerck, L. A., Malmstrom, T., & Peppers, E. (2003). Learning environments and learning styles: Non-traditional student enrollment and success in an Internet-based versus a lecture-based computer science course. *Learning Environments Research, 6*(2), 137–155. doi:10.1023/A:1024939002433

Bulach, C. (1993). A measure of openness and trust. *People and Education, 1*, 382–392.

Burbules, N. C., & Callister, T. A. (2000). *The risky promises and promising risks on new information technologies for education. Watch IT: The risks and promises of information technologies for education.* Boulder, CO: Westview Press.

Burns, R. A. (1985, May). *Information impact and factors affecting recall.* Paper presented at Annual National Conference on Teaching Excellent and Conference of Administrators, Austin TX. (ERIC Document Reproduction Service No. ED 258 639)

Cappicie, A., & Desrosiers, P. (2011). Lessons learned from using Adobe Acrobat Connect in the social work classroom. *Journal of Technology in Human Services, 29*(4), 296–302. doi:10.1080/15228835.2011.638239

Cascaval, R. C., Fogler, K. A., Abrams, G. D., & Durham, R. L. (2008). Evaluating the benefits of providing archived online lectures to in-class math students. *Journal of Asynchronous Learning Networks, 12*(3-4), 61–70.

Casinghino, C. (2011). *Moving images: Making movies, understanding media*. United States: Delmar Cengage Learning.

CAST (Center for Applied Special Technology). (2008). *Universal design for learning (UDL) guidelines – Version 1.0.* Retrieved from http://www.cast.org/publications/UDLguidelines/version1.html

Caulfield, J. (2011). *How to design and teach a hybrid course*. Sterling, VA: Stylus Publishing.

Center for Instructional Technology. (n.d.). *Student video fellowship: Biomedical engineering capstone video project*. Retrieved from http://cit.duke.edu/blog/2010/03/student-video-fellowship-biomedical-engineering-capstone-video-project/

Center for New Designs in Scholarship (CNDS). Georgetown University. (n.d.). *Digital story multimedia archive*. Retrieved May 19, 2012, from https://pilot.cndls.georgetown.edu/digitalstories

Center for New Designs in Scholarship (CNDS). Georgetown University. (n.d.). *Visible knowledge project*. Retrieved May 19, 2012, from https://cndls.georgetown.edu/about/grants/vkp

Chambers, S. M., & Wickersham, L. E. (2007). The electronic portfolio journey: A year later. *Education, 127*(3), 351–360.

Charmaz, K. (2006). *Constructing grounded theory*. Thousand Oaks, CA: Sage.

Chatham-Carpenter, A., Seawel, L., & Raschig, J. (2010). Avoiding the pitfalls: Current practices and recommendations for eportfolios in higher education. *Journal of Educational Technology Systems, 38*(4), 437–456. doi:10.2190/ET.38.4.e

Chen, N., & Ko, H., Kinshuk, & Lin, T. (2005). A model for synchronous learning using the Internet. *Innovations in Education and Teaching International, 42*(2), 181–194. doi:10.1080/14703290500062599

Chickering, A. W., & Ehrmann, S. C. (1996). Implementing the seven principles: Technology as lever. American Association of Higher Education. *AAHE Bulletin, 49*(2), 3–6.

Chickering, A. W., & Gamson, Z. (1987). Seven principles for good practice in undergraduate education. *AAHE Bulletin, 40*(7), 3–7.

Chilsen, P. J., & Wells, C. R. (2012, June). *Media and the moving image: Creating those who thrive in a screen media world*. Paper presented at EdMedia World Conference On Educational Media & Technology, Denver, CO.

Christopher, A. N., Walter, J. L., Marek, P., & Koenig, C. S. (2004). Using a "new classic" film to teach about stereotyping and prejudice. *Teaching of Psychology, 31*, 199–202.

Clarke, A. E. (2005). *Situational analysis: Grounded theory after the postmodern turn*. Thousand Oaks, CA: Sage.

Clark, R., Nguyen, F., & Sweller, J. (2006). *Efficiency in learning: Evidence-based guidelines to manage cognitive load*. San Francisco, CA: John Wiley & Sons. doi:10.1002/pfi.4930450920

Coghlan, E., Futey, D., Little, J., Lomas, C., Oblinger, D., & Windham, C. (2007). *ELI discovery tool: Guide to podcasting*. Retrieved April, 2012 from http://www.educause.edu/Guidetopodcasting/12830

Cole, N. (1990). Conceptions of educational achievement. *Educational Researcher, 19*(3), 2–7.

Collie, L., Shah, V., & Sheridan, D. (2009). *An end-user evaluation of a lecture archiving system*. Paper presented at the 10th International Conference NZ Chapter of the ACM's Special Interest Groupon Human-Computer Interaction.

Collins, A., Seely Brown, J., & Holum, A. (1991). Cognitive apprenticeship: Making thinking visible. *American Educator, 15*(3), 6–46.

Commons, C. (n.d.). *About*. Retrieved May 17, 2012, from Creative Commons: http://creativecommons.org/about

Conference on College Composition and Communication. (2004). *CCCC position statement on teaching, learning, and assessing writing in digital environments.* Retrieved from http://www.ncte.org/cccc/resources/positions/digitalenvironments

Conoway, T. (2011, June 15). Lecture capture can change classroom dynamics for the better. *Faculty Focus: Focused on Today's Higher Education Professional.*

Conrad, R., & Donaldson, J. (2004). *Engaging the online learner, activities and resources for creative instruction.* San Francisco, CA: Jossey-Bass.

Coogan, D. (2006). Service learning and social change: the case for materialist rhetoric. *College Composition and Communication, 57*(4), 667–693.

Council of Writing Program Administrators. (2008). *WPA outcomes statement for first-year composition.* Retrieved from http://wpacouncil.org/positions/outcomes.html

Coutu, D. (2007, June). We Googled you. *Harvard Business Review, 85*(6), 37–47.

Craig, J., Gregory, S., El Haggan, A., Braha, H., & Brittan-Powell, C. (November, 2009). *Lecture capture systems: Are they worth it?* Paper presented at the Educause Mid-Atlantic Regional Conference, Philadelphia, PA.

Creative Commons. (n.d.). *Attribution-NoDerivs 3.0 United States* (CC BY-ND 3.0) Retrieved from http://creativecommons.org/licenses/by-nd/3.0/us/

Creative Vado HD Pocket Video Cameras - Capture & share moments. (n.d.). Retrieved May 29, 2012, from http://www.creative.com/myvado/

Crews, T., & Wilkinson, K. (2010). Students perceived preference for visual and auditory assessment with e-handwritten feedback. *Business Communication Quarterly, 73,* 399–412. doi:10.1177/1080569910385566

Crouch, C., & Mazur, E. (2001). Peer instruction: Ten years of experience and results. *American Journal of Physics, 69*(9), 970–977. doi:10.1119/1.1374249

Curzon-Hobson, A. (2002). A pedagogy of trust in higher education. *Teaching in Higher Education, 7,* 265–276. doi:10.1080/13562510220144770

Cutliff, J. R. (2000). Methodological issues in grounded theory. *Journal of Advanced Nursing, 31*(6), 1476–1484. doi:10.1046/j.1365-2648.2000.01430.x

Daft, R. L., & Lengel, R. H. (1986). Organizational information requirements, media richness and structural design. *Management Science, 32,* 554–571. doi:10.1287/mnsc.32.5.554

Dagen, A., Matter, C., Rinehart, S., & Ice, P. (2008). Can you hear me now? Providing feedback using audio commenting technology. *College Reading Association Yearbook, 29,* 152–166.

Dahlstrom, E., de Boor, T., Grunwald, P., & Vockley, M. (2011). *The ECAR national study of undergraduate students and information technology, 2011 (Research report).* Retrieved from http://educause.edu/

Davis, C. (2010). Using student-centered discussion forums to enhance student participation in online courses. In *Proceedings: 26th Annual Distance Teaching and Learning Conference,* (pp. 1-5). Madison, WI.

Davis, C., & Froriep, K. (2009). Using multi-media for modeling reading instruction in teacher education. In *Proceedings: 25th Annual Distance Teaching and Learning Conference,* (pp. 485-488). Madison: WI.

Davis, E. (2010). Math tops list of most failed at UTM. *The UT Martin Pacer, 82.*

Davis, J. M., & Farina, A. (1970). Humor appreciation as social communication. *Journal of Personality and Social Psychology, 15,* 175–178. doi:10.1037/h0029202

Dean, B. C. (2007). *Dynamic homework annotation.* First International Workshop on Pen-Based Learning Technologies. Retrieved July 15, 2012, from http://www.cs.clemson.edu/~bcdean/vgrade.pdf

Deans, T. (2009). *Requiring revision.* Retrieved March 15, 2012, from http://www.insidehighered.com/views/2009/06/25/deans

DeLeng, B., Dolmans, D., & van de Wiel, M. (2007). How video cases should be used as authentic stimuli in problem-based medical education. *Medical Education, 41*(2), 181–188. doi:10.1111/j.1365-2929.2006.02671.x

Dennett, D. (2007). There aren't enough minds to house the population explosion of memes. In Brockman, J. (Ed.), *What is your dangerous idea?* New York, NY: Harper Perennial.

Denton, P., Madden, J., Roberts, M., & Rowe, P. (2008). Students' response to traditional and computer-assisted formative feedback: A comparative case study. *British Journal of Educational Technology, 39*, 486–500. doi:10.1111/j.1467-8535.2007.00745.x

DeVoss, D., & Porter, J. (2006). Why Napster matters to writing: Filesharing as a new ethic of digital delivery. *Computers and Composition, 23*(2), 178–210. doi:10.1016/j.compcom.2006.02.001

Dewey, J. (1990). *The school and society and the child and the curriculum*. Chicago, IL: The University of Chicago Press.

Dey, E. L., Burn, H. E., & Gerdes, D. (2009). Bringing the classroom to the web: Effects of using new technologies to capture and deliver lectures. *Research in Higher Education, 50*(4), 377–393. doi:10.1007/s11162-009-9124-0

Dey, I. (1999). *Grounding grounded theory*. San Diego, CA: Academic Press.

Diaz, D. P. (May/June 2002). Online drop rates revisited. *The Technology Source*. Retrieved from http://technologysource.org/article/online_drop_rates_revisited/.

Diaz, D. P., & Cartnal, R. B. (1999). Students' learning styles in two classes: Online distance learning and equivalent on-campus. *College Teaching, 47*(4), 130–135. doi:10.1080/87567559909595802

ds106. (n.d.). Retrieved August 10, 2012 from http://ds106.us

DuCharme-Hansen, R., & Dupin-Bryant, P. (2005). Course planning for online adult learners. *TechTrends, 49*(2), 31–39. doi:10.1007/BF02773969

Duke University Digital Storytelling. (n.d.). *Social pedagogy*. Retrieved from https://pilot.cndls.georgetown.edu/digitalstories/social-pedagogy/

Dziuban, C., Hartman, J., Juge, F., Moskal, P., & Sorg, S. (2005). Blended learning: Online learning enters the mainstream. In Bonk, C. J., & Graham, C. (Eds.), *Handbook of blended learning environments: Global perspectives, local designs*. Hoboken, NJ: Pfeiffer Publications, a division of John Wiley and Sons.

Economist. (2011). *Flipping the classroom: Hopes that the internet can improve teaching may at last be bearing fruit*. September, 2011. Retrieved May 1, 2012 from http://www.economist.com/node/21529062

Educause Learning Initiative (ELI). (2006). *7 things you should know about lecture capture*. Retrieved May 21, 2012, from http://net.educause.edu/ir/library/pdf/ELI7044.pdf

EDUCAUSE. (2008). *Seven things you should know about lecture capture*. Retrieved April 1, 2012, from http://net.educause.edu/ir/library/pdf/ELI7044.pdf

EDUCAUSE. (n.d.). *Student engagement*. Retrieved from http://www.educause.edu/EDUCAUSE+Quarterly/EQVolume322009/EDUCAUSEQuarterlyMagazineVolum/192952

Edwards, C. M., & Gibboney, E. R. (1992). *The power of humor in the college classroom*. Retrieved from ERIC Document Reproduction Service No. ED 346 535.

Eidenmuller, M. E. (2012). *American rhetoric*. Retrieved May 17, 2012, from http://www.americanrhetoric.com/

Ellington, A. J., & Hardin, J. R. (2008). The use of video tutorials in a mathematical modeling course. *Mathematics and Computer Education, 42*(2), 109–117.

Ellis, R., & Childs, M. (1999). The effectiveness of video as a learning tool in on-line multimedia modules. *Journal of Educational Media, 24*(3), 217–223. doi:10.1080/1358165990240305

Encyclopedia of Life Learning + Education Group. (n.d.). *What is EOL?* Retrieved May 17, 2012, from http://education.eol.org/who/what_is_eol

Engstrand, S., & Hall, S. (2011). The use of streamed lecture recordings: Patterns of use, student experience and effects on learning outcomes. *Practitioner Research in Higher Education, 5*(1), 9–15.

Facione, P. A. (1990). *Critical thinking: A statement of expert consensus for purposes of educational assessment and instruction*. Millbrae, CA: The California Academic Press.

Felder, R. M., & Brent, R. (1996). Navigating the bumpy road to student-centered instruction. *College Teaching*, *44*(2), 43–47. doi:10.1080/87567555.1996.9933425

Fenrich, P. (1997). *Practical guidelines for creating instructional multimedia applications*. Fort Worth, TX: Harcourt Brace.

Fenton, C., & Watkins, B. (2010). *Communication is key. Fluency in Distance Learning* (p. 240). Charlotte, NC: Information Age Publishing, Inc.

Fiedler, R. L., & Pick, D. (2004). *Adopting an electronic portfolio system: Key considerations for decision makers*. Association for Educational Communications and Technology, 27ᵗʰ Conference.

Fink, L. D. (2003). *A self-directed guide to designing courses for significant learning*. San Francisco, CA: Jossey-Bass.

Fink, L. D. (2003). *Creating significant learning experiences: An integrated approach to designing college courses*. San Francisco, CA: Jossey-Bass.

Fischer, C. (2010). *Made in America: A social history of American culture and character*. Chicago, IL: University of Chicago Press.

Fleming, N., & Baume, D. (2006). Learning styles again: VARKing up the right tree! *Educational Developments*, *7*(4), 4–7.

Foertsch, J., Moses, G., Strikwerda, J., & Litzkow, M. (2002). Reversing the lecture/homework paradigm using e-teach web-based streaming video software. *Journal of Engineering Education*, *91*(3), 267–274. doi:10.1002/j.2168-9830.2002.tb00703.x

Fontaine, G. (2002). Presence in teleland. In Rudestam, K. E., & Schoenhotz-Read, J. (Eds.), *Handbook of online learning: Innovations in higher education and corporate training* (pp. 21–52). Thousand Oaks, CA: Sage.

Forbes, C. (1996). Cowriting, overwriting, and overriding in portfolio land online. *Computers and Composition*, *13*, 195–206. doi:10.1016/S8755-4615(96)90009-2

Foreman, J., & Jenkins, R. (2005). Full-featured web conferencing systems. *Innovate: Journal of Online Education*, *1*(4). Retrieved from http://www.webcitation.org/5YbMitWTt

Foreman, J. (2003, September/October). Next-generation educational technology versus the lecture. *EDUCAUSE Review*, *35*(5), 12–22.

Frand, J. K. (2000, September-October). The information-age mindset: Changes in students and implications for higher education. *EDUCAUSE Review*, *35*(5), 15–24.

Frederickson, N., Reed, P., & Clifford, V. (2005). Evaluating web-supported learning versus lecture-based teaching: Quantitative and qualitative perspectives. *Higher Education*, *50*, 645–664. doi:10.1007/s10734-004-6370-0

Free Video Chat and Video Conferencing from ooVoo. (2012). *University partner program*. Retrieved May 29, 2012, from http://www.oovoo.com/edu/

Frymier, A. B. & Wanzer, M. B. (Nov 1998). *"Make'em laugh and they will learn": A closer look at the relationship between perceptions of instructors' humor orientation and student learning*. Retrieved from the ERIC Document Reproduction Service No. ED 427 377.

Fullen, M. (2001). *The new meaning of educational change* (3rd ed.). New York, NY: Teachers College and University Press.

Gabbard, J., & Desrosiers, P. (2012, June). *Effective pedagogical strategies for engaging students in online learning*. Paper presented at the meeting of the Teaching Professor Conference, Washington, DC.

Gannod, G. C., Burge, J. E., & Helmick, M. T. (2007). Using the inverted classroom to teach software engineering. In *Proceedings of the 30th International Conference on Software Engineering* (Leipzig, Germany, 2008) ICSE '08, (pp. 777-786). New York, NY: ACM.

Ganter, S., & Barker, W. (Eds.). (2004). *Curriculum foundations project: Voices of the partner disciplines*. Washington, DC: Mathematical Association of America.

Gardner, H. (2003). *Multiple intelligences after twenty years*. Retrieved from http://www.pz.harvard.edu/PIs/HG_MI_after_20_years.pdf

Gardner, H. (2006). *Multiple intelligences: New horizons.* New York, NY: Basic Books.

Garrison, D. R. (2007). Online community of inquiry7 review: Social, cognitive, and teaching presence issues. *Journal of Asynchronous Learning Networks, 11*(1), 61–72.

Garrison, D. R., Anderson, T., & Archer, W. (2000). Critical thinking in text-based environment: Computer conferencing in higher education. *The Internet and Higher Education, 2*(2), 87–105. doi:10.1016/S1096-7516(00)00016-6

Garrison, D. R., Anderson, T., & Archer, W. (2001). Critical thinking, cognitive presence, and computer conferencing in distance education. *American Journal of Distance Education, 15*(1), 7–23. doi:10.1080/08923640109527071

Garrison, D., & Archer, W. (2003). A community of inquiry framework for online learning. In Moore, M. (Ed.), *Handbook of distance education.* New York, NY: Erlbaum.

Gee, J. P. (2000). The new literacy studies: from: "socially situated" to the work of the social. In Barton, D., & Ivanic, R. (Eds.), *Writing in community.* London, UK: Sage.

Gibbs, G. (1992). *Improving the quality of student learning.* Bristol, UK: TES.

Giest, H. (2010). Reinventing education: New technology does not guarantee a new learning culture. *E–Learning and Digital Media, 7*(4), 366–376. doi:10.2304/elea.2010.7.4.366

Gillespie, M. K., & National Institute for Literacy, Washington, D. C. (2002). *EFF research principle: A contextualized approach to curriculum and instruction.* EFF Research to Practice note. Jessup, MD: Ed Pubs.

Gillespie, D. (2007). On-demand video system enhances visual learning. *District Administration, 43*(9), 25–26.

Glaser, B. G. (1978). *Theoretical sensitivity.* Mill Valley, CA: The Sociology Press.

Glaser, B. G. (1998). *Doing grounded theory: Issues and discussions.* Mill Valley, CA: The Sociology Press.

Glaser, B. G. (2001). *The grounded theory perspective: Conceptualization contrasted with description.* Mill Valley, CA: The Sociology Press.

Glaser, B. G., & Strauss, A. L. (1967). *The discovery of grounded theory.* Chicago, IL: Aldine.

Gleason, M. (1986). Better communication in large courses. *College Teaching, 34,* 20–24. doi:10.1080/87567555.1986.10532325

Goldsmith, K. (2011). *About UbuWeb.* Retrieved May 17, 2012, from http://www.ubu.com/resources/

Goodman, J. (1983). How to get more smileage out of your life: Making sense of humor, then selling it. In P. E. McGhec & J. H. Goldstein (Eds.), *Handbook of humor research: Vol. 11. Applied studies* (pp. 1-21). New York, NY: Springer-Verlag.

Goodman, S. (2003). *Teaching youth media: A guide to literacy, video production, and social change.* New York, NY: Teachers College Press.

Google. (n.d.). *Google | Inside search: Tips & tricks.* Retrieved May 17, 2012, from http://www.google.com/insidesearch/tipstricks/

Gopnik, A. (2011, February 14 and 21). The information. *New Yorker,* (pp. 124-30).

Gorham, J., & Christophel, D. M. (1990). The relationship of teachers' use of humor in the classroom to immediacy and student learning. *Communication Education, 39,* 46–62. doi:10.1080/03634529009378786

Gosper, M., McNeill, M., & Woo, K. (n.d.). *Web-based lecture recording technologies: Do students learn from them?* Retrieved May 29, 2012, from http://www.caudit.edu.au/educauseaustralasia07/authors_papers/Gosper.pdf

Gosper, M., Green, D., McNeill, M., Phillips, R., Preston, G., & Woo, K. (2008). The impact of web-based lecture technologies on current and future practices in learning and teaching. *ALT-J, 16*(2), 81–93.

Gratton-Lavoie, C., & Stanley, D. (2009, Winter). Teaching and learning principles of microeconomics online: An empirical assessment. *The Journal of Economic Education, 40*(1), 3–25. doi:10.3200/JECE.40.1.003-025

Gray, D. (2008, May 22). *Web log message.* Retrieved from http://www.davegrayinfo.com/2008/05/22/why-powerpoint-rules-the-business-world/

Graziadei, W. D., Gallagher, S., Brown, R. N., & Sasiadek, J. (1997). *Building asynchronous and synchronous teaching-learning environments: Exploring a course/classroom management system solution.* Retrieved from http://horizon.unc.edu/projects/monograph/CD/Technological_Tools/Graziadei.asp

Green, K. C. (2011). *2011 campus computing project.* Retrieved May 1, 2012, from http://www.campuscomputing.net/sites/www.campuscomputing.net/files/Green-CampusComputing2011_4.pdf

Greivenkamp, D., Stoll, C., & Johnston, H. (2009, April 21). *Demystifying invisible processes using mediated feedback.* Paper presented at the 2009 Teaching and Learning with Technology Conference.

Griffin, M. M. (1995). You can't get there from here: Situated learning, transfer and map skills. *Contemporary Educational Psychology, 20*, 65–87. doi:10.1006/ceps.1995.1004

Griffiths, M., & Graham, C. (2009). Using asynchronous video in online classes: Results from a pilot study. *Instructional Technology and Distance Learning, 6*(3), 65-75. Retrieved March 22, 2012, from http://www.itdl.org/journal/mar_09/article06.htm

Grobart, S., & Rusli, E. M. (2011). For Flip video camera, four years from hot start-up to obsolete. *New York Times.* Retrieved April 12, 2011, from http://www.nytimes.com/2011/04/13/technology/13flip.html

Grooms, L. (2000). *Interaction in the computer-mediated adult distance-learning environment: Leadership development through on-line distance education.* Unpublished doctoral dissertation, Regent University, Virginia Beach.

Grunert, J. (2000). *The course syllabus: A learning-centered approach.* Bolton, MA: Anchor Publishing.

Hall, Strangman & Meyer (2009). *Differentiated instruction and implications for UDL implementation.* Retrieved from http://aim.cast.org/learn/historyarchive/backgroundpapers/differentiated_instruction_udl

Halpern, D. F. (1998). Teaching critical thinking for transfer across domains: Dispositions, skills, structure training, and meta-cognitive monitoring. *The American Psychologist, 53*(4), 449–455. doi:10.1037/0003-066X.53.4.449

Han, H. (2011, October). *Video-casting, social presence, interactions, and learning achievement in synchronous online learning.* Paper presented at the World Conference on E-Learning in Corporate, Government, Healthcare, and Higher Education 2011, Chesapeake, VA. Retrieved from http://www.editlib.org/p/38785

Harper, R. E., & Rogers, R. E. (1999). Using feature films to teach human development concepts. *The Journal of Humanistic Counseling, Education and Development, 38*, 89–97. doi:10.1002/j.2164-490X.1999.tb00067.x

Haythornthwaite, C., Kazmer, M. M., Robins, J., & Shoemaker, S. (2000) Community development among distance learners: Temporal and technological dimensions. *Journal of Computer Mediated Communication, 6*(1). Retrieved May 1, 2012, from http://jcmc.indiana.edu/vol6/issue1/haythornthwaite.html

HD Ultra Compact Digital Video Camcorder | Samsung HMX-U20 - Camcorders. (n.d.). Retrieved May 29, 2012, from http://www.samsung.com/us/photography/camcorders/HMX-U20BN/XAA

Hechinger, J. (2008, September 18). College applicants, beware: Your Facebook page is showing. *Wall Street Journal*, p. D1.

Hee Jun, C., & Johnson, S. D. (2005). The effect of context-based video instruction on learning and motivation in online courses. *American Journal of Distance Education, 19*(4), 215–227. doi:10.1207/s15389286ajde1904_3

Hee Jun, C., & Johnson, S. D. (2007). The effect of problem-based video instruction on learner satisfaction, comprehension and retention in college courses. *British Journal of Educational Technology, 38*(5), 885–895. doi:10.1111/j.1467-8535.2006.00676.x

Henderson, C. (1999). *College freshmen with disabilities: Statistical year 1998.* Washington, DC: American Council on Education. Retrieved May 1, 2012, from http://www.answers.com/topic/college-students-with-disabilities-accommodating#ixzz1wAhcakla

Henri, F. (1992). Computer conferencing and content analysis. In Kaye, A. R. (Ed.), *Collaborative learning through computer conferencing: The Najaden papers* (pp. 116–136). Berlin, UK: Springer-Verlag. doi:10.1007/978-3-642-77684-7_8

Herring, D. F., & Notar, C. F. (2011). Show what you know: ePortfolios for 21st century learners. *College Student Journal, 45*(4), 786.

Herrington, J., & Oliver, R. (2000). An instructional design framework for authentic learning environments. *Educational Technology Research and Development, 48*(3), 23–48. doi:10.1007/BF02319856

Herrington, J., & Standon, P. (2000). Moving from an instructivist to a constructivist multimedia learning environment. *Journal of Educational Multimedia and Hypermedia, 9*(3), 195–205.

Hesburgh Libraries University of Notre Dame. (n.d.). *Keyword generator*. Retrieved May 17, 2012, from http://wwwtest.library.nd.edu/reference/keyword_generator/

Hill, D. J. (1988). *Humor in the classroom: A handbook for teachers (and other entertainers!)*. Springfield, IL: Charles C. Thomas.

Hiltzik, M. (2012, February 4). Who really benefits from putting high-tech gadgets in classrooms? *Los Angeles Times*, p. B1.

Hobbs, R. (2006). Non-optimal uses of video in the classroom. *Learning, Media and Technology, 31*(1), 35–50. doi:10.1080/17439880500515457

Hockman, W., & Palmquist, M. (2009). From desktop to laptop: Making transitions to wireless learning in writing classrooms. In Kimme Hea, A. C. (Ed.), *Going wireless: A critical exploration of wireless and mobile technologies for composition teachers and researchers* (pp. 109–131). Cresskill, NJ: Hampton Press.

Hodges, D. (2006). *Laugh lines for educators*. Thousand Oaks, CA: SAGE Publications.

Holden, J., & Schmidt, J. S. (2002). Inquiry and the literary text: Constructing discussions in the English classroom. [Reading, English and Communication Clearinghouse.]. *Urbana (Caracas, Venezuela)*, IL.

Houghton Mifflin. (n.d.). *Project-based learning space: The basics*. Retrieved from http://college.cengage.com/education/pbl/background.html

Hung, D. (2001). Design principles for web-based learning: Implications for Vygotskian thought. *Educational Technology, 41*(3), 33–41.

Hung, D., & Nichani, M. (2001). Constructivism and e-learning: Balancing between the individual and social levels of cognition. *Educational Technology, 41*(2), 40–44.

Hurren, B. L. (2001). *The effects of principals' humor on teachers' job satisfaction*. Dissertation, University of Nevada, Reno.

Ice, P., Curtis, R., Phillips, P., & Wells, J. (2007). Using asynchronous audio feedback to enhance teaching presence and students' sense of community. *Journal of Asynchronous Learning Networks, 11*(2), 3–25.

Ice, P., Swan, K., Diaz, S., Kupczynski, L., & Swan-Dagen, A. (2010). An analysis of students' perceptions of the value and efficacy of instructors' auditory and text-based feedback modalities across multiple conceptual levels. *Journal of Educational Computing Research, 43*(1), 113–134. doi:10.2190/EC.43.1.g

Im, Y., & Lee, O. (2003-2004). Pedagogical implications of online discussion for preservice teacher training. *Journal of Research on Technology in Education, 36*(2), 155–170.

Institute for the Future. (2012). *The future of video: Becoming people of the screen*. Retrieved May 24, 2012, from http://www.iftf.org/node/3584

Intel. (n.d.). *Technology literacy*. Retrieved from http://www.intel.com/education/technologyliteracy/index.htm

ISTE. (2008). *National educational technology standards for teachers – NETS-T* (2nd ed.). International Society for Technology in Education.

Jackson, M. J., & Helms, M. M. (2008). Student perceptions of hybrid courses: Measuring and interpreting quality. *Journal of Education for Business, 84*(1), 7–12. doi:10.3200/JOEB.84.1.7-12

Jameson, D. A. (2007). Literacy in decline: Untangling the evidence. *Business Communication Quarterly, 70*, 16–33. doi:10.1177/1080569906297923

Jenkins, H. (2008). Learning from YouTube: An interview with Alex Juhasz. *Confessions of an Aca-Fan*. Retrieved July 13, 2012, from http://henryjenkins.org/2008/02/learning_from_youtube_an_inter.html

Jenkins, H., Purushotma, R., Clinton, C., Weigel, M., & Robison, A. (2006). *Confronting the challenges of participatory culture: Media education for the 21ˢᵗ century*. Project New Media Literacies. Retrieved May 18, 2012 from http://www.newmedialiteracies.org/files/working/NMLWhitePaper.pdf

Jennifer, L. W. (2001). *Funny you should ask, what is the effect of humor on memory and metamemory?* Dissertation, The American University.

Johnson, C. (2007, January). Clickers in your classroom. *Wakonse-Arizona E-Newsletter, 3*(1), 71–77.

Johnson, C. G. (2005). Lessons learned from teaching web-based courses: The 7-year itch. *Nursing Forum, 40*(1), 11–17. doi:10.1111/j.1744-6198.2005.00002.x

Johnstone, A. H., & Percival, F. (1976, March 01). Attention breaks in lectures. *Education in Chemistry, 13*(2), 49–50.

Jonas, P. M. (2009). *Laughing and learning: An alternative to shut up and listen*. Lanham, MD: Rowan and Littlefield.

Jonassen, D. H. (1999). *Constructing learning environments on the web: Engaging students in meaningful learning. EdTech 99: Educational Technology Conference and Exhibition 1999: Thinking Schools*. Learning Nation.

Jones, P., Kolloff, M., & Kolloff, F. (2008). Students' perspectives on humanizing and establishing teacher presence in an online course. In K. McFerrin et al. (Eds.), *Proceedings of Society for Information Technology & Teacher International Conference 2008* (pp. 460-465). Chesapeake, VA: AACE.

Jones, A. (2004). *A review of the research literature on barriers to the uptake of ICT by teachers*. British Educational Communications and Technology.

Juwah, C., Macfarlane-Dick, D., Mathew, B., Nicol, D., Ross, D., & Smith, B. (2004). *Enhancing student learning through effective formative feedback*. York, UK: Higher Education Academy.

Kalantzis, M., & Cope, B. (2008). *New learning: Elements of a science of education*. Port Melbourne, Australia: Cambridge University Press. doi:10.1017/CBO9780511811951

Kaleta, R., Skibba, K., & Joosten, T. (2007). Discovering, designing, and delivering hybrid courses. In Picciano, A. G., & Dziuban, C. D. (Eds.), *Blended learning: Research perspectives* (pp. 111–143).

Kaplan, R. M., & Pascoe, G. C. (1977). Humorous lectures and humorous examples: Some effects upon comprehension and retention. *Journal of Educational Psychology, 69*, 61–65. doi:10.1037/0022-0663.69.1.61

Katz, V. J. (2007). *Algebra: Gateway to a technological future*. Washington, DC: Mathematical Association of America.

Kear, K. (2010). Social presence in online learning communities. *Proceedings of the 7ᵗʰ International Conference on Networked Learning*. Retrieved April 23, 2011, from http://www.lancs.ac.uk/fss/organisations/netlc/past/nlc2010/abstracts/PDFs/Kear.pdf

Kehrwald, B. (2008). Understanding social presence in text-based online learning environments. *Distance Education, 29*(1), 89–106. doi:10.1080/01587910802004860

Khan Academy. (2012). Retrieved from http://www.khanacademy.org

Khan, S. (2011, March). *Salman Khan: Let's use video to reinvent education*. TED 2011. Retrieved from http://blog.ted.com/2011/03/09/lets-use-video-to-reinvent-education-salman- khan-on-ted-com/

Knapezyk, D., Chapman, C., Kelly, M., & Lu, Li-Fen (2002). *Using web-based conferencing to promote interactivity and collaboration in teacher preparation*. Society for Information Technology and Teacher Education International Conference (SITE).

Kolb, D. A. (1984). *Experiential learning: Experience as the source of learning and development*. Englewood Cliffs, NJ: Prentice-Hall, Inc.

Ko, S., & Rossen, S. (2010). *Teaching online: A practical guide* (3rd ed.). New York, NY: Routledge.

Krathwohl, D. R. (2002). A revision of Bloom's taxonomy: An overview. *Theory into Practice, 41*(4), 212–220. doi:10.1207/s15430421tip4104_2

Krathwohl, D. R., Bloom, B. S., & Masia, B. B. (1964). *Taxonomy of educational objectives; The classification of educational goals. Handbook II: The affective domain.* New York, NY: Longman, Green.

Kress, G., & van Leeuwen, T. (2001). *Multimodal discourse: The modes and media of contemporary communication.* New York, NY: Oxford University Press.

Krovitz, G. (2009). Increasing instructor presence in an online course. *Educator's Voice, 10*(4), 1-7. Retrieved March 19, 2012, from http://www.pearsoncollege.com/Newsletter/EducatorsVoice/EducatorsVoice-Vol10Iss4.learn

Kryder, L. G. (2011). EPortfolios: Proving competency and building a network. *Business Communication Quarterly, 74*(3), 333–341. doi:10.1177/1080569911414556

Kuhn, V. (2010). Speaking with students: Profiles in digital pedagogy. *Kairos: A Journal of Rhetoric, Technology, and Pedagogy, 14*(2). Retrieved from http://kairos.technorhetoric.net/14.2/interviews/kuhn/index.html

LaFontana, V. R. (1996). Throw away that correcting pen. *English Journal, 85*(6), 71–73. doi:10.2307/819831

Lage, M. J., & Platt, G. J. (2000). The Internet and the inverted classroom. *The Journal of Economic Education, 31*(11). Retrieved from http://www.jstor.org/stable/1183338

Lage, M. J., Platt, G. J., & Treglia, M. (2000). Inverting the classroom: A gateway to creating an inclusive learning environment. *The Journal of Economic Education, 31*, 30–43.

Lambert, J. (2010). *Digital storytelling cookbook.* Retrieved May 18, 2012, from http://www.storycenter.org/storage/publications/cookbook.pdf

Lauer, C. (2009). Contending with terms: 'Multimodal' and 'multimedia' in the academic and public spheres. *Computers and Composition, 26*, 225–239. doi:10.1016/j.compcom.2009.09.001

Lave, J., & Wenger, E. (1991). *Situated learning: Legitimate peripheral participation.* Cambridge, UK: University of Cambridge Press. doi:10.1017/CBO9780511815355

Lawson, T. J., Bodle, J. H., & MacDonough, T. A. (2007). Techniques for increasing student learning from educational videos: Notes versus guiding questions. *Teaching of Psychology, 34*(2), 90–93. doi:10.1080/00986280701291309

Lee, K. M. (2004). Presence, explicated. *Communication Theory, 14*, 27–50. http://www.fineminddesign.com/site/media/Readings/Week%2010/Lee(2004)_Presence%20Explicated_CT.pdfdoi:10.1111/j.1468-2885.2004.tb00302.x

Lehman, R. M., & Conceicao, S. C. O. (2010). *Creating a sense of presence in online teaching: How to "be there" for distance learners.* San Francisco, CA: Jossey-Bass.

Levin, B., He, Y., & Robbins, H. (2004). Comparative study of synchronous and asynchronous online case discussions. In C. Crawford et al. (Eds.), *Proceedings of Society for Information Technology and Teacher Education International Conference 2004* (pp. 551-558). Chesapeake, VA: AACE.

Levine, A. (2012). *50+ web 2.0 ways to tell a story.* Retrieved May 18, 2012, from http://50ways.wikispaces.com http://50ways.wikispaces.com

Levine, J. (Ed.). (2006). *Motivation in humor.* New Brunswick, NJ: Transaction Publishers.

Liao, W. C. (2012, February). Using short videos in teaching a social science subject: Values and challenges. *Journal of the NUS Teaching Academy, 2*(1), 42–55.

Library Copyright Alliance. (2008). *Comments of the library copyright alliance and the music library association on proposed exemptions.* Retrieved May 1, 2012, from http://www.ftc.gov/os/comments/drmtechnologies/539814-00705.pdf

Lipman, M. (1988). Critical thinking: What can it be? *Educational Leadership, 46*(1), 38–43.

Lombard, M., & Ditton, T. (1997). At the heart of it all: The concept of presence. *Journal of Computer-Mediated Communication, 3*(2). Retrieved April 19, 2011, from http://jcmc.indiana.edu/vol3/issue2/lombard.html

Lorenzo, G., & Ittelson, J. (2005). *An overview of e-portfolios*. Educause Learning Initiative. Retrieved from http://net.educause.edu/ir/library/pdf/ELI3001.pdf

Lucas, G. (2004, September 14). *Interview by J. Daly [Personal Interview]. Life on the screen: Visual literacy in education. Edutopia*. Retrieved from http://www.edutopia.org/life-screen

Lund, C. R. F. (2008). *Moving lectures out of the classroom to make room for learning* [PowerPoint slides]. Retrieved May, 2012 from http://www.ubtlc.buffalo.edu/workshops/handout.asp?titleID =170&eventID = 639

Lunt, T., & Curran, J. (2010). Are you listening please? The advantages of electronic audio feedback compared to written feedback. *Assessment & Evaluation in Higher Education, 35*(7). doi:10.1080/02602930902977772

Lutzer, D., Rodi, S., Kirkman, E., & Maxwell, J. (2007). *Statistical abstract of undergraduate programs in the mathematical sciences in the United States: Fall 2005 CBMS survey*. Providence, RI: American Mathematical Society.

Madoc-Jones, I., & Parrott, L. (2005). Virtual social work education—Theory and experience. *Social Work Education, 24*(7), 755–768. doi:10.1080/02615470500238678

Malamud, C. (2012). *Chunking information for instructional design*. Retrieved from http://theelearningcoach.com/elearning_design/chunking-information/

Manninen, T. (2000). Interaction in networked virtual environments as communicative action – Social theory and multiplayer games. In *Proceedings of CRIWG2000 Workshop*, Madera, Portugal, (pp. 154-157). IEEE Computer Society Press.

Manning, S., & Johnson, K. E. (2011). *Technology toolbelt for teaching*. San Francisco, CA: Jossey-Bass.

Mannix, M. (1994). Your credentials plus a song and dance. *U.S. News & World Report, 117*(17), 102.

Mark, K. P., Vogel, D. R., & Wong, E. Y. W. (2010). *Developing learning system continuance with teachers and students: Case study of the Echo360 lecture capture system*. Paper presented at the PACIS.

Marshall, B. (April 2000). *"How laughter works" 01*. HowStuffWorks.com. Retrieved July 17, 2012, at http://science.howstuffworks.com/environmental/life/inside-the-mind/laughter.htm

Marton, F., & Saljo, R. (1976). On qualitative differences in learning: Outcome and process. *The British Journal of Educational Psychology, 46*(1), 4–11. doi:10.1111/j.2044-8279.1976.tb02980.x

Mathie, V. A., Beins, B., Benjamin, L. T., Ewing, M. M., Hall, C. C., & Henderson, B. … Smith, R. A. (1993). Promoting active learning in psychology courses. In T. V. McGovern (Ed.), *Handbook for enhancing undergraduate education in psychology,* (pp. 183–214). Washington, DC: American Psychological Association.

Matlin, M. W. (2002). Cognitive psychology and college-level pedagogy: Two siblings that rarely communicate. In Halpern, D. F., & Hakel, M. D. (Eds.), *Applying the science of learning to university teaching and beyond* (pp. 87–103). San Francisco, CA: Jossey-Bass. doi:10.1002/tl.49

Matthews-DeNatale, G. (n.d.). *Reflecting for learning*. Retrieved August 10, 2012, from https://northeastern.digication.com/master_of_education_eportfolio_resources/Reflecting_for_Learning

Matthews-DeNatale, G. (2008). Digital Story-Making: Understanding the Learner's Perspective. Session presented at The *Educause Learning Initiative Annual Conference, San Antonio, TX*. Retrieved May 19, 2012 from http://www.educause.edu/Resources/DigitalStory-MakingUnderstandin/162538

Mayer, R. E. (2009). *Multimedia learning*. Cambridge, UK: Cambridge University Press. doi:10.1017/CBO9780511811678

Mayes, R. (2004). Restructuring college algebra. *International Journal of Computer Algebra in Mathematics Education, 11*, 63–74.

McBride, T., & Nief, R. (2011). *The mindset lists of American history*. Hoboken, NJ: John Wiley and Sons.

McClure, A. (2008). Lecture capture: A fresh look. *University Business, 77*. Retrieved April 1, 2012, from http://www.universitybusiness.com/article/lecture-capture-fresh-look

McGhee, P. E. (1988). Introduction: Recent developments in humor research. *Journal of Children in Contemporary Society, 20*(1-2), 1–12. doi:10.1300/J274v20n01_01

McKeachie, W. J. (2002). *McKeachie's teaching tips: Strategies, research, and theory for college and university teachers* (11th ed.). Boston, MA: Houghton-Mifflin.

McKinney, D., Dyck, J. L., & Luber, E. S. (2008). iTunes University and the classroom: Can podcasts replace professors? *Journal of Computers & Education, 52*(3). Retrieved from http://www.fredonia.edu/department/psychology/pdf/CAE1263.pdf

McLaren, C. H. (2004). A comparison of student persistence and performance in online and classroom business statistics experiences. *Decision Sciences Journal of Innovative Education, 2*(1), 1–10. doi:10.1111/j.0011-7315.2004.00015.x

McLuhan, M. (1964). *Understanding media: The extensions of man.* New York, NY: McGraw-Hill.

Mediasite by Sonic Foundry - Create Online Multimedia Presentations, Briefings and Courses Automatically | Sonic Foundry. (2012). Retrieved May 29, 2012, from http://www.sonicfoundry.com/mediasite

Medina, J. (2008). *Brain rules: 12 principles for surviving and thriving at work, home, and school.* Seattle, WA: Pear Press.

Mehrabian, A. (1969). Some referents and measures of nonverbal behavior. *Behavior Research Methods and Instrumentation, 1*, 203–207. doi:10.3758/BF03208096

Mehrabian, A. (1971). *Silent messages.* Belmont, CA: Wadsworth Publishing Company.

Mehrabian, A. (1981). *Silent messages* (2nd ed.). Belmont, CA: Wadsworth.

Mellen, C., & Sommers, J. (2003). Audio-taped responses and the two-year-campus writing classroom: The two-sided desk, the guy with the ax, and the chirping birds. *Teaching English in the Two-Year College, 31*, 25–39.

Melton, M. (2007). *An investigation of the relationship between supervision quality, quantity, and type with client outcomes in therapy.* Graduate thesis. Retrieved April, 2012 from: http://etd.auburn.edu/etd/bitstream/handle/10415/924/MELTON_MICHELE_53.pdf?sequence=1

MERLOT ELIXR. (n.d.). *Nurturing student creativity – Critical writing.* Retrieved from http://elixr.merlot.org/case-stories/teaching-strategies/nurturing-student-creativity-with-video-projects/nurturing-student-creativity-with-video-projects4/

MERLOT ELIXR. (n.d.). *Visual legal advocacy course with Regina Austin.* Retrieved from http://elixr.merlot.org/case-stories/teaching-strategies/nurturing-student-creativity-with-video-projects/student-video-projects-in-law-school2

MERLOT ELIXR. (n.d.). *Welcome to MERLOT ELIXR.* Retrieved from http://elixr.merlot.org/merlot_elixr?noCache=730:1349067763

Merriam, S. B., & Caffarella, R. S. (1999). *Learning in adulthood: A comprehensive guide.* San Francisco, CA: Jossey-Bass.

Merry, S., & Orsmond, P. (2007). *Students' responses to academic feedback provided via mp3 audio files.* Paper presented at the Science Learning and Teaching Conference in Stafford, UK. (accessed May 8, 2012).

Meyer, C., & Jones, T. B. (1993). *Promoting active learning: Strategies for the college classroom.* San Francisco, CA: Jossey-Bass.

Meyer, J. (1990). Ronald Reagan and humor: A politician's velvet weapon. *Communication Studies, 41*(1), 76–88. doi:10.1080/10510979009368289

Middendorf, J., & Kalish, A. (1995). *The "change-up" in lectures.* Retrieved May 26, 2012, from http://www.iub.edu/~tchsotl/part3/Middendorf%20&%20Kalish.pdf

Miller, G., & Williamson, L. (2009). *Best practices for teaching via interactive video conferencing technology: A review of the literature.* Society for Information Technology and Teacher Education International Conference (SITE).

Millis, B. J., & Cottell, P. G. (1998). *Cooperative learning for higher education faculty*. Phoenix, AZ: American Council on Education & Oryx Press.

Minow, N. (1961, May 9). *Speech to the National Association of Broadcasters*. Retrieved August 5, 2012, from http://www.terramedia.co.uk/reference/documents/vast_wasteland.htm

Montgomery, K. (2000). Youth and digital media: A policy research agenda. *Journal of Adolescent Youth, 27S*, 61–68. doi:10.1016/S1054-139X(00)00130-0

Montgomery, K., Gottliev-Robles, B., & Larson, G. O. (2004). *Youth as e-citizens: Engaging the digital generation*. Center for Social Media.

Moore, K. (2011). *71% of online adults now use video-sharing sites*. Retrieved May 28, 2012, from http://pewinternet.org/Reports/2011/Video-sharing-sites/Report.aspx

Moore, M. G. (1989). Editorial: Three types of interaction. *American Journal of Distance Education, 3*(2), 1–6. doi:10.1080/08923648909526659

Moore, M. G., & Kearsley, G. (1996). *Distance education: A systems view*. Belmont, CA: Wadsworth Publishing Company.

Moore, N. S., & Filling, M. L. (2012). iFeedback: Using video technology for improving student writing. *Journal of College Literacy and Learning, 38*, 3–14.

Morreall, J. (1983). *Taking laughter seriously*. New York, NY: State University of New York Press.

Morris, N. (2006). *Using technology to enhance the quality of the student experience*. Bioscience Education Research Group. Faculty of Biological Sciences. Retrieved April 1, 2012, from http://www.sddu.leeds.ac.uk/uploaded/hotf/HOTF_morris_2012_no_video.pdf

Morrison, G., Ross, S., & Kemp, J. (2007). *Designing effective instruction* (5th ed., p. 218). Hoboken, NJ: John Wiley & Sons.

Moskal, P., Caldwell, R., & Ellis, T. (2009). Evolution of a computer-based testing laboratory. *Innovate: Journal of Online Education, 5*(6). Retrieved from http://www.innovateonline.info/index.php?view=article&id=672

Moskal, P.D., Dziuban, C., Upchurch, R., Hartman, J., & Truman, B. (Fall, 2006). Assessing online learning: What one university learned about student success, persistence, and satisfaction. *peerReview, 8*(4), 26-29.

Mossberger, K., Tolbert, C. J., & McNeal, R. S. (2008). *Digital citizenship: The internet, society, and participation*. (1 ed., Vol. 1). Hong Kong: Massachusetts Institute of Technology.

Murray, M. (2012). *Laughter is the "best medicine" for your heart*. Retrieved September 27, 2012, at http://www.umm.edu/features/laughter.htm

Myers, D. (2006, 2009, 2011). *Psychology*. New York, NY: Worth Publishers.

Nagel, D. (2008, September). Lecture capture: No longer optional? *Campus Technology*. Retrieved May 1, 2012, from http://campustechnology.com/articles/2008/09/lecture-capture-no-longer-optional.aspx

Nass, C., & Sundar, S. S. (submitted). Is human-computer interaction social or para-social? *Human Communication Research*. Retrieved from http://www.stanford.edu/group/commdept/oldstuff/srct_pages/Social-Parasocial.html

National Center for Education Statistics (NCES). (2008). *Digest of education statistics*. Washington, DC: U.S. Department of Education.

National Council of Teachers of English. (2005). *NCTE position statement on multimodal literacies*. Retrieved from http://www.ncte.org/positions/statements/multimodalliteracies

National Council of Teachers of English. (2008). *NCTE definition of 21st century literacies*. Retrieved from http://www.ncte.org/positions/statements/21stcentdefinition

National Survey of Student Engagement (NSSE). (n.d.). *Student engagement*. Retrieved from http://nsse.iub.edu/html/about.cfm

Navarro, P. (2000). Economics in the cyber classroom. *The Journal of Economic Perspectives, 14*, 119–132. doi:10.1257/jep.14.2.119

Nelson, A. (2009). *ARKive*. Retrieved May 17, 2012, from HP Labs: http://www.hpl.hp.com/research/ssrc/services/publishing/arkive/

Newby, T. J., Stepich, D. A., Lehman, J. D., & Russell, J. D. (1996). *Introduction to instructional technology. Instructional Technology for Teaching and Learning.* Englewood Cliffs, New Jersey: Educational Technology Publications.

Newman, F., & Scurry, J. (2001). Online technology pushes pedagogy to the forefront. *The Chronicle of Higher Education, 47*(44), B7.

Newmann, F. (1996). *Authentic achievement: Restructuring schools for intellectual quality.* San Francisco, CA: Jossey-Bass.

Nicholson, J., & Nicolson, D. B. (2010). A stream runs through IT: using streaming video to teach information technology. *Campus-Wide Information Systems, 27*(1), 17–24. doi:10.1108/10650741011011255

Oakland Unified School District Urban Dreams Video Project. (n.d.). *Urban dreams video project video library.* Retrieved from http://urbandreams.ousd.k12.ca.us/video/index.html

Okoro, E. A., Washington, M. C., & Cardon, P. W. (2011). E-portfolios in business communication courses as tools for employment. *Business Communication Quarterly, 74*(3), 347–351. doi:10.1177/1080569911414554

Online Meeting | GoToMeeting. (2012).*Citrix online GoToMeeting.* Retrieved May 29, 2012, from http://www.gotomeeting.com/fec/online_meeting

Oomen-Early, J., Bold, M., Wiginton, K. L., Gallien, T. L., & Anderson, N. (2008). Using asynchronous audio communication (AAC) in the online classroom: A comparative study. *Journal of Online Learning and Teaching, 4*(3).

Overbaugh, R. C., & Schultz, L. (n.d.). *Bloom's taxonomy.* Old Dominion University. Retrieved from http://ww2.odu.edu/educ/roverbau/Bloom/blooms_taxonomy.htm

Owston, R., Lupshenyuk, D., & Wideman, H. (2011). *Lecture capture in large undergraduate classes: What is the impact on the teaching and learning environment?* Retrieved May 29, 2012, from http://www.yorku.ca/rowston/AERA2011final.pdf

Paas, F., van Gog, T., & Sweller, J. (2010). Cognitive load theory: New conceptualizations, specifications, and integrated research perspectives. *Educational Psychology Review, 22*(2), 115–121. doi:10.1007/s10648-010-9133-8

Page, M. S. (2002). Technology-enriched classrooms: Effects on students of low socioeconomic status. *Journal of Research on Technology in Education, 34*(4), 389–409.

Palloff, R. M., & Pratt, K. (2007). *Building online learning communities: Effective strategies for the virtual classroom.* San Francisco, CA: Jossey-Bass.

Papadopoulos, C., Santiago-Roman, A., & Portela, G. (2010, October). *Developing and implementing an inverted classroom for engineering statics.* Paper presented at the annual meeting of the 40th ASEE/IEEE Frontiers in Education Conference, Washington, DC. Retrieved from http://fie-conference.org/fie2010/papers/1741/pdf

Partnership for 21st Century Skills. (2011). *Framework for 21st century learning.* Retrieved from http://www.p21.org/overview/skills-framework

Paulus, T. (2007). CMC modes for learning tasks at a distance. *Journal of computer-Mediated Communication, 12*(4). Retrieved, January 7, 2012, from http://jcmc.indiana.edu/vol12/issue4/paulus.html

Penrod, D. (2007). *Using blogs to enhance literacy: The next powerful step in 21st-century learning.* Lanham, MD: Rowman & Littlefield Education.

Performance Juxtaposition. (1999). *Bloom's taxonomy of learning domains.* Retrieved from http://www.nwlink.com/~donclark/hrd/bloom.html

Phillips, R., Preston, G., Roberts, P., Cummins-Potvin, W., Herrington, J., Maor, D., & Gosper, M. (2010). Using academic analytic tools to investigate studying behaviours in technology-supported learning environments. *Curriculum, Technology & Transformation for an Unknown Future: Proceedings ASCILITE Sydney 2010* (pp. 761–771). Sydney, Australia.

Phillips, D. (2000). *Constructivism in education.* Chicago, IL: University of Chicago Press.

Piaget, J. (1971). *Genetic epistemology.* New York, NY: W. W. Norton & Company, Inc.

Picciano, A. G. (2002). Beyond student perceptions: Issues of interaction, presence, and performance in an online course. *Journal of Asynchronous Learning Networks, 6*(1), 21–40.

Pinder Grover, T., & Groscurth, C. R. (2009). Principles for teaching the millennial generation: Innovative practices of UM faculty. CRLT Occasional Papers. Center for Research on Learning and Teaching, University of Michigan, No. 26.

Pollatsek, H., et al. (2004). *Undergraduate programs and courses in the mathematical sciences: CUPM curriculum guide 2004*. Washington, DC: Mathematical Association of America. Retrieved April 6, 2010, from www.maa.org/cupm

Ponti, M., & Ryberg, T. (2004). Rethinking virtual space as a place for sociability: Theory and design implications. In *Proceedings of Networked Learning Conference 2004*, Sheffield University.

Powell, A. (2012). *Why online courses matter*. Retrieved April 1, 2012, from http://www.online.colostate.edu/blog/posts/why-online-courses-matter

Prensky, M. (2001). Digital natives, digital immigrants — A new way to look at ourselves and our kids. *On the Horizon, 9*(5), 1-6. Retrieved from http://www.marcprensky.com/writing/prensky - digital natives, digital immigrants - part1.pdf

Prensky, M. (2001). Digital natives, digital immigrants part ii: Do they really think differently? — Neuroscience says yes. *On the Horizon, 9*(6), 1-8. Retrieved from http://www.marcprensky.com/writing/prensky - digital natives, digital immigrants – part2.pdf

Provine, R. (2000). *Laughter: A scientific investigation*. New York, NY: Penguin Books.

Purcell, K. (2010). *The state of online video*. Retrieved from http://pewinternet.org/~/media//Files/Reports/2010/PIP-The-State-of-Online-Video.pdf

Pursel, B., & Fang, H. N. (2012). *Lecture capture: Current research and future directions*. Retrieved April 1, 2012, from http://www.psu.edu/dept/site/pursel_lecture_capture_2012v1.pdf

Rainie, L., & Fox, S. (2012). *Just-in-time information through mobile connections*. Retrieved from http://pewinternet.org

Ramaswami, R. (2009, June 1). Capturing the market. *Campus Technology*. News. Retrieved August 23, 2012, from http://campustechnology.com/Articles/2009/06/01/Lecture-Capture.aspx

Ramirez, C. M. (2002). What is the impact of humor, message content and the leader's gender on perceptions of credibility of a leader? *Dissertation Abstracts International, 63*(05), 1864. (UMI No. 3053070).

Reddi, U. V., & Mishra, S. (Eds.). (2003). *Educational multimedia: A handbook for teacher-developers*. New Delhi, India: The Commonwealth Educational Media Centre for Asia.

Renaud, C. (2012). *Creating a digital media curriculum for the high school*. Unpublished Master's thesis. Carthage College, Wisconsin.

Resnick, L. B. (1987). Learning in school and out: 1987 presidential address. *Educational Researcher, 16*(9), 13-20+54. Retrieved from http://links.jstor.org/sici?sici=0013-189X%28198712%2916%3A9%3C13%3ATIPALI%3E2.0.CO%3B2-X

Reynolds, K. C., & Nunn, C. E. (1997). *Engaging classrooms: Student participation and the instructional factors that shape it*. ASHE Annual meeting paper on 11/6-9/97.

Rice, R. E., & Bunz, U. (2006). Evaluating a wireless course feedback system: The role of demographics, expertise, fluency, competency, and usage. *Studies in Media & Information Literacy Education, 6*, 1–10. doi:10.3138/sim.6.3.002

Richert, R. A., Robb, M. B., & Smith, E. I. (2011). Social partners: The social nature of young children's learning from screen media. *Child Development, 82*(1), 82–95. doi:10.1111/j.1467-8624.2010.01542.x

Ring, G., Weaver, B., & Jones, J. H. (2008). Electronic portfolios: Engaged students create multimedia-rich artifacts. *Journal of the Research Center for Educational Technology, 4*(2), 103–114.

Roblyer, M. D. (2006). *Integrating educational technology into teaching* (4th ed.). Upper Saddle River, NJ: Pearson Prentice Hall.

Rodrigo, R. (2009). *Motivation and play: How faculty continue to learn new technologies* (Doctoral dissertation). Retrieved from ProQuest. (1790315301)

Rodrigo, R. (2011). Mobile teaching versus mobile learning. *EDUCAUSE Quarterly, 34*(11). Retrieved from http://educause.edu/

Rourke, L., Anderson, T., Garrison, D. R., & Archer, W. (2001). Assessing social presence in asynchronous, text-based computer conferencing. *Journal of Distance Education, 14*(3), 51–70.

Rovai, A. P. (2002). Sense of community, perceived cognitive learning, and persistence in asynchronous learning networks. *The Internet and Higher Education, 5*(4), 319–332. doi:10.1016/S1096-7516(02)00130-6

Rowntree, D. (2000). *Back to the future with distance learning: From independent learning from interdependence.* Retrieved from http://www-iet.open.ac.uk/pp/D.G.F.Rowntree/future_dl.htm

Salomon, G., & Perkins, D. N. (1996). Learning in wonderland: What computers really offer education. In S. Kerr (Ed.), *Technology and the future of education.* (p. 111-130). NSSE yearbook. Chicago, IL: University of Chicago Press.

SANYO: Dual Cameras: VPC-PD2BK Full HD 1080 Pocket Movie Dual Camera with 10MP Digital Photos and 3X Optical Zoom. (2012). Retrieved May 29, 2012, from http://us.sanyo.com/Dual-Cameras/VPC-PD2BK-Full-HD-1080-Pocket-Movie-Dual-Camera-with-10MP-Digital-Photos-and-3X-Optical-Zoom

Schaefle, S., Smaby, M., & Liu, Li Ping (2006). Counselors attitudes toward video editing technology. *American Counseling Association Vistas.* Retrieved May, 2012 from: http://counselingoutfitters.com/Schaefle.htm

Schank, R. (1992). *Tell me a story: Narrative and intelligence.* Evanston, IL: Northwestern University Press.

Schlosser, C. A., & Burmeister, M. (2006). Audio in online courses: Beyond podcasting. *Proceedings of E-Learn 2006 World Conference on E-Learning in Corporate, Government, Healthcare, and Higher Education,* Honolulu, HI. Retrieved March 22, 2012, from http://www.scribd.com/doc/27071823/Audio-in-Online-Courses-Beyond-Podcasting-Schlosser-Burmeister

Schroeder, B. (2009). Microsoft live meeting 2007: Web conferencing system for virtual classrooms. *Innovate: Journal of Online Education, 1*(1). Retrieved from http://innovateonline.info/pdf/vol1issue1/Rethinking Space and Time-The Role of Internet Technology in a Large Lecture Course.pdf.

Schwartz, D. L., & Hartman, K. (2007). It's not video anymore: Designing digital video for learning and assessment. In Goldman, R., Pea, R., Barron, B., & Derry, S. J. (Eds.), *Video research in the learning sciences* (pp. 335–348). New York, NY: Erlbaum.

Scriven, J., & Hefferin, L. (1998, February). Humor: The "witting" edge in business. *Business Education Forum,* 13–15.

Settle, A., Dettori, L., & Davidson, M. J. (2011). *Does lecture capture make a difference for students in traditional classrooms?* Paper presented at the 16th Annual Joint Conference on Innovation and Technology in Computer Science Education, Germany.

Shade, R. A. (1996). *License to laugh: Humor in the classroom.* Westport, CT: Teacher Ideas Press.

Shea, P., Li, C. S., & Pickett, A. (2006). A study of teaching presence and student sense of learning community in fully online and web-enhanced college courses. *The Internet and Higher Education, 9*(3), 175–190. doi:10.1016/j.iheduc.2006.06.005

Sheridan, D. M., & Inman, J. (2010). *Writing center work, new media, and multimodal rhetoric.* Cresskill, NJ: Hampton Press, Inc.

Shuttleworth, M. (2009). *Hawthorne effect.* Retrieved May, 2012 from: http://www.experiment-resources.com/hawthorne-effect.html

Silva, M. L. (2012). Camtasia in the classroom: Student attitudes and preferences for video commentary or Microsoft Word comments during the revision process. *Computers and Composition, 29,* 1–22. doi:10.1016/j.compcom.2011.12.001

Simmons College. (n.d.). *Multidisciplinary core course.* Retrieved May 18, 2012, from http://www.simmons.edu/enews/orientation_061809/core.html

Simonson, M., Smaldino, S., Albright, M., & Zvacek, S. (2009). *Teaching and learning at a distance: Foundations of distance education* (4th ed.). New York, NY: Pearson.

Simonsson, M., Kupczynski, L., Ice, P., & Pankake, A. (2009, April). *The impact of asynchronous audio feedback in the dissertation advising process.* Paper presented at the American Educational Research Association Annual Meeting, San Diego, CA.

Simpson, E. J. (1972). *The classification of educational objectives in the psychomotor domain.* Washington, DC: Gryphon House.

Sitzmann, T., Kraiger, K., Stewart, D., & Wisher, R. (2006). The comparative effectiveness of web-based and classroom instruction: A meta-analysis. *Personnel Psychology, 59,* 623–664. doi:10.1111/j.1744-6570.2006.00049.x

Slavin, R. E. (1990). *Cooperative learning theory, research and practice.* Needham Heights, MA: Allyn & Bacon.

Smaldino, S., Lowther, D., & Russell, J. (2012). *Connecting learners at a distance. Instructional Technology and Media for Learning* (pp. 144–172). Boston, MA: Pearson.

Smith, A. (2012, March). *46% of American adults are smartphone owners.* Retrieved from http://pewinternet.org/

Smith, A., Rainie, L., & Zickuhr, K. (2011). *College students and technology.* Retrieved from http://pewinternet.org/

Solvie, P., & Kloek, M. (2007). Using technology tools to engage students with multiple learning styles in a constructivist learning environment. *Contemporary Issues in Technology & Teacher Education, 7*(2), 7–27.

Sony Handycam Camcorders | Sony Store USA. (2012). Retrieved May 28, 2012, from http://store.sony.com/webapp/wcs/stores/servlet/CategoryDisplay?catalogId=10551&storeId=10151&langId=-1&identifier=S_Video_Camcorders&SR=nav:electronics:cameras_camcorders:video_cameras_camcorders:shop_compare:ss

Soong, S. K. A., Chan, L. K., & Cheers, C. (2006). Impact of video recorded lectures among students. *Proceedings of the 23rd Annual ASCILITE Conference: Who's Learning? Whose Technology?* Retrieved May 29, 2012, from http://www.ascilite.org.au/conferences/sydney06/proceeding/pdf_papers/p179.pdf

Sorell, W. (1972). *The facets of comedy.* New York, NY: Grosset and Dunlap.

Sorensen, C. K., & Baylen, D. M. (2009). Learning online. In Orellana, A., Hudgins, T., & Simonson, M. (Eds.), *The perfect online course: Best practices for designing and teaching* (pp. 69–86). Charlotte, NC: Information Age Publishing.

Sparrow, L., Sparrow, H., & Swan, P. (2000). Student-centered learning: Is it possible? In A. Hermann & M. M. Kulski (Eds.), *Flexible Futures in Tertiary Teaching: Proceedings of the 9th Annual Teaching Learning Forum.* Perth, Australia: Curtin University of Technology. Retrieved from http://lsn.curtin.edu.au/tlf/tlf2000/sparrow.html

Spinuzzi, C. (2009). The genie's out of the bottle: Leveraging mobile and wireless technologies in qualitative research. In Kimme Hea, A. C. (Ed.), *Going wireless: A critical exploration of wireless and mobile technologies for composition teachers and researchers* (pp. 255–273). Cresskill, NJ: Hampton Press.

Squared 5. (n.d.). *Squared 5: MPEG Streamclip for Mac and Windows and more...* Retrieved May 29, 2012, from http://www.squared5.com/

Stannard, R. (2007). Using screen capture software in student feedback. *The Higher Education Academy.* Retrieved July 15, 2012, from http://www.english.heacademy.ac.uk/explore/publications/casestudies/technology/camtasia.php

Sternberg, R. J., & Grigorenko, E. L. (2002). The theory of successful intelligence as a basis for instruction and assessment in higher education. In Halpern, D. F., & Hakel, M. D. (Eds.), *Applying the science of learning to university teaching and beyond* (pp. 45–54). San Francisco: Jossey-Bass. doi:10.1002/tl.46

Stern, L., & Solomon, A. (2006). Effective faculty feedback: The road less traveled. *Assessing Writing, 11,* 22–41. doi:10.1016/j.asw.2005.12.001

Stigler, J., & Hiebert, J. (1999). *The teaching gap: Best ideas from the world's teachers for improving education in the classroom.* New York, NY: Free Press.

Stone, L. L. (1999, Summer). Multimedia instruction methods. *The Journal of Economic Education,* 253–258.

Stowell, J. R., & Nelson, J. M. (2007). Benefits of electronic audience response systems on student participation, learning, and emotion. *Teaching of Psychology, 34*, 253–258. doi:10.1080/00986280701700391

Straub, R. (2000). The student, the text, and the classroom context: A case study of teacher response. *Assessing Writing, 7*(1), 23–55. doi:10.1016/S1075-2935(00)00017-9

Strauss, W., & Howe, N. (1992). *Generations: The history of America's future, 1584 to 2069*. New York, NY: Quill.

Stuart, J., & Rutgersford, R. J. D. (1978, September 2). Medical student concentration during lectures. *Lancet*, 514–516. doi:10.1016/S0140-6736(78)92233-X

Sugar, W., Brown, A., & Luterbach, K. (2010). Examining the anatomy of a screencast: Uncovering common elements and instructional strategies. *International Review of Research in Open and Distance Learning, 11*(3), 1–20.

Sutton-Smith, B. (1997). *The ambiguity of play*. Cambridge, MA: Harvard University Press.

Symonds, S., Jamieson, A., Bell, A., Wood, B., Ryan, A., & Patterson, L. (2010). Taking sociology online: Boosting teacher presence and student engagement through rich media. In C. H. Steel, M. J. Keppell, P. Gerbic, & S. Housego (Eds.), *Curriculum, Technology & Transformation for an Unknown Future: Proceedings ASCILITE Sydney 2010* (pp. 948-950).

Taylor, D. M. (2007, November 5). *Let's not kill the classroom experience*. University Affairs. Retrieved May 29, 2012, from http://www.universityaffairs.ca/lets-not-kill-the-classroom-experience.aspx

Techsmith (n.d.). *The student demand for lecture capture solutions*. Techsmith Corporation. Retrieved May 30, 2012, from http://download.techsmith.com/relay/docs/CampusTech_whitepaper.pdf

TechSmith. (2012). *Jing, record and share videos on your computer, by TechSmith*. Retrieved May 14, 2012, from http://www.techsmith.com/jing-features.html

TechSmith. (2012). *Snagit, screen grab for Mac and Windows by TechSmith*. Retrieved May 14, 2012, from http://www.techsmith.com/snagit-features.html

TechSmith. (n.d.). *Camtasia video recording and editing software by TechSmith*. Retrieved May 14, 2012, from http://www.techsmith.com/camtasia-features.html

Telestream. (2012). *Screencasting software - ScreenFlow overview - Telestream*. Retrieved May 14, 2012, from http://www.telestream.net/screen-flow/

Thaiss, C., & Zawacki, T. M. (2006). *Engaged writers, dynamic disciplines: Research on the academic writing life*. Portsmouth, UK: Boynton/Cook.

Thompson, J. L. (2000). Funny you should ask, what is the effect of humor on memory and metamemory? (Doctoral Dissertation, American University). *Dissertation Abstracts International, 61(8-B)*, 4442. (UMI 9983671)

Thompson, R., & Bowen, C. J. (2009). *Grammar of the shot* (2nd ed.). Amsterdam, The Netherlands: Focal Press.

Tomlinson, C. A. (2nd. Ed., 2001). How to differentiate instruction in mixed-ability classrooms (2nd ed.) Alexandria, VA: ASCD.

Traphagan, T., Kucsera, J. V., & Kishi, K. (2010, February 01). Impact of class lecture webcasting on attendance and learning. *Educational Technology Research and Development, 58*(1), 19–37. doi:10.1007/s11423-009-9128-7

Trees, A., & Jackson, M. (2007). The learning environment in clicker classrooms: Student processes of learning and involvement in large university-level courses using student response systems. *Learning, Media and Technology, 32*, 21–40. doi:10.1080/17439880601141179

Tufte, E. (2012). PowerPoint does rocket science. Retrieved August 5, 2012, from http://www.edwardtufte.com/bboard/q-and-a-fetch-msg?msg_id=0001yB

U.S. Department of Health and Human Services. (n.d.). *Health information privacy*. Retrieved April 1, 2012, from http://www.hhs.gov/ocr/privacy/

Udell, J. (2005). *What is screencasting?* Retrieved from http://www.oreillynet.com/pub/a/oreilly/digitalmedia/2005/11/16/what-is-screencasting.html

University of Bristol - School of Biological Sciences News Item. (2011, March 11). *£680K for "ARKive in your pocket" audiovisual wildlife experience*. Retrieved April 3, 2012, from http://www.bristol.ac.uk/biology/news/2011/106.html

Vamosi, A. R., Pierce, B. G., & Slotkin, M. H. (2004). Distance learning in an accounting principles course—student satisfaction and perceptions of efficacy. *Journal of Education for Business*, *79*, 360–366. doi:10.3200/JOEB.79.6.360-366

Van Ness, E. (2005, March 6). Is a cinema studies degree the new M.B.A.? *New York Times*, p. M1.

Van Tartwijk, J., & Driessen, E. (2006, April 26). E-portfolio scenarios. *Insight: Observatory for new technologies and education*. Retrieved from http://insight.eun.org/ww/en/pub/insight/school_innovation/eportfolio_scenarios/portfolios_types.htm

Video Capture and Management Software Company | Panopto. (2012). Retrieved May 29, 2012, from http://www.panopto.com/video-capture-and-management-software-company

Video Chat - Free Online Video Calls - Video Calling - Skype. (2012). Retrieved May 29, 2012, from http://www.skype.com/intl/en-us/features/allfeatures/video-call/

Video Conferencing and Personal Telepresence Solutions – Vidyo. (2012). *Vidyo personal telepresence*. Retrieved May 29, 2012, from http://www.vidyo.com/

Vincelette, E. (2011). *Students' perception of multimodal screencast feedback in the writing classroom*. Unpublished raw data.

Vygotsky, L. S. (1978). *Mind in society: The development of higher psychological processes*. Cambridge, MA: Harvard University Press.

Walker, D., & Lambert, L. (1995). Learning and leading theory: A century in the making. In Lambert, L., Walker, D., Zimmerman, D., Cooper, J., Lambert, M., Gardner, M., & Slack, P. (Eds.), *The constructivist leader* (pp. 1–27). New York, NY: Teachers College Press.

Wandersee, J. H. (1982). Humor as a teaching strategy. *The American Biology Teacher*, *44*, 212–218. doi:10.2307/4447475

Warnock, S. (2008). Responding to student writing with audio-visual feedback. In Carter, T., & Clayton, M. A. (Eds.), *Writing and the iGeneration: Composition in the computer-mediated classroom* (pp. 201–227). Southlake, TX: Fountainhead Press.

Warschauer, M., Knober, M., & Stone, L. (2004). Technology and equity in schooling: Deconstructing the digital divide. *Educational Policy*, *18*(4), 562–588. doi:10.1177/0895904804266469

Waters, J. K. (2009). E-portfolios come of age. *T.H.E. Journal*, *36*(10), 24–29.

Waters, J. K. (2011, June 01). Lights! Camera! Action! *Campus Technology*, *24*(10), 22.

Waterworth, E., & Waterworth, J. (2010). Mediated presence in the future. In Bracken, C. C., & Skalaski, P. D. (Eds.), *Immersed in media: Telepresence in everyday life* (pp. 183–196). New York, NY: Routledge.

Web conferencing software - Conference services | Adobe Connect. (2012). *Adobe Connect*. Retrieved May 29, 2012, from http://www.adobe.com/products/adobeconnect.html

Weimer, M. (2002). *Learner-centered teaching: Five key changes to practice*. San Francisco, CA: Jossey-Bass.

Welcome to FuzeBox — FuzeBox. (2012). *Fuze Box*. Retrieved May 29, 2012, from https://www.fuzebox.com/

Wesch, M. (2008, Oct 21). *Web log message*. Retrieved from http://www.britannica.com/blogs/2008/10/a-vision-of-students-today-what-teachers-must-do/

Wesch, M. (2012, June). *The end of wonder in the age of whatever*. Keynote speech presented at EdMedia: World Conference on Educational Media & Technology, Denver, CO.

WhiteHouse.gov. (n.d.). *Education*. Retrieved from http://www.whitehouse.gov/issues/education

Whithaus, C. (2002). Green squiggly lines: Evaluating student writing in computer-mediated environments. *Academic Writing*, *3*. Retrieved April 1, 2012, from http://wac.colostate.edu/aw/articles/whithaus2002/abstract.htm

Wickersham, L. E., & Chambers, S. M. (2006). E-portfolios: Using technology to enhance and assess student learning. *Education*, *126*(4), 738–746.

Wiggins, G., & McTighe, J. (2005). *Understanding by design*. Upper Saddle River, NJ: Prentice Hall.

Wildscreen. (2011). *ARKive: Images of life on Earth information sheet*. Retrieved from http://www.wildscreen.org.uk/downloads/ARKive.pdf

Wilhelmsson, L. (n.d.). *The healing power of humor*. Retrieved September 27, 2012, from http://www.vitalchristianity.org/docs/New%20Articles/Humor-Healing2.pdf

Williams, S. (2010, April 01). New tools for online information literacy instruction. *The Reference Librarian*, *51*(2), 148–162. doi:10.1080/02763870903579802

Wilson, E. O. (2007, March). *E.O. Wilson on saving life on Earth*. Retrieved May 17, 2012 from http://www.ted.com/talks/e_o_wilson_on_saving_life_on_earth.html

Windows Live Essentials - Download Windows Live Essentials. (2012). *Windows live essentials*. Retrieved May 29, 2012, from http://windows.microsoft.com/en-US/windows-live/essentials-home

Wise, A., Chang, J., Duffy, T., & del Valle, R. (2004). The effects of teacher social presence on student satisfaction, engagement, and learning. *Journal of Educational Computing Research*, *31*(3), 247–271. doi:10.2190/V0LB-1M37-RNR8-Y2U1

Wisehart, R. (2004). Nurturing passionate teachers: Making our work transparent. *Teacher Education Quarterly*, 45–53.

Wlodkowski, R. (2008). *Enhancing adult motivation to learn*. San Francisco, CA: Jossey Bass.

Wyatt, R. (2012). *Tegrity case study: Western Kentucky University*. Retrieved June 1, 2012, from http://www.tegrity.com/sites/default/files/WKU.pdf

Yancey, K. (2004). Looking for sources of coherence in a fragmented world: Notes toward a new assessment design. *Computers and Composition*, *21*, 89–102. doi:10.1016/j.compcom.2003.08.024

Yocom, J., & Bishop, M. C. (2010). *4 Rs in multimedia projects: Rationale, resources, roles, and rubrics*. Board of Regents of the University of Wisconsin System for the 26th Annual Conference on Distance Teaching and Learning, Madison, WI.

YouTube. (n.d.). *Press room statistics*. Retrieved from http://www.youtube.com/t/press_statistics

Yu-Lin, J., Ting-Ting, W., Yueh-Min, H., Qing, T., & Yang, S. J. H. (2010). The add-on impact of mobile applications in learning strategies: A review study. *Journal of Educational Technology & Society*, *13*(3), 3–11. Retrieved from http://www.ifets.info/

Zappe, S., Leicht, R., Messner, J., Litzinger, T., & Woo Lee, H. (2009). *Flipping the classroom to explore active learning in a large undergraduate course*. American Society of Engineering. Retrieved from soa.asee.org/paper/conference/paper-view.cfm?id=10046

Zhang, D. (2005). Interactive multimedia-based e-learning: A study of effectiveness. *American Journal of Distance Education*, *19*(3), 149–162. doi:10.1207/s15389286ajde1903_3

Zhang, S., Olfman, L., & Ractham, P. (2007). Designing ePortfolio 2.0: Integrating and coordinating web 2.0 services with eportfolio systems for enhancing users' learning. *Journal of Information Systems Education*, *18*(2), 203–214.

Zhu, E., & Bergom, I. (2010). *Lecture capture: A guide for effective use*. CRLT Occasional Papers. N. 27. University of Michigan. Retrieved from http://www.crlt.umich.edu/publinks/CRLT_no27.pdf

Zickuhr, K., & Smith, A. (2012). *Digital differences*. Retrieved from http://pewinternet.org/

Zimbardo, P. (2001). The power of the situation. [Video program No. 19] In *WGBH Boston (Producer), Discovery psychology: Updated edition*. South Burlington, VT: Annenberg/CPB.

Zinsser, W. (1993). *Writing to learn*. New York, NY: Harper Perennial.

Zull, J. E. (2002). *The art of changing the brain: Enriching the practice of teaching by exploring the biology of learning*. Sterling, VA: Stylus.

About the Contributors

Ellen Smyth is Austin Peay State University's 2010 Innovative Professor, an honor given by the Center for Extended and Distance Education. In 2011, Ellen received a summer research fellowship for exploratory work in open courseware. She publishes articles with *Faculty Focus* and has presented an online seminar through Magna Publications on the "Nine Essential Traits of the Effective Professor." Ellen has presented conference workshops and information sessions with the Sloan-Consortium, the Teaching Professor, and Wisconsin's Distance Teaching and Learning Conference. Ellen enjoys teaching a balance of face-to-face and online statistics courses where video and lecture capturing are her favorite technology tools, naturally.

John X. Volker, PhD, is a Professor of Management at Austin Peay (AP) State University and currently is developing the AP Business Entrepreneurship program. Dr. Volker earned his PhD in Management from Walden University and also holds an MBA and a BS from Murray State University. Dr. Volker has been involved in the entrepreneurship sector since 1983 and has worked with many entrepreneurs as a consultant over the years. Dr. Volker has numerous publications in entrepreneurship and maintains a steady research stream. Dr. Volker is committed to merging the liberal arts with the practice of entrepreneurship and unleashing the creativity inherent in each of us.

* * *

Marianne Castano Bishop, EdD, is Director of the Center for Distance Education at Indiana University South Bend. She was the Instructional Strategist at the University Center for Excellence in Teaching. From Harvard University, she holds a Doctorate in Human Development and Psychology and a Master's degree in Technology in Education. She has a Master's degree in Educational Foundations from Boston College. She has written several articles and presented at conferences on several topics including instructional strategies, race and ethnicity, diversity, cross-cultural communication, gender equity, technology integration, distance education, evaluation, and assessment. She has served as administrative staff and in leadership roles. Teaching is a passion. She is associate faculty at IU South Bend, and has taught both undergraduate and graduate students in the East Coast. She enjoys spending time with her husband, their three cats and one dog. She creates jewelry mobiles and mixed media art. She also writes poetry.

Darnell J. Bradley, EdD, is an Assistant Professor of Leadership Studies at Cardinal Stritch University in Milwaukee, WI. He earned his BA in Political Science from Eastern Illinois University, MA in Public Administration/American Government from Eastern Illinois University; and his EdD in Adult and Higher

Education from Northern Illinois University. Over the last twelve years Dr. Bradley has been involved in student development as an administrator in Greek Life, Leadership, Volunteerism, and Multicultural Education. His research revolves around the experiences of students of color, LGBT, fraternity/sorority life, and internet and technology ethnography.

Paul Chilsen after receiving his undergraduate degree started his professional film and TV career in Los Angeles as an Assistant Director on Disney films and as a Production Manager on the TV show *Star Search*. He left California to pursue an MFA at Columbia College Chicago, where his thesis film *Gross Ratings* was nominated for a regional Student Academy Award TM. Paul also did post-graduate work at UW-Madison and was a Follet Fellow at Columbia. A working filmmaker, he has directed and written theatrical feature films, numerous documentaries, and an Emmy Award TM winning TV show. Paul has taught at Columbia College, Northwestern University, and Carthage College. His focus is the definition and effective use of screen media and cinematic language, in production and media writing courses.

Christine Davis, EdD, specializes in Instructional Technology and Distance Learning. A retired school administrator, she is currently a contributing faculty member at Walden University. Research and presentations at international, national, and state conferences have focused on the use of multimedia based learning systems to support instruction and best practices in instructional design for teaching and learning with technology.

Julie A. DeCesare is Head of Research and Education for the Phillips Memorial Library at Providence College. Julie has a lifelong interest in film studies, audiovisual collections, and multimedia. Throughout her career, Julie has worked closely with instructional designers and faculty to bring multimedia content to course sites and to create vibrant web-based and physical audiovisual collections. She has recently added multimedia-on-the-web evaluation to her repertoire. In a previous life, Julie has held the positions of Digital Media/Film Studies Reference Librarian at Boston College and Technical Coordinator of Media Services at Brown University. She holds a BA in Comparative Literature with a concentration on Film Studies from the University of Massachusetts, Amherst and a MLIS from Simmons College. Julie also teaches Digital Research Technologies at the Marlboro College Graduate Center in the Educational Technology Master program.

Patricia Desrosiers, PhD, is an Assistant Professor at Western Kentucky University. She has taught in the Master of Social Work program (a weekend program consisting of hybrid and online courses) since 2008. Research interests include online teaching, leadership in social work, and trauma recovery. Dedicated to increasing the quality of instruction in her own classroom and others, Dr. Desrosiers has shared her expertise with others in trainings and presentations across the nation. Expertise in multiple video lecture tools including Tegrity™, Adobe® Connect™, and YouTube has been very useful to her in the context of her teaching.

Patricia J. Euzent received her BA in Social Sciences at Coker College, Hartsville, SC. She received an MA in Economics at Clemson University, Clemson, SC. She is currently an Instructor of Economics at the University of Central Florida, Orlando, FL. With more than 28 years of teaching experience she has increasingly taken on the challenges of new technology and applied it in the classroom. Her main research interests are in the History of Economic Thought and Economic Education.

Steve Garwood, MLS, MCIS, is presently the Director of Instructional Design and Technology for the School of Communication & Information (SC&I) at Rutgers University. In this position he provides instructional technology support and instructional development assistance to instructors for on-campus, online, and hybrid courses. In his career Steve has developed and taught courses in general technology, web-design, and multimedia production and has lead efforts in staff training and development for a large university library and for a library cooperative. Steve has developed and led training programs and, for several years, worked as a librarian in public libraries. Steve is a member of the Sloan Consortium, New Media Consortium, and the American Society for Training and Development and is presently pursuing his EdD at the Graduate School of Education at Rutgers University.

Robert Gibson, EdD, is the Director of Learning Technologies and an adjunct graduate faculty member at Emporia State University in Emporia, Kansas. Rob holds multiple undergraduate and graduate degrees and is currently completing a Master's degree in Business Administration. His professional interests include the application of technology in a variety of curricular areas to improve student learning outcomes. Rob has worked in higher education for nearly twenty-five years and at a variety of colleges and universities ranging from small liberal arts universities to Research I universities. Rob lives in both Emporia, Kansas, and Wichita, Kansas.

Terri Gustafson is the Assistant Director of the Center for Teaching and Technology in the College of Education at Michigan State University. She has worked in the field of multimedia and educational technology for fifteen years and holds a Master's degree in Educational Technology from Michigan State University. As the Assistant Director of the Center for Teaching and Technology, Terri is responsible for faculty development in the areas of online teaching and learning and instructional technology integration in the face-to-face classroom. In addition, she is responsible for implementing and managing instructional technology programs such as lecture capture, e-portfolios, and iOS semester loan initiatives. Lastly, Terri is a Doctoral candidate in the Higher, Adult, and Lifelong Education program at Michigan State University. Her research interests include online and blended learning models for digital natives and policy analysis of state sponsored K-12 virtual schooling.

Peter Jonas, PhD, is a Professor of Research and Chairperson of the Doctoral Leadership Department at Cardinal Stritch University has become well known for his wisecracks and lectures on humor. Beneath the humor is a message: If you get people laughing, you can enhance learning. The Professor has written three books (two of them that were any good) in support of his research on humor including *Laughing and Learning: An Alternative to Shut-up and Listen* (2009) and *Secrets of Connecting Leadership and Learning to Humor* (2004). Peter has been at Cardinal Stritch University for more than thirty years teaching research, statistics, and leadership. He has a keen interest in technology and has made more than a hundred presentations, as well as being actively involved in consulting and writing, authoring more than forty books, manuals, and articles.

Paula Jones, EdD, serves as an Instructional Designer within the Instructional Development Center at Eastern Kentucky University. She also serves as an adjunct faculty member in the College of Education and the Gender and Women Studies Department at Eastern Kentucky University where she develops and teaches online courses. Dr. Jones serves as a Quality Matters (QM) Master Reviewer and an Online Trainer. She has presented at numerous conferences in the past five years including Sloan-C Conference,

E-Learning Guild, Quality Matters National Conference, Wisconsin Distance Education Conference, SITE (AACE) Conference, E-Learn World (AACE) Conference, and the Critical Thinking Conference. She holds an EdD in Instructional Systems Design from the University of Kentucky. She earned a Master of Arts in Education (Counseling).

Fred C. Kolloff, PhD, is Director of the Instructional Development Center at Eastern Kentucky University assisting faculty with online learning through instructional design, media production, and professional development services. He has also developed and conducted training for faculty in how to prepare and present through interactive video. Dr. Kolloff is an Assistant Professor in Communication and teaches online. He received a Bachelor of Arts in Speech and Theater from Kalamazoo College and a Master of Arts in Communications from Michigan State University. He holds a PhD from Indiana University in Instructional Systems Technology. Dr. Kolloff is a frequent presenter at national conferences including the Sloan-C, Wisconsin Distance Education, E-Learn World, SITE (AACE), and AECT Conferences in the areas of distance education and online teaching.

MaryAnn Kolloff, EdD, is an Assistant Professor in the Curriculum and Instruction Department at Eastern Kentucky University. Dr. Kolloff is active in presenting workshops focusing on distance education for university faculty and in-service teachers at national and state conferences. She teaches technology courses as well as adolescent and young adult literature courses in online learning environments. She holds an EdD from Indiana University in Instructional Systems Technology. Other degrees include a Bachelor of Science from Northern Illinois University in Early Childhood Education and a Master of Arts in Special Education from National Louis University located in Evanston Illinois. She has successfully published in many different academic journals and has presented at national conferences including Sloan C, E-Learn World Conference, SITE (AACE), Wisconsin Distance Education Conference, AECT, and the Lily Conferences.

Curtis Kunkel, PhD, was born and raised in rural southwest Minnesota, where he attended the University of Minnesota, Morris. He received a BA in both Mathematics and Computer Science in 2003, before pursuing aspirations of higher education in the area of mathematics. Curtis attended Baylor University in Waco, TX, where he earned both an MS in 2005 and a PhD in 2007. Both degrees were in Mathematics specializing in ordinary differential equations. For the past 5 years, he has been teaching at the University of Tennessee at Martin, where he currently holds the rank of Associate Professor in the Department of Mathematics and Statistics. He continues to pursue interests in both ordinary differential equations and technology related to mathematics education.

Thomas L. Martin, PhD, received a BS in Mathematics and a BA in Economics in 1975 from Wake Forest University, Winston-Salem, North Carolina. He went on to earn a PhD in Economics in 1981 from Rice University, Houston, Texas. There he chose a field of specialization in International Economics. His teaching and research interests are in the areas of International Economics, as well as Applied Microeconomics and The History of Economic Thought.

Gail Matthews-DeNatale, PhD, is a Senior Faculty Fellow at Northeastern University's Graduate School of Education, where she specializes in adult learning and emerging trends in education. Dr. Matthews-DeNatale co-leads the GSE's Pedagogically-Sound, Technology-Savvy group and serves as institutional PI for University's Connect to Learning ePortfolio Initiative. Prior to Northeastern, she held both faculty and academic administrative positions at Simmons College and Emmanuel College in Boston, George Mason University, and the University of South Carolina. She is a founding member of the Board of Trustees for the Association for Authentic, Experiential, and Evidence-Based Learning (AAEEBL), former member of the NERCOMP Board of Trustees, and a recent grants panelist for the National Endowment for the Arts, Arts in Education program.

Tom McBride, PhD, is Professor of English and holds the Keefer Chair in the Humanities at Beloit College. He is a graduate of Baylor University and earned his Doctorate at the University of Illinois at Champaign-Urbana. A veteran of almost four decades in the classroom, he is co-founder of Beloit's program in Rhetoric and Discourse and, for more than a decade, has chaired the college's First Year studies program. He has published both critical essays and creative non-fiction and has been a popular commentator on language for Wisconsin Public Radio. Tom McBride and Ron Nief have been partners in the Mindset List project since its since inception in 1998. They are the coauthors of *The Mindset Lists of American History: From Typewriters to Text Messages, What Ten Generations of Americans Think is Normal*, published last year by John Wiley and Sons.

Ann M. Miller, PhD, teaches in the Department of Counselor Education at Emporia State University in Emporia, Kansas. She is also the Director of the department's counselor training facility/clinic, Community Counseling Services. Ann received both her Master's degree in Community Counseling and her Doctorate in Counselor Education and Supervision from North Dakota State University. Her professional interests include supervising students working with clients at the practicum and internship level, exploring client experiences at counselor education program training facilities, and evaluating professional and ethical standards in counselor education programs and clinical training facilities. She is a nationally certified counselor and a licensed professional counselor in the state of Kansas. In her leisure time, Ann enjoys being with her family and her animals, doing yoga, watching football and basketball, listening to live music, and being outdoors.

Patrick Moskal, PhD, is the Director of Testing and Evaluation in the College of Business Administration at the University of Central Florida. He has over twenty-five years of experience in the field of education, training, and program evaluation, with the past twenty-three years at the University of Central Florida. Dr. Moskal coordinates the collection and analysis of student data to support course and degree program improvement as well as accreditation in the college. He also conducts research related to instructional technology within the college. His teaching experience includes statistical methods, program evaluation, learning and memory, and introductory psychology. He received his PhD from the University of Notre Dame.

Patsy Moskal, EdD, is an Associate Director of the University of Central Florida (UCF) Research Initiative for Teaching Effectiveness. She is currently working with UCF faculty to evaluate the effectiveness of their online and traditional courses. She also has worked as a consultant for the Brevard, Volusia, and Orange County Public Schools, as well as the Miami Desegregation Center. This work consisted of evaluating programs and providing research design and statistical analysis expertise. She has served as a consultant to government contract firms providing both research design and instructional design services. Patsy serves as an adjunct faculty member in the Educational Foundations department where she teaches graduate statistics. She received her BS and MS degrees in Computer Science, and her EdD in Curriculum and Instruction from UCF.

Ron Nief, PhD, is Director of Public Affairs Emeritus at Beloit College, retiring in 2009 after more than forty years of communicating the work of higher education. He has served his alma mater, Boston College, as well as Brandeis and Clark universities, and Middlebury College. He has written for the *New York Times*, the *Boston Globe*, and the *Christian Science Monitor* and has been honored by both the Public Relations Society of America and the Council for the Advancement and Support of Education. He created the Mindset List in 1998 and joins Tom McBride in appearances and talks around the country throughout the year.

Kristopher (Kris) Purzycki is a graduate student at Old Dominion University where he is currently pursuing his Master's degree in Rhetoric & Composition. Kris' background rests predominantly in the professional area of digital design and composition. Although interested in digital rhetoric of a myriad of forms, Kris focuses his research on how electronic media impacts self-identification. With an eye towards issues of social justice in the information age, he is beginning work on his thesis which examines altruism and compassion in virtual negotiations.

Rochelle (Shelley) Rodrigo is Assistant Professor of Rhetoric & (New) Media at Old Dominion University. She was as a full time faculty member for nine years in English and film studies at Mesa Community College in Arizona. At MCC she also served as instructional technologist and faculty professional development coordinator. Shelley researches how "newer" technologies better facilitate communicative interactions, more specifically teaching and learning. As well as co-authoring *The Wadsworth Guide to Research*, Shelley also co-edited *Rhetorically Rethinking Usability*. Her scholarly work has appeared in *Computers and Composition, Teaching English in the Two-Year College, EDUCAUSE Quarterly, Journal of Advancing Technology*, as well as various edited collections. In 2012 she was awarded the Digital Humanities High Powered Computing Fellowship. Shelley currently serves as co-chair on the EDUCAUSE Evolving Technologies Committee and was elected to the Conference on College Composition and Communication Executive Committee. In 2010 she became a Google Certified Teacher.

Sharon Stoerger, PhD, is the Director of the Information, Technology, and Informatics program at Rutgers. Her teaching experience ranges from gender and computerization to instructional technologies to media writing courses. Dr. Stoerger's research areas of interest include computer-mediated communication, social informatics, and educational uses of social media including virtual worlds. She is also interested in online and blended teaching approaches. Dr. Stoerger has presented her work on the educational uses of technology at a number of national and international conferences including Association for Library and Information Science Education (ALISE), New Media Consortium, the eLearning Forum Asia, and Online EDUCA Berlin. She has also written several articles and book chapters on the educational uses of social media, rich media, and virtual worlds.

Elizabeth Vincelette, PhD, is a Lecturer in the English department and the Director of the Writing Center at Old Dominion University in Norfolk, VA. Her research interests include writing assessment, editing, genre, and the representation of American literature in digital spaces. Dr. Vincelette is a member of the Modern Language Association and the National Council for Teachers of English and has presented at a number of conferences, including the MLA, the Conference on College Composition and Communication, and the American Literature Association.

Christine Wells began her career in education in the North Shore area of Chicago after receiving her undergraduate degree at Illinois Wesleyan University. Now a National Board Certified Teacher and Department Chair in general and vocal music in Deerfield, Illinois, she focuses on teaching and integrating technology in K-12 curricula. Christine earned an MEd from Carthage College in Creative Arts and Learning, and now teaches screen media and education courses at Carthage. She helped to develop and establish the Rosebud Institute in 2009. As Program Manager of the Rosebud Institute, Christine works on promotions and research, conference presentations, program and curriculum development, and teaching screen media literacy to a wide variety of constituencies.

Jim Yocom, Director of Instructional Media Services at Indiana University South Bend, is a lifelong communicator. Beginning with a love of writing and photography, he spent a decade teaching video production in higher education while playing out his summers as a freelance video producer. Jim now advises students, faculty, and schools on how to communicate effectively through video and multimedia. His intuitive approach and knack for explaining technology in easily understandable ways have resulted in frequent invitations to speak at local and international conferences on topics related to learning, technology, and media. When not working, Jim will be performing indigenous music, photo trekking in nature, or setting up a new art exhibit in his home gallery.

Index